Pukhtun Economy and Society

First published in 1980, this groundbreaking *Routledge Revival* is a reissue of an original and authentic anthropological account of Pukhtun society by Professor Akbar Ahmed. Combining extensive fieldwork data collected among the Mohmand tribe in the Northwest Frontier Province of Pakistan with historical and literary sources, Professor Ahmed's study seeks to construct an ideal-type model of Pukhtun society based on the ideal Code of the Pukhtuns and to analyse the conditions of its maintenance and transformation.

The author's thesis is that this ideal model exists within Pukhtun society when interaction with larger state systems is minimal and in poor economic zones. In this way he posits an opposition between the Tribal Agencies along the border with Afghanistan, where ecological conditions are poor and state influence minimal, and the Settled Areas under state administration where Pukhtun society is forced away from its ideals.

Pukhtun Economy and Society

Traditional structure and economic development
in a tribal society

Akbar S. Ahmed

Routledge
Taylor & Francis Group

First published in 1980
by Routledge & Kegan Paul

This edition first published in 2011 by Routledge
2 Park Square, Milton Park, Abingdon, Oxon, OX14 4RN

Simultaneously published in the USA and Canada
by Routledge
711 Third Avenue, New York, NY 10017

Routledge is an imprint of the Taylor & Francis Group, an informa business

© 1980 Akbar S. Ahmed

Publisher's Note
The publisher has gone to great lengths to ensure the quality of this reprint but
points out that some imperfections in the original copies may be apparent.

Disclaimer
The publisher has made every effort to trace copyright holders and welcomes
correspondence from those they have been unable to contact.

A Library of Congress record exists under LC Control Number: 79041205

ISBN 13: 978-0-415-68795-9 (hbk)
ISBN 13: 978-0-203-35743-9 (ebk)
ISBN 13: 978-0-415-68811-6 (pbk)

International Library of Anthropology

Editor: Adam Kuper, University of Leiden

Arbor Scientiae
Arbor Vitae

A catalogue of other Social Science books published by Routledge &
Kegan Paul will be found at the end of this volume.

Pukhtun economy and society

Traditional structure and economic development in a tribal society

Akbar S. Ahmed

Routledge & Kegan Paul

London, Boston and Henley

First published in 1980
by Routledge & Kegan Paul Ltd
39 Store Street, London WC1E 7DD,
Broadway House, Newtown Road,
Henley-on-Thames, Oxon RG9 1EN and
9 Park Street, Boston, Mass. 02108, USA
Set in IBM Press Roman by
Hope Services, Abingdon, Oxon
and printed in Great Britain by
Redwood Burn Limited,
Trowbridge & Esher

British Library Cataloguing in Publication Data

Ahmed, Akbar Salahudin

Pukhtun economy and society. – (International
library of anthropology).
1. Pukhtuns
I. Title II. Series
301.29'549'12   DS380.P8   79-41205

ISBN 0 7100 0389 7

To Babar
with love

Contents

Illustrations

Maps

Figures

Tables

Acknowledgments

This book is based on a doctoral thesis in anthropology accepted by the University of London in 1978 and entitled 'The economic and social organization of selected Mohmand Pukhtun settlements'. To Professor A.C. Mayer, my supervisor at the School of Oriental and African Studies, goes my deepest gratitude for his supervision and encouragement in the preparation of this work from its very inception in 1974. I also wish to thank Professor E. Gellner, Dr H. Alavi and Dr R. Tapper for reading the manuscript and making valuable suggestions. The involvement and sympathy of Mr P. Hopkins has been a constant source of encouragement. My debt to my wife in the preparation of the study is immeasurable. Not only was she an indefatigable field assistant but she typed the thesis and its drafts. I wish to record my gratitude to the Central Research Fund, University of London, the Scholarships Committee, School of Oriental and African Studies and the Ford Foundation for making available funds to support my university attachment. I would like to dedicate this book to my son, Babar, with love.

Dramatis Personae

The following names of male living persons appear frequently in the text and are reproduced below in order to introduce them to the reader who may also wish to relate them to each other in the social universe. Females, often the wives and daughters of the following, were also interviewed formally and informally by my wife and her sister.

	Shati Khel	*Bela Mohmandan*
senior lineages:	Shahzada Malik Mazullah Khan	Shamshudin Hamesh Gul
junior lineages:	Dilawar Khan Kabil Khan	Mehr Gul
affiliated lineages:	Haji Hassan	Hussain Khan
religious groups:	Mian Jalil	Imam of Bela
occupational groups:	Aziz Ingar (blacksmith)	Morcha Khel (carpenter)
young groups (*kashar*):	Feroz Akbar Jan	Ihsanullah Shamshur Rahman Amin Khan

The field-work was conducted primarily in Shati Khel and Bela Mohmandan and I would like to clarify a possible source of confusion. Shati Khel is a section of the Halimzai clan and also the name of the geographical area where they live in the Mohmand Agency. Similarly Kado Khel, the dominant Tarakzai sub-section of Bela Mohmandan which lies in the Peshawar District, gives its name to an area called Kado Khel or Kado Korona (houses of Kado) a mile north-west of Bela but inside the Agency. I will refer to Mohmands in the Agency as Tribal Area Mohmands, TAM, and those in the Settled Area of the District as Settled Area Mohmands, SAM. TAM and SAM in the text also refer to their respective areas.

Part one

Introduction

1 Introduction

I Problem

(a) *The problem*

The problem before me is to construct an ideal-type model of Pukhtun[1] society primarily from field-work data and based on the ideal Code of the Pukhtuns (*Pukhtunwali*). The central features of *Pukhtunwali* are locally perceived as agnatic rivalry (*tarboorwali*) and the preservation of the honour of women (*tor*). Honour and status are conferred by society on its members through acts approximating to the ideal especially in these two features. In the ideal matters relating to social behaviour and organization such as household settlements, marriage and expenditure patterns are also affected by *Pukhtunwali*. The discussion of the ideal-type will raise questions about the causal variables that create conditions among tribal groups for maintaining, or deviating from, *Pukhtunwali*.

I will attempt to illustrate the high degree of similarity between the ideological model and the immediate or empirically observed model. The study will attempt to prove that the behaviour and organization of social groups approximate to the ideal model. My main aim is to put forward the thesis that the ideal model exists within Pukhtun society when interaction with larger state systems is minimal and in poor economic zones.

My study further sets out to establish that *Pukhtunwali* continues to be operative for Pukhtun groups in spite of the severe constraints of an encapsulated situation implying different jural and administrative sanctions and various points of moral disjunction. Tribal Area Mohmands (TAM) will allow us to examine how the model appears in the ideal; Settled Area Mohmands (SAM) will provide an opportunity of actually testing the hypotheses by allowing us to view how the model behaves in an encapsulated condition. The complexity and extent of deviance from the model may be measured in the SAM situation and the thesis tested; verification or refutation of the thesis is thus possible.

(b) *The problem restated*

The study will examine tribal groups and their changing internal and external relations to exogenous economic and political situations. The thesis postulates that *Pukhtunwali* survives political and administrative encapsulation. Two groups of the Mohmand tribe will be examined to test the thesis, one, TAM, unencapsulated due to special administrative arrangements deriving from its geo-political situation and organized largely to approximate to its original tribal model, and the other, SAM, encapsulated within larger state systems. An examination of the problem will enable us to see how unencapsulated tribal social organization presupposes a political situation which in turn antecedes its form.

I am distinguishing and conceptualizing two polar methods of encapsulation; the one I call encapsulation and the other 'penetration' based on tacit tribal agreement; the end results are often the same – integration of the smaller into the larger system. They are thus aspects of the same phenomenon. Encapsulation as discussed in general anthropological literature involves larger state systems based on different organizational principles encapsulating smaller systems, which does not preclude but does not necessarily imply the naked use of force. None the less it involves encirclement, absorption and enveloping, and provides the encapsulated society with little choice and limited strategies. It is therefore encapsulation both in a metaphorical and literal sense. It assumes larger and more powerful systems engaging weaker and smaller structures in which encapsulation is an inescapable factor and ineluctable destiny. The concept of encapsulation implies the absorption of a smaller system by a larger one and presupposes the surrender of a certain loss of identity of the former system. The terms and pace of encapsulation are decided by the encapsulators and their putatively higher civilization or culture with its symbols of dress, speech, diet, etc., is henceforth dominant (Bailey, 1957, 1960, 1961; Caplan, L., 1970; Caplan, P., 1972; Fürer-Haimendorf, 1939, 1962, 1977; Vitebsky, 1978; Yorke, 1974). In such situations 'the modernizing elite may wade in regardless of the consequences and the cost' (Bailey, 1970: 177). A certain moral disjunction of values is inherent in the situation which could either lead to integration or expressions of local self-assertion.

Anthropologists have seen tribal societies as passive recipients of exogenous pushes in the form of developmental and technical changes (Sahlins, 1968, 1969). I am arguing that TAM are not passive recipients of exogenous pushes. In the Tribal Areas military encapsulation failed over the centuries but from 1974 onwards began what can only be termed as economic penetration; it was encapsulation in economic terms but with major distinctions. The terms and pace were set by the TAM; the penetrators wore the clothes, spoke the language and ate the food of the penetrated. In a sense the encapsulators were allowing themselves to be encapsulated. However, this is palpably a temporary and strategic phenomenon for in the end the results will most likely be the same as that of the encapsulation of SAM, although the method has been diametrically different.

Encapsulation of tribal societies assumes the reordering of certain vital features of social organization such as settlement patterns, marriage rules pertaining to endogamy and exogamy, lineage politics and the two key components, *tarboorwali* and *tor*. The thesis will attempt to show that this is not always so.

It is axiomatic that social structural change can be measured or examined in relation to an anterior form of social reality. Hence the need to construct from historical accounts, case-studies and field-work data a model of Pukhtun tribal society. The economic situation predetermines the social situation and acts to underline the principles of agnatic equality, relationships which subsume agnatic rivalry. I will be showing through case-studies how social organization is affected by the geographical situation and economic constraints. For instance, shooting during feuds cannot last for more than a few days at a time especially when one party has captured the water-well, the key to the village, of the other party. Victory is then assumed and conceded and some sort of agreement invariably reached. A political point has however been clearly made, the point of lineage hegemony. The poor economic base, one half-nourished crop if it rains that year, along with their geopolitical situation, have brought together a combination over the last centuries to create three survival patterns for the tribals which help us to understand tribesmen and their strategy *vis-a-vis* encapsulating systems: 1 emigration; 2 unorthodox and often illegal sources of income such as smuggling and dacoity; 3 political allowances by encapsulating or larger societies in return for concessions in the form of penetration.

What then are the fundamental principles of Pukhtun social organization? The underlying principles are threefold and interconnected: the primary principle rests on *tarboorwali* which in turn crudely ensures a ceiling to the wealth and power an individual may accumulate and therefore more or less forces the second principle, which is an intense spirit of democracy that finds ratification in the tribal charter. The third principle is that of honour deriving from certain features of the Pukhtun Code particularly regarding women and their chastity (Chapters 4 and 7). The model as built through the case-studies reveals a man's world in the most chauvinistic sense of the concept. There is manifest and constant glorification of *machismo*. The entire concepts of Pukhto revolve round the concept of manhood (*saritob*) and honour which in turn involves man's ideal image of himself. The highest compliment is 'he is a man' (*saray day*). The three key and prestige conferring symbols of tribal society, the male guest house (*hujra*), the gun (*topak*) and the council of elders (*jirga*), are exclusively the reserve of Pukhtun males. In the most profound sense it is a man's world.

The central issues in Pukhtun society revolve around the pursuit of power, status and honour, a pursuit that is closely related and limited to agnatic kin on the tribal genealogical charter. The symbolism of unilineal descent from a common apical ancestor is effective in articulating a great deal of the organizational functions of these groups. As I hope to illustrate in the study, the operative segment of the tribe which defines the genealogical and geographical boundaries, the arena of conflict, and produces its leaders and alliances, is the sub-section. I shall analyse tribal social organization and political activity in terms of the sub-section as the operative lineage. The single most important feature of society with far-reaching socio-economic ramifications is that of agnatic rivalry. As Freudian man is charged with hostility towards his father and Malinowskian man against avuncular authority, the object of hostility to the Pukhtun is his Father's Brother's Son (*tarboor*).[2] The answers to questions underlying both psychological and sociological motivation invariably lie in agnatic kin or *tarboor* relationships and at the core of the concept of agnatic rivalry translated in society as *tarboorwali*. There is thus a significant dividing line between true siblings and classificatory siblings. 'Balanced opposition' in tribal structure means the opposing subgroups of cousins, usually of that generation.

The Pukhtun model presupposes that politics is a central activity involving competition for power and as a mode for acquiring honour and status in society. I will be arguing that *Pukhtunwali* survives and that its main aim is political domination at a certain lineage level and not economic aggrandization. Political domination gives political status which in turn affords access to political administration, which may or may not give direct economic benefits. The implications for agnatic rivalry are obvious: while appropriating power agnatic rivals are excluded from it. It is a 'zero-sum' situation (Barth, 1959). The structure of political domination is at once a behavioural and an ideological pheno-menon. Briefly, the problem concerns the Pukhtun view of his world and the changes set in motion within it as a consequence of encapsula-tion. Deviance from and compromise of the Pukhtun model are social mechanisms of adjustment. The awareness of deviance poses an acute dilemma for the Pukhtun: either he rejects his Code or removes him-self to those unencapsulated areas where he can practise it. The dilemma is still unresolved, as the study will illustrate.

Tribal life on varying social and political levels is a constant struggle against attempts to capture, cage or encapsulate it by larger state systems. However, it is already totally imprisoned in the bonds of its own Code. For SAM the test is severe; the Code still survives to an extent in the face of the rather shabby symbols of and feeble attempts at encapsulation. The encounter debilitates the tribal system by attacking it at its most vulnerable and yet vital spot: the Code — the very core and essence of Pukhtunness and that which forms and defines a Pukhtun. In this encounter there can be no synthesis, no harmonious absorption of one system into another; there can be only stages of rejection. I am arguing that SAM is an *aspect* of TAM as a consequence of political operations.

I will show how lineages, particularly the operative lineage, interact with each other in conflict and alliances around the concept of *tarboor-wali* through extended case-studies from TAM and SAM over three and four generations (Chapter 7). How one lineage emerges and in direct proportion the other lineages decline, resulting in changing settlement arrangements, marriage patterns, economic and political activity, is thereby made clear (Chapters 8 and 9). The important variable is the interaction with the colonizing power and its vast resources (Chapters 3, 5 and 10). Administrative patronage confers status and income as it creates a broker role for the Maliks (petty chiefs or headmen). Another important factor is the expulsion from the Tribal Areas into the Settled Areas of groups who over two or three generations make their fortune, first as tenants then as subinfeudators and collaterals of land, and return to reinvest it in the continuation of lineage feuds. In short, I shall show the relationships of lineages to changing political situations, which, in turn, involve changing attitudes towards each other and towards social and cultural values. Pukhto is still *spoken* (*wai*) but more difficult to *do* (*kai*). I will relate the shifting lineage positions and con-flicts to encapsulating systems and, in turn, to tribal strategy, which will illuminate theoretically how lineage structures and Pukhto concepts

undergo changes as a result of such encounters. Part of the thesis involves
the concept of encapsulation which in turn brings with it the awareness
of Mohmandness in the act of migration, an awareness successfully
manipulated for political or professional purposes, as I shall show
through case-studies (Part Three).

The total period during which I was studying the Mohmands, between
1974 and 1977, confirmed part of my thesis that *Pukhtunwali* survives
in its ideal form if given the right ecological environment and the condition of political unencapsulation. With changing economic factors,
such as development schemes bringing new sources of income and a
form of encapsulation through penetration, values even in TAM have
begun to change (Part Three). In 1973, the year the development
schemes began, the last agnatic killing was committed. A certain correlation is apparent. If the peace in Shati Khel becomes a permanent
condition it would, paradoxically, imply deviant Pukhtun behaviour if
we are able to refer to the ideal-type.

However, the thesis that Pukhtun social structure and Code survive
encapsulation is partly refuted and partly substantiated by the very
application and nature of the model in TAM and SAM respectively and
its geo-political requirements, as I will show. Diachronic analysis of the
model will enable us to examine the historical and structural circumstances of its appearance, reproduction and, finally, processes of alteration and reduction in SAM as epiphenomenon. The two important
features making for its empirical validity are the *stability* of the model
and its capacity to *reproduce* itself successfully over some four centuries
at least. These features provide the basis for the formulation of the
problem: what social and cultural criteria determine the transmission of
values from one generation to the next? Or, through what social mechanism does a society prevent breakdown of transmission in the face of
encapsulating systems that herald social and economic change? The
answers are central to my study.

II Methodology

(a) *Method in the field*

The study will be worked out within a framework of Pukhtun life
that includes both the grand symmetry of tribal lineage structure
with its varying and interconnected arches and spans, and also, on
another level, the trivia and minutiae of daily existence: the cold

geometrical arrangements and precision of anthropological tribal lineage charts combined with the smells and sounds of everyday village life. I will not be concerned only with the area of the village, heads of animals, extent of rural credit, lineage charts, etc., in themselves, but as part of larger structural arrangements of social organization. I wish to present the whole range of ethnographic data reflecting the humdrum of every-day life that the average informed reader may wish to see for himself in order to learn about the Pukhtuns, but at the same time I will order the data in such a manner as to illustrate clearly the underlying principles of Pukhtun social organization. The former without the latter is to my mind heuristically an unrewarding and even incomplete anthropological exercise. But the latter without regard to the former risks the danger of becoming a rarified model and losing touch with social reality.

First, a few words about my field-work areas. It is important to understand clearly the distinction between Tribal Areas and Settled Areas, as it provides the basis of division among the Mohmands with far-reaching ramifications. The Tribal Areas of the North-West Frontier Province of Pakistan consist of seven Political Agencies (Map 1). They differ from the Settled Areas in that:

(1) no criminal or civil procedure codes of Pakistan apply;

(2) they are not subject to the payment of taxes or rents of any kind. Many peripheral Islamic tribes like the Kababish Arabs pay taxes (Asad, 1970:154) and there are officially appointed Sheikhs to collect them;

(3) they are loosely administered through a political administration whose main aim is to ensure general tribal peace, especially in head-quarters and on major roads. The administrative arrangement of 'Pax Britannica', confirmed in the tribal treaties of 'accession' at the turn of the century, that whatever happens 100 yards off the road on either side is no concern of the administration, was respected by the government of Pakistan. The designation of the head of the Agency, the Political Agent, underlines the contractual and political nature of the relationship. His designation contrasts with the officer in charge of a Settled District who is called by three names and wears three hats: for purposes of taxes he is District Collector, for administering law, the District Magistrate and for maintenance of law and order, the Deputy Commissioner. The Tribal Areas are federally administered but are attached to the Provincial Government of the North-West Frontier Province for administrative purposes because of geographical and historical reasons;

(4) no political parties or modern politics are allowed as stipulated in

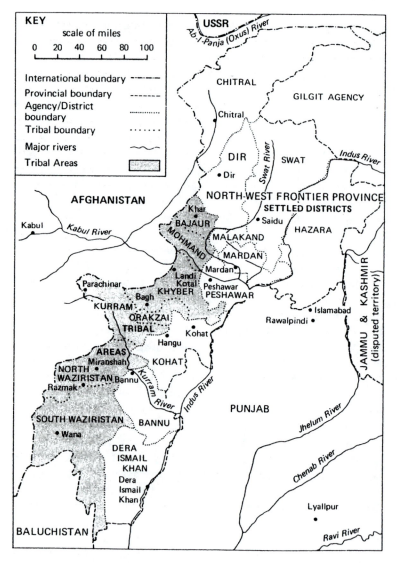

KEY

scale of miles

0   20   40   60   80   100

International boundary ---·---
Provincial boundary ·········
Agency/District
boundary ················
Tribal boundary ········

Major rivers ~~~~

Tribal Areas

USSR

Ab-I-Panja (Oxus) River

CHITRAL

GILGIT AGENCY

Chitral

DIR   SWAT

Swat River

Indus River

• Dir

AFGHANISTAN

NORTH-WEST FRONTIER PROVINCE
SETTLED DISTRICTS

Khar

BAJAUR   • Saidu

MOHMAND

Kabul   *Kabul River*   MALAKAND   HAZARA

MARDAN

Mardan•

Landi
Kotal
Parachinar•   KHYBER   Peshawar•
Bagh   PESHAWAR

KURRAM

ORAKZAI

TRIBAL   • Islamabad

Kohat   Rawalpindi •

Hangu

AREAS   KOHAT

Miranshah•
NORTH   •
WAZIRISTAN Bannu

Razmak•   *Kurram River*   *Indus River*

SOUTH WAZIRISTAN   BANNU   PUNJAB

• Wana

DERA
ISMAIL
KHAN

Dera
Ismail
Khan

BALUCHISTAN

Jhelum River

Chenab River

JAMMU & KASHMIR
(disputed territory)

Lyallpur
•

Ravi River

MAP 1 *The North-West Frontier Province of Pakistan*

the original tribal treaties. The voting right is reserved for the officially
listed Maliks.

Living in one or other Area is a political condition of which the tribal people are explicitly aware. Tribesmen contrast *ilaqa Sarkar* (literally Government Area) with *ghair ilaqa* (outside the Area) and conceptualize the two as antithetical forms of social and political organization. *Ghair* literally means alien, foreign or strange. *Ghair ilaqa* tribesmen live in a state of *siba* or 'institutionalized dissidence' (Gellner, 1969a:1). I prefer the description of such tribal societies as living in 'institutionalized dissidence' to the more usual reference to them in anthropological literature as 'ordered anarchies' (Fortes and Evans-Pritchard, 1970; Middleton and Tait, 1970). 'Dissidence' implies an outside authority which the tribe disagrees with, rebels and rejects in order to keep it at bay. Dissidence is thus implicit in rejection. 'Anarchy', on the other hand, implies a state of chaos within the tribal universe although segmentary societies may be structurally 'ordered'. I will be arguing that to maintain and perpetuate its own social organization based on its tribal normative standards and Code, Pukhtun social history is one of dissidence implying rejection of larger systems.

For purposes of the study I shall define the Mohmand universe geographically as restricted to those lineages living in the Mohmand Agency or conterminous with and along the Peshawar border. Mohmands in Afghanistan, forming half of the entire Mohmand population, and the large groups in the Settled Areas of Mardan and Charsadda, fall outside the scope of my study.

I should now like to say something about my field-work schedule. The idea of conducting a micro-level survey in the Mohmand Agency first came up in 1972 when I was Deputy Secretary, Home and Tribal Affairs Department, to the North-West Frontier Province Government and as a result of my dealing with information on the Tribal Areas. When I was appointed Registrar of the Cooperative Societies, NWFP, in early 1973, I decided to focus my study on economic problems related to kinship structures and selected two sets of Mohmand villages, one in the Mohmand Agency and one in the Peshawar District, after visiting many settlements in the summer of 1974. My primary aim was to select an 'all-Mohmand' village in the Settled Area which, because of its isolated situation, still retained its tribal social customs and structure but was nevertheless in a broader administrative structure, and to draw comparisons with unencapsulated Mohmand villages deep in the Tribal Areas: a comparison between those approximating to the ideal-type and those exposed, juxtaposed or susceptible to encapsulating systems and social change. A largely simplified cause-and-effect study of encapsulation and its impact and ramifications on tribal structure could thus be made.

ions arise as to how and why I finally selected Shati Khel and ~~Be~~ hmandan. The tribal settlements were selected after detailed discussions with the Commissioner of the Peshawar Division and the Political Agent, Mohmands. As this was to be the first study of its — or any — kind in the Agency these officials were keen to suggest villages near the main, and only, road of the Agency, which ran in a direct northerly direction up to the Nahakki mountain range. In any case, travel into the Agency beyond Ekka Ghund, the Agency headquarters, requires clearance from the political authorities for non-locals and an official escort of tribal levies (*badragga*). Traffic, which began as a result of the general opening of the Mohmand road in 1974, comes to a stand-still before dusk when people try to return to the sanctuary of their homes. There are at least four check-posts on the main road between Michni and Nahakki (one at Michni, two at Ekka Ghund and one at Yakh Dand) manned by the Frontier Scouts (in the Agency) and the Frontier Constabulary (at Michni) which scrutinize travellers and transport for smuggling, kidnapping and unauthorized entry.

My concern was to select a village away from the road so as to approximate to as pure a picture of tribal life as possible. The road itself was no international or commercial highway. It was brought up to the Nahakki Pass in 1935 by the British as a strategic military move and triggered off the Mohmand campaign of that year. After this event the authorities tacitly let the road fall into disuse and no further attempts were made either to repair or extend the road until 1974. I finally decided on the Shati Khel area, which touches the main road at one end but is about two miles off the road and almost at the foot of the Nahakki range, which symbolized the furthest point of penetration until then. As this area was virtually untouched it promised a rich source of original anthropological material. My hopes were not to be disappointed and during field-work I found myself constantly checking a tendency to be prejudiced in favour of concentrating on TAM to the detriment of SAM.

Structurally and empirically TAM society fitted into the now classic mould of segmentary and acephalous tribal systems in anthropological literature (Fortes and Evans-Pritchard, 1970; Middleton and Tait, 1970). Here was a patrilineal and egalitarian society with segmentary groups arranged in symmetrical order, dividing and subdividing to exhibit 'nesting attributes'. Territorial boundaries corresponded to tribal segmentary boundaries.

The selection of Bela Mohmandan presented a different type of problem. Many of the Mohmand villages in the Peshawar District which I visited were ethnically mixed and often contained two or more tribes. A selection of any of these would have distorted the comparison and severely affected the variables involved. Bela Mohmandan served the purpose admirably. Although it was remote enough not to have electricity, tube-wells, etc., it was located in the Province's foremost district and was about a furlong from the Agency border. Administratively Bela was part of the Daudzai Police Station which is one of the few areas in the Province selected for the Integrated Rural Development Programme.

Full-time field-work was conducted between August 1975 and March 1976. From March 1976 to August 1976 I was able to continue part-time field-work in my official capacity as instructor in rural sociology and applied anthropology at the Pakistan Academy for Rural Development, Peshawar. The ethnographic present is 1975-76 in the study. Between August 1976 and August 1977 I was posted as Political Agent in the Orakzai Agency which enabled me to complement my field-work by a macro-view of tribal Pukhtun society. My contact with the Mohmands did not cease. They came to stay with me at my headquarters in Hangu from both TAM and SAM and it was a rare week when I did not have a Mohmand, often with his family, staying for a few days. This kept me up to date with fresh developments in my field-work areas.

As there is a need to be precise in spatial terms in describing field-work areas and universe, so there is an equally important need for precision in delineating time-periods and their wider socio-historical context. My study in diachronic analysis uses historical data to place in context the synchronic study of 1975-76. A study in the ethnographic present almost by anthropological definition precludes historical diachronical analysis and as a result reinforces conceptualization of social structure based on consensus and harmony. The very vocabulary of structuralism and functionalism is indicative of this: structure, harmony, equilibrium. The two outstanding exceptions are, of course, the studies of Cyrenaica (Evans-Pritchard, 1973) and highland Burma (Leach, 1977). On the ground, societies on the Indian subcontinent are subject to changes with the various dynasties, rulers and invasions in Indian history. Lord Curzon, the creator of the North-West Frontier Province, once reflected that 'no man who has ever read a page of Indian history will prophesy about the Frontier' (Curzon, 1906:43).

If there is an anthropological lesson that one learns about tribal social life during field-work it is that social networks on various levels at one point or the other are interconnected. This was dramatically brought home to me by a murder that was committed during my field-work in 1975 outside Bela Mohmandan by a closely related agnate of the Subdivisional Officer of the Public Works Department at Hangu, Orakzai Agency. Although the murderer was in jail, the officer had become the prime target, partly because of his eminence, and could not visit his home area in 1977 until the time I was in Hangu.

Added to the problem of open hostility to surveys or official inquisitiveness (Ashraf, 1962; Hussain, 1958:1-2) is the problem of shortage of archival material. There are almost no records, either local or foreign, on the Mohmand, except for routine troop movements recorded by British punitive expeditions with little of ethnographic interest. The only available account was written by an officer, part of whose charge included the Mohmand. Although it is an incisive monograph, it was written by someone who knew little of the social organization in the interior of the Mohmand country and therefore concentrated almost entirely on the history of the hierarchical Khan-type Mohmand organizations in Lalpura in Afghanistan (Merk, 1898). Worse still, there were almost no learned men with special knowledge who could talk about Mohmand history or culture. Those learned Mohmands living in Peshawar or Mardan had little or no knowledge of their cousins in the Agency. Even the Political Agents and Political Officers, who were often knowledgeable on their tribes in other Agencies, administered the Mohmands until 1973 from outside the Agency in Peshawar.

Not surprisingly the Mohmands are the least known Pukhtuns and their Agency 'one of the most isolated areas along the Frontier' (Dichter, 1967: 66). They are among the Pukhtun tribes that have discouraged 'ink-blot tests, anthropometrics, and statistical anthropology' because of 'their ferocity and inaccessibility' (Spain, 1963: 63). Mohmand inaccessibility is mainly responsible for incorrect ethnographic descriptions of their social lives and deviances from Pukhtun custom. They are accused, for instance, of inhospitality and their villages are supposed not to contain male guest rooms (Spain, 1963: 45-6). The accusation of Mohmand inhospitality was found incorrect by my assistants and myself and also by the first wave of officials in 1974-5. Chapter 8 will show that every settlement, however small, has its own *hujra*. Statistical mistakes continue to crop up: for instance there is an incorrect genealogical addition in the Mohmand genealogy published by the Border Publicity Organization (May 1975: 14) which differs from my own investigations which are corroborated by Merk (1898) and General Staff

(1926). Wrong ages (by ten to fourteen years) have been shown on electoral rolls prepared for the Agency in 1977: Shahzada, seventy-four, is shown as sixty and Dilawar, forty, as thirty. The Rural Academy in its publications has quoted Bela Mohmandan as having 153 households and a population of 1,013, both more than double the actual figures (Khan and Shah, 1973: 4). It is conceptually as well as factually erroneous to categorize Mohmand landlords living in the style of the Yusufzai Khans in Mardan as Mohmand tribesmen of the Agency (Spain, 1962: 81-93). Needless to add that none of the above authors actually visited the interior of the Agency.

Matters are made worse by the general inaccessibility of literature on the Tribal Areas for various reasons, often because they contain politically 'sensitive' material. For example, the authoritative monographs by Howell on the Mahsuds (1931), King on the Orakzais (1900) and Merk on the Mohmands (1898) are practically unknown and are not found in the bibliographies of standard works on the Frontier (Barth, 1972; Elliott, 1968; Miller, 1977; Spain, 1962, 1963).

Anthropological surveys in Muslim tribal societies confront a problem regarding the interviewing of women (Barth, 1953: 29; 1970, 1972). I was fortunate in having my wife and her sister present to act as interviewers of women and interpreters of their cultural codes, which helped add an important dimension to my study. My wife and her sister were probably the first outside women to enter the Agency as far as Shati Khel, and certainly the first beyond the Nahakki Pass and as far as the Safi Habibzai Kandahari areas where the ancestors of their agnatic ascendant, the Akhund of Swat, are said to be buried. It would not surprise many people if I were to state that females do play a full part in the political and economic life of the Pukhtuns. As the case-studies in Chapters 5 and 7 will show, women are often in the forefront of upholding Pukhtun ideology, an aspect of society that can be overlooked for lack of data and therefore remain unanalysed.

My data were collected mainly from 101 formal questionnaires: twenty questionnaires were subsequently excluded as fifteen were of women of households already included in the interviews (seven from TAM and eight from SAM) and five were rejected as they appeared to be faulty and inaccurate. The remaining eighty-one households have a total population of 802: Shati Khel[3] 321 (twenty-four households including four entire settlements of its twenty), Kado Korona 117 (twelve of the village's seventy-seven households), Bela 260 (thirty-two of its sixty households) and Kodo 104 (thirteen of the village's thirty-four

households). Of the total population of 1,031 in Shati Khel, 253 people
of the 321 involved in my investigation represent the four settlements
I investigated intensively and the rest are religious and occupational
groups living outside Shati Khel but socially connected to it. As the
above figures show, I also interviewed people from the other nuclear
settlements in the Shati Khel area (Map 5, iii). I also visited Shabkadar,
the other house (*kor*) of many Shati Khel elders and the two villages
near Bela, Kado and Kodo. Some households of the Kado lineage of
Kado Korona and Bela share property, keep in close contact and refer
to each other as the other *kor*. The important point to remember is that
though Kado is only about a mile from Bela it is in the Agency (Maps 2
and 3). Certain data I considered injurious to the interests of the individuals and groups I studied have been omitted and anonymity has been
preserved where it was felt necessary.

   Methodologically I am in full agreement that 'we begin to realise
that the ideal model of the small-scale isolated primitive community is
a myth' (Cohen, 1974: 51). Astraddle across the Agency-District
border and the international border, the Mohmands interact with the
state to their own advantage and when and how it suits them. Reference
to the encapsulating system or state is an integral part of tribal social
organization even if it merely re-defines their unencapsulated condition.
For purposes of methodology 'the anthropologist must *deliberately* for-
mulate his problems in such a way as to make reference to the state a
necessary part of his analysis' (ibid.: 129). Unfortunately, apart from a
few exceptions this acceptance of the larger state or region has been
largely ignored in anthropological studies of small-scale primitive and
tribal societies (ibid.: 126; Velsen, 1969: 145). I agree that for purposes
of methodology 'in tribal studies the tribe has too often been treated as
if it were factually isolated from external cultural, economic and political
influences' (Velsen, 1969: 145). For instance, Professor Bailey records
of his village: 'I was able to isolate Bisipara from its surroundings'
(Bailey, 1960: 5). I maintain that to study a village in 'isolation' is to
risk the danger of reductionism. Certain outstanding studies may be
mentioned as having extended beyond the spatial universe of the village
as a social unit and linked it to the region and wider networks (Asad,
1970; Barth, 1972; Boissevain, 1974; Cohen, 1969, 1972; Epstein,
1962, 1973; Gellner, 1969a; Mayer, A. C., 1966) both among the
individualist and holist anthropologists. Indeed at one point both
analyses require a knowledge of 'linkages' and 'networks' to encapsulating systems (individualist) or superstructure (holist). Unfortunately,

too few studies extend diachronically over time. This is one of the reasons I find the studies of the Sanusi (Evans-Pritchard, 1973) and the Burmese (Leach, 1977) to be among the most effective tribal analyses. In these two examples, both space and time are extended to explain synchronic social phenomena and organizations. Social reality becomes polychrome. I will therefore consciously extend my own study spatially and temporally, without which a full understanding of tribal social structure would not be possible. Encapsulating systems and their links, both over time and space, subsume social history in a connected series of on-going social events that give meaning to and help us to understand the logic behind such fundamental Pukhtun social activity as agnatic rivalry. If I turn to the question of social causality I will in part be turning to historical processes.

I hoped to avoid either an 'ethnocentric' or a 'synecdochic' bias in my study (Ahmed, 1976). I therefore ensured information from and communication to the various groups and strata among my field-work areas by subdividing them thus: men (elders and *kashar*), women, Pukhtun, non-Pukhtun, religious and occupational groups. I was fortunate to interview some of the oldest men in Shati Khel, like Shahmat (Musa) who died during my field-work at what was claimed to be an age over 110 years, Umar Gul (Malok) now said to be the oldest man in TAM at over 100 years old, and Noor Mohammad the oldest man in Bela. From these I learned of social conditions prevalent at the turn of the century. It is fair to point out that Pukhtun society is patrilineal, male-orientated and comprises a population that is self-consciously and almost entirely homogeneous, descended as it is from a common apical ancestor apart from limited religious and occupational groups. Young or old, rich or poor, the Pukhtun sees it as his world and upholds his social values by the prevalent Pukhtun ideology. I shall show by a combination of 'the extended case-method' (Gluckman, 1961) and 'situational analysis' (Velsen, 1964, 1969) based on information provided by informants from various strata and groups, and making allowances for their value judgments, that in certain features, specially those which revolve around the two key concepts of agnatic rivalry and chastity of women, ideal and empirical Pukhtun behaviour coincide to a large degree.

This is not a study of a society 'before' and 'after' (Epstein, 1962, 1973; Firth, 1936, 1959) or of 'hills' versus 'plains' tribes, but a simultaneous study of two groups belonging to one tribe living in differentiated administrative environments. The latter situation creates problems of choices of action and limitations of strategy, both for individuals and groups. I will be arguing that TAM and SAM are not alternative models of social organization but aspects of the same model. The study should allow us to see for ourselves the intervening *processes* of change and not merely the *stages* of change. These will give occasion through extended case-studies to examine normative and deviant behaviour as well as showing up social regularities and irregularities. The influence of modernization (roads, schools, electricity, etc.) on social morphology through the changing economic balance in traditional symmetrical tribal order activate conflicting norms which are themselves a symptom and consequence of the encapsulating process. A section on methodology could not have a more appropriate closing statement than the following: 'These demands are for a synchronic analysis of general structural principles that is closely interwoven with a diachronic analysis of the operation of these principles by specific actors in specified situations' (Velsen, 1969: 149).

(b) *Role of the field-worker*

The role of the field-worker has been insufficiently dealt with in analytical anthropological monographs. I think it is necessary to know why he is there, who sent him, what his relationships are with his respondents, for whom he will write up his study and what specific problems he faced in the field. I am in full agreement that for

> the processes of feedback ... nowadays it becomes essential to know a great deal more about the way in which the field anthropologist has gone about his task: how well he knew the local language; whether he lived among the people as a prince or a beggar or like an 'ordinary' person; who were his friends and who told him what and when and why, and what, if anything, he did about the things he was told (Gluckman, 1969: xviii).

The answers to these questions may provide insight into the mind of the researcher and his own relationship with the topic of his study. From the reader's viewpoint, they may increase empathy with the study and create sympathetic understanding of the problems faced by the field researcher.

'Field-work is an extremely personal traumatic kind of experience' (Leach, 1971a: 1) which can even be 'painful and humiliating' (Wax, 1971: 19), and the first weeks invariably produce a 'feeling of hopelessness and despair' (Malinowski, 1964: Introduction). One is in a sense always *asking*: asking for information, for time, even for social acceptance however temporary and superficial. In return there is palpably so little to give. In terms of reciprocity a sophisticated monograph produced a couple of years later will neither change the lives of the people studied nor be read by them generally. I agree that 'the personal involvement of the anthropologist in his work is reflected in what he produces' (Leach, 1971a: 1) and that 'Anthropologists are also influenced to an enormous extent by the nature of their field experience' (Winter, 1973: 171).

In my own case I found I was pushing myself physically almost beyond endurance. I was beginning to be socially cut off from my service colleagues and friends and even family. My service colleagues were advancing to better jobs while I felt frozen in my study, a victim of a feeling of suspension which bordered near alienation and even depression. In identifying and living with marginal groups one runs the danger of becoming marginal. I found myself asking what I was doing, a question which I am sure was reflected in the minds of many who knew me. Was it the honour and challenge of obtaining a Ph.D degree alone? Was it some instinct in me to serve a less privileged people by documenting their life and bringing their condition to light? Was it simply to understand people and through them myself? Or was it a form of escape? Perhaps, as with all anthropologists, it was a combination of these factors. None the less, in retrospect and as with many anthropologists, I found that some of my happiest moments of companionship were spent in the villages and some lasting friendships were made during my field-work.

The difficulties of method in survey work in the Tribal Areas are mentioned by the author of *Tribal People of West Pakistan: a demographic study*:

It was often heart-breaking to find the interviewee absent from his hut after the enumerator had walked all the long and difficult miles of a mountain country. One way out would have been to hold the interviews in the evening when the interviewee was expected to be back from work. But, in many cases, this was not possible, firstly, because the difficult terrain made it hard to find the way after sunset, and secondly, because, a stranger, despite all peace and calm in these regions, still could not expose himself to the danger of moving about at night (Ashraf, 1962: 12).

The above quotation is from one of the few surveys conducted in the headquarters of the 'open' and 'safe' Tribal Areas. It did not involve residence or 'participant observation' and was limited to a formal questionnaire. In contrast, mine was the first survey of any kind on any scale in the Mohmand Agency, far from the headquarters, in a closed area and especially significant as it involved full participant observation.

The actual physical dangers of doing work in the trans-Indus tribal tracts cannot be minimized. At least one anthropologist, Robert Pehrson, died recently in Baluchistan due to the severity of the field-work conditions (Pehrson, 1966). Scarcity of water, lack of electricity, sanitation, etc., make life difficult and uncomfortable. My wife and I contracted a species of body lice called scabies from sleeping in the beddings provided in TAM that took months to cure, and drew a withering comment on the physical filthiness and standards of sanitation of their hill cousins from the elders of Bela.

Apart from physical discomfort there is always the presence and undercurrents of what the British termed in the last century 'the Great Game'. Shots fired at officials or kidnappings are not uncommon in the Tribal Areas as a result of international political tension. I was conducting my field-work from 1975 to 1976 when relations along the international border were more tense than normal.[4] Very few outsiders ever stayed the night in Shati; officials would either hurry home to Peshawar before dusk or, as in the case of some junior officials after 1973, to Ekka Ghund to their quarters.

In spite of the difficulties mentioned, I had few problems conducting my field-work. The reasons, as I can see them, were that I had no problem of assuming the kinship role offered to me as a field-worker, nor was I working within an alien culture. Above all, I was introduced to TAM and SAM areas before my actual field-work through my contacts with them in the summer of 1974. I had, in fact, appointed two sub-inspectors of cooperative societies from among my field-work groups, the grandson of Shahzada Malik,[5] and Shamshur Rahman of Kado, and tried to help others in various ways. Shati and Bela elders (*mashars*) had visited me in my office and home. Through the tribal network I was quickly known, accepted and therefore assisted. After the initial reservations expressed by those I had not met earlier I was taken into complete confidence. Thus there was no 'pre-involvement', 'introductory' or 'probationary period' (Firth, 1966: 307). When I started field-work in August 1975 the stage was set and waiting. I could therefore 'put aside camera, note-book and pencil' and 'plunge' into and participate in the 'imponderabilia of actual life', which afforded me the opportunity 'to grasp the native's point of view, his relation to life, to realize his version of his world' (Malinowski, 1964: Introduction).

A remarkable sociological characteristic is the almost poker-faced truthfulness of tribesmen. Facts about sensitive issues that were difficult to accept at face value because of their startling frankness were repeatedly cross-checked and invariably found to be accurate. Perhaps social life in *ghair ilaqa* does not create the inhibitions and complexes which cause people to conceal things or lie about them in more civilized social environs. In such an open and face-to-face society there are no secrets. I found that at the slightest hint of deviance from the truth, whether in genealogical lines or in inflated figures about property or income, there would be an immediate and normally good-humoured rebuke either at that moment if an elder were present, or later should I happen to counter-check or my assistants inquire in cases of doubt. This is not to deny that many Mohmands were probably responding to me in the hope that I would take over as their Political Agent or be appointed to some other senior job and therefore be in a position to grant patronage. While not exactly sure of what I was about initially, many would 'humour' my mundane and tedious questioning and regarded me as a harmless and eccentric type of officer.

It may be significant to point out that I lived and travelled throughout my field-work period unarmed and unescorted, a rare attribute shared perhaps only with the Mians and the occupational groups among the Mohmand. For even the Political Agent, like the most minor official, had some form of armed escort, if only for prestige. Like the Mians, members of religious groups, I was unanimously placed in a 'neutral' category and could go and come as I pleased.

During the initial stages of my study the two groups of informants expressed their anxieties in ways which reflect their particular political contexts. TAM groups wondered why I was so interested in sociological questions and not the usual political ones, for instance regarding 'Pukhtunistan'. Was my questioning the prelude to abolition of the institution of the Maliks? Was I noting names of wanted criminals, the Proclaimed Offenders, who escaped the arms of the law and sought refuge in the Agencies? Were we working for the Intelligence Department in an attempt to assess and check international smuggling? However, in SAM fears reflected those of agriculturalists: was this a survey to end the revenue remission they traditionally enjoyed, or to impose a new tax?

By the summer of 1974, I had settled down to a 'pseudo-kinship role' in both areas. The assignment of this role by TAM and SAM is of interest in revealing the attitudes of the two areas. For TAM I became a younger 'brother' of two of the Shati Maliks and pseudo-kin on the lineage charter as a classificatory sibling. I was defined in terms of the tribal charter involving the creation of a fictitious lineage link on it. To the people of Bela I became a 'Belawal', a villager or a person belonging to the village and defined in a spatial sense.

I was acutely aware that as a local officer I could become, however unwittingly, an agent of change – a role I wished to avoid, initially at least, for purposes of academic neutrality and purity. I therefore minimized my role as an official and accepted passively the role allocated to me by TAM and SAM.

I was also conscious of the anthropological need to retain a strict neutrality and objectivity during my field-work. The ideal anthropologist in the field in his relation to the people he is studying 'does not want to improve them, convert them, govern them, trade with them, recruit them or heal them. He wants only to understand them' (Mead, 1974: 57). There were advantages and disadvantages in my being a local officer. From an academic point of view I attempted to be as dispassionately objective as possible. However, it would be unnatural to claim that the extreme problems of economic poverty did not move me subjectively and spur me into hoping that my study would throw some light on these problems and in this way bring them to the notice of the concerned authorities for solution.

III Theory

In this section I shall briefly make three theoretical points in an attempt to place my study within a relevant theoretical framework. The first concerns traditional structural tribal studies in British social anthropology. Following from the consensual models above and in opposition to them we arrive at the second point, a discussion of conflict and cleavage models as represented in Marxist anthropology. Finally I will touch on the debate in the social sciences between methodological holism and methodological individualism. My position will be clearly stated and I hope to substantiate it through the ordering of my data and arguments as the study proceeds.

Professor Leach in *Political Systems of Highland Burma* complained 'that British Social Anthropology had rested too long on a crudely oversimplified set of equilibrium assumptions derived from the use of organic analogies for the structure of social systems' (Leach, 1977: ix). British anthropologists tended to borrow their concepts from Durkheim rather than Marx, Pareto or Weber. Consequently societies revealed 'functional integration', 'social solidarity', 'cultural uniformity' and 'structural equilibrium'. Societies that displayed symptoms of internal conflict leading to structural change were suspected of 'anomie' and pathological decay. At present, however, iconoclasts tear down the old gods of anthropology. Evans-Pritchard's work among the Azande (1937) is a 'romantic and myopic version ... [he] lived for many years as a prince – not a commoner amongst them' (Lamb, 1977: 712). Nadel (1942, 1947) in the field emerges as an offensive, unsympathetic character 'bullying' his Nuba informants. Apparently he had access to a police squad in the Nuba mountains to summon his respondents and was contemptible of their customs. He is the anthropologist as tool of imperialism and oppression *par excellence* (Faris, 1973: 153-70). Evans-Pritchard gets away lightly symbolizing 'the anthropologist as reluctant imperialist' (James, 1973). This is, of course, unfair. I cannot imagine a more sympathetic treatment of the subject than his *The Sanusi of Cyrenaica* (Evans-Pritchard, 1973).

In a recent reprint of the same book Leach felt that the pendulum had swung too far: 'The pendulum has now swung so far over in the opposite direction that I am obliged to present it as a defence of empirical observation against the encroachments of structuralist Marxist fantasy!' (Leach, 1977: xvii). I would agree that the pendulum may have swung too far. This is a deductive not a polemic statement and is based on field-work data. While Swat provides a neat example of a 'conflict tribal model' (Asad, 1972) Mohmands, ecologically and historically, present a different picture, an opposing ideal model. Conflict exists on two levels in society and works in opposite directions: external conflict with imperial forces reinforce ideal Pukhtun values, and internal conflict, exacerbated as a result of British-backed Maliks, interacts with agnatic rivalry to widen divisions in society (Chapters 3, 5 and 7). In spite of this the Mohmand model of an acephalous, segmentary, egalitarian tribal society is in the classic mould of British social anthropology. To illustrate my point I would like to borrow a description of one such African society which Leach uses as a model to attack:

At every level of Tale social organisation ... the tendency towards an equilibrium is apparent.... This does not mean that Tale society

was ever stagnant. Tension is implicit in the equilibrium.... But conflict could never develop to the point of bringing about complete
disintegration. The homogeneity of Tale culture, the undifferen-
tiated economic system, the territorial stability of the population,
the network of kinship ties, the ramifications of clanship, and especially the mystical doctrines and ritual practices determining the
native conception of the common good – all these are factors,
restricting conflict and promoting restoration of equilibrium (Fortes,
quoted in Leach, 1977: x).

I would like to postulate that Mohmands in the ideal-type model conform to the description of a tribal society in equilibrium as described
above. In Chapter 4 I shall give a fuller account of this type of unencapsulated Pukhtun society revolving around concepts of *nang* (honour) as
opposed to Pukhtun groups ordering their social organization around
qalang (taxes and rents) that imply encapsulation, hierarchy and deviance from the Pukhtun ideal-type. The point of anthropological interest
is that this is a picture of social reality as it exists today and not *circa*
1940 when *African Political Systems* was compiled.

Following from the discussion of equilibrium models, there is a
tendency in anthropological literature to speak of the tribe as a unit, a
whole. For example, Nuer or the Tiv are conceptualized as if they are
contained and defined by their distinct genealogical charters (Bohannan,
L., 1952, 1970; Bohannan, L. and Bohannan, P., 1953, 1968; Evans-
Pritchard, 1940, 1970; Fortes and Evans-Pritchard, 1970). The social
boundaries of the universe embrace the tribe in its entirety. Empirically
I found the concept of the 'tribe' limiting for purposes of theoretical
analysis. My data in TAM and SAM pointed to a lower level of the
genealogical chart as the actual, effective social universe. As I posited
in the opening statement of the study, the operative lineage in tribal
society is the sub-section within which marriage and political alliances,
and, above all, agnatic rivalry, are contracted, as I shall illustrate by
case-studies. The Mohmand is at the centre and aware of three concentric tribal and diacritical circles, the blueprint of which he carries in his
mind: the operative lineage, the sub-section as the immediate and
cognitive socially relevant universe, a larger Mohmand circle that defines
him as a member of the tribe and finally the phyletic boundary that
defines him as a Pukhtun. Similarly three levels have been discerned for
membership of castes in India: 'The lowest is that of an effective local
subcaste population, which I call the kindred of co-operation' (Mayer,

A.C., 1970: 4). We may conceptualize the tribal sub-section as the 'effective local subcaste population' and could term its members 'the kindred of co-operation'. However, in view of the intense agnatic rivalry that is generated in the sub-section, perhaps 'the kindred of competition' may be a more apt description.

The concept of the operative lineage for analysis of social and political life poses a logical and interesting question: is the operative lineage to be translated in terms of economic activity as the 'lineage mode of production'? (Godelier, 1977). I shall deal with this at length in later chapters but the short answer is in the negative. The intense spirit of individualism and egalitarianism that permeates tribal groups vitiates any concept of sustained or institutionalized, joint or communal economic activity. Income, production and consumption are entirely a function of the household and the family, usually nuclear and in some cases compound families where a patriarch organizes economic activity and is a polygamist. Male married siblings living within the walls of a joint family settlement operate individual budgets and balance their own books (as will be seen in Chapters 8 and 9). The economic and consumption unit is the 'hearth' or *kor*. The 'mode of production' may be called 'familial' or 'domestic' (Sahlins, 1968: 75–81).

With reference to the second point of this section the pendulum of 'equilibrium models' has indeed swung in the opposite direction and conflict models are popular in anthropology today. There is a growing body of Marxist anthropological literature. Professor Godelier's illuminating analysis of Marxist anthropology and reference to the brands of 'vulgar Marxism' (Godelier, 1977), which was probably anticipated by Marx himself and prompted him to utter his prophetic disclaimer 'Je ne suis pas Marxiste', reflects that there is perhaps a band-wagon quality in this trend. Where do I stand for purposes of my study? From a pure and simple academic point of view (if such a view – to borrow a Wildean phrase – can be pure or simple) British social anthropology is still inclined to concepts centring around structure, function, consent and unity in primitive and tribal societies, an academic and almost psychological predilection rooted in its imperial history and the genesis of the discipline. Therefore Marxist anthropology with its emphasis on class, cleavage and conflict is a healthy intellectual corrective and the encounter can only be good for the discipline. For instance, it is interesting to note that Marxist anthropologists see the debate between Substantivist and Formalist economic anthropologists not only as having little actual content but with the two positions coalescing (Godelier,

1977: ch. 1). Unfortunately Marxist analysis of South Asia still largely ignores tribal societies (Blackburn, 1975; Gough and Sharma, 1973) while Marxist analysis of African tribal societies remains simplistic and unsatisfactory (Rey, 1975; Terray, 1972, 1975a, b) — what Godelier has termed 'vulgar Marxism' (Godelier, 1977).

In the Mohmand situation, if we are to perceive transformation of the class becoming *for* itself (political) *from* in itself (economic), we must ask which class we are referring to and then define it. Is it the majoritarian population of Pukhtuns constituting 92 per cent of the population who are small landowners, or the religious groups who consider themselves both socially and economically equal if not better than the Pukhtuns, and who with the socially inferior but economically equal non-Mohmand occupational groups constitute 8 per cent of the population? In the SAM situation, for purposes of Marxist analysis, we could ask the question: who is the exploiter? Though SAM are developing peasant attributes there are still no landlords or other exploiting agents. I agree with Terray that so far Maxist theories of segmentary societies 'are only hypotheses which must be verified, enriched, and completed' (Terray, 1975b: 133).

The Mohmand model is almost classic in its structural simplicity, depictive of balancing lineage arches and spans and derived from the segmentary, acephalous democratic tribal formations of British anthropology. But this is palpably a conceptualization of tribal democracy. In fact there are inequalities: between seniors and juniors, men and women, Mohmand and non-Mohmand and, since the impact of the British, sharpened cleavages within segments as agents of change in the articulation of various political demands between *mashar* and *kashar*. None the less these differences among the Mohmand are not wide enough to justify an application of a Marxist conflict framework as has been done successfully for Swat where large landowners are in a position to exploit their tenants (Asad, 1972). In TAM, Shahzada of the senior lineage, the most powerful political figure, owns 7 acres[6] of land where the average land ownership of household heads is about 4½ acres. The biggest landlord in SAM, Hussain, owns some 9 acres, and that recently acquired, whereas the average ownership is about 2 acres of land (Chapters 8 and 9). Obviously the sources of power and exploitation do not derive from control of the purely economic means of production.

Third, within the theoretical framework of the study, I shall try to work out an analysis to illustrate the need in the social sciences for

some form of synthesis between the methodological holist and individualist frames of analyses, a point I have raised in an earlier work
(Ahmed, 1976) and which has been argued by anthropologists:

> Our problem is, therefore, to search for a framework of analysis
> which might transcend that dichotomy and the associated mecha-
> nistic conceptions of relationship between man and society, so that
> we might conceptualize man in society as a dialectical unity, neither
> being prior to the other (Alavi, 1973: 50-1).

The individual and society do not presuppose each other and neither
precedes nor is prior to the other. Temporal and spatial boundaries are
as complex as they are shifting. Synthesis of the major compartments
rather than particularistic analysis is suggested.

I will be arguing that for Pukhtun tribal groups one or other analysis
may be heuristically useful at different times in their history and in
different geographical situations.

The study will attempt to illustrate that the generalized motivations
to 'strategize' or 'maximize' of 'Barthian man' (man as entrepreneur:
Barth, 1963, 1971a, 1972) or 'Leachian man' (political man: Leach,
1977) are not universally applicable. The translation of 'maximizing
man' from economics into anthropology in many ways diminishes and
subtracts a dimension of social man. A metaphor is a poor surrogate for
social reality. I will show from case-studies that tribal man does not
necessarily act out his life deciding between alternative strategies and
scarce means in order to maximize. Mohmand man embodies the *aspects*
of politics (pursuit of political power), economics (pursuit of economic
gain) or religion (pursuit of religious status – or, as one result, even a
rejection of it). His actions are explained by one or more of these
motivations at different times and in different conditions.

If there is competition between agnates, there is some scarce commodity. This scarce commodity is political power and status: it is
defined in sectional leadership, in recognition of status by the group
and the political administration, and it involves official patronage. At
the risk of oversimplifying, if TAM can be generally classified as 'political' man then SAM may be 'agricultural' man. I shall illustrate this
point through various case-studies particularly concerning the two key
features of society, agnatic rivalry and the chastity of women. In certain
areas and in certain situations TAM is subjected to groups limiting and
curtailing his alternative choices and strategies. On the other hand and
in certain other situations he is in a position to order or reorder his

strategy, limited only by the scarcity of means and not by group pressures. He may be said to be in pursuit of 'maximization' in one form or other. I will show that Mohmand man is in a social position to 'attack', 'seize' and 'oust', etc., and that 'group commitments may be assumed and shed at will' (Barth, 1972: 2). TAM maximizes political power and sees life in political terms, within the context of the cognitive symbols of his society especially involving agnatic rivalry. He is not restricted by the laws of the state, as is the Swat Pukhtun, or by those codified by national government, like the Pukhtuns in the Settled Districts of Pakistan, but only by the structure of his tribe and its Code. But his group, in a different situation, may be in a position to frustrate or block him.

For TAM, time is invested in hospitality and building alliances. There are few other sources of material and non-material investment; land is limited and barren and marketing and trading are traditionally non-Pukhtun activities. In the TAM model in Shati Khel, when he stands a chance of participating with some possibility of success, the Mohmand participates, but when he assesses that the time is not propitious he retires from the arena. Retirement can be of two sorts: like that of the Malok lineage, living in one of the four villages studied, who have deliberately rejected participation in agnatic rivalry and have turned to economic activity to channel their energies, at a stroke illustrating their political position by resorting to traditionally non-Pukhtun activity such as trade. The second form of retirement is temporary: when they are no longer in a position to defend themselves in agnatic enmity, their settlements are 'seized' and they are 'ousted', as in the cases of Atta Khan or Mazullah Khan. Such gladiators repair to outside the Agency, usually to Shabkadar, but watch the situation carefully with a view to returning at the opportune moment. Expulsion does not end the game. It merely adds a new dimension to it (Chapters 5 and 7).

Characteristically TAM may be best analysed in 'wholes' or 'groups' when the Pukhtun Code is involved or evoked. Social action or reaction is almost mechanistically determined by what the group *expects*, as in cases regarding the chastity of women. The agnatic kin of a dishonoured female cannot shrug off the holist demands of society without risking severe opprobrium and ostracism (Chapter 7).

TAM 'attack', 'seize' and 'oust' but not in a manner that would depict a breakdown in society or annihilate their universe. There is a predictable rhythm in the pattern of agnatic movement, action activates reaction, point activates counterpoint. Underneath the semblance of anarchy lie structural principles that perpetuate and maintain stability in society and correct deviance or instability with an almost scientific predictability. There is thus always an implicit tribal structural limit to explicit choices of strategy.

In contrast SAM runs up against the laws of the land if they do not correspond to the laws of his tribe or its customs. He is man eking out a meagre livelihood from the soil and politics is relegated to one of the various objectives of life and not the major or overriding one.

In terms of our model SAM may wish to pursue political power as Barthian Swat man or the Leachian Burmese or even his TAM cousin, but with an important qualification. He finds this increasingly difficult within the laws and administrative framework of the state. For instance, Shamshudin and Hamesh Gul, the SAM elders of the senior Kado Khel and Madar lineages, are not playing the power game. They admit there is no profit in attempting traditional Pukhtun activity. They are hospitable but cannot convert it into a political asset or status. Both are caught up in the trivia of daily life and its immediate problems. They are opting out of games of power or prestige. Whether they are hospitable or not does not substantially change their status or social standing. Hussain Khan, an elder of the junior Jano Khel lineage, not noted for his hospitality, finds a viable alternative to investing resources in hospitality by acquiring land or loaning money on credit. The SAM village has little to offer in terms of political rewards or their possible conversion to economic profit.

I would like to conclude this section by reproducing the relevant part of a comment I made elsewhere:

> The masters of a theory — whether 'holist/individualist', 'substantivist/ formalist', etc. — risk becoming its slaves. Intellectual traditions and thought systems tend to go sour and even sterile if confined to watertight categories. Social ontology and its manifestation — human society — in the 20th century are polychrome, changing, and complex. The fundamental strength of anthropology remains in fieldwork data, allowing reexaminations and reassessments (Ahmed, 1978a: 222).

IV Model

In this section I shall follow the Oxford Dictionary in the definition of 'model': 'design to be followed, style of structure, person or thing proposed for or worthy of imitation, exemplary.' Following this definition, the study will attempt to build a model of Pukhtun social organization drawn from historical and archival material but mainly based on field-work data (Chapters 4 to 9). I will build a Weberian ideal-type model and examine it in an 'as if' situation: as if there is a timeless, unchanging, ethnographic present (Chapter 4). The creation of a model and the empirical study of two tribal groups provide ideal laboratory conditions for an inductive experiment: if an alteration is effected in the political variable while other variables, such as religion, language, culture, etc., are held constant, we will be in a position to assess the emergent differences in the two groups. Thus TAM remain unencapsulated while SAM are encapsulated in political terms (although the difference is in kind not degree, the validity of the experiment is unaffected). In building an ideal-type model there is a danger of over-simplification which I shall risk. The various Pukhtun categories of normative behaviour will help to throw crucial features of the ideal-type into relief, features important to the 'native exegesis' or apperception of the model. In a similar experiment Epstein examined two villages in India where variables such as the political, ritual and cultural were held constant but the economic variable was altered, thus allowing an assessment of increasing changes and widening differentiation in the other (constant) variables in the two village societies (Epstein, 1962, 1973). Just as Epstein argued that economic change was the determining variable in changes in political, ritual and social life, so I argue that it was changes in the political situation in 1951 which produced changes in economic, ritual and social life. The changes in economic life will emerge from statistics and their analysis in later chapters. However, neither the experiment nor the results are so simple and a multilineal system of trajectories is perceptible. The deeper structure which we are brought to face when we consider the process of tribal transformation from TAM to SAM is one whose properties can be defined only with respect to time. Thus, changes in modes of production and consumption cannot be understood in terms of technological constraints alone but partly through organizational possibilities afforded by changed and changing political situations. A fuller discussion of these possibilities will follow in Parts Two and Three.

The critical date for the alteration in the political variable, the date that may be considered as the baseline of change in and between TAM and SAM, is 1951. Until then both groups lived within similar economic and political situations and responded alike to similar external or internal stimuli. After 1951 social, economic and political differentiations, as reflected in kinship organization, political leadership and deviance from the tribal Code and customs, begin to emerge. The gap between ideal and actual Pukhtun behaviour with reference to the model widens in direct proportion to the extent of political encapsulation. Conversely *Pukhtunwali* goes through a process of increasing attenuation in the encapsulated group.

As I will explicate, my model is cognate and theoretically aligned to Barth's 'generative models' (Barth, 1971a). The models

> are not designed to be homologous with observed social regularities; instead they are designed so that they, by specified operations, can *generate* such regularities or forms.... Thus by a series of logical operations, forms can be generated; these forms may be compared to empirical forms of social systems, and where there is correspondence in formal features between the two, the empirical form may then be characterized as a particular constellation of the variables in the model. [Generative models] have three important uses: 1) ... to discover and describe the processes that generate the form. 2) They provide the means to describe and study change in social forms as changes in the basic variables that generate the forms. 3) Finally, they facilitate comparative analysis as a methodological equivalent of experiment (ibid.: v).

Barth summarizes his argument: 'our theoretical models should be designed to explain how the observable frequency patterns, or regularities, are generated' (ibid.: 1).

I have partly dealt with Barth's 'models of process' elsewhere in a study (Ahmed, 1976) in which I attempted to draw a 'model of process' over time in order to examine the changing social organization of a tribal group diachronically and as a result of certain historical sequences. In the present study I shall also employ the useful concept of 'models of process' and add the dimension of space to that of time. I shall take two sets of tribal groups at one moment in time and examine the effects encapsulation and concomitant administrative processes have on them; that is, the determinants of form and their impact on social organization, particularly in institutions I see as vital to Pukhtun society such as agnatic rivalry as a consequence of changes in basic variables. Aggregates of social regularity create social reality and help us understand it, but instances of social irregularity illuminate that reality and help us comprehend it and measure the extent of deviance. Therefore case-studies from TAM and SAM will help us to understand what an original 'conscious', 'home-made' (Ward, 1969) Mohmand model would look like and where and how far deviances have occurred from it. The model will show how encapsulation affects social structure in the two most vital institutions of society, agnatic rivalry and chastity of women, and how this, in turn, affects their views of themselves and of each other.

In SAM already the two most important institutions *tarboorwali* and *tor* are partly affected as a result of three decades of encapsulation (Chapter 7). The model is *depictive* of social reality *over time*; it has reproduced itself successfully over historical periods and in spite of changing historical sequences. It is also to an extent predictive. It can predict forms of social changes and the directions they are likely to take given certain conditions. The creation of an ideal-type model will therefore 'facilitate comparative analysis as a methodological equivalent of experiment'.

In large, like other models, mine will be part myth. The model will allow us to measure, assess, examine and finally analyse changes in Pukhtun social organization, by allowing us to view SAM against TAM. The latter will provide us with the model and point of reference; the former will enable us to examine the forms of change and the deter-minants of change. For purposes of defining the essential components of the model I will restrict myself to case-studies involving two key features of the Pukhtun Code, *tarboorwali* and *tor*. However, directly cognate patterns in settlement, marriage and expenditure will also be examined to support my argument. It should be possible to conduct an examination of the underlying logic of social phenomena beyond and behind the apparent visible logic and symmetry of structure. We have almost laboratory conditions for an experiment that will allow us to see the processes of change and, because of our two-village situation, simul-taneously to analyse the *forms* of change (Barth, 1971a). The attempt will enable us to show changes as a result of alteration in one variable, the political. The forms of change subsume a degree of complexity in the situation in spite of the small-scale society with its limited techno-logy and rudimentary division of labour.

The model will be a dynamic one possessing social components that are in constant action and subject to shift and change in response to external stimuli as will be seen through case-studies. Pukhtun ideology itself anteceding encapsulation legitimizes and perpetuates Pukhtun activity. The analysis will therefore be diachronic and take in the sweep of Mohmand history over the last hundred years where it is relevant to the argument and concerns our groups.

The model itself will coalesce various factors: micro-level field-work data based on the Mohmand, with macro-level data gathered from my period as Political Agent among the Orakzais. Although it will be synchronic and based on an ethnographic present, it will simultaneously be diachronic with reference to the ongoing sequences of social history. Although set within a theoretical framework discussed in the last section, a deliberate attempt to place hard ethnographic data in the foreground will be made in support of my belief in the nature of ethnographic accounts.

The plan of the study is as follows: Part One, Chapters 1 to 3 state the theoretical and methodological framework of the study. The geopolitical situation and historical sequences provide the variables that help to define, conceptualize and even explain the model and the causal factors that have contributed to its unbroken continuity over the last four centuries. About two-thirds of the study concentrates on the construction of an ideal-type *nang* Mohmand model and its normative demographic, social and economic organization based on data gathered during field-work (Part Two: Chapters 4 to 9). The main aim of Part Two is to establish the parameters of the model and to distinguish the permanent and underlying principles of social organization and elaborate on the major features of structure that constitute it. Part Two may be considered the core of the study, supported by the equally important earlier and later parts whose focus may not be as direct and as central to the model but help place it in relief. Changes that may be predicted in the model affecting traditional symmetry, structure and function following penetration in the form of various governmental development schemes resulting in a form of encapsulation are discussed in Part Three (Chapters 10 to 12).

The model will be an accurate microcosm of larger tribal life of segmentary, acephalous groups with similar economies and political structures in the Tribal Areas of Pakistan. It will enable generalization about tribes living in similar conditions elsewhere. From a practical point of view, the tribal study should be an addition to the general knowledge of the Tribal Areas with its hard data, especially as this will be the first of its kind and of interest to planners both in national and international agencies, especially those connected with rural development, agriculture, economic programmes, etc., and of course to the political authorities interested in implementing these projects. Second, it will be a theoretical and ethnographic addition to the knowledge of tribal structure and systems.

2 The Mohmand ecological and administrative framework

The general aspect of the Mohmand country is, with few exceptions, wild, rugged and desolate. It consists of a dull monotony of brown rocky hills alternating with dusty sun-baked plains, which are, for the most part, scored in every direction by deep dry *nalas* (streambeds) (General Staff, 1926: 10).

In this chapter I shall discuss the geographical environment and administrative system within which Mohmands organize their lives and how these factors affect social organization and help to explain differentiation between the two groups I am studying. Two sets of factors have shaped politics and society through history: first, the Mohmand Agency as it lies in a low rainfall zone with few sources of water is a low production area. Second, the Mohmand tribe straddles two borders, one international, and the other between two distinct administrative systems of the North-West Frontier Province (Maps 1 and 2). The implications for population mobility and exploitation of the geo-political situation for purposes of my theme will be discussed below.

1 Mohmand ecology

In this section I shall outline briefly the geographical situation, the physical features and the population deployment of the Mohmand clans related to the study.

The Agency which is 887 square miles in area lies between $34°$–40 and $33°$–30 lines of latitude and $70°$–30 and $71°$–30 longitude. It is bordered by the Bajaur Agency in the north (with its perennial snow-capped peaks visible from the Agency) and divided from the Khyber Agency by the Kabul river in the south. The western boundary lies along the international border dividing the Mohmands in half, and has never been visited by any official boundary commission including the Durand Commission of 1893-4 responsible for creating the border. Turn of the century correspondence speaks of this as 'the presumptive

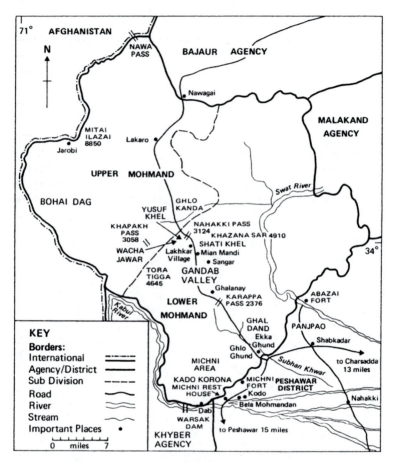

MAP 2 *Mohmand Agency: geographical and administrative features*

border' (Baha, 1968). To the east the Agency shares an arbitrary and
sometimes shifting border with Peshawar District (Maps 1 and 2). Crossing from the Agency into the District either towards Shabkadar or
Peshawar does not involve crossing an ethnic border since the Halimzai
and Tarakzai have spilled over from the Agency for at least 10 to 15
miles inside the District. For instance, there are other Tarakzai villages
like Bela Mohmandan in the District, like Nilawai, Danglakhtai in the
Daudzai Thana and up to Joganni situated along the Kabul river and its
branches. Mohmands call the Mardan and Charsadda region *maira* (flat,
settled plains); they associate it with tenant farming over the last genera-

tions and consider it an important area of political and economic refuge. The four seasons are divided distinctly and equally through the year and have characteristic features. November, December and January are the winter months (*jamay*). February, March and April form the most pleasant season of the year, spring (*sparlay*). Regular dust-storms and hazy air mark summer (*oray*), in May, June and July. The latter two months (*har, pashakal*) which are hot, humid and enervating precede the autumn season (*manay*). Temperatures range from maximum averages of 105–110 °F in summer and drop to 30–40 °F in winter.

The Agency is *barani* (entirely dependent on rainfall for its agricultural needs). The scant annual rainfall of about 6–8 inches, mainly in spring and early autumn, produces one poor crop of barley, and where spring or Persian wheel (*arat*) water is available, maize and wheat on small plots. The situation in Bela is somewhat better. Rainfall has averaged 12 inches for the last seven years (Office of Executive Engineer, Warsak Canals Division, Peshawar) and irrigation water, though restricted, is provided by a system of water channels from the Kabul river and shared by several adjoining villages. The main crops of Bela Mohmandan are sugar-cane, maize and wheat. Barley is grown for animals.

A description of Mohmand country written in the last century is still valid today: 'The aspect of the Mohmand hills is exceedingly dreary, and the eye is everywhere met by dry ravines between long rows of rocky hills and crags, scantily clothed in coarse grass, scrub wood and the dwarf palm (*mazari*)' (Merk, 1898: 1). The dwarf palm has since disappeared, increasing denudation: 'In summer great want of water is felt, and the desert tracts radiate an intolerable heat; this, coupled with the unhealthiness of the river low-lands, probably accounts for the inferior physique of Mohmands as compared with Afridi and Shinwari neighbours' (ibid.).

The recently completed main road passing through the middle of the Agency and connecting it from north to south divides its geographical area into three zones that correspond to clan localities: the Safi area in the north, lying south of the Bajaur Agency and extending to the Halimzai area separated by Ghlo Kanda; the Halimzai area in the centre between Ghlo Kanda and the Karappa Pass (2,376 feet) (the Nahakki range from 2,500 to 3,500 feet divides Kamali and Gandab Halimzai); and the Tarkazai area in the south between the Karappa Pass and Ekka Ghund on the borders of the Agency (Maps 2 and 4). The Safi area has large, flat, dry valleys cut by perpendicular ravines. The Gandab of the Halimzai has a few spots of green wherever there is a

Persian wheel in the belly of the valley where water is closest to the earth at about 50 feet; otherwise its small barren valleys are dominated by equally barren mountain ranges. Nuclear settlements are clustered around features such as the *arat*. Shati Khel is some eight miles from the international border to the west. The Baezai and, below them, the Khwaezai clans lie on both sides of the border, and are still largely inaccessible. The Tarakzai area is an unending range of desolate and broken mountains. In this zone no population is visible. Occasionally one may catch a glimpse of a woman or boy with a donkey carrying fodder for cattle, appearing and disappearing from nowhere to houses miles out of sight. Standing on the Karappa Pass with the Peshawar valley faintly visible in hues of misty green and blue to the south-east, it is not difficult to analyse why the Tarakzai have moved further south and south-east, first to around the Michni area and then beyond and, as at Bela Mohmandan, into the District.

Shati Khel is situated in the northern end of the Gandab valley which contains the central routes from and to the Agency and may be considered the key to the Agency. The Halimzai valley area starts at Ghlo Kanda in the north and ends at Ghal Dand in the south: it thus begins and ends with *ghal* (which means thief). The historical derivation of these names is not difficult to guess. The Gandab was one of the trading routes to the Indian subcontinent and caravans had to pay 'protection money' at the rate of 3 rupees[1] per camel, Rs. 2 per horse and Rs. 1 or half per man in the last century (Holmes, 1887: 1470; Merk, 1898), not unlike that collected by local sectional leaders, *aaban*, in certain African societies (Bohannan and Dalton, 1962: 369-71). The total sum was scrupulously and equally divided between the clans through whose territory the caravans passed. 'Unprotected' caravans were at the mercy of local tribal groups. The insecurity of the Gandab was inimical to trade, a situation familiar in other tribal societies and areas (ibid.). Even today traffic slows down in the afternoon and comes to a standstill by dusk. The word Gandab itself means dirty water, and my Bela assistants would privately complain to me of the quality of the water and its effects on their stomachs.

Lineage and settlement boundaries are important in Shati Khel to delimit individual and sectional ownership and reflect the contemporary strength of lineages. Currently the Musa Khel of the Shati Khel dominate the Shati area which is about 2 square miles. Although Sangar and Ghazi Kor are in the centre of the Gandab valley where water is found at a depth of 50 feet while at Shati it is found between 200 to 250 feet, the latter is strategically situated from a military point of view being surrounded on all sides except one by high mountains. Sangar lies in the valley and is therefore unprotected and more vulnerable. The choice of Shati as the home of the dominating lineage is thus partly explained. Chapters 5, 7 and 8 will discuss present settlement deployment as a consequence of historical processes.

The location and history of Bela Mohmandan are related to the Tarakzai area west of the Michni rest house and fort. Between the Michni rest house and the Michni Frontier Constabulary fort, but in the Agency to the west, are the houses of the progenitors of the Bela lineages. Indeed, as we saw earlier, the dominant lineage, Kado Khel, has given its name to the geographical area called Kado Korona. The entire area is about 8 miles from west to east and about 10 miles north to south and lies at the foot of the barren Tarakzai hills described above. It is densely populated, one of the effects of the Left Bank Canal from the Warsak Dam on the Kabul river, begun in 1956 and completed in 1960, which irrigates its fields.

Michni, a name loosely applied to the area, was so called, I am told by the elders, because of the number of domestic hand-mills (*maichans*) for grinding wheat in that area. Today there is only one – at the carpenter's in Bela – which is usually used to grind salt and is made available free. I shall be calling the region just described the Michni area generally for purposes of my study. The Michni area is shared by the two major sub-clans of the Tarakzai, the Dadu and Kasim Khel, in clearly demarcated geographical areas corresponding to their sections: from south to north, the Dadu Khel, representing the senior lineage, are placed in a strategic position along the Kabul river. The Kasim Khel sub-clan, to which all the five out of six Bela Mohmandan sub-sections trace their lineage, occupies the other half of the Michni area. The Zarif Khel, another section of the Kasim Khel, live in the northern area and are represented in Bela Mohmandan by two houses. Among the Kasim Khel the Kado sub-section is dominant in the central area which is commonly called Kado Korona. Baz Mohammad, Shamshudin's wife's paternal uncle, and a Kado senior, lives here as does Habibur Rahman, the elder, and only brother of Shamshudin. This gives people, like Shamshudin, the opportunity to place themselves in a *dwa-kora* (two houses) category and to transfer conflict or awkward situations within the administrative framework of the district to their other *kor* in Kado. Shamshur Rahman, another assistant in my study and a nephew of Shamshudin, also lives here. It will be seen in the case-studies in Chapter 7 how the above people and lineages living *both* in Bela Mohmandan and Kado Korona could subvert the laws of the Settled Districts by a tacit understanding that the *arena* of conflict and rules would be of and in the Agency.

Historically the Michni area has felt the full brunt of the British presence from the beginning of the colonial encounter, as the record of these tribal sections, referred to as the Michni Mohmands in official records, testifies (Chapter 3). Villages, like Dab on the banks of the Kabul river, were repeatedly destroyed over the hundred years of the British presence in this area. The Michni Mohmands were at one stage excommunicated from British India by an electric fence running from the Michni rest house 17½ miles to the north, as we will see below. But as the barren Tarakzai hills pushed them inexorably to the Michni area two to three centuries ago, the demographic trends in the context of the larger historical framework discussed in Chapter 3 from the middle of the last century pushed the Michni Mohmands further east across the changing and ill-defined boundary into the Settled Areas. The population shifts assumed a symmetrical pattern as the arrows in Map 3 show. So while the Dadu Khel moved to lands around the Michni rest house, the Kasim Khel shifted to and built villages like Bela Mohmandan in the initial thrust. The symmetry was maintained at various levels of segmentation and within the sub-clan the Khalil remained in the villages around Bela while the Zarif occupied villages down the river. This is, of course, a schematized map and on the ground and after a hundred years of acquiring and loosing land (through marriage, sale, mortgage default, etc.) there is a tendency towards intermingling of sub-sectional land ownership, as indeed Bela Mohmandan illustrates.

A less dramatic population shift, but one that is partly explained by my thesis of tribal strategy *vis-à-vis* the larger state system, began in the last three decades *after* the creation of the Agency. This time the shift, from the District to the Agency, was of tribal groups wishing to reactivate their interests in the Agency; this is illustrated by the broken lines in Map 3. The irrigation waters from the Warsak Left Bank Canal in the 1960s have made the Michni area into a highly fertile one producing excellent varieties of sugar-cane and wheat. Fear of floods and actual flooding, as in Zor Mandi, have also encouraged reverse migration. I have interviewed some groups from Bela who returned to the Agency in the 1960s and their answers partly confirmed my thesis of tribal groups consciously adopting a strategy to exploit political and administrative arrangements (tribal strategy *vis-à-vis* encapsulating systems will be discussed in Part Three).

Bela Mohmandan, like the Michni rest house almost a mile away, lies on the banks of the Kabul river in the District. The main road from Peshawar runs parallel to the Agency border but in the District between the rest house and the Frontier Constabulary fort at Michni. The road divides into two at Pir Qila (still in the District): west to the Mohmand Agency -- Shati Khel is 20 miles from Pir Qila and just over 40 miles from Peshawar -- and north across Subhan Khwar, the boundary between the Tarakzai and Halimzai, to Shabkadar the stronghold of the latter. Bela is about 8 miles from Shabkadar and 16 miles from Peshawar (Map 2).

The role of water in Mohmand lives must be emphasized: severe

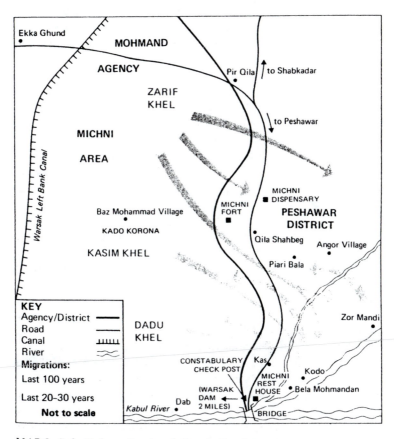

MAP 3 *Bela Mohmandan in relation to the Agency*

scarcity of it in TAM, and often excess of it, in the form of floods, in
SAM. Tribal strategy in conflict is based on capturing the well or water
tank of the opponents. TAM settlements relate directly to the strategy
of tribal warfare while Bela, on the other hand, with the Mohmand
villages situated along the Kabul river, probably finds itself where it is
for reasons of economic and agricultural strategy (Chapters 8 and 9).
For four summer months Bela becomes an island when the otherwise
dry channel, some 120 yards in width, to the north-west of its area is
flooded by waters of the melting snows in the Kabul river (Map 6).
There is no road to Bela and buses and cars cannot visit the village.
Jeeps can make the journey only during the dry months and through
the channel. One of the major and persistent demands of the villagers
has been for a bridge over this channel and an all-weather road.

In Bela village boundaries delimit land in the face of encroachments
by the landowning non-Mohmand Arbabs across the river towards
Peshawar and to record the alluvial and diluvial activities of the river.
Seasonally reclaimed land (called *tapo*) is worked by junior and poor
lineages. I have seen members of the juniormost and poorest lineage
(Sabah Khel) like Tor Gul, the brother of Mehr Gul, working for days
to reclaim bits of land once the summer waters recede. In winter the
edge of the village can be almost 7 yards above water level and a
considerable area of land is temporarily reclaimed until the spring rains.

Floods are a real threat and some two decades ago the village Zor
Mandi, on the banks of the river about 3 miles downstream from Bela,
was largely destroyed and its population uprooted to new and safer
localities to the north. Bela was hit by the river in the late 1950s and
terrible tales of flooded and destroyed houses are still told. The few
two-storeyed towers (*bruj*) in the village, like the one in Hamesh Gul's
house, were built not for agnatic defence but for safety in case of
floods. Hamesh Gul has every right to fear the river. He has lost almost
10 acres in the last three decades and today owns only 1½ acres. The
regulation of the Kabul waters by the Warsak Dam has all but eliminated the threat of floods to the riverside villages. The heavy spring rains
convert the lanes of Bela into slush and mud and make transport even
of animals a difficult and messy business. However, the inside of houses
are kept clean and dry by spreading sand on the mud floors.

Without wishing too much to be read into it I would like to mention
different place-names that exist in and around my field-work areas of
TAM and SAM (Maps 2, 3 and 4). It is interesting that the Mohmands
themselves contrast the two areas within which they live through the

names they have chosen to give to places. The TAM see their areas as abounding in places where thieves may seek refuge or congregate: *Ghlo Ghund* (hillock of thieves), *Ghlo Kanda* (ravine of thieves), *Ghal Dand* (pond of thieves); furtive, *Ghalanay*; barren, *Gandab* (dirty water), *Wacha Jawar* (dry depression); dark, *Tora Tigga*, *Tor Gat* (black rocks) and forbidding, *Sangar* (defence breast-works). SAM names reflect different aspects of social organization: agricultural, *Zor Mandi* (old market); productive, *Angor Kilay* (village of grapes), *Michni* (hand-mills); orthodox, *Pir Qila* (stronghold of holy men).

Ecological systems, how geographical environment is related to social systems, are critical in understanding Mohmand politics and partly explain segmentary fissures. Pukhtun ideal behaviour reflects a close relationship between the geographical environment and the population it can support and may therefore be seen as a social mechanism to prevent population saturation point. Politics, social structure and ecology relate closely among the Mohmand:

> with the exception of favoured parts of the Gandab and Kabul valleys, agriculture here is largely dependent on the winter and autumn rains; should these fail great hardship ensues. Some experts on the Frontier suggest that times of maximum tribal unrest can be directly correlated with these periods of hardship; an idea well worth substantiating in any future tribal development plans (Dichter, 1967: 69).

Records as far back as 1884 relate the harsh geographical environment to Mohmand migration to the Peshawar District (Mason, 1884: 228).

Demographic surveys, like most other census information in the Tribal Areas, are based on answers provided by 'leading Maliks' and are usually collected and collated at the Agency headquarters or in Peshawar. The statistical accuracy of such surveys may be gauged from the fact that they are officially labelled 'estimates' or 'enumerations'. The first enumeration in the Tribal Areas took place in 1881 and only included British troops and their followers in the Khyber Pass. In 1911, 1921 and 1931 estimates of tribal population were made. In 1941 the Malakand Division was included in the census. In the first census in 1951, after the creation of Pakistan, population for the Tribal Areas was also based on estimates. The position remained unchanged for the census of 1961 (Ashraf, 1962: 18-20) and the latest census, in 1971.

Exaggeration of male and deflation of female numbers in questions regarding demographic or domestic statistics is common tribal practice.[2]

In the eyes of tribesmen this interconnected formula is explained thus: inflated male numbers increase political (military) prestige and social status and thus command that much more attention, and allowances, from political administration. The subject of females is strictly private and information regarding their lives an infringement of this privacy. Concepts of shame, highly developed regarding chastity among women, may be evoked. The inflation of population figures may also have a

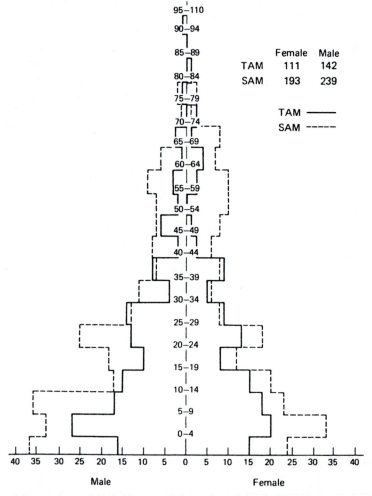

FIGURE 1 *Age and sex breakdown of TAM/SAM population*

valid explanation. The *dwa-kora* system that many Mohmands maintain (Chapter 8) may result in double counting. According to the population census there should be 432 people per square mile in the Agency. However, a superficial visit to the Agency with its vast, desolate areas will indicate the considerable inflation in the population figures.

In the summer of 1974, in my early surveys I was repeatedly assured that the population of Shati Khel's twenty hamlets was 3,000 whereas it turned out to be about 1,031. Similarly Bela Mohmandan was said to have 2,000 people when the actual number is about 432. Inflation of population figures by three- or fourfold should emphasize my earlier caution regarding figures, population, age and even dates, unless substantiated. Figure 1 gives the age and sex breakdown of the four settlements I studied in depth among TAM, Shahzada, Ranra, Malok and Lakhkar villages (Map 5 (iii)) and the entire village of Bela Mohmandan.

Because of the rather rough and ready method of estimating population in the Tribal Areas, I reproduce the official *Census Report of Tribal Agencies* (1961, 1971) population figures for the Mohmand Agency with some circumspection. In the latest census conducted in 1971 there were 382,885 Mohmands, 200,418 males and 182,467 females; in 1961 there were 294,215 Mohmands, 154,400 males and 139,815 females. Another estimate then put the total Mohmand population at 400,000, half on either side of the international border (Spain,

TABLE 1   Mohmand Agency population, 1971

i	Tarakzai	:	31,183
ii	Halimzai	:	
	a. Gandab	:	16,986
	b. Kamali	:	11,426
iii	Baezai	:	38,000
	a. Musa Khel	:	28,859
iv	Khwaezai	:	28,412
v	Utman Khel	:	62,100
vi	Safis	:	86,506
vii	*Others* Burhan Khel Isa Khel	:	79,413

Mohmand Agency Total = 382,885

1963: 44). In 1951 estimates of Mohmand population were 129,300. The tribal breakdown in 1972 (FATA Census) is given in Table 1 and may be used with Map 4 to assess population deployment in the Mohmand Agency.

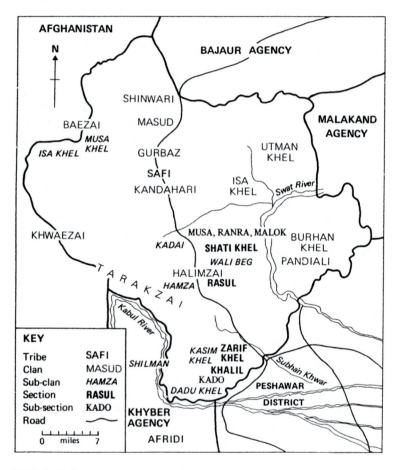

MAP 4 *Mohmand Agency: tribal map*

Sectional boundaries correspond to geographical regions and were probably fixed and allocated at the time of the first migrations. The Halimzai are divided territorially into the Gandab and Kamali Halimzai, the former inhabit the Gandab valley and the latter are placed north of the Nahakki. The Halimzai clan is genealogically divided into three sub-clans, Hamza, Kadai and Wali Beg. The population of the Wali Beg, roughly a third of the Gandab Halimzai, is mainly concentrated in Shati Khel (2,355) and around Sangar (2,953). The area and clans to the north of the Nahakki Pass are considered Upper Mohmand for administrative purposes. The clans that I studied, the Halimzai and the Tarakzai, are in Lower Mohmand. However, this is an arbitrary and shifting administrative division.

It is important to point out that no local memory or history exists of autochthonous groups encountered during the sixteenth-century Mohmand migrations in these areas. Occupational groups generally *accompanied* the Pukhtun clans and subscribe to its preponderate ideology. The absence of an autochthonous population with a history of military conquest or economic exploitation by an outside elite does not create the resentment generated in Swat (Barth, 1972: 68-9).

It is also important to point out that no outsiders live in the Agency. Pukhtun or non-Pukhtun groups coming from outside to live among the Mohmand do so only under the direct protection of a patriarch of a settlement and as clients (*hamsayas*). These groups may arrive escaping agnatic competition or the arms of the law in the districts. Their honour is directly tied to that of their host (see also Chapter 6).

The importance of geography is shown by the way the mountains and the gorges acted as a geographical barrier that underwrote the cultural barriers between *ilaqa* and *ghair ilaqa*. The ecology determined Mohmand population movements. The ecological and geo-political situation, and the absence of central government itself a consequence of that situation, created certain problems, but these presented an eminently plausible and elegant solution, that of creating and maintaining an ideal-type Pukhtun society where structural boundaries corresponded to administrative ones. The differentiation in the ecological systems of TAM and SAM is accentuated by administrative arrangements as I shall show in the next section.

II Administrative systems and the Mohmand

The head of the newly formed North-West Frontier Province, the Chief Commissioner, argued in an official note in 1908 to the Foreign Secretary of India for the creation of a Political Agency for the charge of the Mohmands. At present they are under the control of the Deputy Commissioner, Peshawar, who has so much work in his district that for many years he has been unable to devote that attention to them which is necessary.... Although the Mohmand tribe has been nominally under the Deputy Commissioner, Peshawar, its management has in practice been left to a very junior Assistant Commissioner, usually a Probationer, and even he has been burdened with many other duties and has allowed his work to slide into the capable but sometimes unscrupulous hands of some Native officer of the Border Police (H.D., T.R.C., File 181, C.C. to F.S.: 25 August 1908).

Although the British were in India for almost another forty years the Mohmands were not to get their Agency. They remained an anonymous part of the tribal territory[3] attached to Peshawar District. Pakistan was created in 1947 and four years later, on 1 August 1951, the Mohmand Agency came into being for the Mohmand tribes with its headquarters at Peshawar.

If 1951 may be considered the base-line dividing TAM and SAM, an earlier base-line ought to be mentioned. The first base-line was created in 1901 when the Province was created from the Punjab as a result of Curzon's famous and historical Minute (NWF: 1901). From a remote part of a vast Province controlled from Lahore, 'the trans-Indus Districts' became an administrative entity, the North-West Frontier Province. None the less the Tribal Areas or tribal territories continued untouched and unaffected by this administrative change and both TAM and SAM successfully subverted and/or diverted the resources of the encapsulating systems to their own ends, and managed successfully to maintain their unencapsulated condition unaffected to a large degree until 1951.

Until 1951 the Deputy Commissioner, Peshawar, head of the most important District and the capital of the Province, was in charge of the Mohmands who were the least of his worries. Little wonder that from the early days of the creation of the new Province 'they have always felt that they were regarded by the Deputy Commissioner, Peshawar, more as step-children than as his own, and they have frequently expressed a wish to be separated from the District' (H.D., T.R.C., File 181, C.C. to F.S.: 25 August 1908). The other major tribes like the Afridis, in the Khyber Agency, or the Mahsuds and Wazirs in the North and South Waziristan Agencies who had their Agencies around 1895-96 looked down on the Mohmands: 'You are politically not important enough for government to give you your own Political Agent.' These rebukes can still be heard when leaders representing different tribes argue. I have heard Afridi and Mahsud Maliks, representing older Agencies, haughtily put down Orakzai and Mohmand Maliks with withering comments on their political insignificance as reflected by their recently created Agencies.

A more significant yardstick of measuring the political importance of a Pukhtun tribe or clan as seen and assessed by tribesmen themselves is the extent of its geographical and administrative encapsulation. For instance, the Orakzai clans are landlocked in the Orakzai Agency having no access to the international boundary line, and as a consequence are constantly reminded of their inferior situation by the other tribes. Access to the international border is a key factor in remaining in a state of unencapsulation and being able to play off one state against another politically. The Tarakzai clan of the Mohmands is largely encapsulated, a fact thrown in their face in any dispute with Mohmand sections who live on both sides of the border like the Baezai and Khwaezai, or even the Halimzai who lie close to the border.

From 1901 until 1951 both TAM and SAM were subject to more or less one administration. More or less, as Bela found itself on the periphery of an unimportant part of an important District. By tacit administrative agreement it was allowed to continue a penumbral existence; not quite tribal and not quite settled. This administrative neglect allowed SAM to remain structurally and culturally close to TAM and to approximate in their behaviour to the ideal-type, as the long saga of agnatic rivalry ending in numerous deaths illustrates (Chapter 7). TAM and SAM reacted to the colonial presence with equal fervour. This is an important point in confirming that SAM were to be and felt encapsulated later. The similitude in society and culture remained undisturbed. Tarakzai (Bela) and Halimzai (Shati) were equal nuisances to the British. A typical notification of the period proclaims:

Whereas the following Mohmand tribes, viz. Tarakzai, Halimzai of Gandab, Burhan Khel and Isa Khel of Pandiali are acting in a hostile and unfriendly manner towards the British Government and towards persons residing in British India, the Deputy Commissioner is pleased to — 1) debar the said tribes from all access to British India; and 2) to prohibit all persons within the limits of British India from all intercourse or communication of any kind what so ever with any members of these tribes (H.D., T.R.C., File 191, Secretary to the Chief Commissioner: 18 October 1916).

Although technically part of Peshawar District the laws of the land did not apply to SAM until 1933 and they ordered their lives according to Pukhtun custom (*riwaj*). After this date legislation was passed in the NWFP Assembly that Islamic law (*shariat*) should replace *riwaj* in the entire Province. The significance of changing from *riwaj* to *shariat* in 1933 meant that daughters and wives could legally inherit land (shared in the ratio of two sisters to inherit the share of one brother). This was rarely practised and I have given the rare and rather unique exception to the rule in the case of female inheritance forty years after the law made it legal in Chapter 9.

In spite of the legislation administrative preoccupation allowed SAM to lead traditional lives. The boundary between the District and the tribal territory in which the Mohmands lived was vague and undefined. It was easy to keep open and allowed Kado and Bela to maintain close social and economic links in the *dwa-kora* system.

Officials were not enamoured of the Mohmands and their ability to slip across the border to the tribal belt where they could live with impunity and not be extradited as this frank assessment illustrates: 'The Upper Mohmands domiciled in the District are the most aweful swine being treacherous, crooked and unreliable to a degree. Also they can always run away to Upper Mohmand Tribal Territory where we cannot get at them' (H.D., T.R.C., F.C. Reports, 5 March 1934).

To placate the Mohmands even that *sine qua non* of imperialism, land revenue, was exempted by the British for Halimzais living in Panjpao, around Shabkadar, and Tarakzai villages, like Bela Mohmandan. In the last century the former yielded about Rs. 3,000 per annum to the Halimzai and the latter about Rs. 5,000 to the Tarakzai (MacGregor, 1873: 474). The Tarakzai had thirteen revenue-free villages in the Peshawar District, including Bela Mohmandan. They were even allowed to continue their traditional toll at Michni for goods coming down the Kabul river for a short while. Cash allowances for both clans from the Kabul and British Governments also supplemented income (Merk, 1898: 9), as I shall show in Chapter 5.

Even today Halimzais living on the Panjpao lands and Tarakzais around Michni, both in the District, do not pay either revenue taxes (*malya*) or irrigation taxes (*abyana*). To balance accounts the Political Agent, Mohmands, pays land revenue, a nominal sum, on behalf of

these groups in the District at a rate of Rs. 4.50 per acre for cultivated land.

The elevation from tribal territory attached to a District to a fullfledged Agency in 1951 did not contain administrative implications only. It implied far-reaching social and political ramifications. As mentioned earlier no regular criminal and civil laws apply in the Agency, nor are there taxes, courts or municipal councils of any kind. Officials from the elite Indian Political Service Cadre (two-thirds from the Army and one-third from the Indian Civil Service) manned the Tribal Agencies (Coen, 1971; Woodruff, 1965). The priority given to Agency matters is reflected in its chain of command which links the Political Agent directly to the Governor who, as Agent for the Tribal Areas, reports directly to the President of Pakistan. The Political Agent's counterpart, the Deputy Commissioner, operates along established hierarchical lines. He reports to the Commissioner, who in turn reports to the Chief Secretary who informs the Chief Minister and the Provincial Government, who in turn may inform Islamabad. Administratively, too, an Agency is part of a separate 'special' category, the Federally Administered Tribal Areas, and distinct from the districts of the Province.

The Peshawar District has a population of 1.7 million living in 549 villages spread over an area of 1,646 square miles, compared to a population of 382,885 and an area of 887 square miles in the Mohmand Agency. The Deputy Commissioner has to cope with every conceivable problem from malaria eradication to student demands. With his work load he will barely know the names of the villages in his charge before his transfer, let alone their elders and tribal sections. It is not surprising that Bela Mohmandan can only remember the visit of three Deputy Commissioners in the last thirty years. The third visited Bela in early 1976 during my field-work.

The Deputy Commissioner, Peshawar, heads a phalanx of bureaucrats: the Additional Deputy Commissioner, four Assistant Commissioners, thirteen Extra Assistant Commissioners and numerous additional posts such as Tehsildars and Naib-Tehsildars. Bela is part of the jurisdiction of the Assistant Commissioner, Peshawar, the most heavily worked Assistant Commissioner of the District. Its administrative significance in the District bureaucratic hierarchy may be gauged by the fact that there is neither a headman nor any official posted in the village or even near it. In contrast, the Political Agent, as his name and that of his staff implies, is to administer 'politically', or not to administer his clans as he thinks wise. Most tribes are aware of the contractual nature through treaties of their original association and absorption into British India. There will be a fuller discussion of the role of the Political Agent in tribal society in Chapter 10.

The history of Mohmand administration of TAM since 1947 has been one of proliferation of administration and penetration into the Agency as Figure 2 shows.

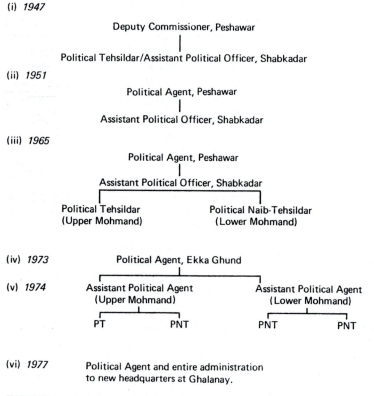

(i) *1947*

Deputy Commissioner, Peshawar

Political Tehsildar/Assistant Political Officer, Shabkadar

(ii) *1951*

Political Agent, Peshawar

Assistant Political Officer, Shabkadar

(iii) *1965*

Political Agent, Peshawar

Assistant Political Officer, Shabkadar

Political Tehsildar   Political Naib-Tehsildar
(Upper Mohmand)   (Lower Mohmand)

(iv) *1973*   Political Agent, Ekka Ghund

(v) *1974*   Assistant Political Agent   Assistant Political Agent
                 (Upper Mohmand)   (Lower Mohmand)

                 PT   PNT   PNT   PNT

(vi) *1977*   Political Agent and entire administration
                 to new headquarters at Ghalanay.

FIGURE 2 *Mohmand administrative changes*

As Figure 2 illustrates, both the Deputy Commissioner, at Peshawar – an exceedingly busy public figure – and the Tehsildar, at Shabkadar – a relatively junior official – were posted *outside* the Agency. The post of Tehsildar was later upgraded to that of an Assistant Political Officer[4] when the Agency was created in August 1951. By 1965 two posts, those of Tehsildar and a Naib-Tehsildar, were added. The Tehsildar was in charge of the tribes in the Upper Mohmand area: Baezai, Khwaezai, Safis and Musa Khel. The Naib-Tehsildar was in charge of the Lower Mohmand: the Halimzai, Tarakzai and Pandiali tribes. The entire staff, apart from the Political Agent's office in Peshawar, was still in Shabkadar. The Tehsildar, Upper Mohmands, never visited his charges in their area and they had to come down to him individually and in *jirgas* during fixed monthly times. This ensured continuity of tribal behaviour and organization in the Agency even after its creation.

In late 1973 the Political Agent moved to Ekka Ghund just inside the Agency boundary with his entire staff. The first major penetration was effected. In October the Political Agent crossed the Nahakki Pass north of the Gandab valley and roughly dividing the Upper from the Lower Mohmands. The crossing of the Pass beyond which no road or trace of the twentieth century existed was of immense psychological significance (Chapter 11; Ahmed, 1977a). Far-ranging and numerous development schemes followed the road (Chapters 10 and 11).

By 1974 the Political Agent had two Assistant Political Agents and four Tehsildars/Naib-Tehsildars to assist him and property was being bought for the new Agency headquarters in Ghalanay. In mid-1977 the final step was taken. The Political Agent and his staff moved in to their new headquarters inside the Agency at Ghalanay (Figure 2). Since the creation of the Mohmand Agency in August 1951 and up to August 1977 there have been twenty Political Agents. The average tenure is about one year and four months.

In spite of success in penetration, the Mohmand Agency remains what is called in the Tribal Areas a 'no-family station' for army and civil officials. Tension and shooting may suddenly close the main road and few officials are prepared to involve their families in this exercise. Travel to and from the Agency is regulated and no unauthorized visitors, without permission of the Political Agent, are allowed. Coming from Peshawar to Shati Khel (via Michni) along the main road all vehicles are stopped at four check-posts. Traditionally in most Agencies there were 'road open days' when *bona fide* travellers carrying an 'official permit' signed by the Political Agent were provided with an armed tribal escort. Under no conditions were women allowed (Allen, 1977: 203). The question of issuing 'travel permits' into the Mohmand area did not arise. Even the staff worked from outside the Mohmand areas and in Shabkadar. The single Mohmand road was disused and dangerous, passing through and terminating in the Halimzai area, a clan renowned as unruly in the area.

It was only in 1951 with the birth of the Agency that SAM perceived the death of certain aspects of their Mohmandness, a negative realization that stemmed from a positive act; as their Agency kin were unencapsulated they were encapsulated and finally defined as Settled Mohmands.

Until 1951 TAM and SAM were with the same Deputy Commissioner after which TAM were given their own Political Agent and in a sense formally de-encapsulated: a unique situation in the history of encapsulation. It was an official confirmation of an established situation for, even when attached to Peshawar District, TAM were free to live and organize their own lives. In 1951 Kado and Bela were suddenly separated by the Frontier Constabulary posts, a physical symbol of the finality of their rupture. However, Shabkadar in the Settled Area for TAM and Kado in the Tribal Agency for SAM provided both with reference points and an escape-valve through which they could carry on sundry activities otherwise restricted or difficult. For instance, the word smuggling has been incorporated into the Pukhto language as *sparling* and understood in the length and breadth of the Agency. The crossing of the international border is not seen as smuggling by the Mohmands. They argue, with a certain logic, that neither were they consulted regarding its lines nor do they see the point in dividing clans into two halves, and wide tribal networks are mobilized and trade organized through them by passing formal and legal frontiers and customs posts (Ahmed: forthcoming a).

Administration has its own priorities. The Agency Mohmands were penetrated and therefore sweetened. Their every whim was treated as a demand. With every shift in the administrative chart above there was a corresponding increase in allowances and grants to TAM. Shati Khel got its cement school and an eight-bed hospital in the early 1960s. With the crossing of the Nahakki Pass, Shati Khel was given electricity in 1973. Today as the momentum of the thrust pushes administration further north beyond the Nahakki and among the Safis, the Halimzais are beginning to feel neglected and aggrieved. For instance, of a total number of 8,955 Maliks and *lungi* (individual allowance) holders in the Mohmand Agency, Safis accounted for 3,200 (Home Department Figures, June 1976). The significance of this proliferation of Safi Maliks may be brought into relief by explaining that when the voting lists were made earlier in the year there were still only some 6,000 Mohmand Maliks including a few dozen Safis. Since then almost 3,000 new Maliks were made, almost entirely from among the Safis. The aim was obvious – to

help in the process of integrating and thereby moving the Safis closer to encapsulation. The inflation of the number of Maliks also diminished their importance and role both in society and with the administration. However, the *lungi* allowance, even if it comes to half a rupee, carries social and political prestige which I shall consider in Chapter 5.

The question of non-tribals administering tribals has been successfully solved by Pakistan. In 1977, for instance, four tribesmen from the Tribal Areas were Political Agents in the Agencies: in the Mohmand Agency a Wazir; in Bajaur a Mahsud; in the Khyber a Mohmand; and in Malakand an Afridi. The junior staff of the Agencies is almost entirely tribal and usually local. The tensions generated between local and non-locals in other situations of encapsulation have been minimized (Bailey, 1957, 1960, 1961, 1970; Fürer-Haimendorf, 1939, 1962, 1977; Vitebsky, 1978; Yorke, 1974).

For SAM encapsulation brought with it only its negative symbols in the form of visiting police and revenue officials. Today, three decades later, Bela Mohmandan still awaits its turn in the long queue for electricity, roads and official buildings.

I shall briefly describe the agricultural land and revenue situation as it exists in Bela. The Bela revenue official's (*patwari*) area includes Bela Mohmandan, Kas Korona, Zor Mandi, Piari Bala and Qila Shahbeg, villages around Bela (Map 3). The *patwari* confirmed that the first Revenue Settlement of this area was made in 1870, the second in 1895-6 and the third in 1926-30. Of these records almost the entire papers of the first and the second have been burnt in accidental fires. Two years ago a fire in the Deputy Commissioner's office in Peshawar burnt most of the present records. *Patwaris* may be of great assistance in decreasing revenue returns. For instance lands shown in the Second Settlement in 1895-6 as 'uncultivable' and therefore revenue-free may now be cultivable. Given suitable incentives, the *patwari* will continue to record the area as uncultivable. This device is of little use to him in Bela where the villagers pay no revenue in any case. Consequently the *patwari* rarely, if ever, visits Bela and certainly did not do so in the one year I was conducting field-work.

Bela Mohmandan and its surrounding fields, according to revenue records (*jamabandi*), totalled 1,488 acres of which 316 acres were cultivable, 261 *barani*, 784 were uncultivable and 127 were wasteland (Khan and Shah, 1973: 10). The *jamabandi* is to be compiled every four years but was last completed in 1967-8. For purposes of my study it is important to clarify that although much more than 316 acres are cultivable today, Bela lands have slowly passed out through sale, mortgage, etc., to other neighbouring kin groups. The village is encircled by non-Bela owners of originally Bela lands. Belawals own less than 70 acres of cultivable land, apart from those categorized as waste and uncultivable. Administratively Bela is part of the Daudzai Police Thana with its headquarters at Nahakki Police Station 14 miles away via Shabkadar (Map 2).

In this chapter we have seen how the two groups operate within generally similar low-production geographical zones but were differentiated once formally divided by the creation of an Agency and separate status for its clans. The Agency formally differentiates TAM from SAM. Having provided a baseline in 1951 I can move on to consider its long-range implications. In this chapter I am suggesting that administrative changes provide a fundamental explanation for an entire set of widening social differences and structural arrangements between the two groups. Deviance from the ideal Pukhtun model is thus implicit in the administrative arrangements of SAM after 1951. That they still retain various essential features of *Pukhtunwali* in spite of their situation supports the thesis which I will substantiate in the following chapters. My concern in the next chapter is to provide a historical framework with theoretical implications which will consider the questions and attempt the answers central to my study.

3 Tribal society and the historical process

History and Social Anthropology . . . the two disciplines are *indissociables* (Evans-Pritchard, 1962: 65).

'Any theory about social change is necessarily a theory about historical process' (Leach, 1977: 227). I am in agreement with this position as the contents and method of this chapter will illustrate. For purposes of my study I am arguing that historical process partly explains continuity and stability in social structure in *nang* society, of which the Mohmand are part. In this chapter I am concerned with history not as a string of dates, events and dynastic periods but as a means of discovering principles which determine social processes and change form: in short, history as 'social history', an extension of cultural forms and an articulation of social systems. Those aggregates of historical sequences will be examined that form, conform or alter the determinants of the Pukhtun ideal-type model, its Code and empirically observed social reality. I shall show how *external* historical sequences explicitly reinforce *internal* cultural tradition and structural arrangements, partly explaining social form.

Firstly, I shall argue that it was the intensity of external pressures that reiterated and reconfirmed the need for Pukhtun society to preserve traditional social structure and values in the Pukhtun heart-lands and it was the nature of these pressures that partly determined the population shifts from and to the Tribal Areas over the centuries, especially in the context of the rise and fall of empires in India. I will examine the impact of the colonial encounter on the participants, which will partly explain present Mohmand attitudes to governmental schemes and presence in their areas. In the second section I will be showing that *tarboorwali* finds homologous parallels in historical sequences by an example from early this century in my field-work areas. The example involves ascendants of some of my respondents and illustrates the point that *tarboorwali* remains the key to political motivation, diverting and subverting larger, and in this case imperial, issues to its own arena of conflict and ends. I will discuss separately the 'mystification' and 'romanticization' of the colonial encounter, a persistent historical phenomenon on the Frontier, and its social causes rooted in middle and upper-middle class British attitudes at the turn of the century (Ahmed, 1978b).

Placing societal sequences and extraordinary events within dynastic or 'period' frameworks as in traditional history would be a sterile exercise for *nang* societies since they do not have any dynasties. To me, as an anthropologist, history exists in society and not vice-versa, and some of the finest monographs (Evans-Pritchard, 1973; Leach, 1977) and theses (Balandier, 1974) in the discipline prove this view. Methodologically my approach to the past is summed up thus: 'I can see no vital difference between sociological history and what some anthropologists like to call social dynamics or diachronic sociology' (Evans-Pritchard, 1962: 62).

Mohmand historical memory is vague about dates and periods beyond three generations although agnatic links to the apical ancestor can be reconstructed. As elsewhere in stateless acephalous societies no kingly dynasties mark the beginning and end of particular historical periods, no literature or discrete priest category exist to record and observe historical sequences. I am perhaps tempted to agree with the view propounded for the Nuer:

> Valid history ends a century ago, and tradition, generously measured, takes us back only ten to twelve generations in lineage structure. ... Time is thus not a continuum but is a constant structural relationship between two points, the first and last persons in a line of agnatic descent (Evans-Pritchard, 1940: 108).

Unfortunately we have almost no extant record of Mohmand origin that survived the Pukhtun diaspora in the fifteenth and sixteenth centuries. From the sixteenth century to the early twentieth century the main themes of *nang* society articulated in Pukhtun ideology, *Pukhtunwali* and confronted by successive encapsulating and aggressive imperial systems, retained traditional ones revolving around religion and the politics of a patrilineal tribal society and its Code. The colonial encounter, though unsuccessful in vanquishing Pukhtun *nang* areas, succeeded in creating ambivalence and ambiguity in certain areas of life, especially social leadership (Chapter 5), which are still unresolved. We

are in the midst of seeing the emergent phase of society, and its implications for it will be the theme in the last part of this study.

I Colonial encounters and tribal strategy

In this section I will attempt

> to determine the number and range of compatible possibilities within a system of conditions and constraints, and ... reconstruct ... the limited number of transformations that such structures, or combinations of structures, can perform ... [so that history does not appear as] an immense, meaningless mass of facts ... [but] a science of human populations, from which the fetishized compartmentalization and arbitrary divisions of the social sciences will have been abolished. A science that will serve not only to interpret history but also to make it (Godelier, 1975: 22-3).

This section will extensively use 'sociological history' or 'diachronic sociology' for method. It will begin with an attempt to reconstruct the possible 'conditions and constraints' of the first Mohmand migrations to their present tribal tracts; it will then divide into three further and interconnected sub-sections: firstly, the implications for Pukhtuns, specifically with reference to the tribal tracts, of the disintegration of the Mughal Empire. Secondly, following the collapse of the Mughal Empire, the increasingly ethnic and religious nature of the Pukhtun struggle. Finally, a brief and diachronic aggregate of historical sequences of successful tribal struggle against colonial expansionism that is embedded in the social consciousness of Pukhtun society and ideology in the dominant period of history and which partly explain them in the present emerging period. It is hoped that the various strands in the argument will fall into place to explain largely the stability of Pukhtun social structure and ideology. The historical argument will substantiate my thesis contention that a pure and ideal-type structure exists in the tribal belt.

If the cardinal principle in the social history of the subcontinent is clash between different systems producing synthesis (Ahmad, A., 1964; Datta *et al.*, 1956; Nehru, 1960; Smith, V. A., 1958) then the Tribal Areas are the exception. In the Pukhtun *nang* heart-lands Indian imperial systems, native or foreign, have produced no social or cultural synthesis. The encounters have been mechanical and their ferocity merely helped to confirm existing social reality and cultural boundaries. Mohmand history may be seen as a general confirmation of my *nang* thesis: Pukhtun segmentary, acephalous tribes in low-production areas contain penetration by larger imperial systems and perpetuate their own system based on certain key concepts successfully within a world they conceptualize as *ghair ilaqa* or *yaghistan* (land of rebellion). It is important to underline that *ghair ilaqa* or *yaghistan* was conceptualized as a political philosophy in opposition to the expansionism of larger states.

Chronologically Mohmand history may be seen as battle sequences between encapsulating systems and tribal society. From the known beginning of Mohmand history in the first half of the sixteenth century the pattern of raid, by tribesmen, and reprisal, by the state, is established. I wish to suggest that this pattern is rooted in their historical experiences in Afghanistan, the area of provenance of the Mohmands before their arrival at their present locations in the Frontier hills, and confirmed by the poor geographical areas that they finally settled in. There is little known of them before their migration from Afghanistan with their Ghoriah Khel cousins, the Khalils, Daudzais and Chamkanis.[1] The Mughal Emperor Babar mentions encountering them in their ancestral homes in the Kandahar-Mukur region after the Yusufzais were in the Peshawar valley early in the sixteenth century (Babar, 1922; Caroe, 1965).

Our interest, however, is social and we shall examine the Mohmands as we know them empirically and on the basis of history as it is known to them. We do know that along with their senior cousins, the Yusufzai, they were driven out of their Afghan homelands. We also know, from both TAM and SAM elders, that Mohmand Baba,[2] the apical ancestor of the tribe and after whom the tribe takes its name, is buried in the Tarakzai area near Ekka Ghund and not in his ancestral home in Afghanistan. This would argue that the Mohmands were pushed out of their ancestral homes fairly early in their history. The genealogies of the elders of my two areas, Shahzada in Shati Khel and Shamshudin in Bela Mohmandan, trace ten generations, including themselves, to Mohmand Baba (Figure 5). Allowing for the conventional thirty years for each generation, this would take us to about 1677. If we can allow for four generations to be 'lost' through 'genealogical telescoping' (Bohannan, L., 1952; Evans-Pritchard, 1973: 46–61; Fortes and Evans-Pritchard, 1970; Freedman, 1958; Lewis, I. M., 1961: 144–52; Peters, 1960: 32–3) or 'genealogical amnesia' (Geertz, C. and H., 1964), Mohmand genealogies do indeed confirm historical sources of their appearance in the Peshawar valley around the early part of the sixteenth century.

Combining our genealogical arithmetic and Babar's observations we may place their first migrations to the Peshawar valley between 1500 and the 1550s. In any case their arrival in Peshawar is later than that of the Yusufzais who arrived between 1485–1500. This would explain why the Yusufzai took possession of the finest lands in the valley and the Mohmands were left with the barren hills they still inhabit.[3] The unfair division of land cannot be explained except by the arrival of the Mohmands two or at least one generation after the Yusufzai. Tribal divisions of land are scrupulously fair to those sections party to the act of settling or acquiring new lands. For instance, the Mandar and Yusuf clans of the Yusufzai tribe divided Swat and Mardan between them and conceptualized equality through a system of periodic redistribution of land (*wesh*). The Mohmand geographical situation is all the more remarkable because the Mohmands are the only major tribe descended from Sarban, the senior son of Qais, the putative ancestor of the Pukhtun tribes, in the Tribal Areas. The other tribes in these generally low-production mountain areas are descendants of Ghurghust and Karlanri, other and junior sons of Qais. In terms of my *nang* and *qalang* social categories mentioned earlier, the Mohmands are aware of their rich *qalang* Yusufzai cousins and their own position in the poor *nang* areas. Other *nang* tribes like the Afridis, Orakzais, Mahsuds or Wazirs have no such kin yardstick to measure their economic condition. The continuing agnatic rivalry between Yusufzai and Mohmand may have as much a psychological base as a social one though we shall restrict ourselves to the latter.

Thus Mohmand history begins with the facts of existing social grievance. Mohmand history may be seen as a battle on two levels: their antagonism to the Yusufzai *within* phyletic boundaries as not only the richer cousins but as those who have blocked them from better lands; and on a different level and *outside* phyletic boundaries the attempts of the rulers of Peshawar, the Mughals, Durranis, Sikhs and British to incorporate them into their domain. The former is a complex, involuted socio-psychological relationship only comprehensible within the Pukhtun ideological framework and its emphasis on agnatic rivalry, but the latter is a straightforward clash on the field of battle between opposed, defined and unambiguous positions.

Let us briefly look at the former conflict and how it affects Mohmand population shifts. Mohmands arriving late in the Peshawar valley soon began to upset and challenge the status quo with the Yusufzai as its primary tribe through raids. A decision regarding their permanent settlement and definition of spatial tribal boundaries had to be made sooner or later and after biding their time the Yusufzai gathered an army of 100,000 and shattered the Mohmands, and their Ghoriah Khel cousins, in 1550 at the famous battle of Shaikh Tapur near Peshawar (Caroe, 1965: 186-9). The Mohmands learned one lesson they never forgot, to avoid pitched battles. As a consequence of their defeat they were finally repulsed to their present locations and denied the rich lands of Hashtnagar and Mardan. They now combined martial qualities with location in inaccessible mountains, that crossed unsettled international borders, to raid villages in the Peshawar valley and levy taxes and tolls on caravans passing their country as the well-known saying testifies: 'a single Momund will pass a whole caravan' (Elphinstone, 1972, II: 41).

'My brother's enemy is my friend', an extension of the philosophy of agnatic rivalry, was the basis of inter-tribal policy *vis-à-vis* imperial systems. In 1586 the Mohmands met and allied with Akbar, the Great Mughal, in his battle with the Yusufzai and later, particularly in the next century, when the Yusufzai had reconciled with the Mughals, changed sides to harass Mughal armies in the Frontier passes. In 1673 and 1674 they defeated Aurangzeb's Mughal armies in the Gandab valley, the Khapakh Pass and at Karappa (Map 2):

When to Karappa rolled the crimson tide
Karappa to Bajaur the mountains shake
With noise of battle and the valley quake (Howell and Caroe, 1963: 49).

The Mughal chroniclers complained of 'the tumult-raising Afaghinah of this mountainous tract, outwardly obedient servitors, but inwardly delighting in disorder and ever ready to plunder and molest' (Elliott, 1968: 73).

The disintegration of the Mughal Empire was partly caused by the constant drain on its resources by the unceasing rebellions among the Frontier tribes (Datta *et al.*, 1956: 494-5). Between the collapse of the Mughals in the early decades of the eighteenth century and the annexation of Peshawar by the British in 1849 lie a hundred years of unparalleled political turbulence and uncertainty on the subcontinent. Only one equation was crystallizing: every stage of the contraction of the Mughal Empire was in inverse proportion to the expansion of British territory. Pukhtun soldiers of fortune discovered that the times were not propitious for their particular talents. Many of the emergent powers like the Sikhs and Marathas were assuming an anti-Muslim stance due to their opposition to the Mughals. The British themselves in the middle of casting off the role of peaceful trader and assuming one of military adventurer, had little time for other military adventurers. A significant and new phenomenon that began to emerge in the eighteenth-century dynasties was their consciously ethnic and religious nature. Empires like the Marathas and, later in the century, the Sikhs were based on an ethnic and religious homogeneity that propagated the superiority and cohesion of a particular ethnic group to the exclusion of extra-ethnic groups. This contrasted strongly with earlier Indian social history where ethnic and religious affiliations were often secondary considerations. To make matters worse for the Pukhtun the rise of the Sikh kingdom coincided with the collapse of the Durrani Empire after Taimur Shah's death in 1792. The Pukhtun was forced to sit at home with the avenues of traditional employment blocked to him. His last and perhaps most traditional source of income, raiding and/or taxing caravans and military groups in the Frontier passes on their way to India, dried up. There were no rich caravans or conquering armies plying these routes.

In terms of Pukhtun *nang* history, as seen from their hills, the encounter between imperial invasion and their tribal resistance has never ceased. As I mentioned earlier it would be heuristically sterile to divide these periods into conventional compartments of Mughal, Durrani, Sikh or British sequences. The forms of imperial expansionism and its impact on social process override religious or ethnic considerations. Political reprisals, mobile columns, large garrisons and exploitation of tribal conflicts, on the one hand, followed by allowances, estates and titles on the other, have been the dual standard strategies of every imperial power encountering the tribes. Liberal allowances were part of imperial policy whether Mughal,[4] Durrani[5] or British.[6] Nothing worked in the *nang* areas of tribal society. Afghanistan's Amir Abdur Rahman, the Iron Amir and himself a Pukhtun, found his Pukhtun tribes, especially the Lalpura Mohmands, equally difficult to subjugate and encapsulate (Fraser-Tytler, 1969; Gregorian, 1969; Kakar, 1968; Rahman, 1900).

Perhaps a structural pattern may be discerned of stronger attempts at encapsulation with firm government at Delhi and a forced tolerance of tribal inroads with the weakening of reins at Delhi. The insouciance with which small tribal bands constantly and casually raided imperial Mughal or British India was all the more remarkable for the savagery and bitterness of the encounters. British India after 1857–8 was militarily subdued and a mood of awe hung over the subcontinent created by the savagery of the reprisals in the wake of the 1857 holocaust. Yet this mood failed to communicate itself to the Frontier. In 1852 the Tarakzai Mohmands had made an early entry into British records by killing Lt Boulnois near Michni.[7] Between 1855 and 1860 the Mohmands organized eighty-three major raids, consisting of raiding parties 300 to 400 strong, and forty minor raids into British India. In 1864 they fought an engagement near Shabkadar in which 40 Mohmands were killed. In 1873 they murdered Major Macdonald, the Commandant of Michni fort, for which the Tarakzai were fined Rs. 10,000 (Mason, 1884).

Raids into British settled districts from tribal territory now became a regular occurrence. The historical explanation for the raids was no longer economic as in the past but lay in a combination of three factors: the tribal Code that provided the Pukhtun with an ideological reference to fight religious war (*jihad*); physical environment which provided him with refuge to escape to; and finally his geo-political situation which allowed him to play a version of the Great Game, then so important to British India, and to balance great nation-states to his advantage.

The entirely different political situation and the unchanged position of the British after 1849 eliminated any possibility of military adventurism in India. The Pukhtun tribesman in the middle of the nineteenth century stood face to face with the social realities of a changed world. He now migrated not to faraway Bihar or Bengal with dreams of kingdom and superior social status, but to Mardan or Charsadda as a tenant of inferior status to his Yusufzai landlord cousin. From a free *qabail* (tribesman) he became a *hamsaya*, a *faqir* or a *dehqan* (tenant) — terms loaded with connotations of inferior social status.

It is not difficult to reconstruct Mohmand social history in the middle of the last century within the historical frame. If they were denied the richer Hashtnagar land as owners 300 years ago, the Mohmands began to migrate to these areas in the last century to work as tenants on the demesnes of Yusufzai landlords. Mohmand migration was noted as early as 1873: 'Even in ordinary times the hills are unable to support the surplus population, which is steadily emigrating to the Yusufzai and Hashtnagar *mairas* in the Peshawar district' (ibid.: 228). Agnatic rivalry in their own areas remained an important cognitive social force and their fortunes made through hard work and subinfeudation in the *maira* were partly diverted to continuous vendettas. This continued connection took on an interesting residential aspect as most Mohmands became *dwa-kora* (Chapters 7 and 8). The case of Dilawar Khan is an apt illustration of agnatic rivalry diverting fortunes made by tenant farming to its perpetuation and operating over time, three generations, and space, from Shati Khel in the Agency to the Swabi Subdivision and back to the Agency (Chapters 7 and 8; Figure 14).

What caused these migrations in the last century? Barren land is one answer only and an incomplete one, for geographical conditions had remained unchanged in the Mohmand areas for the last four hundred years. I have posited an explanation that has required a large canvas. I am suggesting that scarcity of traditional Pukhtun employment as soldiers of fortune in India, itself a consequence of unsettled political times as a result of the disintegrating Mughal Empire in the mid-1700s, forced the tribesman to sit idly at home. Over a century this produced a population explosion which the naturally poor soil could not support and which, in turn, produced the hardship necessary to eject less resilient groups from their tribal homes and seek positions of inferior status as tenants in the *maira*. The hardship would have been severe, otherwise no Pukhtun would easily place himself in a position of subordination to another Pukhtun, conscious as *both* would be of their kinship on the tribal charter and given the bitter historical relationship.

The population movements late in the last century were given further impetus by the irrigation systems that the British introduced towards the end of the century in the Mardan and Peshawar Districts, and by the introduction of cash-crops. The Yusufzai landlord needed as much farm assistance as he could find. The tensions generated in this situation are not to be viewed in simplistic landless peasant versus landlord terms. Initially landlords may have had complete suzerainty over their tenants but by the mid-twentieth century Mohmands through hard work, personal deprivation and shrewd investments had accumulated considerable *independent* properties in the *maira*. They felt strong enough to assert themselves politically, partly by joining militant parties like the *Mazdoor Kisan* (labourer/tenant) against their landlords (Bangash, 1972; Dupree, 1977: 514-16). They were now *middle peasants* and not poor landless tenants and in their new economic condition they were *militant* rather than revolutionary, demanding *social equality* not an overthrow of the social order, important distinctions made by Alavi and Wolf (Alavi, 1965; Wolf, 1969a and b). Lineage and kin networks continued to sustain and support them as in other parts of the subcontinent whether in Punjab (Alavi, 1972) or Bengal (Nicholas, 1963, 1965).

The ethnic and religious factor lent a particular bitterness to the last colonial encounter. For all the twentieth century and post-colonial 'mystification' of the British–Pukhtun encounter, Mohmand clashes with the British from the earliest days were severe and savage. Almost immediately after officially inheriting Peshawar from the Sikhs in 1849

> the Supreme Government deemed it necessary to direct that the Mohmand fiefs in the Doaba should be confiscated, that the defensive posts should be strengthened and that British troops should operate against the offending Mohmands, and destroy their chief villages (Mason, 1884: 233).

The 'chief villages' were in the Michni area and inhabited by the ascendants of Kado and Bela Mohmandan. Dab (Map 3) is repeatedly mentioned as 'destroyed' in these early reports. Often indiscriminate burning of border villages followed tribal raids. Mohmand raids and imperial reprisals form the ebb and flow of Mohmand history until the departure of the British in 1947.

The ethnic nature of the struggle was never allowed out of sight. With Sir Colin Campbell in 1851–2, when he camped in the Michni area to subjugate the Mohmands, were regular British and crack Gurkha troops (66th Gurkha Regiment). Shortly afterwards, the 1st Sikh Infantry was moved to the area and by 1864 the British fielded the 2nd and 6th Bengal Cavalry, 2nd Gurkha Regiment and the 4th Sikh Infantry. In 1879 the 10th and 11th Bengal Cavalry, the 4th Gurkha and a Bhopal battalion had joined their brothers for duty on the Mohmand border between Michni and Shabkadar (ibid.). The full-scale operation against the Mohmands in 1897 involved three brigades consisting of Punjab (20th), Gurkhas (2nd and 9th), Dogras (37th), Bengal (13th), Bombay (28th), Patiala and Nabha units (Wylly, 1912: 248–9).

The tradition of employing extra-ethnic troops was carried into the next century and during the 1935 Mohmand campaign newspapers carried headlines such as 'Tora Tigga crest occupied by Baluchis and Punjabis' (*Statesman*, 17 September 1935). In retaliation one of the major targets of Mohmand raids was invariably Shankargarh (a Hindu name) situated by the Shabkadar fort and a stronghold of Hindu and Sikh traders and money-lenders. Even today it is called locally *Sikho derai* (the home of Sikhs). I wish to make an important point here. Non-Muslim groups lived, and are still living, in complete social harmony in the Tribal Areas as accepted *insiders* (Ahmed, 1977a). Attacks such as on Shabkadar are justified as attacks on *outsiders*; non-Muslimness only strengthens that conviction but does not motivate it. The nature of the colonial encounter was marked by a high degree of truculence. In 1897 the Frontier erupted in what can be seen as local response to promises by visionary religious leaders of a millennium and utopia in the near future. This was a consequence of various factors which need not concern us here and have been dealt with elsewhere (Ahmed, 1976). Mohmands attacked and burned Shabkadar but were driven out after losing 300 men. The failure of the uprisings saw the three brigades of the Mohmand Field Force in 1897[8] roaming at will in the most inaccessible areas of the Agency up to the Baezai Jarobi glen destroying villages, water tanks and grain stores. This was the first and last invasion of the deepest area of Mohmand country in history. Churchill, who accompanied the force, was moved to write: 'Far beneath was a valley upon which perhaps no white man had looked since Alexander crossed the mountains on his march to India' (Churchill, 1972: 81). It was to be almost another seventy-six years before outsiders would be permitted to visit the areas north of the Nahakki again (Part Three).

During the 1908 Mohmand expedition[9] into the Gandab valley 38,000 maunds of grain were destroyed (H.D., T.R.C., File 258, 8 January 1927: 4) and the British lost eighty-nine dead and 184 wounded. 1916 saw the high-water-mark of determination to keep the Mohmands from the Empire (also see notification in the last chapter). Two wires, one of which was charged with electricity, were strung up between the Kabul and Swat rivers and along the Michni fort, a length of over 17 miles. The Belawals were literally severed from their Kado kin. Four hundred Mohmands were electrocuted that year. In between and at every 600 yards strongly guarded block-houses were constructed and as a 'final solution' nearby villages were destroyed. Mohmands still carry a bitter memory of this period and date events from the 'year of expulsion' (*sharonkay kal*). For instance Khushal Baba (Do Khel), an elder of Bela, could not tell me the actual year of his birth but said he was born in the *sharonkay kal*.

The economic consequences of blockade had far greater impact on society than a military defeat:

> a blockade of the Mohmands had been proclaimed by the Chief Commissioner in August, and its effect was beginning to be most seriously felt. Cloth was soon practically unobtainable in Lower

Mohmand country, the Upper Mohmands only obtained it at great cost through Kana and Kunar; salt was being sold in Pandiali and Kamali at two seers per rupee as compared with the normal price of nine seers per rupee, and the cost of soap, tea, sugar and other commodities had risen in proportion. Above all, the annual winter migration to the Peshawar Valley for labour and trade, upon which the Khwaezai, Baezai and other up-country clans depend in great measure for their subsistence during the rest of the year, was stopped. Numerous arrests of Mohmands had also been made, and property of considerable value seized by the Frontier Constabulary, who were constantly engaged in patrolling the Mohmand border by night in search of tribesmen attempting to evade the blockade, was sold by auction and the proceeds credited to Government (H.D., T.R.C., File 191, nos 6-13, Political Branch, Proceedings, July 1916: 7).

The standard *Military Report on the Mohmand Country* recommends that 'the only means by which the submission of the tribes can be secured are the temporary occupation of the country and the destruction of crops and villages' (General Staff, 1926: 33) and has sections entitled 'Best seasons for opérations [which recommend autumn so that] the chief harvest of the year can then be taken for the use of the expedition, any surplus destroyed and the sowing of the next crop disturbed or prevented' (ibid.: 34).

In a 'top-secret' assessment called 'Secret Appreciation of Officer Commanding No. 2 (Indian) wing of the possibilities of the coercion of the Mohmand tribes by air action' water tanks (the store of the year's water in the village mud and clay pond from rains), whole villages and towers were listed. Also listed was Chamarkand in the Safi area where a report, still haunted by the ghost of the Russophobic elements in the Great Game, suspected Russian influences (H.D., T.R.C., File 258, 8 January 1927: 5-7). In the 1933 and 1935 campaigns air strikes and tanks were used against the Mohmands. In 1933 the Governor of the Province (Griffiths) wrote a letter to the Foreign Secretary (Fraser-Tytler) containing proposals to bomb the Mohmands from the air:

> as you will see, the proposals amount to the deliberate bombing of selected villages within a defined area ... [the Governor called for a general preemptive strike]. I must make it clear that to bomb these villages merely on seeing them in actual use by *lashkars* [war parties] would take the whole essence out of the scheme (H.D., T.R.C., File 220, Gov. to F.S., 4 September 1933).

A leader titled 'Ethics of bombing' in the *Statesman* supported such action by concluding 'if the Government of India have to teach the marauders a lesson − what, from the point of view of the party attacked, is the difference between being bombed from above or shelled from opposite or being attacked by machine-gun or rifle fire?' (9 September 1935).

In the last major campaign against the Mohmands in 1935 General Auchinleck led over 30,000 British troops into their country (*Statesman*, 17 September 1935). The fighting strength of the Mohmands as officially assessed may be gauged by the fighting men of their two major clans: the Gandab Halimzai had 3,500 and the Tarakzai had 3,100 fighting men (General Staff, 1926: 38).

The Mohmands, hard by Shati Khel, mauled regiments of the 5th/12th Frontier Force, the Guides, killing thirty-five and wounding sixty in the battle of hill point 4080 (Elliott, 1968; *C & MG*, 6 October 1935). Captain Meynell[10] was awarded the V.C. posthumously for the action and Auchinleck promoted to Major General.[11] Extensive coverage was given to the campaign, and the range overlooking Shati Khel, Khazana Sar (Maps 2 and 5), a tribal stronghold from where Mohmands sniped, was mentioned in *The Times* (17 September 1935).

The Mohmand had learned to avoid pitched battle. Tribal strategy is based on raids over the borders and elusive guerrilla tactics on home ground. Mohmands like *nang* Pukhtuns are masters of guerrilla war. One of the reasons for the successful maintenance of their spatial boundaries by tribesmen was the fact that they never fell into the trap that other tribal groups were falling into at the end of the last century: making grand, romantic and futile gestures by charging into British squares with spears and scimitars to be mowed down by superior fire-power like the classic example of the Sudanese Dervishes (Churchill, 1972). Defeat does not exist in the vocabulary of the *nang* Pukhtun. He never fights a pitched battle, he chooses the time and the place. He is not armed as well as his adversary and does not possess artillery pieces, but his .303 is deadly and effective in the mountains and most adult Pukhtuns own one. 'A curious feature' of an engagement with the Mohmands on 18 April 1915 was that they were 'so well armed' and estimated to have used 1,200 .303 rifles (H.D., T.R.C., File 181, C.C. to F.S., 23 April 1915). The Gulf, Afghanistan and even small pockets in the Tribal Areas produced a steady stream of weapons, illegal in the rest of India (Keppel, 1911). Even after the invasion of his territory the Pukhtun does not accept defeat. He disappears into the mountains and after the enemy has left, burning and blowing up his villages and water tanks, he returns quite unrepentant and as determined as ever to carry on his way of life.

Not unnaturally the Mohmands were the victims of a bad imperial press. The British found 'their courage is open to doubt' (Mason, 1884: 229); 'they have a bad-name for treachery and cruelty' (General Staff, 1926: 15) and 'are the most aweful swine' (H.D., T.R.C., F.C. Reports, 5 March 1934).

Bitterness towards twentieth-century civilization and modernization in Mohmand minds results from their association of these processes with the colonizing British. An American scholar comments:

> As far as the Frontier is concerned, however, the story throughout is one of struggle for control – a control which was never completely established and a struggle which ended only when the British departed in 1947. In this context, the political history of the Frontier under British rule hangs more on milestones of suppression than on those of reform (Spain, 1963: 145).

Structurally, the British bolstered and encouraged the growth of a 'chiefly' Malik class in the Tribal Areas. Their efforts met with little success. But the foundation of conflict, contradiction and dysfunction in Mohmand society between the *mashars* and *kashars* was created. The very core of tribal democracy was touched. Nevertheless the Maliks with all their secret allowances and political privileges remained little more than glorified tourist chiefs. In the interior of the Agency the weight of their word depended to a great extent on their personal influence. The Agency remained a closed system. However, this class did open up a window to the Tribal Areas and one through which the British could not only peer but make their voices heard. Those Mohmands who could manipulate and relate *internal* agnatic and *external* politics successfully were to emerge as the Musa in Shati Khel (as I show later). However, it is important to note that at the slightest sign of political trouble with the British it was the Mullahs who took the initiative and emerged as leaders stressing religious themes. British Maliks would be their first targets, as we shall see in the next section. It was no secret that the Mohmand Maliks and leaders resented the intrusion of the Haji of Turangzai or his sons from Lakaro, which involved them with or without willingness in the tribal uprisings against the British (*The Times*, 16 September 1935).

In terms of our two areas of study, Shati Khel and Bela Mohmandan were both fully exposed to the rough and tumble of the border politics of tribal raids and imperial reprisal as this chapter illustrates. The model of society for these two areas was maintained and affected by the same historical experiences and ecological situation. Changes in the two areas began only after the creation of Pakistan and that of the Agency in 1951.

In this section I have argued that history is seen as part of social process and as a direct result of larger historical sequences, which in turn reorder local social structure, and not as 'an immense, meaningless mass of facts'. The stream of events do not exist as autonomous social sequences but as part of interconnected and integrated social processes. I have argued that Pukhtun social history adopted two polar attitudes as a consequence of the colonial encounter: a positive attitude which helped to consolidate and preserve the Pukhtun ideal-type within society, and a negative attitude permeated with suspicion of the outside world and its developments. To the Mohmand it meant a complete rejection of the twentieth century which in his eyes the British represented: in 1947 there was not a single electric bulb, school, tube-well or government post in what is now the Mohmand Agency. It took almost three decades after the British had left for the suspicion to be altered.

II Historical process and agnatic rivalry

A section on historical processes and agnatic rivalry could not begin better than with the examples of two of the greatest Pukhtun kings, illustrating the credo intrinsic to *tarboorwali*, that no Pukhtun is better than another, a belief to be established even at the cost of mutual and far-reaching losses to the community. Sher Shah Suri replaced the Mughals and ruled with wisdom and success until his accidental death in 1545 which was a signal for intense internecine kin rivalry to begin. His grandson was killed by an uncle who seized the throne. A series of revolts and counter-revolts among agnatic kin opened the way for the return of Humayun, the Mughal, in 1555. A similar sequence was enacted by the descendants of Ahmed Shah Abdali. The twenty-three sons of Taimur, his son and successor, fought among themselves and the Durrani Empire was plunged into a state of total chaos with tribal centrifugal forces asserting themselves until the emergence of Amir Abdur Rahman in 1880 almost a hundred years later.

The example in this section is taken from Frontier events in 1915 in

the Gandab valley. It is not restricted to intra-sectional agnatic rivalry
of the type which will be examined in Chapter 7, but is an example of
how intra-lineage agnatic rivalry functions within larger tribal and state
structures and politics creating highly complex and interconnected
relationships. The case-study will show how each party, on its own
operative level and with its own specific goals in view, attempts to
divert and subvert the larger situation for its own purposes. Such agnatic
rivalry set in an earlier period has ramifications through to the next
generation of descendants, as we shall see in Chapters 5 and 7. The
material in this section is based on historical archives, official records
and personal information obtained from the descendants of the main
actors involved. The example may be taken as typical of tribal and
Frontier politics.

I do not propose to approach the case-study by drawing up a chrono-
logical list of dates and events in support of what I am saying. I shall
restrict myself to pointing out the structural mechanism and underlying
principles in such situations. The focus of analysis is fixed on the
agnatic rivalry between Malik Anmir, the father of Shahzada Malik,
from Shati Khel, and his Wali Beg sectional cousin Inayatullah Khan,
the grandfather of Khanzada Khan, living at Sangar, both emergent
leaders of their sub-sections (Figure 6). In the spring of 1915 various
Mullahs led by Haji Chaknawar and Babra, themselves rivals for power
among the Upper Mohmands, attempted to rally the Baezai and Khwaezai
against the British in a *jihad*. The timing of such political movements
with the agricultural seasons is of utmost importance. Chaknawar's
initial call met with a poor response:

> the Chaknawar Mullah had sent envoys to the Baezais and Khwaezais
> to prepare them for Jehad, but he had received unsatisfactory replies,
> the tribes objecting on the ground that the time of harvest was at
> hand and that they could take no part in any movement that would
> endanger their crops (H.D., T.R.C., File 181, no. 48, APA to C.C.,
> Shabkadar, 6 April 1915).

Shortly afterwards the crops were harvested and the Upper Mohmands
were ready for *jihad*. In the meantime the hostility between Anmir and
Inayatullah had degenerated into shootings in which several deaths
occurred but events overtook their personal animosity when the *jihad*
was declared (ibid.).

Muhasil, Kuda Khel of the Baezai clan and an inveterate enemy of
the British, was opposed in his section by his cousin Bazwan who would

normally oppose Muhasil's politics. However, when Muhasil joined Chaknawar Bazwan, fearing the accusation of soft-peddling against the British and being labelled *kafir* (unbeliever) by the Mullahs, also joined in. Muhasil, related to Anmir and Inayatullah on the larger tribal genealogical span, had an old-standing enmity with them which had been exacerbated by their attempts to block his raiding gang in Gandab on its return from Shabkadar earlier in the year. Muhasil and the Mullahs had already dubbed the two Gandab leaders 'British agents' and *kafirs* as the *jihad* fever mounted. Afghan Mohmands began to cross the border to join the *jihad* and the Viceroy of India entered into urgent correspondence with the Amir of Afghanistan. The stage was once again abruptly set for an international crisis.

I would like to pause and attempt an initial demarcation of the participants, their situational levels of conflict and their relationships to each other with the aid of Figure 3.

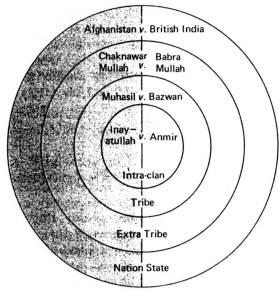

FIGURE 3 *Levels of tribal conflict*

As we see there are four clear and differentiated levels of involvement: intra-clan, inter-clan, extra-tribal and state. The shaded half of the figure indicates general traditional alliance patterns along the four levels and at each stage of conflict. Thus Muhasil would support Chaknawar who, in turn, would expect support from Afghanistan. Anmir and Inayatullah could expect British support against the Mullahs. No tribal situation is patently so simple: as we know at each level there are bitter and primordial rivalries ready to subvert the grander design of alliances.

In this particular case the lines of conflict criss-cross over different levels and even change over different times. For instance, Muhasil is opposed to Anmir and as he is inclined to the Chaknawar Mullah, Anmir by the same logic finds support with Babra Mullah who in normal times opposes him. The elements are highly complex; there is conflict based on agnatic rivalry within the sub-clan and clan, there is conflict based on religious leadership and there is the continuation of the Great Game involving international politics. Events can swiftly out-pace local rivalries and rationality or sanity. The situation is made worse by the knowledge that at every stage of the crisis attempts to sabotage the enemy whether he is presently in alliance or not are made. Agnatic rivalry remains the supreme expression of tribal politics.

In the present example the final state level was not activated and a crisis was averted as a result of intense and successful international diplomatic activity (H.D., T.R.C., File 181, no. 81, Viceroy-Amir Correspondence, 1915). British Military Intelligence summed up the situation:

> operations against the Mohmands present all the typical peculiarities of warfare against the uncivilised tribes of the North-West Frontier. The advantages which they enjoy from their mobility, excellent intelligence and powers of endurance are largely neutralised by lack of cohesion and absence of any effective system of command (General Staff, 1926: 33).

The authors need not have studied anthropology to arrive at the two key concepts of segmentary social organization among Pukhtun tribes: agnatic rivalry leading to 'lack of cohesion' and intense individual democracy resulting in the 'absence of any effective system of command'; both concepts derive from *Pukhtunwali* and its relationship to the genealogical charter.

I shall now briefly show the complicated and changing sequence of events. Chaknawar had declared *jihad* simultaneously against the British and the pro-British, Anmir and Inayatullah *kafirs*. A *lakhkar* was prepared to burn the Gandab villages of Anmir and Inayatullah en route to crossing the administrative border. Mohmands from Lalpura and Goshta had already arrived to join the *lakhkar*. At this stage, Babra Mullah

challenged Chaknawar by announcing that *jihad* could only be technically justified theologically if the British invaded the Mohmands and
not vice-versa, but he was over-ruled. Inayatullah and Anmir found
themselves opposed by a formidable combination of their own immediate sub-sectional first cousins, Muhasil's Kuda Khels and the Mullahs.
The axe was temporarily buried between Anmir and Inayatullah (something that was not done in 1932 in a similar situation involving similar
levels of politics and with almost the same actors and their direct
descendants) and they contacted the British at Shabkadar. For Anmir,
Inayatullah and their Halimzai supporters the dilemma was acute: if
they remained neutral in *jihad* they would be disgraced and punished
through fines and burnt houses by the larger tribe; on the other hand, if
they participated against the British they would be the first to be
chastised by a retaliatory expedition as they were geographically first in
the line of defence. Little wonder they are fond of quoting the following proverb: 'On this side the staff, on that side the panther' (Ahmed,
1975: 58). In such a situation tribesmen resort to diplomacy by keeping secret lines of communication open to *all* parties: the tribe was
assured of their support and so were the British. The British understood
their dilemma: 'The only tribes whose territorial limits are directly concerned are the Kamali Halimzai and the Gandab Halimzai.... Their helplessness to resist the Mullah is evident, and the passive attitude they
adopted was all that could be expected from them' (H.D., T.R.C.,
File 181, no. 74, APA to DC, 28 April 1915: 27).

Over 4,000 men assembled at Ghalanay and Muhasil led them across
the border. In the clash some 100 Mohmands were killed including a
nephew of Chaknawar, a brother of Muhasil and a son of Bazwan: 'The
enemy displayed unexpected gallantry and dash, and assisted by considerable advantages of terrain, inflicted substantial losses on our troops,
namely fourteen killed and fifty-seven wounded. Among the former
were included three British officers' (ibid., no. 71, C.C. to F.S. Peshawar,
23 April 1915: 23).

Chaknawar had been using the Amir of Afghanistan's name to support his call for *jihad*. However, correspondence between the Viceroy
and the Amir assured the former:

> With regard to the attack that Your Excellency has written about, I
> had heard rumours that the Mohmands of places outside the terri-
> tory of the sublime God-granted Government of Afghanistan and
> Mohmands of territory in dispute were assembling for the purpose

of waging war. I therefore sent stringent orders enjoining on the Governors of the eastern districts to effectually prevent Afghan subjects of those parts from joining the frontier tribes (ibid., no. 81, Amir to Viceroy, 28 April 1915: 32).

The Amir's active interest defused the situation; Chaknawar's property was attached in Afghanistan and the authorities issued orders for his arrest. Chaknawar's major source of support dried up and he was forced into retirement in Upper Mohmand. None the less he still had one final card up his sleeve: to demolish his rival Babra. He declared that Babra had taken Rs. 30,000 from the British to keep out of the fighting. The only proof of innocence that Babra could hope to give in tribal eyes was to call for *jihad* which he himself would lead. But for the moment the crisis was over.

The Mohmands were fined Rs. 23,000 (compared to Rs. 18,000 in 1897 and Rs. 10,500 in 1908) but the three sub-clans of the Halimzai were rewarded Rs. 1,000 each. Anmir and Inayatullah emerged with the highest rewards:

> I would recommend that a sum of Rs. 5,000 (five thousand only) be presented to Anmir and Inayatullah to cover the losses they will suffer by reason of the fine and confiscation of allowances, and, in recognition of their individual good work, I would propose that a substantial increase be made in the *lungi inams* they now receive (ibid., no. 10, APA, 1 May 1915: 30).

In Chapters 5 and 7 the importance of alliance with the British for politics within the operative lineage is clearly illustrated. Within two decades Anmir's sons would dominate Shati Khel, reversing a situation in which they had been dominated by their cousins, the Ranra, for at least three generations.

In 1932 a similar combination of balanced opposition on all four levels almost escalated into a full-scale tribal war with international ramifications. The political administration succeeded in patching up the differences between Anmir and Abdullah, the son of Inayatullah, to block a large Baezai and Khwaezai *lakhkar* of some 2,000 Upper Mohmands from crossing the Gandab on its way to the British border. At a Tarakzai/Halimzai *jirga* it was decided that Anmir, with his men, was to hold Nahakki and Abdullah was to hold the Pass at Karappa and the Tora Tigga. After counsel with their leader, Abdullah's men felt they had been deliberately given the more dangerous position to hold and returned to their villages the same night leaving the Gandab exposed. Elements of the *lakhkar* immediately moved into the valley where the Hamza Khel sub-clan of the Halimzais crossed sides. Anmir learnt of Abdullah's move and as his flank was wholly exposed requested him to join his position on the Nahakki range. Abdullah moved up and soon both were surrounded and outnumbered by the *lakhkar* and firing began. After several hours of firing Anmir's ammunition ran out and as a *coup de grâce* his water supply was cut. Anmir's party was allowed to leave for Shati Khel on a safe-conduct agreement which was promptly broken and several casualties resulted. The Lower Mohmand tribes had gathered in Anmir's villages in Shati Khel. First the non-Shati Halimzai and finally Anmir with his party bolted from Shati Khel. The hostile *lakhkar* arrived by midnight and burnt the villages of Anmir and his relatives. Accusation and counter-accusation further soured relations among the Gandab Halimzai. Official reports agreed that the debacle was due largely to the 'jealousy and dissension' among the Gandab Halimzai (H.D., T.R.C., File 220, DC Peshawar, 11 May 1932: 4). The events briefly described above were to be repeated in 1935 and involved the British in a full-fledged campaign.

The symmetry and pattern of tribal agnatic conflict with its major and characteristic components perpetuates itself over generations. Today the descendants of Anmir and Inayatullah are rivals and Amin, Muhasil's descendant, is their enemy; and so the symmetry of agnatic antagonism is maintained. The lessons of history are clear: agnatic rivalry will allow cutting off the nose to spite the face.

In concluding the chapter on history I wish to emphasize, for purposes of my argument in the study, that the British left tribal structure largely untouched. Whether they could or could not occupy and hold the Tribal Areas is not the point. As a logical result of various factors, including a certain romantic attitude to the Frontier in colonial eyes, tribal structures were allowed to function uninterrupted and untouched; their anthropological 'purity' was thus ensured. We have seen in this chapter how external imperial expansionism worked in two opposing directions within Pukhtun society. External pressure created homogeneity within the tribe which ensured safeguarding and preservation of tribal cultural values. An aspect of this pressure applied as 'big-power' strategy had another and opposite effect: allowances, estates and titles exacerbated and deepened internal conflict based on agnatic rivalry. External history is seen locally as unending sequences to aggrandize, interfere or encapsulate and in the main accounts for suspicion regarding official schemes sponsored by larger state systems. Having stated the ecological and historical framework of the Mohmand, which largely explains how society successfully maintained and perpetuated internal structure, my concern in the next chapters is to construct what may be called the Pukhtun ideal-type model.

Part two

Tribal models

4 Segmentary tribes and models of Pukhtun social organization

These Powers (who dominate and oppress the young nations of the Third World) often make it seem that tribal conflicts are modern contradictions which have their origin in the functioning of pre-colonial structures: in fact, these conflicts are explainable primarily by reference to colonial domination (Godelier, 1977: 96).

In this chapter my main concern will be to construct an ideal-type Pukhtun model in order to illustrate the major theme of my study: namely that Mohmand social behaviour and organization approximate to the ideal and therefore there is little disjunction between concepts of the actual and ideal in society. Subsequent chapters will provide the data enabling me to argue and show clearly whether, and if so to what extent, deviance has occurred from the model in the two tribal groups, TAM and SAM.

A brief discussion on tribes in anthropology will be followed by a discussion of the major features of the model both as an ideological and empirically observed form. In Section III a taxonomy of Pukhtun societies within a larger framework than the Tribal Areas will be attempted to enable me to place the model in its proper social and political context in order to bring its main features into relief.

I The tribe

One of the major contributions of anthropology to knowledge has been the detailed study and classification of tribal societies. For purposes of my study I shall place tribes that possess the common religious denominator of Islam in a separate category (see, for example, Asad, 1970; Barth, 1953, 1959, 1961, 1972; Evans-Pritchard, 1973; Gellner, 1969a; Hart, 1976; Leach, 1940; Lewis, I. M., 1961, 1962a and b, 1969a; Pehrson, 1966; Peters, 1960; Stirling, 1965; Tapper, 1971; 1974a, b). The Islamic factor will not raise theological, eschatological or ecclesiastical issues but those of interest to a social anthropologist. The interest is primarily in social analysis of the Islamic tribe. How does religious symbolism function to invoke, inhibit, predicate or perpetuate values in society? What are the important cognitive values discerned by the various groups of the tribe? How are these values ranked in order of precedence by different age, sex and status groups? The answers to these questions will be attempted in Section II. I will be arguing that Islamic symbolism is intrinsic to society whether dormant or activated by outside religious groups and is fundamental to the sociological understanding of Islamic groups however geographically or politically remote. I shall return to this point with reference to my field-work data in the next section and in Chapter 6.

Briefly *African Political Systems* (Fortes and Evans-Pritchard, 1970) distinguishes three types of tribal social organization and I shall begin my discussion of tribal society from that work: the Bushmen, where political relations equal kin relations (ibid.: 6–7), the second type, called Group A, are unitary states with kings or paramount chiefs ruling centralized states with societies that are ranked. The third type, Group B, are segmentary lineage systems, characterized by: 1 segmentation of tribal groups, 2 unilineal descent from a common eponymous ancestor. Patrilineal descent is of primary importance as against matrilineal descent in other societies (Leach, 1971b); 3 monadism; 'the smaller group is the embryo tribe, the tribe is the smaller group writ large' (Gellner, 1969a: 48); and finally 4 egalitarianism or an acephalous form of political organization. To these categories of tribal systems may be added another classification, that of the 'segmentary state' (Southall, 1953).

Having briefly introduced the subject of tribal societies, I will attempt the difficult task of defining a tribe as I do not consider the definition of a tribe as given, axiomatic or tautologous. This simple task is at the core of a larger controversy that is not confined to semantics and definitions:

> Thus, the term 'tribe' while literally obtruding in all the writings and discussion of anthropologists seems not to have entered the most bitter theoretical combat zones. For a decade now, doubt, concern, criticism and sometimes outright rejection have gradually been creeping in with regard to the term; and today we are faced with a conflict of opinion (Godelier, 1977: 71).

The term tribe is used with 'scandalous imprecision' (Neiva, 1964: 302), as 'an exceedingly ill-defined, catchall' (Steward, 1955: 53), while 'the wide variety in the meanings assigned to the term tribe, either explicitly or by implication, gives one the impression of individual caprice' (Dole, 1971: 83). The discipline itself comes under attack for 'notoriously lacking in precision in the logical definition of its units of empirical study' (Southall, 1953: 22).

If there is imprecision and ambiguity regarding the definition of a tribe, there is logically little unanimity in classifying or delimiting tribal groups:

> Gluckman's attached list of tribes includes the Bushmen and the Eskimo as well as Nuba and Dahomey (xv-xx). He also applies the term 'tribal' to Scots, Welsh, Irish, French, Jewish, Lebanese, and African denizens of British towns, on the ground that they 'have their own associations, and their domestic life is ruled by their own national [sic] customs insofar as British law and conditions allow' (Gluckman, 1971: 292) (Fried, 1971: 17).

I shall briefly discuss what I discern to be the characteristics of tribal society in order to define my terms of reference and field-work groups.

The relationship between the concept and structure of tribe and kin-organized groups is recognized:

> The Latin word *tribus* was used to refer to each of the independent 'gentile' groups (Tities, Ramnes and Luceres) that together formed the population of early Rome. Also in the archaic Attic dialect of Greece any group of uncivilized people was referred to as *trittus*, and as *trippus* in the dialect of the Aeolian emigrants to Asia Minor (Dole, 1971: 90).

Tribal groups, like the Bedouin, since Ibn Khaldun, are defined by the term *asabiyah* or solidarity of kinship groups (Watt, 1961: 36-7) which 'is the spirit of the clan. It implies boundless and unconditional loyalty to fellow clansmen and corresponds in general to patriotism of the passionate, chauvinistic type' (Hitti, 1977: 27).

The relationship between kin and politics is cognate and important:

> An Indo-European tribe referred to the largest kind of social and political community which existed before the appearance of the city state. More elementary social units were included in it, from the smallest, the Greek *genos* and the *phratra* and the Latin *gens* and *curia*. It is important to establish here that all these terms (apart

from *curia*) belonged *both* to kinship and political terminology; this means there was an internal relationship, real or implied, between kinship and political organisation (Godelier, 1977: 72).

The Royal Anthropological Institute's Committee of experts included the concept of territory in its definition (RAI, 1971: 66).

In synopsis form the main features emphasized of tribes as examined over the last hundred years are placed in Table 2 (chronologically to date of work). The recurring characteristics of tribal society in Table 2 appear to be common territory, common name, common language, common culture, common descent and some form of political organization. For purposes of my study I will define a tribe as possessing the above characteristics but will include a common religious belief. A Mohmand tribesman is therefore one living on common territory (the Mohmand Agency, or having migrated but still in contact with kin in the Agency), possessing a common name (Mohmand),[1] speaking a common language (Pukhto), living within a common cultural code (*Pukhtunwali*), descended from an eponymous ancestor (Mohmand), possessing a form of political organization and a common religion (Mohmands are orthodox Sunni Muslims). This is a rudimentary definition largely applicable to Tribal Area society. It will raise certain problems when discussing Pukhtun groups *outside* the Tribal Areas. For example, do Pukhtun groups not owning exclusive territory or not speaking their common language in various parts of India, like the Yusufzai in Rampur, cease to be Pukhtun? This leads us to important related questions: is a Pukhtun/Pathan by definition a 'tribesman' as the Penguin English Dictionary defines him? Does the act of losing his language or culture in the Pukhtun areas lose him his claims to Pukhtunness? Or is the descent principle crucial and able to sustain his Pukhtun identity?

I shall define a Pukhtun, whether he is living in the Pukhtun areas or not, speaking Pukhto or not, as one who can trace his lineage through the father's line to one of the Pukhtun tribes, and in turn to the apical ancestor. A Mohmand may migrate from the Agency or Province and lose his paternal land or may be expelled for an act involving the honour of women, but he cannot be de-Mohmandized. Nothing can strip him of his place on the tribal charter to which he is recruited by birth. The kinship chart provides him with a permanent set of terms and techniques for allocating people around him to their social positions and preventing him from becoming anomic (Durkheim, 1951). As

TABLE 2   Tribal characteristics

	Morgan, 1878	Evans-Pritchard, [1940] 1970: 278	Elkin, 1943: 23	Hoebel, 1958: 661	Naroll, 1964	Honigmann, 1964	Middleton/ Tait, 1970
common territory	Yes	Yes	Yes		Yes	Yes	
common name	Yes	Yes	Yes			Yes	
common language	Yes		Yes	Yes	Yes	Yes	Yes
common culture		Yes	Yes	Yes	Yes	Yes	Yes
unilineal descent	Yes	Yes				Yes	Yes
economic self-sufficiency		Yes			Yes		
common rites, beliefs			Yes				Yes
political organization	Yes	Yes		No	Yes		Yes
no European contact/local community structure					Yes		Yes

suggested for Swat society (Barth, 1972) dispossession of land does not cancel his Pukhtunness. The single most important criterion for the definition of a Pukhtun tribesman is patrilineal descent from Pukhtun ascendants. A man possesses *droit de cité* in virtue of occupying a given niche in the social structure and membership of a tribe is a consequence of this place in the lineage. A place on the charter confers legitimacy while creating barriers between Pukhtun and non-Pukhtun; as it includes, it excludes. Non-Pukhtun groups living in Pukhtun areas, like Muslim Punjabis and Kashmiris in Peshawar or non-Muslim Hindus and Sikhs in the Tirah, Tribal Areas, speaking, behaving and dressing like Pukhtuns, are not considered Pukhtun. They do not feature on the tribal charter. The above definition approximates to the Pukhtun definition. As an example of my point, Pukhtuns generally take immense pride in naming Sher Shah Suri, one of the greatest rulers of India (Datta *et al.*, 1956; Smith, 1958), a Pukhtun, although he was born in India and maintained no lingual or cultural contact with his ancestral home. The common linking factor between the King of India and the ordinary tribesman in the Frontier hills is mutual placement on the tribal charter, which at the moment of relating them reduces them to equal status. Definition of a Pukhtun or of why and when he is one, or not one, is not a spurious anthropological exercise. It is debated and discussed in earnest and constantly in *hujras*. Pukhtuns appear obsessed in establish-ing the purity of their Pukhtunness while doubting that of those belonging to other groups or tribes (Caroe, 1965; Spain, 1962, 1963).

Although Indian studies are still not unanimous in defining a tribe (Dube, 1960; Guha, 1951; Hitchcock, 1958, 1966; Majumdar, 1958; Mandelbaum, 1956; Srinivas, 1952) Indian tribal groups generally speak the Dravidian language indicating pre-Aryan and autochthonous origin, and are largely animist and not Hindu in religious beliefs (Bailey, 1957, 1960, 1961; Fürer-Haimendorf, 1939, 1962, 1977; Vitebsky, 1978). In contrast Pukhtun tribes speak Pukhto, a language cognate to the main-stream Islamic languages, Persian and Arabic, and on the subcontinent, Urdu. The script is Arabic in character. The Pukhtuns belong to the orthodox and main sect of Islam, the Sunnis. The Hindi equivalent terms for tribal are either *adivasi* (aborigines or first inhabitants) or *pahari* (hill people). Pukhtun migrations from Afghan areas to their present localities began between the fifteenth and sixteenth centuries and are part of recorded history and they are therefore not *adivasi*. Pukhtuns could be said to be *pahari* but there are large and important tribes, like the Khattak, not living in the mountain ranges.

The division between town-dwellers and countrymen distinguishing tribals from non-tribals (Mayer, P., 1961) does not help us define Pukhtuns who have lived in towns like Peshawar and Kabul for generations in large groups. For certain anthropologists 'tribes occupy a position in cultural evolution' which '*illustrates* humanity's condition in a *barbarian state*' (Morgan, 1871: 122) and are morphologically shifting along a social trajectory to 'more advanced cultures we call civilizations' (Sahlins, 1968: 4; Service, 1966). As I hope to show in the following pages Pukhtun tribal society is not a stage in a typological sequence, band–tribe–chiefdom–state, but in its exclusive core *nang* areas it presents a discrete self-sufficient socio-cultural category that has successfully perpetuated itself over centuries, while simultaneously exhibiting various complex forms in other areas as a result of changing economic and political situations.

Perhaps I will be more successful in defining a Pukhtun tribesman negatively, in terms of what he is not, than in terms of what he is. A common definition of a tribe categorizes it as 'pre-literate', 'pre-industrial' and possessing an 'egalitarian economy, with relatively simple tools to produce and primary goods to consume' (Gluckman, 1971: xv). But can Pukhtun tribes be classified as 'pre-literate' when their greatest and most prolific poets were contemporaneous to John Milton? And would the Afridi 'arms factories' flourishing in Darra Adam Khel and producing exact replicas of sophisticated international guns and ammunition since the turn of the century qualify them as producers of primary goods only? Another definition includes the absence of law and tribal councils (Evans-Pritchard, 1970: 293-4). Pukhtun society not only adheres to general Islamic law but also its own, the *Pukhtunwali*, with its institution of *jirga*. The decision of the *jirga* is final and the tribesman faces severe punishment, like the burning of his house, if he wilfully disobeys its decision. I disagree with colonial administrators when they refer to Pukhtun tribal society as unstable and without law (Caroe, 1977: 352). On the contrary, tribal society is highly stable and has defined laws within which it operates, as I shall show in the following chapters. The fact that society has perpetuated itself over 400 years seems to bear this out.

I will conclude this section with a reflection on the sterility of a formal discussion of tribes:

It now seems clear that, in this whole region, the concept 'tribe' is of quite negative utility from the viewpoint of social analysis. The

significance of particular features of particular tribal organisations
cannot be discovered by functional investigations of the more usual
kind. It is rather that we come to understand the qualities of 'Tribe
A' only when we measure these qualities against their antithesis in
'Tribe B' (as in the *gumsa-gumlao* case) (Leach, 1977: xv).

I am in general agreement with this position; for the discussion to be
meaningful and heuristic, tribal groups can only be studied or analysed
with reference to other antithetical groups within their own ethnic
boundaries (Section III). I now propose to construct an ideal-type
Pukhtun model in the following section.

II The Pukhtun ideal-type model

In this section I shall establish a sociological Pukhtun ideal-type model
of social organization so that observable frequencies of social behaviour
and societal processes may be brought out in relief. The sources are
based on Pukhtun literature (native model), historical material (foreign
model) and my field-work notes during the ethnographic present. As in
other models irregularities will be smoothed out and structure and
unity emphasized. Leach justifiably criticized equilibrium models: 'the
presentation is one of *stable* equilibrium; the authors write as if the
Trobrianders, the Tikopia, the Nuer are as they are, now and for ever'
(ibid., 7). However, I should clarify at this point that my ideal-
type model *is* a timeless one and the Pukhtuns in it 'are as they are,
now and for ever'. We may presume to construct a timeless model that
will depict Pukhtun social reality as it has existed uninterrupted, stable
and in equilibrium for over four centuries at least. Only as an antithesis
to an unchanging model can we measure deviance among the Mohmands.
Although I shall be building a ideal-type model and describing its
structure as part of an overall equilibrium, I will accept Leach's advice
that 'the fictional nature of this equilibrium should be frankly recog-
nised' (ibid.: 285).

What is the nature and function of the Weberian 'ideal-type' in
formulating societal models? 'The ideal type ... does not describe a
concrete course of action, but a normatively ideal course, assuming
certain ends and modes of normative orientation as "binding" on the
actors. It does not describe an individual course of action, but a "typical"
one' (Parsons, 1947: 13). To Weber the ideal-type allows the social
analyst to examine empirical reality: 'The construction of a purely

rational course of action in such cases serves the sociologist as a type ("ideal-type") which has the merit of clear understandability and lack of ambiguity' (Weber, 1947: 92).

> The construction of a purely rational course of action ... serves the sociologist as a type ... by comparison with this it is possible to understand the ways in which actual action is influenced by irrational factors of all sorts ... in that they account for the deviation from the line of conduct which would be expected on the hypothesis that the action were purely rational (ibid.: 92).

It is important that the ideal-type implies the 'pure-type' (ibid.: 89) and that it is 'ideal' or 'pure' as conceived by the actor not the observer. Ideal-types are therefore subjective or native exegeses of their social systems. I am in agreement with Weber that 'theoretical analysis in the field of sociology is possible only in terms of such pure types' (ibid.: 110).

If in the Weberian context the ideal-type person in ancient China was the Mandarin, in ancient Greece the scholar-gymnast, in Islam the warrior (Weber, 1947, 1960, 1961, 1966, 1968) then the ideal Pukhtun is one who upholds *Pukhtunwali*. I shall now discuss what is generally understood to be the ideal-type model, its main features, how these are interpreted in society and how and if they are *actually* practised.

(a) *Pukhtun ideal-type*

Pukhtun ideal-type social organization and behaviour revolve around the concepts of *Pukhtunwali*, translated as the Pukhtun Code or the way of the Pukhtuns. *Pukhtunwali* is the core of Pukhtun social behaviour. Although unwritten and precisely undefined it is the theme of song, proverb, metaphor and parable and never far from men's minds; like most codes it is part-fiction and part-reality. A Mohmand sociologist observed of the Mohmands: 'Pukhto operates in every aspect of their social and cultural life' (Mohmand, 1966: 44). One hundred per cent agreement was recorded in both TAM and SAM questionnaires that *Pukhtunwali* was practised in their villages. It is remarkable how native and foreign models coincide with regard to the main features of *Pukhtunwali* and its relevance and sanctity in society. It is equally remarkable how similar the ideological model is to the actual immediate model of empirically observed social behaviour and organization as I shall illustrate below. Missionaries,[2] doctors,[3] soldiers,[4] administrators,[5] scholars[6] and women[7] have contributed over a century to a multi-dimensional and intimate account of Pukhtun social and political life. The main institutions of *Pukhtunwali*, and as culled from the literature on the Pukhtuns by Pukhtuns and non-Pukhtuns, appear to be:

(1) *Badal*: translated as revenge, feud and vendetta, forms the primary law of *Pukhtunwali*. It is to be wreaked regardless of time, space and cost. A proverb sums up attitudes to revenge: 'He is not a Pukhtun who does not give a blow for a pinch' (Ahmed, 1975: 57). The Pukhto concept of revenge emphasizes ends rather than means; the end overrides the means. That is how and why the system perpetuates itself.

(2) *Melmastia*: hospitality to guests. Mohmand *mashars* equate a Pukhtun with 'a friend of guests' (*da melma dost*) and 'miser' (*shoom*) is a term of abuse. The custom of hospitality is still strong especially in TAM and even today the proudest of Maliks will personally serve his guest tea or meals. As a mark of deference he will rarely sit with his guest. His sons in any case will not sit with the father or guests but help serve the meals. Ideally the village should share the burden of the guest's expense but in fact this usually falls upon the TAM patriarch or senior lineage *mashars* like Shamshudin in SAM.

(3) *Nanawatee*: from the verb 'to go in' and an extension of *melmastia*. It is evoked when an enemy 'goes in' or 'comes in' to sue for peace, usually with the Holy Koran in hand. The act implies supplication and must be honoured by showing reciprocal magnanimity. Examples of *nanawatee* still abound in Shati Khel. For instance Mazullah a few years ago sought *nanawatee* from Shahzada after his Ranra village was occupied. More recently, when the son and grandsons of Shahzada fired on Mazullah in Mian Mandi, Shahzada swallowed his pride and asked for *nanawatee* rather than see one of his offspring killed. On both occasions *nanawatee* was granted with the traditional slaying of goats and cows.

(4) *Jirga*: assembly of elders who are called to decide specific issues and whose decisions are binding on parties in conflict. The *jirga* has been called 'the closest thing to Athenian democracy that has existed since the original' (Spain, 1963: 69). In a society where there is no written or formal law the importance of an assembly is crucial in ordering society and preventing it from collapsing into anarchy. The *jirga* regulates life through decisions ranging from the location of a mosque to the settling of conflict within sub-sections, to larger issues such as regulating foreign relations with other tribes and even conveying decisions of the tribe to government. Decisions are based on a combination of Islamic law and

Pukhto custom. The *jirga*'s sanctions may include ostracism, and disobedience would result in extreme opprobrium leading to fines and might even include burning of the house. Membership of the *jirga*, which is not fixed and may range from five to fifty depending on the importance of the issue, is restricted to Pukhtuns. Members are called *jirgaeez*. Non-Mohmand and religious groups are excluded from it. A *jirga* member must be either a respected *mashar* or, if young, someone who has inherited the Maliki from his father. The *jirga* as an institution exists and functions among the Mohmands.[8]

However, my own findings, which I shall elaborate below, lead me to the conclusion that the two most important operative features of *Pukhtunwali* as locally understood are *tarboorwali* and *tor* (Chapters 5 and 7). *Badal*, the primary law, is freely translated to mean *tarboorwali*. The very concept of *nang* is equated and reduced to *tarboorwali* and *tor*. It is in the pursuit of these two that the other principles of *Pukhtunwali* may be tacitly suspended. Considerations of *tarboorwali* and *tor* override sanctions of custom, Code and even religion. Around these two social features the boundaries are clear and unambiguous. There is no compromise in practice. They refer to acts of commission as well as omission. For example, 'He killed his *tor* daughter and did Pukhto' or 'He did *not* kill his daughter and he has not done Pukhto'. In the practice of these two features actual social behaviour and ideal behaviour correspond; together they form the Pukhto paradigm (Chapter 7). I shall give due weight to the traditional features of *Pukhtunwali* discussed above but will concentrate on *tarboorwali* and *tor* as forming the kernel of the cognitively accepted ideal-type. Taken together, the above characteristics may be thought of as the 'conscious' or 'homemade' or 'native' model (Ward, 1969) of the Pukhtun.[9]

In the ideal, the pursuit of an honourable life, in the eyes of the actor, is equated with a life approximating to the features of *Pukhtunwali*. *Pukhtunwali* may be freely equated to *nangwali* or the Code of Honour. It is abbreviated also to 'Pukhto' and thus equated with the language of the Pukhtuns, or *jaba* (literally meaning tongue or word of honour). 'Pukhto [the tongue or language] is one's word' (*Pukhto jaba da*) is a common expression. This Code is the idiom through which the Pukhtun expresses his Pukhtunness.

It is this pursuit and theme of *nang* that is at the core of Pukhto poetry and literature[10] and military and social action. Khushal Khan Khattak (1613–89), probably the greatest of the Pukhto poets, wrote in a famous couplet:

I despise the man who does not guide his life by honour
The very word 'honour'drives me mad (Spain, 1963: 63).

Khanzada told me that his grandfather, Inayatullah (who featured in
the last chapter), would constantly quote the proverb 'If Pukhto were
the highest mountain I would climb it', which he interpreted to mean
badal, tarboorwali and *tor*.

To the Pukhtun in the Tribal Areas where he still lives largely
according to his concepts of *nang* and in the fastness of his mountain
eyrie there is no contradiction in the world as it is and as it should be.
It is his world and politically it has never been conquered. Pukhtuns
in the *nang* areas have never been conquered and are aware that they
have humbled the armies of two of the greatest empires known in India,
the Mughal and the British. *Nang* Pukhtuns, in Afghanistan and before
their assimilation by Amir Abdur Rahman later in the century, provided
British military history with one of its most dramatic and chilling
moments with the appearance of the half-dead and half-crazed Dr
Brydon on a cold January morning in 1842 at the Jalalabad garrison.[11]
The doctor was the sole survivor of the grand Army of the Indus. The
impossible had happened in the Victorian era and at the high-noon of
British military might: an entire British army had been wiped out. In
1672, a similar fate had overtaken an entire Mughal Army in the Khyber
Pass where 10,000 soldiers were killed and 20,000 people, including
families, taken prisoner. The Emperor Aurangzeb's Governor, Amin
Khan, survived with four others to make his ignominious way to
Peshawar.

The three key passes into the subcontinent are in the *nang* areas, the
Gandab valley through the Mohmand Agency, the Khyber through the
Khyber Agency, and the Kurram valley through the Kurram Agency,
which allows these tribes an opportunity to exploit their strategic
situation which they rarely miss. Historically, passage through these
routes, under the eyes of the clan deployed on the peaks and with its
permission after due payments, was always a tense affair. The toll
respected no social hierarchy. In the eighteenth century the Persian
Emperor Nadir Shah found the Khyber Pass blocked to him on his
return from the conquest of India and after shattering the Mughal
Empire; he had ignominiously to come to terms with the tribes. Anyone wandering off the road was subject to their mercy. Even at the
high-noon of Empire, Pax Britannica existed on the main roads and
up to a hundred yards on either side; in this case the Khyber and

Kurram roads only, as the Gandab road was almost immediately closed after the 1935 campaign to open it. *Nang* Pukhtuns reconcile with difficulty to an imposed non-*nang* situation. It is not surprising that the assassin of Lord Mayo, the Viceroy of India, in 1872 was an Afridi, and the case almost typically began years prior to the incident with the killing of a woman involved in a case of *tor*. Another Afridi assassinated Mackeson, the first Commissioner of Peshawar. As we saw, the Mohmands made an early appearance in British records by killing Lt Boulnois, in command of a company of Sappers, in 1852 near Michni. The list of political and army officers, symbols of the Raj, killed in the nineteenth and twentieth centuries is a long one, especially in Waziristan.[12] Even for a Pukhtun king the *nang* tribesman is a formidable subject to dominate and equivalent versions of the immortal *cri de coeur* in 1879 of Yaqub Khan, King of Afghanistan, as he confronted the tribes gathering in Kabul to topple him, must have passed through the minds of many a ruler of Pukhtuns: 'I would rather be a grasscutter in the English camp than ruler of Afghanistan' (Spain, 1963: 135). History is rooted in the *nang* Pukhtun's social consciousness (Chapter 3). Indeed 'it is the last free place on Earth' (Moynahan, 1976).

The modern world and its dilemmas are neither comprehended nor caricatured by the *nang* Pukhtun. There is no need to conjure away or abjure the modern world, it simply has not arrived. Whether returning from distant cities or neighbouring districts, he returns to an area of retreat, of recognizable and familiar symbols of social life. In society he confronts oneness, a supreme monism. In the ideal, his world is undamaged by the intrusion of alien elements that could compromise the Code or distort its translation in society. The following passage captures the essence of junction between tribal Code, Islam and the influences of the greater world:

> This people was black and white not only in vision, but by inmost furnishing: black and white not merely in clarity, but in apposition. ... With cool head and tranquil judgement, imperturbably unconscious of the flight, they oscillated from asymptote to asymptote (Lawrence, 1962: 36).

The ideal-type model creates a clear web of polyadic kin relationships around the individual which are partly regulated by the Code. For instance if he murders outside the recognized laws of revenge, rapes a woman, or thieves from a kin he will be severely dealt with by society through the *jirga*. He is thus not free to 'attack', 'seize' and 'oust' in his pursuits, political or otherwise, as the Swat Pukhtun (Barth, 1971a, 1972). However, he may 'attack', 'seize' and 'oust' in the pursuit of those elements of the Code involving *tarboorwali* and *tor*. In such cases the Code will not interfere. On the contrary, if he avoids normative behaviour he will be condemned as not doing 'Pukhto'. In his freedom he is a slave to the Code.

To dismantle *Pukhtunwali* is to reorder the basis of social life and the world. The Settled Area Mohmand and his *Pukhtunwali* is a parody of his Tribal Area self, an ideological mimicry; it assuages his loss of freedom as it assures him of his identity. At its core is the increasing awareness of a changing world, the re-ordering and redundancy of the two key components of his socio-psychological consciousness: the tribal charter and the Code. The dilemma is acute for the Pukhtun in an encapsulated condition, and there are times when he appears able to parody the ideal or pure idea of himself. Parody and sometimes un-conscious mimicry. For instance, Shamshudin the elder of Bela, gentle and wise, long past feuds and murders, approached me with the only favour he asked in the last four years: could I arrange bail for a man imprisoned in a *tor* case in Charsadda so that he could return to the Agency and allow Shamshudin's relative, the husband of the woman, a chance to shoot him? Honour would be redeemed. Weber suggested that in the ideal-type

> the actor is treated not merely as responding to stimuli, but as making an 'effort' to conform with certain 'ideal', rather than actual, patterns of conduct with the probability that his efforts will be only partially successful, and there will be elements of deviation (Parsons, 1947: 12).

On one level tribal life may be conceptualized as almost Hobbesian, 'solitary, poor, nasty, brutish and short'. Democracy is almost total, it can come close to anarchy: 'Every man is a Khan' (*har saray khan day*). Cousin rivalry levels as it consumes the Pukhtun. The Father's Brother's Son is the bane of his existence and main rival for power and status. On another conceptual level there is a placidity, symmetry and equilibrium. The Pukhtun utopia is now, and consequently his society is static; it discourages change as it perpetuates itself.

As there is security in terms of larger systems, there is no cultural xenophobia or chauvinism in the *nang* lands as among other societies confronting larger systems (Bailey, 1973: 302). There is a sense of social security and personal confidence. This confidence allows the Pukhtun to laugh at himself and he is known for his sense of humour. A threat to local culture helps create xenophobia, a form of reaction to an alien and hostile presence, on which it feeds. In the Tribal Areas there is no alien or hostile presence. The social world is in harmony and within it, in carefully balanced symmetry, are the smaller worlds of the lineages and sections each aware of its territory and boundary. No contradiction or conflict has developed in society. A potential source of conflict results from the imperial encounter and the role of the Maliks and their attendant privileges. However, tribal social mechanism and administrative policy tend to deflate that role. Conflict comes into being but is neither sharpened nor developed.

Tribal democracy, the very fundamental of Pukhtun society, is not embodied in a set of scriptures or a Magna Carta. It is conceptualized and draws its life and sustenance from the two key factors of social life: the Pukhtun Code and the tribal charter, these two are connected, and ratify each other. They also set up boundaries within which the Pukhtun organizes and articulates his social functions. Beyond these boundaries lies an unchartered world where the Code is suspended and the charter irrelevant.

There is no ritual or magic associated with passage from one age-group to another, from boyhood into manhood, as in Africa (Fortes and Evans-Pritchard, 1970: 288-9). The three generally recognized stages of man are: when he is a boy (*halak*) up to twelve to fourteen years and looked on with tolerance; when he is a man (*saray*) and expected to live up to the Code and uphold it (it is the *saray* who inherits the duties and enjoys the privileges of social life); and third, generally between fifty and sixty years and over, when he is a 'whitebeard' (*spingiray*) and expected to be a repository of wisdom and sensible advice based on experience and Pukhto custom.

Pukhto ritual and custom are bare and simple and do not involve mystical or complex arrangements. There is decorum in public life and a general respect for elders, even those in opposing political camps. There are no dances communal or otherwise in which men and women take part, or any social occasions permitting orgiastic behaviour.

Nang is pure democracy for the Pukhtuns. The social and ecological structure act in unison to limit the growth of individual power. I am not only speaking of an ideal-type that exists in the minds of men and is restricted to folk-lore and stories. It is democracy in its purest form. I have seen eminent men such as (retired) General Jamaldar, a Sandhurst officer, in 1977 a Central Cabinet Minister and a man of standing in Pakistan politics, bullied and harried by his *nang* cousins in the Orakzai Agency and helpless before their threats to burn down his house in the Agency. The motivation was agnatic jealousy. It is this belief, based on intense cousin rivalry and underlined by poor economic and limited land-holdings, that almost eliminate the other Weberian concept, that of 'charismatic authority'. It is no surprise that historically Pukhtuns only rise to great political heights *outside* their *nang* areas.

The Pukhtun is free in the most profound political sense. The main thesis contained in *Oriental Despotism* is that in hydraulic societies power is total and therefore terror is total (Wittfogel, 1957). Everything belongs to the ruling elite. Government is the largest land-owner. In contrast, in the Tribal Areas land and/or the house belong to the individual and he is responsible to no one as long as he does not violate the Code. In this sense Pukhtun society is at the opposite end of the conceptual spectrum of political freedom based on economic divisions of land. Once he has identified the landmarks on his social landscape (*badal, melmastia, nanawatee, tor*) he can manoeuvre and manipulate other large unspoken areas. The democracy the Code implies is in a sense real, no Pukhtun is master of another. He is not bounden by tedious daily ritual or commensal rules that can defile him. He interprets for action the fundamental requirements of the Code and the larger ones of Islam, often reduced to formal prayers, and apart from these is largely free to organize his life for himself. For instance, there is little societal shame attached to a smuggler, murderer or drug addict as there would be in any village society on the subcontinent. If he smuggles that is *his* business, he recognizes no formal borders in his lands, they were neither made nor accepted by him; if he kills that is part of *his* Code; if he takes opium that is *his* weakness. Society may not approve but it will not act against him as long as he does not violate the Code. He alone is responsible for the laws of revenge. There is no concept of a group or lineage collectively responsible for injury and death like the '*dia*-paying group' among the Somali (Lewis, I. M., 1969a: 256). In *tor* or *badal* cases the father, husband or son are individually responsible for implementing or seeking revenge.

Apart from the bloody demands of *tarboorwali* and *tor*, a Pukhtun is defined by dignity and decorum in his affairs whether in public or private. The personal and social indignities, religious or temporal, that often degenerate into confusion and exhaustion on the subcontinent as depicted by native writers (Chaudhuri, 1965; Moraes, 1960, 1974;

Naipaul, 1964, 1977; Narayan, 1956, 1969) and often result in 'cringing subservience' to authority (Asad, 1970: xv), do not exist in the Tribal Areas. This attitude contrasts sharply with the dignity and decorum of public and private life among the Pukhtuns, whether interacting with outsiders or themselves (Caroe, 1965; Howell, 1931; King, 1900; Merk, 1898; Spain, 1962, 1963). The patriarch is a model of Apollonian behaviour, dignified and sombre. Dionysian behaviour is as rare as it is unexpected of him (Benedict, 1961). How he speaks and comports himself is important to him and his family. As patriarch of the house he is the model of Pukhtunness and normative values are exemplified by his behaviour.

Nang is a Pukhtun world. In the Mohmand universe (TAM and SAM) 92 per cent of the total population are Pukhtuns and land ideally belongs to them (Holmes, 1887: 1,453). It is also a man's world. The direct laudatory equivalent to 'Pukhto' is manhood (*saritob*). Descent is reckoned through male ascendants; residence after marriage is virilocal, preferred marriages are to patrilateral parallel cousins and potential foes and friends are agnatic kin. Other groups, like religious groups, the Mians and Mullahs, exist to perform obligatory Islamic functions during the *rites de passage*, and the occupational groups (*qasabgar*) exist to cut the Pukhtun's hair (the barber), build his house and make his hoe (the carpenter). A third group, often non-Muslim, organizes trade, credit and itinerant markets. The word shopkeeper (*dokandar*) is used with contempt when a Pukhtun indulges in such non-Pukhtun activity. None of these three groups is allowed to disturb the precise symmetry of the social order as none of them exists on the genealogical charter. However, the dominant Pukhtun ideology permeates all social groups. Non-Pukhtun groups carry on feuds, although in less violent and sustained manner, and are as strict regarding women as Pukhtuns. The Ganjian or the Ghunda Khel settlements in Shati Khel have a long history of feuding and agnatic rivalry among themselves, almost in the Pukhtun mould (Map 5). The Mians in Mian Kassai also have similar problems, the difference being that they rarely resort to shooting and violence. Compromising behaviour in women is severely dealt with. For instance, I have cited a case among the Mians where both the girl and boy concerned were shot in a *tor* case (Chapter 7).

There is no subjugation or tyranny of one group over another and boundaries are known and respected by contracting parties. The hierarchy is social, not economic. In theory segmentary societies may be democratic but politics, where politics concerns decision-making, in reality is allocation and transmission of authority which is invariably hierarchical (Smith, M. G., 1956). The importance of social roles and decision-making is apparent in the key issues of Pukhtun politics; for instance, who sits in a *jirga*, or is the spokesman of a section, or is the employer of a Mullah or decides to give the call for battle? None of the religious or occupational groups qualify for any one of these positions. The Pukhtun would say, and the groups would agree, that this is not a form of suppression. After all, they all agree it is the Pukhtun only who is privileged to 'carry a gun' (*topak garzai*), which defines him in the Tribal Areas and is a burden he is not unaware of: 'Though arms are heavy their carrying is essential' (Ahmed, 1975: 56). The ideal-type model may demand conformity even at the cost of rationality: 'It certainly does not involve a belief in the actual predominance of rational elements in human life' (Weber, 1947: 92). It is the Pukhtun who is 'maddened' by *nang* and the Pukhtun who gives his life to uphold *nang*. Pukhtuns themselves are acutely conscious of this madness and quote the saying 'Pukhto is half-madness' (*Pukhto nim liwantob day*) which is illustrated by the case-studies in Chapter 7. The axiom is also quoted by non-Pukhtuns regularly and with conviction. Non-Pukhtuns speak of Pukhtun activity such as agnatic rivalry thus: 'They are unintelligent because they kill one another' (*kamakal dee yaw bal wajni*) and by doing so 'perform anti-religious acts' (*bedina kar kai*) since 'the Prophet never commanded Muslims to kill one another'.

Apart from political pursuit which remains the monopoly of the Pukhtun, and agnatic rivalry as its recurrent and manifest expression, all groups live, eat, dress and speak alike, including the non-Muslim groups (Chapters 6, 8 and 9). In certain spheres which the Pukhtun consider ungentlemanly, like trade and marketing, these groups have had a monopoly, and have accumulated sizeable wealth. In Chapter 9 I shall illustrate through income and consumption expenditures, after 'weighting' them, that the differences between senior lineages and junior ones, Pukhtuns and non-Pukhtuns, are not all that wide. Indeed in certain cases where senior lineages still invest money in non-economic activity like hospitality they are being steadily overtaken by junior and non-Pukhtun groups. After all, the Code of honour is expensive to maintain in terms of life and wealth and never more so than today when a bullet could cost up to Rs. 20 and a gun over Rs. 10,000. The Pukhtuns consider agriculture as a somewhat secondary and demeaning occupation in TAM, and even the senior lineages of Bela will speak of themselves as agriculturalists (*zamindar*) with reluctance. In TAM, 'agriculturalist' has a derogatory ring to it. Shahzada or Mazullah who 'carry the gun' would sneer at kin making a full-time living as agriculturalists. This contrasts with village societies on the subcontinent where an agriculturalist is socially considered as belonging to the highest occupation (Mayer, A.C., 1970: 75).

Nang external political history has been a constant struggle to maintain its boundaries against larger state systems attempting to capture, cage, subjugate or encapsulate it. If history is to be seen as a Marxist dialectical encounter between the exploiters and the exploited, the harassers and the harassed, the Mohmand gave as good as they got in terms of military encounters. Apart from one major military incursion in 1897 into their heart-lands, in the last four hundred years they have been left untouched and no symbols of larger states existed in their areas until 1947: administrators, missionaries, tax-officials or police force. On the contrary they may be said to have a rather successful record of harassment of larger state systems.

Why were these areas left to themselves by the two greatest empires of Indian history, the Mughals and the British? Apart from the problem of actually inflicting military defeat on the highly martial tribes, there was the difficult terrain which the tribesmen made use of to maintain military superiority; there was also little prospect of economic gain in the barren Tribal Areas and, finally, the tribesmen played their own version of the Victorian Great Game to perfection: Kabul against Delhi, Moscow against London. It was the obverse version of the Imperial dictum: 'Divide and you will not be ruled'.

The Independence of Pakistan in 1947 changed little in the Tribal Areas. But for once in their history there was no military barrier between the Agency and District border. The message was clear. It was their country. Pakistan did not *go* to the tribes but the tribes began to *come* to Pakistan: in government service, the army, in business, in the professions. Today there are over a million Pukhtuns living in Karachi. By the 1970s, in almost the third decade of Independence, there was a feeling among tribesmen of all groups that perhaps the time was ripe to come to terms with the modern world. Pakistan responded by placing massive development schemes at the disposal of the tribes who remained aware that they called the tune and set the pace (Part Three). Abruptly, and in a totally unexpected manner, the ideal-type model faced its most formidable threat in recorded history. This form of willing encapsulation poses an even more acute dilemma for TAM than if accomplished by the force of arms. It is awareness in the actor of the finality of a *hara-kiri* act as it is self-imposed. Today encapsulation in the political and administrative sense brings no extra-ethnic or extra-religious dominating classes with it. At a stroke the Pukhtun world is re-ordered. Now groups drift to towns or migrate abroad looking for work rather than remaining in the villages. Occupational groups appropriate land and income surpassing that of Pukhtun neighbours as in SAM. Pukhtuns themselves take up government employment and no longer wish to 'carry the gun'. The democracy of Bela is indeed complete. There are no landlords, no factory owners and no petty officials to harass the villager. There is no real significance in senior lineage or junior lineage, Pukhtun or non-Pukhtun group. They are simply 'Belawals', agricultural peasants, about the business of making two ends meet on small land-holdings.

(b) *Social diacritica: diet and dress*

Diet and dress are locally perceived as important social diacritica distinguishing ideal from non-ideal Pukhtun life.

Diet The extreme material poverty among Pukhtuns forces on them a diet which is in many ways ideal. Although I am not qualified to speak specifically of the health qualities of various foods I will comment in a general manner. Protein is commonly eaten in lentil (*dal*) and iron in spinach. A great deal of garlic and onions are eaten which are medically beneficial for the heart. On the other hand, eggs or sweetmeats are rarely, if ever, eaten which keep cholesterol levels low. Brown bread (*dodai*) is eaten unhusked and contains vitamin B. Bread is eaten without vegetable oil and 'dry'. Milk products, like curds, are a regular feature of diet. There is no debilitating counter-presence of such factors as alcoholism and venereal diseases. Despite a tendency to exaggerate age, healthy patriarchs are as voluble as they are visible.

Although life is physically hard there are no signs of starvation. On the contrary, simple regular diet and hours combined with an absence of debilitating weaknesses such as smoking or drinking confirm my impression of longevity and good health. Heights and weights of 100 randomly selected males in my field-work area in TAM and SAM confirm my impression of tribal health. The average height is 5 feet 4½ inches and weight almost 147 pounds, by no means substandard or sub-normal averages. I therefore agree with an important point raised in economic anthropology regarding tribal societies: 'Now, in the time of the greatest technical power starvation is an institution. Reverse another venerable formula: the amount of hunger increases relatively and absolutely with the evolution of culture' (Sahlins, 1974: 36).

In SAM various types of spinach are grown most of the year and form a common food. However, barley is cultivated mainly for animals, unlike in TAM where it is eaten by poorer people. Milk products are common as almost all houses keep cattle or goats and produce the following at home: animal fat and oil (*ghwari*), buttermilk (*shomlay*), cheese (*bagora*), cream (*payraway*), curds (*masta*), milk (*pai*) and a semi-solid milk product called *warga*. Shahzada would repeat the secret of his superb health like an incantation: 'I eat only garlic and barley bread, I never drink tea. Salt and tomatoes ruin health and I never eat them'. Shahzada recalls that he was about ten years old when tea (*tor chay*) was introduced to Shati Khel although he never drank it. Haji Umar claims that he and Anmir were the first to bring tea pots (*chaynak*) from the Settled Area to Shati Khel. Today Pukhtuns drink 'mixed' (*gadwad*) tea: water, tea leaves, milk and sugar boiled together. Black or English tea is drunk during the day and green tea (*shnay chay*) at night and are now common and popular. In 1918 snuff (*niswar*), ground tobacco leaf and ash, was introduced and in 1928 Isa Khan brought opium (*charas*) to the area. Shahzada abstains from these innovations and boasts that although his grandsons feel the cold in winter he is still healthy enough not to feel it. Shahmat, the oldest man in Shati and, like Anmir, a grandson of Saida Mir, like the other Shati elders singled out the tomato as a major cause of ill-health. 'Tomato,' he would joke, 'causes impotence.'

Shahzada recounts the days of his youth when diet revolved around barley and some wheat bread eaten with a paste of onion or garlic. He ascribes his perfect health to this basic diet. At seventy-four his handshake and the strength of his hands in a squeeze or playful embrace around the waist can still make able-bodied men fifty years younger wince in pain. His firm body, unlined face and ruddy complexion give him the appearance of a healthy man of fifty. His generation, who do indeed appear good physical advertisements for this diet, still speak of 'tomatoes' as a symbol of soft and decadent living. Shahzada and his generation would often complain that the days of Pukhto were over, correlating this with new dietary habits: 'Can you imagine? Mohmands in the Gandab are eating tomatoes these days!'

Haji Hassan explained the old days and contrasted them with the new ones and their symbols:

In the old days people spoke truth. Such things as sweetmeat were never seen and eaten. In the old days people ate plain *dodai*, lentils and only on special occasions and for guests perhaps cooked chicken. Today people eat vegetables like tomatoes. They enjoy themselves and loaf. Today everyone has become a king.

Feroz recalls that as a child up to 1954 he never saw fruit except a few pears or walnuts brought from Shabkadar and in any case never saw or tasted the sweetmeats so popular in the Settled Areas. *Mashars* constantly quote 'fatness is a disease' (*ghatwalay yao kisam bimari da*), although it does signify a certain amount of affluence and social status deduced from the fact that the fat person does not have to work with his hands in the fields. Diet is largely common to TAM and SAM. In Bela, as men work in the fields during certain seasons lunch is brought to them by children.

Fish in Bela is a popular and free diet, though the method of catching fish is illegal and dangerous involving the use of crude dynamite which costs Rs. 5 to 6 per stick. The dynamite is cut in half, wrapped in a dirty cloth, then tied to a rock with phosphorous which is lighted and can burn under water, and is hurled into the river. The fish are attracted to the light and the explosion stuns or kills them. Quite a few Belawals have lost fingers and hands as a result of badly-timed explosions. Alternatively, fish are caught with a small net tied around a piece of wood (*jal patray*).

I carried out a survey and discovered that almost 95 per cent of the male population take *niswar* and many elders smoked the hubble-bubble (*chilam*). About 15 per cent of males smoked *charas* in both areas. As males take *niswar* their teeth spoil at an early age and they are compelled to spit every few minutes. In the *hujra* people frequently lean over to spit. It is widely admitted that *niswar* is 'the work of the devil' (*de shatan kar day*). Khan Mohammad, the son of Hussain, proudly claims that, except for his father, no one in his family is addicted to *niswar*. The *niswar* is kept in a tin with a mirror on it. Males are constantly displaying their vanity by examining their faces in it and combing their beards.

Dress   Head-wear symbolizes the age, lineage and occupation of the individual. Senior lineages and Maliks often wear the *kullah* which is a semi-formal head-dress. A cap made of lamb skin (*karakuli*) is usually worn by younger and middle-aged men who have either served in the army or in other parts of Pakistan. An ordinary turban without a *kullah* is worn by poorer *mashars* as those of SAM. An ordinary skull cap costing Rs. 5–10 is worn by almost all agriculturalists, particularly those working in the fields, whether occupational groups or junior lineages. Only the very destitute or the young would be 'black head' (*sar tor*) and appear with uncovered heads. The sheet used as rope, pillow, trousers, prayer-mat, head-dress and for protection against the cold is becoming a symbol of less sophisticated *mashars*. Younger males will say 'my position would be spoilt (if I were seen carrying a sheet)' (*posishan may kharabaygi*).

Males and females never reveal some parts of their body which are wrapped up in sheets (*sadar*) in winter. At the height of summer, males will not take off their shirts either to relax, or to take part in activities such as wrestling or volley ball, or just to lie under the trees in the heat, as many do in the Punjab. Only the face and the hands remain uncovered. Winter, the Mohmands say, is a 'bad time' for poor people as they need warm clothes and burn wood fuels (*khashak*) at night to keep them warm. During the day they often sit or work where they are exposed to the sun.

Shamshudin's clothes, which I have seen him wearing for the last four years, are dark grey baggy trousers (*partog*) and shirt (*kames*) of the cheapest cloth (*militia*), and the same rubber moccasins and a white sheet on his shoulders. Sometimes he wears his old, worn waistcoat. On his head is a skull cap costing Rs. 5–10 or a *Chatrali* cap costing Rs. 20–30. Chisti Gul of the junior lineage wore no slippers or shoes. In winter, which is sharp and cold, people are wrapped in sheets but few wear socks, even old or torn ones. Some have sweaters under their well-worn shirts but most do not. Mohmands wear shoes (*saplai*) costing between Rs. 30 and 40 which last them four to five years and are regularly repaired and patched. *Kames partog* worn by men and women take up to about six or seven yards of cloth, the women's one extra yard; they are worn for a couple of years and are often patched. Haji Umar claims he was one of the first to wear the new tighter *partog*. The old *partog* was very wide, often ten to twelve yards. Shahmat confirmed that the old *partog* could be about twenty yards in length whereas today it was four yards. Haji Hassan again contrasted the old and the new: 'People wore rough home-spun (*kadar*) clothes, with no collars or coats, which are called English clothes (*angrazi jamay*), but now they lie (*darogh wai*), they just pass time aimlessly (*taam pass kayi*).' In the old days all males shaved their heads but today they leave hair on their heads, a style called 'English'.

Women wear well-worn *kames partog* too but if young they prefer brighter colours. The veil (*lopata*) is also colourful but in the presence of men or when going out a large white *sadar* is worn. Older women always wear the white *sadar* which covers the head, breasts and waist fully. Rubber shoes or sponge slippers are worn by women but younger women also wear sandals. Clothes and sandals are given at marriages and last for years. Kohl powder for their eyes and walnut bark (*dandasa*) for their teeth may be used once a week by women. A certain amount of cheap make-up is also now used, usually by newly weds. Henna (*nakriza*) is commonly used for hands and feet by both young and old, and older women use it for dyeing their hair. Bangles, rings and other jewellery, whether real or artificial, are always worn. The *partog* of the older women are much larger and younger girls tend to wear tighter ones.

For males personal hygiene is restricted to bathing about once a month. When Feroz bathed twice a week in Shati Khel he was teased: 'he has made a Punjabi of himself' (*de zan naye Panjabay jor karay day*). He remembers bathing in the pool at Chino as a youth when his eyes would become red because the water was so dirty. Pipes were installed in the 1960s to connect it to the Chino springs. Others like the Malok bathed and drank, as did their cattle, from the mud pond west of the village which collected rain-water. Only two decades ago when men bathed in the house they did so standing on cots so that the water could be collected underneath and given to cattle for drinking as water was so scarce. Men seldom use soap, which is the same type as that used for washing clothes. Scent (*atar*) is sometimes used during the festival of Eed. Eyes are blackened with kohl powder on Fridays as Mullahs suggest it is religiously beneficial (*sawab*). Mustard oil is used for the hair which is combed with wooden combs even today. The barber cuts the hair and finger-nails of males although nail-cutters are becoming common. Women cut their own hair and use blades to cut their nails.

There is a certain correlation between arms as part of dress and lineage status. The senior patriarchs and Maliks, in addition to having a son or grandson carrying a gun as escort, usually carry a revolver themselves. The ordinary Malik carries his own gun. A member of the junior lineage, religious or occupational group, seldom carries a gun.

Symbolism is attached to status even in sitting in the *hujra*. For instance, the central cot usually decorated by an extra, colourful pillow or two is for the most senior *mashar*. On the cot itself there is a head, where the pillow is usually kept, which is reserved for the *mashar*. The other end of the cot is used by younger or junior lineages.

(c) *Religious symbolism among the Pukhtun*

The importance of the larger political framework of the Islamic world for Islamic societies, and their interconnection through universally accepted religious symbols, was one of the main points I wished to make in an earlier work (Ahmed, 1976) and is a recognized social phenomenon (Coon, 1952; Gellner, 1969a: 2; Hart, 1976: 15-16; Tavakolian, 1976). In this section I am concerned simply in stating how sociological roles and normative behaviour are explained *within* society by reference to what are *locally* understood and recognized as symbols derived from the main body of Islamic traditions. By the sociology of religion I mean the location of cognitive and affective referents that determine, at least in part, social action among groups. The Pukhtun social world, its mores and norms, the symbols of its society, are embedded in and often identical to those of the wider world of Islam. Our concern is with religion not as theology but as a cultural system imposing social action that translates symbolic associations with the supernatural into material reality.

The methodology in this section is based on an important assumption: that 'the most obvious basis for religious behaviour is the one which any religious actor tells us about when we ask him – and, unlike some anthropologists, I believe him' (Spiro, 1973: 112). I shall thus examine Islamic symbolism and its relevance in society through the eyes of the actors and accept their interpretation and apperception as a basis for analysis.

In a sociological manner that almost echoes Durkheim, 'Islam is another name for Pukhtun society'. I wish to emphasize my use of the word sociological. The Islamic symbols are clear and easily identified by the actors; perhaps their religious meaning in the ecclesiastical sense may not appear relevant or even comprehensible but their social significance is established by frequent recurrence. Religious groups ensure that these symbols are constantly activated, partly to enhance their own social prestige and to permit them a certain leverage in society. I am examining these symbols through the eyes of the actors and therefore ones that may appear superficial or even trivial remain significant in society. On one level, I listened in the mosque to the Bela Mullah's sermon on Islamic symbolism in society, on the keeping or not keeping of beards as a measure of religiosity, and as I did not have one it proved to be an uncomfortable experience which would have been more so for any local men transgressing this norm. Shamshudin gravely confessed to

me in 1974 'I am a sinner' (*ze gonangar yam*) because he did not sport
a beard. Shortly afterwards he began to make amends and now has a
beard. Old Haji Hassan of TAM, who had recently returned from
pilgrimage (*haj*) and was basking in its glory, unceasingly turning beads
in his hands, asked me one favour only in our long friendship: 'For the
love of God cut those English (*kafir*) side-burns'. When I obliged he was
as pleased as a child given a toy and commented on this ceaselessly, all
the while blessing me. On another level, religious leaders have repeatedly
activated Islamic symbolism in their fight against the British. The Haji
of Turangzai began his proclamation to the Mohmand for *jihad* with
quotations from the Holy Koran, as did his son Badshah Gul when he
tried to prevent the British from constructing a road in the Gandab in
the early 1930s. Badshah's pamphlets argued 'Anyone who makes
friends with the British becomes the enemy of God and His Prophet'
(H.D., T.R.C., File 220: 203).

The unity of *Pukhtunwali* and Islam is symbolized and expressed in
village social life by the physical juxtaposition of the mosque and the
hujra. These two institutions are the focus of life in every settlement
and village. They are built simultaneously and usually share a wall
and/or courtyard. The Pukhtun accepts religion without doubts or
questions, there is no conflict between his Code and Islam. Indeed he
sees the Code as embedded in Islam, and where there is contradiction,
as in the taking of interest for loans or not allowing women their rights,
he accepts his guilt frankly. The reluctance to give property to women
may well be tied up with the importance of fixed geographical areas inhabited and associated with sections and clans, parts of which would run
the risk of alienation through the marriage of women if they inherited
property. In both cases the percentage who accepted they were indulging in un-Islamic practice was 100 per cent of the respondents answering the formal questionnaires. The problem for the Pukhtun is not one
of accepting colonial law or tribal law but one of bringing Pukhtun
custom into focus with accepted Islamic law. Deviances from Islamic
law are partly legitimized in the eyes of society by a frank recognition
of deviance and are explained as Pukhto *riwaj*, as if by such an explanation the guilt would be extenuated or even exculpated. 'Yes there is
contradiction, we are wrong, but can a Pukhtun be anything but a
Muslim?' His attitude to the Almighty is that of a favourite. Native
exegesis rests on the assumption that the Pukhtuns were a favoured
Islamic group. He carries no stigma of forcible conversion. His Islam
reaches back to the origins of the religion. Like the Bedouin whose

tribal structure and sociological environment are so similar, he sees and feels a close affinity to God that needs no translation and interpretation: 'The Beduin could not look for God within him: he was too sure that he was within God' (Lawrence, 1962: 39). Obedience and submission, total loyalty of his will to the infinite power of the Almighty: that is all that is required of him and that is what he gives willingly. He is unburdened with religious dialectics and polemics; that, he says disparagingly, is for the Mullahs and Mians. He is by definition a Muslim just as by birth he obtains the inalienable right to Pukhtunness. His place in society as a Pukhtun and a Muslim is thus secure and defined from the moment of birth. However famous or infamous, high or low, good or bad, he cannot be ousted from this niche.

Islam, with *Pukhtunwali* and patrilineal descent, is seen as an attribute associated with Pukhtun identity (Barth, 1970). The Pukhtun defines himself as a Muslim and as this definition is intrinsically unequivocal it poses him no dilemmas. In any case, the absence of larger non-Muslim groups neither threatens his Muslimness nor prompts him to emphasize it. He may not have come to this conclusion after philosophic debate but to him there is no disjunction in being Muslim and being Pukhtun. This inherent belief in his Muslimness, supported by the putative genealogical links to the Prophet through his apical ancestor Qais, assure him of his special relationship to God which, in turn, has two social consequences. Firstly, the Pukhtun brand of Islam is as sociologically all-pervasive as it is tolerant. This partly explains why non-Muslim groups like Hindus and Sikhs live in absolute security and freedom to worship in Tirah, areas which even non-Pukhtun Muslim groups would find inaccessible. Secondly, the complete confidence in his Muslimness constricts the role of religious groups and explains the continuation of Pukhto custom which contains non-Islamic elements, such as the taking of usury and the denial of certain rights to women.

Pukhtunness and Muslimness do not have to coalesce, they are within each other, the interiority of the former is assumed in the latter. The Pukhtun defines and assesses Islam in terms of two fundamental sets of precepts. The first raises no problem to him and is intrinsic to his Pukhtunness: the belief in the foremost of the five pillars of Islam, the acceptance of the omnipotence and monism of God expressed in the oneness of God and the prophethood of Muhammad (*kalima*). The second has social ramifications and may be defined as containing the other four pillars of Islam:

(1) Prayers (*munz*) five times a day which most Pukhtuns, particularly

after middle age, attempt to fulfil. For instance my assistants Ihsanullah, Khan Wahid, Shamshur Rahman and Feroz, ranging in age from twenty-one to twenty-seven years, would say their prayers five times a day.
(2) Fasting (*rojay*) from sunrise to sunset during the month of Ramadan. Ramadan is universally respected and during this month almost every adult male or female fasts. To be seen eating or smoking during Ramadan would incur serious reprimand from the entire community and those who cannot keep the fast maintain their secret with the utmost discretion. British officers who served in the Tribal Areas testify that they never heard of a man who broke the fast, even in the most severe climatic conditions (Pettigrew, 1965: 35). The position remains unchanged today in TAM. I was told that until a decade ago in SAM if someone did not fast the village would blacken his face, put him on a donkey and take him round the village. Examples of such cases were given to me in Michni. There is a general enthusiasm for fasting among the young. For instance Ghani, the younger son of Shamshudin, who is now 12 years old, has been keeping at least half the feasts, about fourteen to fifteen days, since the age of ten.
(3) Pilgrimage (*haj*) to the land of Arabia once in a lifetime. Economic conditions determine *haj* but it is a major life-long ambition of most men and women and carries a certain amount of social prestige. The *haji*, the title with which he is called after his *haj*, is expected to behave in a manner befitting his newly acquired status. The economic situation of Bela Mohmandan and the changing economic situation of Shati Khel are reflected in the statistics regarding *hajis*. There are no *hajis* in Bela. On the other hand there are at least thirteen *hajis* in Shati Khel and more significantly four of these are women.
(4) *Zakat*, 2½ per cent of the annual savings to be given to the poor. Ideally this is meant to be a personal contribution of money circulated to the poorer of the community, but as it is left to the discretion of the individual it is difficult to assess. Pukhtuns often talk of *zakat* when they house and shelter poorer relatives. Mohmands also translate *zakat* as *ushar* which is a fixed share given to Mullahs or, as in Bela, to the Mian, or the poor after the crop is harvested.

Although *jihad* is not technically considered among the five pillars of Islam described above, Pukhtuns attach great importance to it, which emphasizes their martial tribal tradition and expresses their enthusiasm for Islam. Almost every Mohmand Malik remembers 1947 and 1948 as the years of *jihad* in Kashmir, a fact they still constantly repeat in *jirgas* and meetings to underline their loyalty to Pakistan and the larger cause of Islam. Including senior Maliks like Shahzada and Mazullah, every settlement in Shati was represented by an adult male in Kashmir. They still remember that those were days of 'much emotion' (*der jazba*). Personal habits are explained simply by reference to actions of the Prophet (*sunnat*) or by association with his personal history. Middle-aged men who keep beards in the Tribal Areas will dye them red with henna. The explanation I consistently received throughout the Tribal Areas, and in its most remote regions, was that this was *sunnat*. Amirzada, the son of Shahzada, explained why the fig is called the 'fruit of heaven' (*janati maywa*) and its branches are used in the mosque for the beam but never burned in the house: 'The fig lowered its branches when the Prophet was a child and gave him milk to drink.' Personal names such as the Prophet's, Muhammad, or his agnatic descendants', Hassan and Hussain, or those of his companions, Umar and Ali, are very common among male Pukhtuns just as the names of his female kin like Roqaia, his daughter, are common among females. For instance Shamshudin's daughter is called Roqaia.

In the month when the Prophet was dying, his wives are said to have cooked *chori* (flour, oil and *gur* – non centrifugal sugar) to distribute to the poor and this tradition is still kept alive. *Chori* is cooked and distributed in Mohmand villages during this month. Items of daily diet are affected by the dietary habits of the Prophet. He was said to prefer the simplest of foods and especially onions. Perhaps making a virtue out of necessity, *mashars* would explain the simplicity of their daily diet with reference to the Prophet's life.

Elders quote stories of the evil eye (*nazar*) from the life of the Prophet. Therefore, they argue, *nazar* has social meaning and is effective. Certain traditional measures are taken to avoid *nazar*. For instance a cow's skull or a black flag is placed on a new house so the *nazar* may shift to it and be negated. A black spot made of kohl powder is placed on a child's face to divert *nazar*. Za Gul's *nazar* in Shati Khel is notorious. If he comments that a cow is healthy it will die or dry up. It is said that he recently commented on the number of sheep owned by Jafar, the brother of Sawtar, the Musa village elder, and most of them died.

Considerable veneration and symbolism are attached to the objects associated with the two holy cities of Islam in Arabia, Mecca Sharif and Medina Sharif, that *hajis* bring from the *haj* and distribute in small quantities to their near and dear. 'Holy' water from the spring used by the Prophet (*abayzamzam*) is stored safely to be sprinkled ritually on the coffin; dates (*khorma*); prayer-mats and rosaries; a simple white shroud called *cappan*, for coffin, to be wrapped around the corpse; and when money is scarce, then the soil of Mecca and Medina (*de Maccay-Madinay khawra*) is brought as an object of veneration. Such Arabic objects have a symbolic value far beyond their actual value in terms of money, especially as there is a continuing mystical and emotional attachment to them and they are commonly believed to act as cures for various diseases. Today there are 13 *hajis* from Shati: 3 Musa, 1 Ranra, 7 Malok, 1 Ganjian and 1 Ghunda Khel. The first woman *haji* of Shati Khel is Isa Khan's mother, who performed the *haj* in 1973; in 1975 Isa took his wife as did Sardar. Both Isa and Sardar are Malok. *Hajis* I interviewed talked of feeling spiritually uplifted (*roshani*). The implication for the spread of ideas is fascinating. Haji Abdullah was said to be the first *haji* among the Halimzai and Tarakzai when he performed the *haj* in 1937. Since then he has performed *haj* five times more. This contrasts with his arch-rivals and cousins, Anmir and Shahzada, who could afford to perform the *haj* but refused to do so for reasons discussed below. The first *haji* in Shati Khel was Subedar-Major Sultan Jan who went for *haj* in 1965. Before then, as Haji Hassan succinctly summed up, playing on the nuances of the Islamic framework in society, the dominant Shati lineage were simply Pukhtuns (*Pukhtana woo*).

Locally the newly achieved status of the *haji* is balanced by the status of the Pukhtun *mashar*. I heard Shahzada and other *mashars* in both areas speak cynically about the entire business of *haj*: 'They go to smuggle watches and cloth.' They would quote a saying attributed to the Prophet: 'The *haj* decides a man's course for the rest of his life: he either returns very holy or very wicked', and agree that the *hajis* they know fell into the latter category. Shahzada would pointedly refer to the Malok. It is for this reason, they argue, that they would not perform the *haj*. Nonetheless, and according to both formal and informal interviews, the *haj* remains the main ambition of most people, including women. The general economic situation of Bela is reflected in the fact that not one person has performed the *haj* from the village. Haji Gul, the Bela barber, has appropriated the title though he has not been to *haj*, like the grandfather of Aziz (the Shati blacksmith) who did not perform the *haj* but was called *haji* merely because he was born on a Friday, the holy day of the week.

Shamshudin's wife, as indeed other Mohmand women, would discuss their *haj* plans with my wife endlessly. They were clear in their minds, and their husbands had agreed that as soon as they had enough money they would perform the *haj* rather than buy land or spend it on the education of their children. Though Shahzada and other Maliks may deride *hajis*, they are present at the 'seeing off' and 'receiving of' the *hajis* which are accompanied by a series of feasts and celebrations as participation is considered *sawab*. During this period hostilities are tacitly suspended to permit cross-factional visiting. Large Mohmand crowds gather at the railway station or airport in Peshawar with garlands to see off and receive their kin, arriving in hired buses or cars decorated with bunting and coloured paper otherwise used for marriages.

Pukhto names of days in the week and months in the year are said to contain Islamic symbolism: *Pinzama* (Tuesday), the fifth day, is dedicated to the greatest Sunni Saint, Hazrat Gilani of Baghdad. *Shoro* (Wednesday) is so called as God is said to have begun working on the world on this day. *Ziarat* (Thursday) and *Juma* (Friday) are recognized as the two holy days of the week when good Muslims should attend congregational prayers in the mosque. Thursday is considered auspicious for laying the foundation of a new building or starting cultivation, just as Friday is not. Friday is meant exclusively for prayers (*de munz warz*) and designated in Pukhto as such.

Certain Pukhto months of the year are associated directly with events from early Islamic social history centring around the life of the Prophet; native local exegesis reinforces larger Islamic culture and tradition. For instance there are the months of *Moharram*, generally called *Asan* among the Mohmand after the two grandsons of the Prophet, Hassan and Hussain, who were martyred, *Rabi-ul-awal* in which the Prophet died and *Roja*, the month of Ramadan and fasting when the Holy Koran was revealed to the Prophet. No marriages or celebrations are held in these months. *Warokay Akhtar* (small Eed) celebrating the end of Ramadan and the other month of *Akhtar* are months of happiness (*khushali*). *Lowey Akhtar* (big Eed) derives from the incident when Abraham, the ancestor of the Prophet, almost sacrificed his son Ismail to appease God. Every home is expected to and does make a sacrifice (*qurbani*) which is then divided into three shares: the first is given to the poor, the second to poor kin and the third is kept for the house. Three, five or seven persons, traditionally Islamic numbers, may join to sacrifice one cow. In Shati Khel usually seven males pool together to sacrifice a cow costing about Rs. 1,000. Alternatively one sheep may be sacrified by one man. The skin (*sarman*) of the cow, worth about Rs. 100, is for the Mullah (*de mullah shay day*).

On Eed most of the Musa and Malok males, about 100 to 150,

congregate at Shahzada's to pray. Many Ranra pray at the Mian villages while the Ganjian pray in their own villages. In his Eed sermons the Mullah talks of the unity of Islam and honour and shame (*haya*), the general themes in Pukhto. I attended Eed prayers in Shati and Bela; both occasions reflected social structure. In Bela, I sat quietly and un-noticed in one of the back rows where I felt I could observe better. Khan Mohammad, son of Hussain, on leave from the Mohmand Rifles, was prominent in the front row, usually reserved for *mashars*, wearing his new clothes, leather jacket, and *karakuli* cap. In the mosque of Shahzada I tried to stand in the back-row but was immediately called to the front by Shahzada to stand with him so that the symbolism of hierarchy based on age and lineage status should not be unbalanced. In their selection of the Eed day the two areas reflected their geographical and political situations. Bela celebrated the official government Eed and Shati, except for Shahzada who self-consciously celebrated both, celebrated Eed a day earlier — confusion invariably rising annually from different sightings of the new moon.

Hujras and rooms in houses have bare walls except perhaps for a calendar with the name of 'Allah' or 'Muhammad' calligraphied in colour, or one depicting Islamic rulers, usually the late King Faisal of Saudi Arabia. A popular poster shows him being assassinated, signifying martyrdom (*shahdat*) and immortality in the next world. Symbolism of the transitory nature of human life and the permanence of God, a constant theme of the Mullah, is physically present in the Bela mosque. There is a wooden plank (*takhta*) hanging in the mosque visible to all as a reminder of death in the midst of life, for on it males and females of Bela are placed after death as part of the funerary rites and taken to their graves.

In deference to general religious sentiments no radios or tape-recorders are allowed to be played in Mian Mandi, the market owned and controlled by the Mians. This tradition is not restricted to mere lip-service and on various occasions while being driven through the Mandi by *kashars*, restive of tradition, I have seen them respecting the ban by promptly switching off the car radio. As a symbol of his Islamic post-*haj* stance, Haji Hassan will not allow a radio in his house although his sons are doing good business in transport and own two buses.

There is no question of heresy or heretics among the tribesmen, no doubts such as those raised by the orthodox regarding the Berber tribes-men in Morocco (Gellner, 1969a: 22). Prayers are a sort of social therapy, they externalize and exorcise doubts. God is confronted directly by the Pukhtun without the aid of priests, shamans, secret societies and ecstatic behaviour. The mumbo-jumbo and hocus-pocus of medicine men or priests have no place in his world. Religion is direct, monistic and personal. Not surprisingly there are no Sufi orders in *nang* life: itinerant religious mendicants or temporary religious leaders, yes, but institutionalized Sufic or extra-worldly orders, no. In the *nang* areas there are no mystic or Sufic cults that symbolize extraordinary human experience except among the Shias of the Orakzai.[13] The difference in cognition was illustrated by an interesting confrontation between Ihansullah and some other Mohmands, who were visiting me, and the Orakzai Shias when I took them to a dinner the latter had given for me. The Shias had promised to allow me to witness their special rites near Hangu, in the Settled District Kohat, a privilege rarely afforded to non-Shias and given as a gesture of appreciation for my role in helping to solve the long-standing Shia-Sunni problem regarding the Shia Mian Ziarat dispute in Tirah (Ahmed, forthcoming d). After dinner, the Shias, wearing no shoes, danced themselves into an ecstatic frenzy on an area covered with live and burning coal which they picked up from time to time and put in their mouths. The interesting question raised in the discussion that subsequently followed was: what was the emic view of ecstatic behaviour that transcended human physical pain? The Mohmands had never seen anything like it before and simply had no explanation for it. To them the entire performance was sheer mumbo-jumbo and so much magic (*jado*). The Shias explained their transcendence over physical pain through religious emotion and ecstasy (*jazba*). Like the Mohmands I confess I had never witnessed anything like this before. Was it *jado* or *jazba*?

In an illustrative conversation between Shamshudin and Hussain Khan on mysticism in Islam, Shamshudin often pondered the meaning of Sufism and was attracted to the simple Sufi way of life. When I asked them to define Sufism, Hussain Khan replied 'It is nothing but a state of religious lunacy, madness (*mallangi*).' Shamshudin then turned to me and said 'Hussain Khan is only interested in making money', to which Hussain Khan replied 'God will give me money. This is God's work' (*de de Allah kar day*). Hussain then explained that the Muslims of today had forgotten God but that the people of old were saints (*zbarg*) and martyrs (*shahid*). Today, he said, money counts; Shamshudin did not answer — perhaps he had no reply.

In more complex social systems mysticism may be an acceptable alternative to orthodox Islam but in the *nang* areas it is seen as a surrogate for it and is therefore consciously rejected. Hence the explanation of the Mohmand to the Shia ecstatic trance, 'magic'. Just as the Pukhtun is politically iconoclastic he cannot be religiously hagiolatrous. Both conditions are defined by his social Code and descent structure. It is significant that Islam is alive within tribal society not through the memory of teachings of great scholars or saints or their shrines but as part of everyday tribal lore and common descent memory; this partly explains the lack of hagiolatry or anthropolatory among *nang* tribes in contrast with other Islamic societies (Ahmad, A., 1964; Evans-Pritchard, 1973; Gellner, 1969a and b; Gilsenan, 1973; Trimingham, 1973). The Islam of the Mohmands is puritanical, not syncretic or eclectic.

Sociologially it may be relevant to point out that Islam and Islamic symbolism are over-emphasized by non-Mohmand groups, perhaps to even out or obliterate the elitism of the Pukhtun; similarly junior lineages place heavy emphasis on Islamic symbolism, perhaps to perform the same operation on the elitism of the senior lineages. The maximum number of *hajis* are among the Malok. Haji Hassan, an elder of the affiliated Ganjian lineage, or Haji Umar, an elder of the junior Malok lineage, would constantly use 'if God wills' (*inshallah*) or 'by the Grace of God' (*mashallah*) in their sentences. Haji Umar would speak of the Mians with a reverence unimaginable among the Musa: 'They are pure, they stand for prayers and godliness'. Haji Hassan repeatedly quoted the Prophet: 'To respect a *haji* means you respect me.' He would start sentences with a self-conscious 'I cannot tell lies' (*darogh nasham waylay*).

There is no correlation between economic development and lack of religiosity, as is apparent by a superficial visit to the Tribal Areas. Although the older generation, like Haji Hassan in TAM and Shamshudin in SAM, may talk of the young as being less religious than themselves, the fact is that almost the first investment made by the younger Pukhtuns, earning money especially from the Gulf States, is in a new cement mosque.

Perhaps the social bonds of religion within an extra-tribal framework may best be explained by two personal examples. On my tour as Political Agent of the Mullah Khel area, Badaon, there was considerable tension. I was the first political officer ever to have come as far as Badaon, virtually overlooking the Afridi borders of Tirah, and to spend a night in the local *hujra*. It was no coincidence that this tension, which my junior officers felt so keenly, evaporated after I joined my Mullah

Khel hosts at prayer in their mosque by the *hujra*. In another example, I was at an informal meeting in the evening with the Governor of the Province, when he asked some Mohmand Maliks to join us just as the call for prayer (*azan*) was heard. To the Mohmand, equality in the prayer formation symbolized the sociological importance of a common religious system between those representing encapsulating systems and those in the process of encapsulation. Earlier, when he was Inspector-General, Frontier Corps, the Governor deliberately selected Islamic days, such as Fridays, for special occasions like the raising of the Mohmand Rifles or the crossing of the Nahakki Pass.

Indeed, the respect for *hajis* and their rather self-conscious post-*haj* role, the unceasing sermons of the Mians and Mullahs, the physical and focal presence of the mosque, the regularity of prayers by the *mashars*, and the sound of the *azan* add up to an Islamic social if not religious milieu. Islamic symbols pervade ordinary life and its tenets and universalistic customs regulate it to a remarkable degree.

The history of conversion to Islam by the Prophet himself of Qais bin Rashid, the common Pukhtun ancestor, and of patrilineal descent from him, places religion as a defining factor in the Pukhtun model along with *Pukhtunwali*. The Mohmands must be understood within a phyletic context, that of Pukhtunness and a religious context of being Muslim. From a sociological point of view the *latent* function of *Pukhtunwali* appears to be to integrate and perpetuate *nang* society, while its *manifest* function has been successfully to provide diacritica from other social systems (Merton, 1968), such as the *qalang* societies discussed in the next section.

We may conclude that there is a high degree of similarity in the native and foreign models regarding the Pukhtun ideal-type. The central features of *Pukhtunwali* and determining *nang* are *tarboorwali* and *tor* which, in turn, affect social organization and behaviour. How these features either fade away or take other forms in an encapsulated condition will be examined below. Such deviances are emergent and apparent in SAM. For purposes of the thesis contained in my study, TAM behaviour approximates largely to the ideal-type model. It is an 'as they are, now and forever' situation. None the less as Part Three of the study indicates, social change in the model re-ordering *structure* and *values* may be expected in the future. Prognosis of change is not difficult; the rate of acceleration of change and therefore deviance from the ideal model in terms of my study is more difficult to forecast.

III Typology of Pukhtun social organization

Mohmand Pukhtunness in its polychromic sociological entirety can be
best understood in relation to the ideal-type model constructed in the
last section. For the purposes of my study, only then can the extent of
the morphological changes as a result of contact with or encapsulation
within larger state systems be comprehended. Social analysis without
comparison with antithetical forms will continue to remain problematic
and incomplete. The aim of this section is to provide a framework for
such comparison by working out a fundamental taxonomy of Pukhtun
social organization.

The variety and complexity of Pukhtun social structure has long
required a rigorous exercise in Pukhtun taxonomy, the lack of which
results in imprecision in separating those who 'do' and 'can do' Pukhto
and those who 'speak' it only. The need is further underlined by a
surface similarity in Pukhtun groups, common language, custom, Code
and the impression that there is homogeneity in their social and political
structure. I will attempt a taxonomy of Pukhtun social organization
that takes temporal and spatial factors into account elsewhere[14] (Ahmed,
forthcoming e). The absence of a general societal typology has led
authoritative writers to take *nang* values for granted while analysing
empirically observed *qalang* society (Barth, 1972; Caroe, 1965; Davies,
1975; Ibbetson, 1883; Spain, 1962, 1963).

In general Pukhtun tribes are divided linguistically into those speaking the hard Pukhto, living roughly north of Peshawar, like the Yusufzai
and Mohmand, and those speaking the soft Pashto, mainly south of
Peshawar and in Afghanistan. The former would call the tribe 'Khattak'
while the latter would pronounce it 'Shattak'. There is also a third
variety of speech somewhere in between hard Pukhto and soft Pashto
among the Paktia Pukhtuns in Afghanistan (Misdaq, 1976: 58). Some
Pukhtun tribes, like the Mohmands, are divided into high (*bar*) and low
(*kuz*) which corresponds to the hill versus plain division. I suspect it is
also a conceptualization of descent from the homeland in Kabul. *Bar*
clans like the Baezai and Khwaezai Mohmands are still largely in Afghanistan while *kuz* clans, Halimzai and Tarakzai, are in the Agency and
Settled Areas of Pakistan. Political authorities divide the Mohmand
clans into administrative units roughly coinciding with *bar* and *kuz* as
belonging to the Upper or Lower subdivisions of the Agency. Such
categories as linguistic, administrative or hills versus plains are crude
and, for our purposes, sterile. They tell us nothing of structure or form

and would not allow analysis of the causal factors determining and generating change in structure and form.

In Pakistan there is a tendency to refer to the hill tribes as *qabaili*, a term used by the tribes themselves and meaning tribal. But this leads us nowhere as the Pukhtuns even in the Settled Areas in general refer to themselves as tribal. In India, as we saw earlier, a tribal is a mountain-dweller, forest-dweller (*vanyajati*) or aboriginal. These terms tell us little of what the characteristic economic and social features are likely to be of the groups under consideration. Such categories may prove misleading for the social scientist and, apart from providing limited information about the fundamental bases of difference in social organization, may even be empirically invalid. For instance, where would the Khattak groups, who should, and do, belong to the soft Pashto-speakers in the main, but live in Mardan and speak hard Pukhto, be placed? The hill versus plain or Tribal Areas versus Settled Areas categories are equally crude and neither heuristically fruitful nor illuminating. They tell us little. The Yusufzai, for instance, live both in Tribal Areas, the Malakand Agency, and in Settled Districts like Mardan. In any case, migrations and demographic shifts have taken place on such a scale as to make this division almost meaningless.

In an earlier work I briefly suggested the basis for a typology of Pukhtun social groups resting on the fundamental division between those organized around the principle of *nang* as it is interpreted locally and those organized around *qalang* which divides and creates superior and subordinate positions in society (Ahmed, 1976: 73-83). *Nang* and *qalang* conceptualize two antithetical forms of Pukhtun social organization, the former free and unencapsulated and the latter encapsulated. *Nang* and *qalang* lend themselves easily to analysis in terms of simple binary oppositions. I thought it significant that Pukhtuns themselves have identified these key symbols as diacritica in society in a proverb that reflects the dilemmas arising from both forms: 'Honour, *nang*, ate up the mountains and taxes, *qalang*, ate up the plains' (Ahmed, 1975: 47).

I hasten to add the qualification that *nang* and *qalang* are symbols to differentiate and define two types of Pukhtun tribal structure and that *nang* values in themselves may be of equal importance in *qalang* societies. Murders based on *tarboorwali* or *tor* in the Peshawar District are common (Ali, 1966) and once equalled the number of murders in the entire Punjab Province, which in turn equalled murders for the entire subcontinent (Coen, 1971). Such violence is perhaps a result of the anxiety and tension of *qalang* society wishing to live up to the *nang* ideal but finding it difficult to do so in an encapsulated situation. The violence may reflect the acute dilemma of apperceiving and having to come to terms with the actual but desiring the ideal. Both *nang* and *qalang* Pukhtuns see themselves and define themselves unequivocally as Pukhtun societies upholding Pukhtun values.

Qalang life is qualitatively different to *nang* life in the mountains and the difference creates perceptible social boundaries between two sub-cultures. *Qalang* culture is sophisticated, urban, elite or high culture in comparison with and is antithetical to *nang* culture as the two are distinguished in the literature on tribes and peasants (Dalton, 1971; Fallers, 1971; Sahlins, 1968, 1974; Shanin, 1973). Paradoxically, however, the political ideals and cultural values of the latter have always inspired and provided a model for the literature of the former. *Qalang* society perceives *nang* as approximating to the ideal. This adaptation is made all the more complex as *qalang* society deliberately lays down a social line beyond which *nang* values are not permitted to disturb or challenge *qalang* elitism and hierarchy. *Nang* groups migrating to *qalang* areas also face a dilemma. They either acculturize themselves to *qalang* society by accepting subordinate social positions, compromise *nang* or confront hostility (Chapters 3 and 10).

Churchill records a meeting with a typical *qalang* Khan near Swat:

> He was a fine-looking man and sat well on a stamping roan stallion. His dress was imposing. A waistcoat of gorgeous crimson, thickly covered with gold lace, displayed flowing sleeves of white linen, buttoned at the wrist. This striking costume was completed by a small skullcap richly embroidered, and an ornamental sabre (Churchill, 1972: 76-7).

A contemporary British soldier underlined the contrast with the above by concluding a description of a *nang* Pukhtun thus: 'He is certain to be filthy and he may be ragged, but he will saunter into a Viceregal *durbar* as proud as Lucifer, and with an air of unconcern a diplomatist might envy' (Oliver in Wylly, 1912: 11-12).

I am, of course, like all model-builders, holding constant as many variables as possible so as to exaggerate and bring into relief what I argue to be the determinative factors of change, and am therefore guilty of over-simplifying. With a *nang* society model before us in contrast to one of *qalang* it will not be difficult to place Swat society in the latter category from available data (Ahmad, M. T., 1962; Ahmed, 1976;

Barth, 1959, 1972; Bellew, 1864; Hay, 1934; Miangul, 1962). I am arguing that just as Swat provides a typical societal model for the latter category, the Mohmand may be considered a typical societal model for the former category as my field-work data supported by other literature show (General Staff, 1926; Hamid, n.d.; Howell, 1931; King, 1900; Merk, 1898; Mohmand, 1966). The comparison is an essential exercise as it is an opposition recognized by *nang* Mohmands, acutely aware of its existence, especially because of their situation in the Yusufzai *maira*. It will help bring into relief the ideal-type features of the *nang* model for purposes of my study.

Mohmand model	*Swat model*
economic	
1 scant rainfall, unirrigated land, single crop	heavy rainfall, complex irrigation systems, double-cropping, cash-crops, rice
2 no memory of *wesh*	practice and memory of *wesh*
3 Maliks or their sons cultivate own limited land-holdings	tenants cultivate vast estates of Khans
4 small land-holdings and little income differentiation	vast land-holdings and considerable income differentiation
5 no development of markets or towns	development of market towns and connected facilities
social	
6 sparse population	dense population
7 homogeneous society, majority Mohmands, no autochthonous groups	aristocratic minority Yusufzai elite ruling autochthonous population
8 descendants of common ancestor in settlements	peasant agricultural villages with mixed groups
9 definition of Pukhtun based on lineage membership	definition of Pukhtun based on land ownership
10 fewer and less rigid caste-like groups and notable lineage exogamy but clan endogamy	caste-like social stratification and caste endogamy

11 usually *dwa-kora* settlements	usually one house
12 sub-section operative lineage of social action	tribe the operative lineage of social action

political

13 segmentary, acephalous tribal system, no central authority	politically centralized society
14 blocs and alliances a function of social relations with Father's Brother's Son	blocs and alliances a function of power politics cross-cutting ethnic and consanguineal ties
15 socio-political subordination of 'saints' to Maliks, tribal leaders	importance of 'saints' (Mians, Sayyeds *et al.*) as exemplified by the Akhund and the Wali
16 limited authority of senior agnate, backed by genea- logical charter and Code	considerable power of Khans, backed by coercive authority
17 undefined borders, crossing international lines and main- tenance of Mohmand ethnicity	defined borders of state and emergence of 'Swati' ethnicity based on state
18 (*azizwali, rorwali*) agnatic factions emphasizing lineage kinship of combatants	(*della, taltol*) factions based on political factors

There is a progressively widening and irreconcilable qualitative difference in the life-styles of the two models. Swat cinemas in the towns, electricity in the main villages, hospitals, telephones, schools, cottage industries producing intricately designed shawls and quilts, and now an air-field, are in sharp contrast to the mud houses, barren land-scape and absence of modern amenities in the Mohmand. Among the Mohmand there are no ornate works of art, no developed paintings or music, no intricate marmoreal arabesques in graveyards, in mosque or *hujra*, no central townships or markets. This difference is further under-lined by the fact that while Swat is open to and visited by tourists from all over the world the Mohmand Agency still remains closed and off-limits to any kind of tourist, national or international.

It is important to point out that *nang* Tribal Areas are geo-politically surrounded by other Pukhtun tribes and there is no direct contact with non-Pukhtun groups or a 'shatter-zone' of cultures (Barth, 1953: 9). The boundaries of the Mohmand Agency are not ethnic but simply administrative ones, unlike *qalang* boundaries which often divide Pukhtun from non-Pukhtun groups such as Swatis and Chitralis.

Where does this lead us to? Firstly it establishes the validity of studying different societal forms in positions of binary opposition and provides the basis for model-building in order to understand form. Secondly, by illustrating the antithetical nature of the two societies, I wish to argue that Mohmand society approximates to the *nang* ideal-type model and by the same token Swat society is a deviant form of the model and helps our perception of the former.

The important question centres around the point of passage from *nang* to *qalang* society. What preconditions are necessary and what conditions need to be satisfied for the transition? Empirically we can postulate with some confidence that differentiation originates as a result of a dynamic and direct relationship between ecological and larger political factors. Briefly, I mean the basic mechanism for social change presupposes irrigated or fertile lands juxtaposed with or encapsulated into larger state systems, which interfere in society to create chiefs or Khans and help prepare conditions for transition from one category to another. Large irrigated tracts allowing double-cropping provide conditions for accumulation of wealth and hiring of 'mercenaries' to intimidate tenants (Ahmad, M.T., 1962). It is significant that *nang* areas are almost defined by rain-fed lands producing one crop. However, social organization based on large irrigated tracts is not a sufficient explanation for the emergence of hierarchy in itself, but provides the conditions when and if neighbouring larger state systems become involved. The British affected local structure in their attempts to create chiefs as part of imperial policy and in turn the chiefs gave them support. Churchill describes the situation of the *qalang* Khans at the turn of the century north and outside of the Mohmand areas (Churchill, 1972: 74-5). We see how elites and stratification in society begin to appear and simultaneously people find they speak Pukhto but are often constrained from doing so when larger state systems are at hand to support or create local chiefs. Structural changes in economic and social relationships and their articulation through political hegemony is neither understood nor accepted by the Pukhtun; it has no reference to the history of his ideal-type society and its claims to be a pure democracy.

Revolt is not so much an expression of political philosophy as an assertion of cultural and social history and an act of self-definition.

There is a tendency for Pukhtun society to move uni-directionally from *nang* to *qalang* in acts of migration. There is no oscillation between these two poles as between *gumsa* and *gumlao* society (Leach, 1977). It is a mechanical not dialectic relationship. Uni-directional change, defined in the act of leaving traditional *nang* areas, is in contrast to the oscillation conceptualized between two opposed social forms in society, one, democratic acephalous tribal republics ruled by assemblies and the other ephemeral hierarchical tribal tyrannies as among the Berbers (Gellner, 1969a; Hart, 1976; Montagne, 1930, 1931) and Burmese (Leach, 1977).

Qalang Pukhtuns, whether Muhammadzais in Pakistan or Popalzais and Barakzais in Afghanistan, are mostly descendants of Sarban, the eldest son of Qais which, along with their political and economic situation, places them as *mashar* in the Pukhtun universe. *Qalang* Pukhtuns joined British service and rose to high posts in the army and civil service. The British as elsewhere in the world when confronted with such two choices found the *nang* system 'was tainted with rebellion and thoroughly obnoxious' (Leach, 1977: 198). Pukhtun rulers themselves viewed *nang* Pukhtun systems with similar distaste. Amir Abdur Rahman of Afghanistan always referred to their areas, and especially those of Mohmand clans, as 'the land of rebellion' (Rahman, 1900), and the Wali of Swat categorized earlier pre-state Swat history, 'the Pukhtun period', representing anarchy and chaos (Miangul, 1962).

The Mohmands prove an interesting example of cultural unity covering structural diversity. The Khans of Lalpura and Goshta in Afghanistan lived in and organized their Mohmand subjects/tenants into *qalang* groups. They could do so because they owned lands irrigated by the Kabul river which helped accumulate wealth and create hierarchies; the Afghan and later British Government recognized the Khans. Merk's account of the Mohmands describes how these Mohmand Khans were used as pawns between Kabul and Delhi, and, in turn, themselves played off the two, but organized *qalang* society (Merk, 1898). It is important to point out that the Khans, however powerful in Lalpura in the last century, exercised virtually no power in what is now the Mohmand Agency (Elphinstone, 1972 II: 40–2; Merk, 1898). In contrast to the Mohmand Khans are the other Mohmand sections in what is now the Mohmand Agency organized along *nang* lines. Migrations west to Lalpura or east to Mardan presented the Mohmand with an acute dilemma created by the real and divergent views between ideal and actual. Examples such as the Mohmand allow categorization of important clan and tribal groups with precision, as distinct from imprecise labelling of entire tribes in crude categories such as linguistic or administrative ones.

The *qalang* category differs from the *nang* by the characteristic sanction of larger systems neighbouring on or in the process of encapsulating smaller systems, that of physical force or the threat of it. Hegemony is expressed characteristically 'by the organized exercise of coercive authority through the use, or possibility of use, of physical force' (Radcliffe-Brown, 1970: xiv). Within the framework of anthropological literature ideal Pukhtun *nang* society structurally approximates to the Nuer (Evans-Pritchard, 1940; 1970) and other Group B segmentary stateless societies (Fortes and Evans-Pritchard, 1970; Middleton and Tait, 1970) at one end of the continuum, while the *qalang*[15] categories on the other end to that of the Nigerian emirates (Nadel, 1942, 1947; Smith, M. G., 1960) or the Zulu kingdoms with their standing armies, titled nobility and hierarchies in Group A centralized tribal societies (Fortes and Evans-Pritchard, 1970; Gluckman, 1970, 1971: 123-66). In between there are forms of Pukhtun organization resembling 'segmentary states' as among the Alur (Southall, 1953). The diaspora of Pukhtun clans and groups has fascinating implications for the spread of *nang* ideas to distant areas of the subcontinent. The subject is beyond the scope of this thesis but I am dealing with it elsewhere (Ahmed, forthcoming e).

It is not surprising that a *nang* Pukhtun from Waziristan challenged Barth regarding the *Pukhtunness* of the Swat Pukhtun (Barth, 1970) who forms part of the *qalang* system. The doctor at the Shati hospital, a third generation Mohmand from the Settled Area, with his clean clothes and soft looks represented an aspect of the confrontation between *nang* and *qalang* systems and the anxiety it creates in the latter. He was contemptuous of the Mohmands and their manner of living. He considered 'the people very dirty and mean although they had a lot of money stored away at home'. He confirmed the strict seclusion (*parda*) of women and said only old women ever came to consult him. Although he had been posted in the hospital for at least nine months he did not know the names of the area or sub-section of the tribe, Shati Khel. He was pulling strings to be posted out of the area. Paradoxically, he was selected for his posting due to his Mohmand domicile and origin.

To the elders of Shati Khel excess of money and power was *kofar*, an attribute of the *kafir*; it was un-Islamic. Similarly the elders of Bela Mohmandan would often talk to me with awe of the corrupting influence of too much money and power. I believed them. I maintain this is a typical and genuine native exegesis of the world by a *nang* Pukhtun confronting or contemplating *qalang* systems.

What is anthropologically important and interesting is that the social structure and cultural values of the *nang* model have been repeated and perpetuated in an unbroken line for at least four centuries. Their universe has been whole, homogeneous and structural in a manner that the famed anthropological triumvirate, Evans-Pritchard, Malinowski and Radcliffe-Brown, would have found intellectually gratifying and which would have delighted Durkheim. What is of equal interest is that structurally conflict, not in a Gluckmanian sense where it almost re-assures and re-emphasizes unity, but within the framework of Marxist anthropology (Godelier, 1975, 1977; Meillasoux, 1964, 1972; Rey, 1975; Terray, 1972, 1975a, b) is minimal and restricted to expressions of agnatic cousin rivalry and resentment against the proliferation of headmen-type Maliks largely encouraged by the British.

The successful analysis of *nang* Pukhtun society in a Marxist framework provides it with one of its most interesting challenges and remains problematic. As mentioned earlier, *qalang* society, on the other hand, offers a ready fit for a Marxist model and the analysis has been successfully attempted (Asad, 1972).

In conclusion, for my purposes it is the underlying structural pattern and not the overt cultural pattern that has real significance. We are concerned with the structural localized interpretation of a particular culture, how interpretations there assume a variety of cultural forms and how different structures can be represented by the same set of cultural symbols. The taxonomy of Pukhtun society is an attempt to interpret and understand the variety of cultural and morphological forms social organization may take; the ideal-type provides symbols and acts as a yardstick that helps to enumerate variety of form and measure deviance.

In this chapter I have attempted to construct an ideal-type Pukhtun model in order to measure approximation or the extent of deviance in social organization and behaviour of TAM and SAM groups. I have built the model from written material and field-work data based on empirically observed social behaviour. The model itself reveals a remarkable degree of similarity between native and foreign perception of its essential features. Its application to TAM confirms my thesis that an ideal-type model exists and may be empirically sustained in certain parts of the Tribal Areas. The model not only exemplifies the ideal but reveals the high degree of similarity between the ideological model and the immediate model. Its construction is thus a fundamental exercise for the purpose of my study both to define *Pukhtunwali* and measure deviance from it in TAM and SAM. The following chapters will provide data to enable an understanding of the extent of deviance, if any, from the model. In the next chapter I turn to an examination of unilineal descent as the organizing principle in tribal society and its implications for lineage and leadership organization.

5 Lineage and leadership organization: alliance and conflict

'We are all descendants of one ancestor' (*mong the yaw baba awlad you*) — common Mohmand saying.

In the preceding chapter I endeavoured to construct an ideal-type Pukhtun model based on the concept of *Pukhtunwali* and patrilineal descent. In this chapter I shall illustrate the importance of unilineal descent traced from the apical ancestor of the tribe and how it relates and translates to the idiom of *Pukhtunwali* and determines lineage leadership. I shall be arguing that unilineal descent appropriates certain roles and predetermines conflict patterns in society. I am suggesting for purposes of my central problem that placement on the tribal charter is diacritical in Mohmand social and political life and its continuing importance in society illustrates the validity of the model.

1 Unilineal descent as organizing principle in tribal society

The role of unilineal descent as an organizational principle varies widely in different societies but it is generally agreed that there are certain broad categories of rights and obligations which attach to and are transmitted by descent.[1] In Mohmand society these broad categories relate to jural, social and political status in the widest sense applicable by native definition to those groups who have a place on the Mohmand tribal charter. Although segmentary societies possess unusual diffusion of power and tendency to egalitarianism among collaterals, the democracy is structural rather than ideological and there is no political theory or written principles to support it. Unilineal descent, and the concomitant social behaviour it implies and imposes through the tribal Code, act as diacritica to distinguish Mohmands from non-Mohmands. There is thus an exaggerated social awareness of unilineal descent in tribal society. Ideally identical segments are arranged symmetrically on the genealogical charter and the ascendant or descendant levels structurally reflect one another. Segmentary structure and the principle of unilineal descent pervade the whole system and contribute to social cohesion. The political superstructure of Pukhtun tribes tracing descent from a common apical ancestor is an extension of this segmentary lineage organization. The descent charter defines a hierarchy of homologous groups which can direct fusion or fission of social and political interests within a merging or diverging series of such groups. Ideally Mohmand genealogy 'is a conceptualization of a hierarchy of ordered territorial segments' (Peters, 1960: 31). In the Mohmand Agency at every level of segmentation a high degree of consistency between ecological divisions and genealogical divisions is apparent. We have seen, for instance, that the Shati Khel live in a recognized geographical area called after their section and that on a deeper level of the charter the Halimzai clan exclusively occupy the Gandab valley.

Pursuit of concepts embodied in *Pukhtunwali*, that brings power and status, is restricted to bona fide members of the tribe as defined by lineage membership. In this context I agree with the definition: 'a lineage is a corporate group of unilineal kin, with a formalized system of authority.... It is generally named and within it an accepted genealogical relationship is known between all members. It includes both living and dead' (Middleton and Tait, 1970: 3-4). Lineages are homologous corporate groups based on genealogical maps of unilineal descent that define rights and duties, friends and enemies, kin and non-kin:

> From the structural point of view, then, lineage groups are 'segmentary'. From a functionalist point of view, however, they are 'corporate groups', to use the term invented by British Anthropologists; they hold symbols common to all their members, prescribe distinctive practices and oppose each other, in a sense, as differentiated units (Balandier, 1972: 51).

As briefly discussed in an earlier chapter, for purposes of my study I have come to the conclusion that it is on a shallower level of the charter than 'the lineage' or 'corporate group' that analysis must focus. The operative multi-functional institutional unit or segment of the lineage is the sub-section within which agnates interact. Any pretender to power or status must be able to trace successfully his agnatic ascendants to the apical ancestor of the tribe. The Pukhtun's Code, his descent charter, his agnatic enmities and the alternative choices of action open to him are linked together at one point of the individual's position in his community defined by his affiliation in the patrilineage to which he belongs by birth. The pursuit of *Pukhtunwali* is almost a monopoly shared by agnatic collaterals of the operative lineage which is the main arena for its expression. Pukhtun structural and cultural factors place agnatic collaterals in a perpetual and bitter relation of opposition and rivalry. The articulation of lineage fissure produces a situation in which close agnatic kin are continually transformed into political enemies.

From the point of view of the traditional anthropology of seg-mentary societies, what is of interest among Pukhtuns is that smaller segments do not join with corresponding ones on the same unilineal descent level when threatened or in conflict with other less closely rela-ted segments as in many African societies (Fortes and Evans-Pritchard, 1970; Middleton and Tait, 1970: 21). My Mohmand data support the Swat data (Barth, 1959, 1972). Thus if threatened by the sub-clans Hamza Khel or Kadai (Figure 6), the Ranra, Musa or Malok sub-sections will not make common cause. This was illustrated by the example in Chapter 2 of Hamza Khel joining forces with the Baezai and Khwaezai clans in their attack on the Wali Beg sub-clan. Indeed, agnatic rivalry is so acute that, as our examples below and in Chapter 7 will show, Ranra or Musa would prefer to seek alliances with outside lineages to discomfit each other.[2]

Genealogical memory of descent in both TAM and SAM groups traces clear lines to the eponymous ancestor Mohmand, as calculated in Chapter 3, I, allowing for the manipulative processes that operate in different segmentary lineage societies to 'telescope' or 'fuse' names of less important ascendants (Bohannan, L., 1952; Evans-Pritchard, 1973: 46–61; Fortes and Evans-Pritchard, 1970; Freedman, 1958; Geertz, C. and H., 1964; Lewis, I. M., 1961: 144–52; Peters, 1960: 32-3).

As mentioned in preceding chapters, Pukhtun tribes trace their descent to a putative ancestor Qais bin Rashid of Ghor in Afghanistan. Qais's ancestry is traced to Afghana, hence the name Afghan, the descendant of Saul, the first king of the Jews. The Prophet, pleased with the group, conferred on them the title Malik (Arabic for king). Thus every Pukhtun is technically a Malik. This consciousness underlies societal attitudes to hierarchy and titles and is summed up by sayings like 'every man is a Malik, Khan or Nawab'. Qais married the daughter of Khalid bin Walid, one of the most renowned generals of early Islam. Qais had three sons Sarban, Bitan and Ghurghust and a fourth, Karlanri, was said to have been adopted later. Two important points for Pukhtun society emerge from this almost mythical genealogy: the conversion of the Pukhtun ancestor to Islam by the Prophet and the lineage traced to

Khalid bin Walid. The first ensures that the Pukhtun has no complexes or memory of coercive conversion; the second creates the basis of a mythology of martial descent from Khalid bin Walid. In Figure 4 I have shown the genealogical charter of the important Pukhtun tribes to illustrate their descent from the sons of Qais and their relationship to the Mohmand.

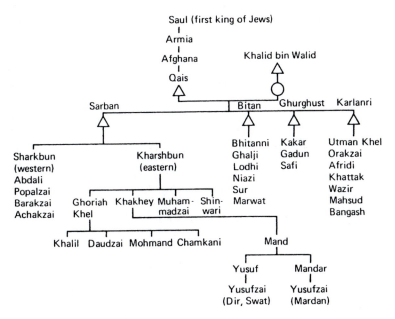

FIGURE 4 *Pukhtun putative genealogy*

The genealogical map linking Shahzada (TAM) and Shamshudin (SAM) to Qais involves some 1,350 years and about forty-five generations and is supported by neither written sources nor named ancestors beyond the tribal eponym. None the less, oral tradition tracing and creating fictitious ancestral links to Qais and beyond is common conversation in *hujras* (Caroe, 1965: 3, 11). I have heard Mohmand elders refer to Khalid Baba (Khalid bin Walid) as the ancestor of Mohmand Baba.[3] In turn, Mohmand is said to have had twelve sons of whom three died issueless and in time the names of the sons except the Baezai, Khwaezai, Tarakzai and Halimzai were forgotten (Raverty, 1888:122 f.n.).

Mohmand elders, especially of senior lineages, can trace their ancestry back to Mohmand Baba with ease, except for 'lost' or 'telescoped'

ancestors. Figure 5 depicts the unilineal descent chart from Mohmand
Baba to Shahzada and Shamshudin as given to me by the informants,
and shows how they relate to each other and on the tribal charter. The
genealogy is corroborated to the sub-sectional level by Merk (1898,
Appendix A: 37) and General Staff (1926).

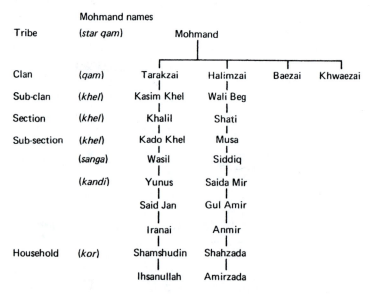

FIGURE 5 *Mohmand genealogy: respondents and their eponymous
ancestor*

In traditional tribal anthropology (Fortes and Evans-Pritchard, 1970;
Peters, 1960: 31) the Tarakzai and Halimzai would correspond generally
to the maximal lineage, eight to eleven generations or primary segments;
the Kasim Khel and Wali Beg to the major lineage or secondary segments; the Khalil and Shati Khel to the minor lineage or tertiary
segment, the smallest political group with its own homeland, water
supplies, pastures and plough-land and genealogical depth of three to
six generations. This lineage level has also been identified as the 'local
descent group' (Leach, 1951: 24). The Musa and Kado form the minimal lineage, the children of one man or village group. Among certain
Islamic tribes the maximal lineage in effect defines the universe beyond
which 'no supra-lineage political authority is developed' (Barth, 1953:
139). This is not true of the Mohmands who are not only highly aware

of other Pukhtun tribes in the *nang* areas with whom they can co-
ordinate in times of crises, as in 1897 when they rose *en masse* in revolt
in the Tribal Areas, but also of *qalang* tribes.

I shall identify tribal divisions, borrowing from these and later
categories (Sahlins, 1968: 15-17) for purposes of my study. I shall
categorize the Mohmand as tribe, Tarakzai as clan, Kasim as sub-clan,
Khalil as section and Kado as sub-section which correspond closest to
Mohmand categorization. To the Mohmand the operative lineage is the
sub-section, Musa in Shati and Kado in Bela, within which he marries,
makes alliances and is in conflict. Mohmands generally call both tribe
and clan *qam*, loosely translated as tribe, the former being large (*star*).
The next three descending generations are usually referred to as *khel*[4]
including the one that concerns us, the sub-section. *Kor* is the smallest
unit and implies habitation with a living grandfather and lineage continuity. The *kor* may be considered as the molecular level of social life
and economic activity. I shall not restrict myself to Mohmand terminology as it is imprecise and may lead to confusion.

The twenty tiny Shati Khel settlements are evidence of the proliferation of segments and fissure in Pukhtun society: 'the principle here is
that every man is the potential founder of a lineage' (Fox, 1967: 128-
9). After the death of the patriarch his sons, if they are able to do so,
invariably exhibit tendencies to fissure and start their own settlements
like those around and in Chino among the Musa Khel in the 1930s after
the death of Anmir. Two interconnected principles operating in society
are set in motion on the death of the grandfather of the *kor*: the
generally recognized rights of the senior agnate to inherit leadership
(symbolic of this status, the eldest son inherits slightly more than the
shares of the other brothers in property, a practice called *masharana*)
and the principle of the legal equivalence and political equality of male
siblings. The seed for demographic fissure are inherent in the system
and ripen on the death of the grandfather.

Unilineal descent confers on the member of the tribe elite status
regardless of his economic position. It is important to note the exclusivity
of this membership. 'Affiliation' and 'grafting' (Peters, 1960) to a
lineage provide only second-rate membership. Until 1977 the National
Assembly Member of the Mohmands was an example of successful
surface assimilation, but whenever I talked of him to Mohmands they
began the conversation by denying his place on the tribal charter and
reminding me of his origin and traditionally non-Pukhtun profession,
trading. Descent and birth from the father's side is the immutable

principle of recruitment to Pukhtunness. As descent is of importance in defining a Pukhtun, seniority of lineage is a factor in planning his settlement arrangements. Perhaps this explains why the Tarakzai, senior to the Halimzai, have access to the better lands along the Kabul river. In my field-work areas senior lineage groups such as the descendants of Ranra and Musa in Shati Khel, and Kado Khel in Bela Mohmandan, live on lands with superior economic, social, and, as in TAM, military value. I shall discuss the correlation of seniority of lineages and settlement arrangements that reflect shifting political power in Chapter 8 with the aid of maps and figures.

Unilineal descent determines marriage and, in turn, endogamous rules underline the importance of descent. Unlike other segmentary societies where exogamous rules define a clan (Mair, 1972: 79), Mohmand women are rarely given outside the clan and a high percentage married within the clan and almost entirely endogamously within the tribe, as will be seen in Chapter 8. Although there are examples of Pukhtuns marrying non-Pukhtun women, there are limited examples of Pukhtuns giving daughters to non-Pukhtuns. The social and economic hierarchy is reflected in the matrimonial circuit which differentiates between wife-givers and wife-takers. Pukhtuns fall strictly in the latter category.

Figures 6 and 7 will show the present major houses in both my field-work areas and the operative lineage groups within which they order their social and political affairs. For TAM the operative lineages are the tribal sub-sections descended from Ranra, Musa and Malok, the three sons of Shati. The numerous Mohmand hamlet-settlements of Shati Khel trace descent from one of these three brothers and agnatic rivalry in every possible sphere of activity involves their descendants. In terms of diachronic political analysis the Ranra dominated Shati Khel until three to four generations ago because of their numbers and were therefore termed descendants of eight fathers (*ata plara*). Opposing them were their cousins the Musa and Malok, with lesser numbers, who together with their allies the Ghunda Khel and Ganjian were called *salor plara* (literally, four fathers).

My three main Shati settlements represent the sons of Shati, the descendants of Ranra living in Ranra or Malik Mazullah village, Musa in Shahzada Malik village and Malok in Malok or Sar Gul Malik village (Figure 6 and Map 5 (iii)). In TAM unilineal descent in the patri-lineage is of key importance to Pukhtun activity. The average adult or young man in Shati Khel questioned by me knew and could trace his ancestry precisely to one of the three sons of Shati, and more often than not relate his age-group agnates to the charter within the operative lineage. Elders in TAM, of the three sub-sections, could trace their links to Mohmand Baba without hesitation. 'Generation recall' is important to tribal society and contrasts with agricultural peasant societies where village and caste boundaries are more important than lineage.[5]

It is of significance that in Shati Khel the settlement patterns approximate to the idealized type. No non-Mohmand groups live in Shati (Chapter 8; Map 5 (iii)) except those affiliated to the charter like the Ganjian and the Ghunda Khel (the latter claim to be Kamali Halimzai). Thus Shati, as a Pukhtun unit, remains pure. The religious Mian group live nearby in Mian Kassai and the occupational groups, the barbers and carpenters, live in Sangar, a few miles south of Shati (Maps 2 and 4). Types of settlement and occupational situations depend directly on being placed by birth on the tribal charter. Figure 6 relates the Shati lineages and reflects consociation and conflict between their members, which will be examined in more detail in Chapter 7.

Examples of 'affiliation' to the dominant Yusufzai tribal charter have been given for Swat (Barth, 1972: 27) and they also exist in both TAM and SAM areas. For instance the Ganjian and the Ghunda Khel have unilaterally declared affiliation with the Shati Khel. The Ganjian,[6] a Safi Pukhtun group, moved to Shati Khel from the northern Safi areas with *hamsaya* status some three to four generations ago and now claim to be Halimzai. In spite of detailed questioning they could not satisfy me regarding their place on the Halimzai charter. None the less they are adamant about their Halimzainess. Haji Hassan, about 70 years old and their elder, insisted the Ganjian were Halimzai, which would provoke Amirzada, son of Shahzada, and other Shati Halimzai to make sure I asked him to trace his ancestry in front of them in order that they might expose him. When openly challenged Hassan would graciously answer 'they are pranksters, they joke' (*tokay kayi*). None the less tribally, to all intents and purposes, the Ganjian are now considered affiliated to the Shati. This assertion is supported by the fact that certain examples of inter-marriages between Ganjian and Shati, albeit with the junior Malok lineage, may be cited (Chapter 8). The Mians among TAM neither claim Mohmandness nor are invited to affiliate. Pukhtun and Mian know their respective social roles and recognize the tribal charter that defines them and acts as a boundary between them.

Consent rather than conflict characterizes society, unlike the situation

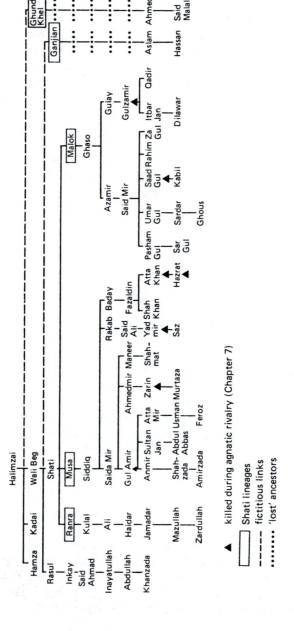

FIGURE 6 *Shati Khel: 'operative lineages'*

in other Islamic tribes such as the Kababish Arabs (Asad, 1970: 245). Among the Pukhtuns consent is largely implicit in society as a result of conceptualization of democracy both in structural and empirical terms. Tension between dominant Shati Khel Pukhtun groups and non-Shati Khel Pukhtun groups is resolved by the social mechanism of affiliation. Similarly non-Mohmands like religious or occupational groups are guaranteed unrestricted freedom of movement, economic security and political neutrality, which compensates for Pukhtun social superiority. In any case, none of the above groups privately accept superiority of Pukhtun genealogy or activity except where it involves agnatic killing in which they are happily neutral. Individual ownership of land and service monopoly further reinforce the concept of democracy in society and every household, Mohmand or non-Mohmand, will say 'I am a Malik/Khan/Nawab'. Such devices ensure stability in a society otherwise without visible forms of government. Consent permeates segmentary symmetry and allows for the mystification of Pukhtun ideology. It is this acceptance or affiliation that allows Shati Khel to give the Ghunda Khel and Ganjian a share in the sectional allowance (*muajib*), albeit a token and small one. None the less this share confirms their Pukhtunness and distinguishes them from religious and occupational groups who have no share in the *muajib*.

Figure 7 depicts the genealogical structure of the Mohmands in the Bela village and reflects the sources of seniority and status within the community. I shall discuss each major group according to its accepted seniority in the village group. I use the word seniority with some caution. It does not imply the political domination and status it does in Shati Khel. In the context of the Bela *mashars* Shamshudin represents Kado, Hamesh the Madar, Majeed the Sabah and Qulamat, Hussain the Jano, Khushal the Do and Morcha the occupational groups.

Kado Khel can trace their lineage directly to Kasim and even beyond to Mohmand himself. This itself reflects the importance they feel the charter gives them and the community recognizes this. The second senior lineage, the Madar Khel, are descended from Madar, the nephew of Kado. They generally ally with the Kado in Bela but often find themselves in opposition to their cousins, especially in instances where division of political allowances affect their sub-sectional kin across the Agency border in the Michni area. As the Kado are a stronger group, especially in the Michni area of the Agency, the Madar often refer to themselves as Kado, thus 'merging' themselves with the better known or senior lineage. In formal questionnaires I was surprised to discover the

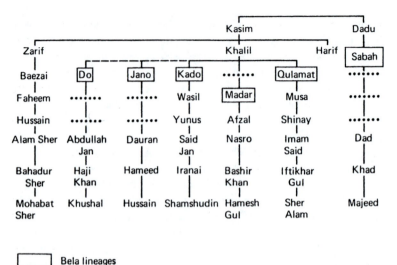

Bela lineages

– – – – fictitious lineage links

• • • • • • • 'lost' ancestors

FIGURE 7 *Bela Mohmandan: 'operative lineages'*

number of Madar, including the Madar elder Hamesh Gul, who defined
themselves as Kado. These are the two senior lineages of Bela.

Qulamat Khel, the third lineage descended from a brother of Kado,
do not actually live in Bela although they own lands around the village.
However, the fourth group, the Sabah Khel, who are related to the
Kado Khel on a deeper span of the genealogy than the Qulamat, and
through Dadu on the sub-clan level, have adopted a social device to
move closer to the Kado. They have forged a fictitious relationship and
thereby identify themselves with Qulamat. For instance, Mehr Gul
(Sabah Khel) who features in later chapters, like others of his group,
would use the word Qulamat interchangeably with Sabah. This may
have brought the Sabah closer to the operative lineage, the sub-section,
in Bela social life, but no elder of Sabah Khel, including their most
senior member Majeed, could trace his ancestry beyond his grandfather. Mehr Gul could not name ancestors beyond his grandfather
either. That leaves us with the Do Khel and the Jano Khel. Both have
created a fictitious lineage beyond their grandfathers that link them to
Kado Khel but which is challenged and denied by the latter. Khushal
and Hussain, the elders of Do and Jano, could not trace their ancestors

beyond grandfathers. In contrast the senior lineage Zarif Khel,[7] living in Bela, like the Kado had no difficulty in recalling the names of agnatic ascendants up to Mohmand Baba, the common eponymous ancestor. In Bela neither are the Kado and Madar strong enough to repudiate the claims of the Do and Jano as their kin, nor are there any rewards to make it a worthwhile exercise. Situated as the village is in the Settled District where no special favours accrue to any particular lineage, the affiliation and fictitious lineage links are allowed to assume a certain validity by tacit agreement in society. To the outsider no Kado or Madar would be impolite enough to challenge the origin of the Jano and Do Khel or question their agnatic links to a mutual ancestor. Economic poverty and lack of political favours have created a sense of social equality that transcends the need for ranking within lineage groups.

Occupational groups like Haji Gul, the elder of Bela barbers, told me they were also descended from Khalil, the ancestor of the main sub-section in the village, Kado Khel, but had neither genealogical maps nor names to prove it. The barber elders could not name Kado's brothers and they would negate their genealogical story by suggesting they migrated from Afghanistan two or three generations ago. However, inter-marriage and proximity have conferred an affiliated status on them.

Morcha Khel, the Bela carpenter, could not name his great-grandfather but insisted he was a Halimzai from Gandab. This fictitious affiliation with a distant clan rather than with a resident clan provides an interesting case. The carpenters migrated from Sangar, in the Halimzai Gandab, to a Tarakzai village, and rather than attempt to affiliate with their local patrons, they claim Halimzai descent. The reasons are not complex to ascertain. Affiliation and creation of fictitious links would be relatively simple in the act of migration, whereas if attempted locally genealogical memory would be sharp. In fact the carpenters claim relationship with the carpenters of Sangar in the Gandab with whom they still have credit dealing. These examples are of upward social mobility but it is important to point out that unlike the Jambal Khel 'carpenters who some 200 years ago so distinguished themselves in war that they were given land and Pakhtun status' (Barth, 1972: 27), neither the Ganjian in TAM nor the carpenters in SAM have won their laurels on the battlefield or in any dramatic manner. Affiliation in these cases is still an incomplete genealogical process and is largely a consequence of services rendered in daily life, reinforced with shows of loyalty over time *vis-à-vis* non-local hostile groups.

The Imam, the religious instructor and supervisor of the mosque of Bela, traced his links to Kasim, father of Khalil, but could not specify the names that linked them. Although Bela elders doubted the veracity of the links, the Imam was generally considered as affiliated to the local genealogy. The Imam's male descendants married Pukhtun girls, a rare example of Pukhtun exogamy. This contrasts with the TAM religious groups, the Mians. The reasons support my thesis: Bela lines of descent are in the process of becoming blurred as they become unimportant. In TAM they are still important and remain firm and clear.

None the less, there are important deviances in Bela from Shati Khel. Firstly, and most important, Bela is 'mixed': the neighbours of Kado, the senior lineage, are barbers. Apart from occupational groups, non-Mohmand Pukhtun groups, like Afridi and Afghans, also live in Bela (Chapter 8; Map 7). Second, occupational groups finding better economic rewards for their services as suppliers of specialized services are investing in land ideally the right of Pukhtuns. The barbers of Bela have acquired houses recently by the north-west channel (Map 6) and the carpenters have a higher income and average land-holdings than any other Bela group (Chapters 6 and 9). Third, as traditional Pukhtun activity cannot be maintained by SAM, the importance of memorizing ancestral links is diminished. Another process is at work, the results of which in genealogical terms are similar to 'fusing' and 'telescoping' names of ascendants. This is a process that corresponds to 'genealogical amnesia' (Geertz, C. and H., 1964) of 'losing' names. It was significant that although all the elders of the six lineages of Bela could trace their ancestry from Khalil to Mohmand Baba *mashars* of the three junior lineages, Sabah, Do and Jano, had 'lost' two or three linking names of direct and near ascendants to Khalil (Figure 7).

Yet another interesting genealogical process is at work in Bela. Weaker or junior lineages 'blur' their lines of descent in order to associate with senior lineages like Kado. As mentioned, some of my formal questionnaires were answered by household heads who ideally should have been able to trace their lineage up to the sectional ancestor without ambiguity and clarity but could not do so. Do Khel often answered as if they were associated with Madar. The Madar 'blurred' their genealogical lines and often talked of themselves as Kado. Do and Madar, Madar and Kado were assumed to be interchangeable lineage names whose lines were blurred. Lineages like Kado retain a vested interest in keeping their genealogical memory alive and clear as it ratifies their seniority and at a stroke denies association with, as it confirms the junior position of, those lineages who deliberately attempt to blur lineage lines.

As suggested earlier, the answers to the questions raised above partly support my thesis. Immediate ascendants are of little benefit to junior lineages of Bela but in the context of the larger lineages in the Michni-Bela area memory of Khalil to Mohmand is still a diacritical factor that allocates broad categories of social divisions based on lands and villages. In this case my findings corroborate those of Peters: 'the evidence that has been examined suggests that the mechanical devices of telescoping, fusion of names, and extinction of lines do not affect orders of segmentation superior to that of the tertiary order' (Peters, 1960: 50). The deduction is clear. Genealogical memory is in the process of becoming irrelevant to social life in SAM evidenced by 'telescoped', 'fused', 'lost' ancestors and 'blurred' lines of descent. Losing ascendants is facilitated by the absence of religious or cultic significance of ancestors. Extraordinary names may be remembered but there is no evidence of ritual significance attached to them as in other systems where the principle of patrilineal descent is objectified and kept alive by patterns of ritual beliefs and practices as, for example, among the Nuer (Evans-Pritchard, 1940); Lugbara (Middleton, 1960); the Chinese (Freedman, 1958, 1966); and the Tallensi of Ghana (Fortes, 1945). Nor is there a presence of esoteric cults, like the Sufis, encouraging hierarchy and memory of religious descent as in other Islamic tribes such as the Cyrenaican Bedouin (Evans-Pritchard, 1973; Peters, 1960) and the Somali (Lewis, I. M., 1961, 1962a, b, 1969a, b).

So far we have discussed the importance of genealogy to the tribes internally but sectional divisions and subdivisions are also important externally. Allowances such as *muajibs* and *lungis* are based on traditional genealogical arrangements and proof of filiation on the charter.[8] How and what allowances were distributed among the Mohmand, by the Kabul and later the British Government, corresponding to tribal clans and sections late in the last century has been discussed in detail by Merk (1898: 15-17).

Mohmand kin terminology, formal and, in brackets, informal is placed in Figure 8. Mohmand kin terminology is largely similar to that of Swat (Barth, 1972: 110) and other Pukhtun groups (Lorimer, 1934). There are no differences in terminology between Pukhtun and non-Pukhtun or TAM and SAM. The areas of potential general conflict are unshaded and those of friendly contact are shaded. Conflict is embedded in relationships between agnatic collaterals and siblings. Patrilateral parallel male cousins are conceptually separated from all other siblings and cousins by a separate term, *tarboor*, which carries the subsidiary connotation of 'enemy' (Morgenstierne, 1927). *Tarboor* relationships, which invariably involve the women of the house, are discussed in Chapter 7. Actual names are rarely used and informal ones preferred, for instance *lala* is a general classification for male elders of ego's generation as *bebey* is for female elders. Younger kin are usually called by their own names.

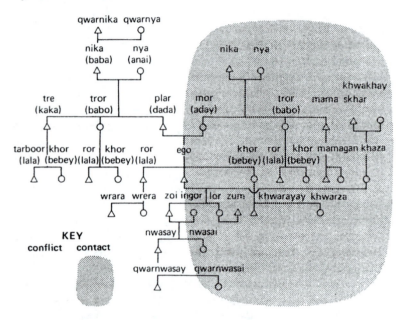

FIGURE 8 *Consanguineal and affinal terms among the Mohmand: formal and informal*

In concluding this section we may summarize unilineal descent as the organizing principle in tribal society thus:

(1) Mohmand groups trace their ancestry through agnatic links to the tribal eponym, Mohmand Baba. Such descent legitimizes claims for lineage leadership.

(2) Adopted and affiliated lineages exhibit surface signs of successful assimilation and politically participate in agnatic rivalry, as they tilt to one or other local faction, but retain *hamsaya* status and are explicitly aware of their exclusion from the local tribal genealogy.

(3) Importance of lineage memory is directly correlated to traditional Pukhtun activity centring around *Pukhtunwali*. In encapsulated systems opportunity for such activity is restricted and therefore genealogical memory is less important resulting in fused, telescoped or lost ancestors. Lineage lines may be deliberately blurred to identify with senior lineages. Having discussed the importance of unilineal descent in society, I turn now to a discussion of types of leadership among the Mohmand.

II Leadership and authority: 'chiefly' model

In the typology of leadership in anthropological tribal literature authority varies from 'big men' and 'petty chiefs' to kings ruling powerful empires combining religious and secular duties (Fortes and Evans-Pritchard, 1970; Gluckman, 1971: 123-66; Sahlins, 1968: 20-7). Mohmand leaders approximate to the former types of leadership, 'big men' and 'petty chiefs', who may build up ephemeral prestige and power because of exceptional personal qualities of leadership, like Shahzada, but this is not hereditary and cannot be passed on to their sons.

The leader of the section or sub-section is almost invariably the living senior agnate. Authority may be classified sociologically as 'patriarchal' (Weber, 1961). The role of the paterfamilias or patriarch is restricted to head of household. Pukhtun ideology, structure and ecology restrict the growth of patriarchal authority to gerontocratic or patrimonial authority, both of which imply formal leadership, hierarchy and a minimum of administrative apparatus (Weber, 1960). Weber saw a certain similarity in the two polar types of authority on the sociological continuum, patriarchal and bureaucratic, in that both were of a permanent nature:

> yet they have in common a most important peculiarity: permanence. In this respect they are both institutions of daily routine. Patriarchal power especially is rooted in the provisioning of recurring and normal needs of the workday life.... The patriarch is the 'natural leader' of the daily routine (Weber, 1961: 245).

Patriarchs may be called Maliks, implying 'petty chief' or 'headman' or, more informally, *mashars*. There is a thin dividing line between the two and Malik denotes only a formalized category of leadership. There are no Khans, Walis or Nawabs in the *nang* Tribal Areas. The prejudice against ranks and titles and the hierarchy they imply is strong in tribal

society and is summed up by the choice the Mahsud *mashar*, speaking
on behalf of the clan elders, gave the British, 'blow us all up with cannon,
or make all eighteen thousand of us Nawabs' (Howell, 1931: 48). As it
implies hierarchy and inequality 'the Mohmands dislike the word Malik'
and prefer *'mashar'* (Merk, 1898: 15).

The British had imposed a uniform framework of administration in
the Empire which was often insensitive to local ethnic and structural
susceptibilities. Administration was based on the principle of utilizing
chiefs or, where there were none, creating them. So as they curtailed
the power of chiefs in Group A societies they created chiefs, even if
none previously existed, in Group B societies in Africa[9] (Fortes and
Evans-Pritchard, 1970: 15-16). In the Pukhtun *nang* areas indirect rule
posed problems not encountered in the *qalang* areas where a hierarchy
of Khans already existed. The precepts of indirect rule presupposed
ignorance of tribal *nang* structure, a point cogently made by British
political officers who knew the Tribal Areas (Howell, 1931: 50). The
colonial encounter with the British resulted in the creation of what is
called 'the Maliki system' in the Tribal Areas. Loyal and suppliant
Maliks and *mashars* were officially given the title Malik and their names
placed by the Political Agent on lists which entitled them to various
favours and imposed certain duties. A profusion of Malik categories
resulted, such as *spin giray* and *lungi*-holders. Inaccessible areas of little
strategic value to the Britsh, such as the Shilman area south of the
Kabul river and in the Khyber Agency, were not given Maliks of any
kind.

This system has continued until today. Official allowances such as
muajib are often very small, starting from half a rupee to a rupee per
year, but they signify political importance and open economic possibilities and are therefore social symbols of status. A Mohmand Malik
described the attraction of the allowance: 'I do not enjoy eating a
carrot but like the sound it makes when munched.' Agnatic rivalry is
touched at its most sensitive if one cousin receives a rupee more than
another. A Political Agent, Mohmands, in the 1970s described an
incident when he was Assistant Political Officer in the mid-1950s
concerning Shahzada and his rival Abdullah. The patriarchs received
their secret allowance of Rs. 100 and left his office. When they discovered
that both had received exact sums they promptly returned to plead
with the APO in private to increase the sum if by half a rupee only.
Agnatic honour and status would be satisfied. A rather dramatic manner
in which agnatic jealousy can be triggered during the half-yearly official

presentation of allowances by the Political Agent was brought home to me while I was distributing allowances in 1977 to the Mullah Khel clan of the Orakzai tribe in Hangu which is in the Settled District of Kohat. Being in the Settled Area, the clan was unarmed and in case of breach of law exposed to police action. Nothing daunted, and within minutes of receiving his sum and discovering it to be less than his cousin's, a Mullah Khel started a fight using bricks which ended in one death and several severely wounded participants.

The offical Maliks in time have grown in wealth with the official favours they receive and a cleavage within society is becoming perceptible. The Malik receives special financial allowances in addition to those meant for his sub-section; only he is allowed to vote for candidates to the National Assembly; he receives quotas for food rations at special prices (sugar, tea, flour); he is given the choice of appointing tribal levies (*khassadars*) from his section (he usually appoints his sons — three of Shahzada's are *khassadars*); he gets all building contracts in his Agency (which he often sub-contracts); his signature, along with that of three other Maliks, attests as to whether a person is a genuine Mohmand and eligible for a domicile certificate which is essential for scholarships and service quotas, etc.; and, of current relevance, groups of Maliks form lobbies to decide who may be given visas for employment abroad, mostly in the Arab States (Chapter 11). Such official benefits accrue on both sides of the border to the successful Maliks. Mohammad Amin, son of Muhasil (Kuda Khel), is a rich man in Afghanistan as a result of his father's role in Mohmand history (Chapter 3).

Duties are as vague as is the term 'loyalty' for which favours are ostensibly given: they are confined to helping keep the main roads open, negotiating return of kidnapped people or outlaws, Proclaimed Offenders, and being available in times of trouble. For instance, a few years ago Shahzada used his influence in the Shati Khel to persuade the Ranra Khel to return a Mian they had kidnapped for ransom from Charsadda. Or more recently Shahzada, Khanzada, Afzal and other Maliks successfully calmed the *kashars* and other Mohmand sections following an incident at the Dand Scouts' picket between the authorities and tribesmen in which three tribesmen were killed. But as they have grown affluent the Maliks have inevitably found it prudent to shift their sphere of activity outside the Agency.

Maliks were created by fiat, producing more problems than they solved for the administration. Even today the Maliks share little of their benefits with their kin, who criticize them as selfish and devious in the

pursuit of personal gain. Internally tribal society is faced with its first
structural crisis. In opposition to the Maliks and *mashars* grew a class of
kashars. *Kashars* may be defined as political 'have-nots' although the
word means young or junior, as opposed to *mashar*. *Kashar* may include
old and rich people and I have therefore preferred to define it in
political terms. Churchill spoke of their intransigence in the first full-
scale invasion of Mohmand country in 1897 (Churchill, 1972: 133) and
they continue to be mentioned until the last major British campaign in
1935 (Elliott, 1968: 183). Government and newspaper reports mention
them too (H.D., T.R.C., File 220).

Opposition to Maliks is not on the level of crude social abuse or
insult but is restricted to political expressions of opposition. The *kashar*
is a militant, not a revolutionary. He wishes to remove what he sees as
the invidious British-created Maliki system and to return to the traditional ideal structure but not to create a new one. His actions may be
translated as a desire for structural change in society, but he is merely
an expression of emergent contradictions within it (a useful distinction
made by Bailey, 1960; Gluckman, 1971). Conflict is seen as an attempt
to change the personnel, not to abolish the leadership structure or the
system it represents (Fortes and Evans-Pritchard, 1970: 13; Gluckman,
1971: xxii). The severity of the crisis has not developed in the structure
because 'the Maliki system' is hardly more than two generations old,
beginning in its present form as it did at the turn of the century.

Shamshur Rahman, son of Noor Rahman, and nephew of Shamshudin,
is a school teacher in the Agency and a *kashar*. He wrote: 'These Maliks
are of the British rule which is a great injustice. Our Maliks destroyed
the qualities of their forefathers, they are toady now and drinking wine
so how they will do the services of their tribe, *khel* or nation?' An
uneducated Halimzai of the junior lineage (Malok) driven from the
Gandab to seek employment as a tenant in the Kado area of Michni
endorsed this view in his answers in a formal questionnaire:

> I am a tenant here. I left my village due to poverty. Our Maliks,
> example, Shahzada, Khanzada get a large amount from the Govern-
> ment. They do not give it to the poor, if they helped me, I will not
> leave my village. These Maliks are of the British reign. Now is
> Pakistan so these should be elected on votes. We poor have no right
> of vote. We have no ration share.

Ihsanullah and Feroz, two of my assistants, are vocal *kashars* but like
other younger Mohmands are models of correct social behaviour in the

presence of elders. Malok or Ranra youngsters though opposed to him as *kashars* in lineage politics would none the less address Shahzada as 'Malik Sahib'. Similarly the youngsters of Musa will refer to Malok and Ranra elders as 'Malik Sahib'; or, in a less formal and more personal manner, uncle (*kaka*) or grandfather (*baba*). In Bela, however acrimonious the dealings among the *mashars*, the *kashar* would still address leaders of opposed factions as *kaka* or *baba*. Even *mashars* like Shamshudin of the senior lineage would always refer to Khushal of a junior lineage but older in years as 'Khushal baba', as indeed did the entire village. In the *hujra* the *kashars* would sit only when there was space on the cots; otherwise they would stand and not speak out of turn in the gathering of elders.

Ordinary household heads who had little contact with administration would complain to me of the official Maliks who they felt diverted facilities meant for the tribe to themselves: 'they eat us up'. But if I asked the head during the course of the conversation who the Malik of the house was he would indignantly reply: 'I am the Malik'. He thus aspires to a position he rejects. Genealogically as we saw in the last section all are 'descended from one ancestor' and are therefore equal. *Mashar* and *kashar*, senior or junior lineage groups, would repeat to me: 'We are like the stalks of wheat – we grow as one – there is no better or worse, faster or slower.' Unfortunately, the actual situation allows room for discontent especially within the framework of ideal expectations and the desire to restore an ideal past order.

What does society see as the ideal qualities of a leader, Malik or *mashar*? The Malik like the Kurd leader 'the Agha likes to think of himself as a military leader rather than as a landlord' (Leach, 1940: 55). Ideally he is brave; in agnatic rivalry or *jihad* against the British he must be in the forefront of the assault. He is generous, concerned for his lineage and wise in council. TAM respondents in the formal questionnaires defined the lineage elder, *mashar* or Malik, as primarily one who helped his sub-section or group, 58 per cent, and equally that he ensured peace among them with justice and wisdom, 58 per cent. Hospitality had a lower priority, 17 per cent. In contrast, SAM reflected their subconscious desire for dependence, itself a consequence of their encapsulated state, on stronger leaders than their structures contain by almost unanimously defining a Malik or *mashar* as one who 'helped the poor', 99 per cent. His hospitality came low in priority, 6 per cent, clearly indicating a deviance from the ideal concept of *Pukhtunwali*. The conclusions were clear. Desire for tribal cohesion in the former and material assistance in the latter are plainly illustrative of the diverging models of society.

Administration has inadvertently connived with tribal demand to negate the effects of the new hierarchy by creating so many Maliks as almost to reduce the 'title' to its former position of household elder and little else. The proliferation of Maliks is reflected in a Malthusian proposition: Maliks grow in geometric proportion to a population that grows in arithmetic proportion. In the Tribal Areas for every 100 people there is one Malik (Ahmed, 1977a: 48). The number of Mohmand Maliks is 8,955 (Home Department Figures, June 1976). One Mohmand Malik thus represents 43 people. Among the Orakzais in 1900 there were 236 official Maliks, in 1972 there were 1,500, in 1976 almost 5,000 and by the time I left in 1977 there were almost 7,000 Maliks for a population of 278,951: one Malik for every 40 people in the Orakzai Agency. The proportionate figures would be even more striking if the basis of calculation was actual populations and not the inflated official estimates we have used. Even without reference to tribal structure and ideology these statistics should suffice to prove no 'chiefly model' has evolved or is possible in the Tribal Areas. Elders yes, petty chiefs for temporary periods possibly, but chiefs, no.

By some fortune or traits of personality an individual may exceed another but none is by right superordinate and none by structure subordinate, all are as good in the sight of man and by their own lights and apt to proclaim the fact at every possible opportunity. Jealous of their own sovereignty, they recognize no greater political cause standing over and against their separate and individual interests. The universal saying 'I am a Malik' is not far from social truth. The corresponding equivalence of Malik, the Khan in the Districts, is similarly levelled by society. When Professor Anne Lambton,[10] whom I took to Bela Mohmandan, asked in the *hujra*, where some fifty Belawals congregated, who was the Khan and how they elected him, the answer was 'every man is a Khan'.

The rule of primogeniture determines the passage of the Maliki in a household and the father's traditional ceremonial head-dress (*patkai*), symbolizing leadership, is placed on the son's head after the burial of the father. From a sample of sixty Tarakzai and Halimzai Maliks primogeniture was observed as the rule in 90 per cent of the cases. This rule may be broken if the son is incompetent or mentally defective or an infant. In such cases inheritance may be filial, ultimogenital or adelphic, in that order of precedence. In an example of filial inheritance being refused among the Halimzai Haji Umar of Malok rejected the Maliki as he felt he was too old and infirm and recommended his brother's son, Sar Gul, who was made Malik. Itbar Jan applied successfully for the transfer of his Maliki to his younger son Dilawar on the plea that his eldest son was not interested in tribal affairs and was occupied with the family lands in the Settled Swabi Subdivision. Among certain families, two siblings may be nominated Maliks as in the case of Yusuf Mohmand (Tarakzai) and his elder brother.

Five kinds of leadership in tribal society may now be identified: traditional Maliks recognized by the lineage; *mashars*; government appointed Maliks, who may be from the first categories; *kashars*; and in times of supra-tribal crisis, religious leaders. The distinction is a legalistic one. The *mashar* requests while the Malik, when backed by government or a *jirga*, can require. The last three categories are essentially extrinsic to society, being a by-product of the colonial encounter; and as we have briefly discussed the government Malik and the *kashar*, I propose to analyse the role of the first two in tribal society. The leadership that regulates daily social life on the molecular and sub-sectional level concerns traditional Maliks, and, if and where they coincide, government Maliks and *mashars*.

Maliks headed the four main TAM villages I studied, as indeed they do all TAM villages: Malik Lakhkar of Malik Lakhkar village, Shahzada Malik of Shahzada Malik village, Malik Sar Gul of Malok or Sar Gul village and Mazullah Khan of Ranra or Mazullah village. The importance of the patriarch may be seen from the fact that villages are usually called after the living senior agnate. The names of the last two villages are commonly interchangeable and often called Sar Gul village and Mazullah village respectively. These Maliks are traditional patriarchal heads of the *kor* and are also recognized officially as Maliks by government. The Malik often sees himself at the receiving end of economic exploitation. To do Pukhto he has to live up to, among other things, the standards of hospitality. In ritual, the *rites de passage*, during festivals such as Eed or on the holy days of the Islamic calendar or when receiving guests and officials, hospitality must be maintained which junior lineages are able to avoid (Chapters 7 and 9).

Bela Mohmandan not being in the Agency has no Maliks, and consequently no sources of patronage such as allowances, rations or privileges for its elders. Elders are called *mashars*. Shamshudin's father Iranai, before the division of the Agency in 1951, was called a Malik and in moments of cordiality and goodwill Bela *mashars* may call Shamshudin a Malik. Even his traditional rival, Hussain, often repeated to me in

private, 'After all, he is the son of a Malik', in a complimentary tone of
voice. Shamshudin's elder brother, Habibur Rahman, being a *mashar* in
the Agency, receives about Rs. 10 annually as tribal *muajib*. Hussain
styles himself a Malik in half-earnest manner. As authority roles in Bela
bring few material or social rewards they are not pursued. Shamshudin's
is a thankless job of living up to the role of village *mashar*. Hamesh Gul,
another *mashar*, is older and ill and simply could not cope with the
extra burdens of contacting police and revenue officials and paying for
their hospitality that leadership implies. In the 1964 Basic Democracy
election he was unanimously elected by the village but kept his promise
of protesting against the choice by disappearing for two days. The
period, he recalls, was of endless loss (*tawan*) and no benefit or gratitude.
The incident also illustrates the spirit of democracy in Bela. The non-
Kado groups had decided to elect a member of any lineage except that
of the Kado, and indeed they succeeded.

The authority of TAM Maliks is reinforced by the administrative
structure as a source of patronage which they use in their struggle with
their cousin rivals. They accept development schemes as a 'favour' and
extract a double advantage: firstly, that of the scheme itself and its
economic benefits, and second, by accepting it they impose a political
obligation on the administration. On the other hand, SAM village
leadership is not reinforced by the state apparatus as we know there is
no headman or *lambardar* in the village. Therefore no *mashar* can
mobilize the state or its symbols to his aid, as Shamshudin discovered
in terms of development schemes when he was left paying for them
from his own pocket. He not only incurred the displeasure of government but the disapproval of his own village (Chapter 11).

What are the rewards for emerging dominant in TAM and SAM? In
TAM the obvious rewards are recognition and contact with administration, which brings with it allowances, prestige, etc. Political officers
have been shot at so that an 'introduction' is effected, however crude.
As, indeed, I was by .303 bullets hitting a spot three feet from me in
Orakzai Tirah. A popular proverb exemplifies the act: 'As no one knew
him he urinated in the mosque and gained notoriety/fame' (*cha pajando
na no pa jumat kay ay michazay ukray*). Quoting my own case I can say
such negative tactics, though not resulting in the conferment of the
status or title of a Maliki, at least succeed as an effective introduction
paving the way for future communication. On the other hand, as in the
case of Shamshudin, contact with officials in the Nahakki Integrated
Rural Development Centre only brought with it diminishing returns in

every sense: debt default, unfinished schemes and unenthusiastic response which subjected him to pressure from above and by officials and from inside the village and from his own groups. Bela *mashars* constantly talk of loss in government schemes. It is not surprising that Hussain Khan by-passes this circuit to concentrate on acquiring land and wealth.

What is the fundamental and structural role of leadership with such limited sources of patronage in a highly egalitarian society? Firstly, the elder or *mashar* represents direct unilineal descent from the tribal eponym and is a symbol of lineage continuity. The patriarch comes to symbolize the living link with ancestors that provides the basis for dia-critica in social life between various groups with its manifold ramifications. Secondly, he symbolizes *Pukhtunwali* and attempts through social practice to uphold its virtues including *badal, melmastia*, etc.

I shall take the latter as an example since Chapter 7 deals with *badal* at length. In TAM Shahzada's name is synonymous with *melmastia*, even at the cost of keeping himself out of pocket. Hospitality is a major feature of leadership roles in most tribal and small communities (Sahlins, 1969: 186-225) especially Islamic societies (Barth, 1968). Shamshudin who was aware that *melmastia* no longer brought honour to the host would invariably assume the burden of paying for the tea, etc., provided for guests visiting Bela. He had almost sunk into the swirling whirlpool of debt from which there is often no return for the villager but he would not compromise the one principle of *Pukhtunwali* he could still uphold in his encapsulated condition (Chapter 9).

Thirdly, the *mashar* represents his *kor* or sub-section in conflict (*shar*)[11] and council. He is usually a member of the sub-sectional council to decide cases arising from disputes within his group. In TAM *shar* can rapidly involve the complex of agnatic relationships and degenerate into full-fledged shooting involving larger groups. The Atta Khan-Shahzada saga discussed in Chapter 7 escalated from the catching of some quail in a Shati Khel field. Elders therefore avoid becoming embroiled in trivial matters. In SAM, on the other hand, conflict generally arises from a petty affair and involves *mashars*. I recorded numerous such cases during my field-work and reproduce some of them in the next section to illustrate the origin and the nature of conflict in tribal society and the mechanism involved to arbitrate and decide disputes. The role of tribal leadership clearly emerges in the case-studies discussed below.

III Tribal conflict

(a) *Intra-lineage conflict: case-studies*

In comparison with TAM cases where the strength of factions is immediately apparent in the *jirga* which is based on *riwaj* decisions, those in SAM are more complex, involving as they do the overlap of three different systems, the tribal *riwaj*, the Islamic *shariat* and the national legal codes. As the latter present more complex factional interests I shall deal with them at greater length. In SAM *mashar* leadership is largely ineffective and no new leadership has emerged. Traditional leadership structure is by-passed and government agencies, such as the police, approached for decisions as a result. Representation of groups may operate thus: if money is required for a communal purpose (for example, the repair of the village boat) then each *mashar* is responsible for collecting equal amounts from his lineage. But there are neither *topaks* nor *mlatars* (factional fighters) in Bela and therefore the intra-village struggles remain mild and low-key. In SAM there is no clash over material wealth or ideological theory and lineage tension can be cemented in times of mutual trouble. For example, when Hussain Khan's son in the Scouts was in trouble Shamshudin saw officials to express village solidarity. Similarly, when Amin Khan was in trouble Shamshudin came to plead his case to my brother, then District Officer, Frontier Constabulary at Bara, and in charge of Amin's platoon. These attitudes are in contrast to TAM where *badal* approximates to the ideal and where there are no limits to enmity and no bounds to agnatic hatred through which it is expressed.

I was present during the following three cases of conflict in TAM, two of which involved Shahzada. In the first case a Kamali Halimzai had borrowed about Rs. 2,000 which he refused to return to the creditor, a Shati Khel, who appealed to Shahzada to form a *jirga*. Shahzada had the man caught and kept him in his *hujra* as a virtual prisoner until relatives turned up to provide security consisting of two guns, worth Rs. 10,000 each, until the money was repaid. The creditor was released after a captivity of eight days and the money was repaid. In another case which took place in a village near Shabana (Map 5, iii) two groups, Mohammad Siddiq and Rahim on one side and Abdul Mannan and Sewaley on the other, quarrelled. One group ejected their opponents from the village in violation of an existing truce. When the ejected group approached Shahzada he gathered a *jirga* party of some forty men and installed the expelled group back in the village. The *jirga* fined the guilty party Rs. 15,000, later reduced to Rs. 2,000, which was divided among the *jirga* members equally. In such cases disputants will prefer to enlist a strong Malik in a *jirga* rather than a powerless Mian whom Pukhtuns would disregard or put off. Alternatively, as in the third case, the aggrieved parties can simply take matters in their own hands as at Shabana, Shati Khel, when creditors captured a relative of the debtor and kept him locked up until the money was paid. In such cases the prisoner is fed and housed like other members of the family and only his movements outside the village are restricted. I now present two examples of cases from SAM.

Case-study no. 1: A dispute in early 1976 that began within the family but almost turned into a sub-sectional clash centred around half an acre of land just outside the limits of the Bela village. It reflects complex and intricate agnatic rivalries and leadership patterns. Yar Mohammad's mother, Basa, had called her cousin Guldar 'brother' and on her marriage was given this land by Guldar as a marriage gift, *lopata* (literally veil). Both belonged to the Madar Khel. Yar had allowed Guldar to cultivate the land on the basis of *nim-kara* (half the produce to be given to the owner). Eventually Yar wanted Guldar ejected and a *jirga* complied with his request. Guldar gathered support and claimed the land. In the meantime, tension between Madar and Kado Khel in Bela was growing due to problems in the distribution of *muajibs* between their respective kin across the Agency border in the Michni area. The Madar Khel therefore made an attempt to present a united front to the Kado by patching up the differences between Yar and Guldar.

Guldar already had a problem with Afsar Khan, the son of a Kado elder Noor Mohammad, and the Madar decided to back him with force. Anybody leaving the fight would be fined Rs. 10,000. Wilayat and Mir Ahmad, nephews of Noor Mohammad from his sister's side, objected to fighting their mother's brothers (*mamagan*). Afsar and Noor Mohammad began to mobilize their support and contacted Yar to offer him assistance against Guldar in the hope of splitting the Madar. Together they challenged Guldar at an appointed time and took up positions with guns by the disputed field. Guldar failed to turn up. Akbar Shah Bacha, representing the religious house of Bela, intervened and declared there would be no cultivation of the land until a decision was reached and imposed a *dazbandi* (literally 'end the shots'). A *jirga* was convened but was postponed due to a death in the family of one of its members. When it assembled Guldar provoked a quarrel which ended in fisticuffs. The *jirga* ordered him to prepare a meal, after killing a sheep (*gad*), to compensate for his untoward behaviour in their presence.

The *jirga* did not come to a decision and Guldar threatened to turn up with a *qulba* (a pair of bullocks and plough) to cultivate the land at sunrise on a certain day. He kept his promise. The Kado were also present in force with Yar and so were the Madar in support of Guldar. In the shooting that followed one bullock was killed and one wounded. Positions behind breast-works (*morchas*) were held until the evening and the Kado gave a general call for battle involving their powerful kin in the Agency. The situation was serious enough for Malik Khaista to arrive from the Agency. He imposed a *dazbandi*, took three guns from each party as security and declared a fine of Rs. 30,000 if the truce were broken. He promised a decision based on *shariat* as requested by both parties.

Shortly afterwards another shooting took place between a Kado and a Madar group. Malik Khaista assembled Mullahs in the Bela *hujra* from Shabkadar, as both factions wished for *shariat* law. The Mullahs inspected the fields and heard the parties after much reading of Koranic verses. They then gave a date for the decision at Shabkadar. On the fixed date Yar with some forty and Guldar with about thirty supporters turned up at Shabkadar. The Mullahs decided in favour of Yar as it was he who had ploughed the land with the *qulba*. Guldar challenged the decision and the Mullahs warned him that the land was now legally declared Yar's and he could be killed if he was seen on the disputed land. They also gave a date fifteen days later to Guldar to travel the length and breadth of Pakistan to locate a legal theocratic challenge to their decision from other religious divines. On that day neither Malik Khaista nor the Mullahs came to Bela. The decision was now accepted as final. The Madar were despondent and the Kado jubilant as they fired shots in the air in joy and prepared to arrange for dancing girls (*tamasha*) for the morrow to celebrate.

Case-study no. 2:   Another case involving conflict between two junior lineages, the Jano and the Sabah, took place during my field-work. Hussain Khan's son after saying his prayers in the mosque forgot to take his snuff box home with him. Mehr Gul's brother, Badshah Gul, found the box in the mosque and later told Yar Mohammad Khan that he did not know who the owner was. Both took a pinch of snuff from the box and Yar Mohammad Khan told him to keep it until the owner claimed it.

The next day at the *hujra* Hussain Khan's son mentioned that he had lost his snuff box at the mosque. Yar Mohammad Khan told him that Badshah Gul had taken it and that they both had taken a pinch of snuff from it. Three or four days later Badshah Gul was returning from his Michni land and was passing Hussain's house. Hussain's two sons and nephews while working in the fields called out to him and asked for the box. Badshah replied that he had given it to Yar Mohammad. A quarrel ensued involving blows and punches. Badshah Gul had the upper hand until Hussain's other sons and nephews joined in. Mehr Gul came to the aid of his brother, Badshah, and joined the mêlée.

In the afternoon Hussain Khan went to Shashti Gul and asked for *nanawatee*. He admitted that his sons had been rough on Shashti's brother and was prepared to do anything if they made up with each other. Shashti refused but with much persuasion from Shamshudin, Hamesh Gul, Dawai Khan and Said Mohammad agreed to make up if Hussain gave him compensation (*uzar*). Hussain agreed.

That evening Badshah Gul's wife came to the house of Shamshudin and said that they would accept the *uzar* but that Badshah Gul 'who is very hot-tempered' – she used the word 'mad' – 'says that he will not forgive Hussain and his sons'. In such a contingency, she said, she would not be able to afford the same *uzar* in return to Hussain Khan. Shamshudin went to Shashti who decided that the *uzar* should be put off for the day and that Shashti Gul would let Shamshudin know of his decision the following evening. The next evening the groups led by Shashti and Hussain made up between themselves.

None the less tension remained among the groups and the Sabah Khel women, led by the women of their *mashar* Majeed, decided to escalate the matter by provoking Hussain Khan's women the following afternoon. Majeed's women asked the women of Hussain Khan to remove their fire-wood which was lying in front of Majeed's house. Upon refusal to do so a fight began and the women hit each other with sticks and stones. Hussain Khan's male relatives soon arrived on the scene and beat up Majeed's wife and women. When Majeed's men heard of this they too joined the fight. Majeed's wife and daughter-in-law were severely hurt as were Hussain's daughter-in-law and two grandsons.

During the fight Hussain's sons fetched their guns and fired shots in the air while Hussain Khan went promptly to the police station fourteen miles away at Nahakki to report the case. Majeed's side, specially

Mehr Gul's son, tried to stop him unsuccessfully. That day both parties reported the case at the station and five people from each were detained for the night and they were released on bail the next day. The village tried to unite them but Hussain refused and again reported Mehr Gul and Majeed; this time nine people from each faction were detained in the police station for the night. Costs involved on both sides were Rs. 600 each. After involving the police a second time the matter came to a close.

To conclude: recently, and especially in SAM cases, there has been talk of *jirga* members taking bribes either to influence or delay decisions. This has shaken confidence in the *jirga* as our cases from SAM show. In any case the institution of the *jirga* will be as strong as the authority and respect in society for the *mashar*. The prestige of the two is interconnected. When a *jirga* fails to solve a local dispute another may be convened from neighbouring groups, related at a deeper genealogical level. In TAM failing *solla* (temporary truce)[12] one of two things can happen and events may take a highly unpredictable turn involving large-scale operations: either a tribal *lakhkar* representing the major clans will impose a *solla* or government will come in to impose a government agreement (*sarkari solla*). A social mechanism has to exist for a neutral body to arbitrate between Pukhtuns. In such cases the Mians may play the mediators (*munsipans*) as in Swat (Barth, 1972: 96). This is all very well in theory. In practice few examples can be cited of factions seeking out Mians to mediate. Their lack of strength is decisive in persuading parties in conflict to seek out neutral but powerful Maliks who could effectively form a *jirga* and thereby bring a halt to the conflict. I shall discuss the role of the Mians in the next chapter.

Theoretically an all-Pukhtun tribal homologue to the sectional *jirga* could form to contain an inter-clan conflict. Such conflicts are rare, especially as they involve considerable groups of people over large areas and can result in many deaths. No such instance among the Mohmand clans has taken place in the memory of the elders. The last time the Baezai and Khwaezai clans attacked the Halimzai was in 1932 and 1935. However, this example is not what I have in mind as the Baezai and Khwaezai were really attacking and accusing certain groups among the Halimzai as British stooges and their aim was to prevent the construction of the government's Gandab road (Chapter 3). An example that illustrates the principles of intra-tribal conflict at the clan level is quoted from the period I was posted among the Orakzais, 1976–7.

When inter-clan conflict flares up it is a combination of Pukhtun *riwaj*, Islamic *shariat* and government pressure that may combine to resolve or settle it, as the case-study below illustrates.

(b) *Inter-clan conflict: case-study*

Three clans, the A'Khel on one side and the Rabia and Daradar Mamozai on the other, of the eighteen clans forming the Orakzai tribe (total population 278, 951) living in the Orakzai Agency clashed suddenly in May 1977. I was told that a clash which assumed such serious proportions last took place over three decades ago. The three clans, and indeed the other clans in the Ismailzai, Central and Upper Tehsils of the four Tehsils in the Agency, are organized along the principles of segmentary acephalous tribal societies living in low-production areas. Their structural, social and cultural situation is typical of Pukhtun *nang* society and identical to the Mohmand in the Agency. According to the Orakzai genealogy these clans are first cousins, like the Halimzai and Tarakzai, and usually on cordial terms.

The cause of the clash was typical of tribal conflict: three acres of a barren but long-disputed plot called the Mullah's field (*Mullah patay*). It began when some Daradar Mamozai quietly built a breast-work (*morcha*) at night on 1 May. Next morning their allies persuaded them to vacate the *morchas* in the face of strong A'Khel protests. The A'Khel now violated the truce and took possession of the area. At this stage the Rabia Khel attacked and three people from their ranks were killed. More than a dozen were wounded in the shooting from both sides. In a counter-attack the Rabia Khel captured six A'Khels. Death is the final dividing line between a casual and serious affair in such conflicts as it involves the irrevocable laws of *badal*. The clans now sat in trenches and took up strategic positions eye-ball to eye-ball along a ten-mile clan border within the Agency. The area of conflict was almost eighty square miles and paralysed transport movements and other activity within half the Agency.

Traditionally, political administration is supposed to interfere in only the most discreet and indirect manner, especially if the conflict is not around or in what are called protected areas such as government roads and property. In practice I found this position difficult to maintain. For a start the other Orakzai clans, each belonging to one or the other faction in the Agency, Gar or Samil, were beginning to show signs of interest. The A'Khel belonged to Gar and the Rabia and Daradar

Mamozai to the Samil. Their involvement could literally have the entire
Agency up in flames. Other non-Orakzai tribes like the Afridis living in
Tirah on the borders of the Orakzai were also showing interest in one
faction or the other. Various *kashar* groups were in contact with political parties, legally excluded from the Tribal Areas, in an attempt to
generally discredit government and tie in with the political turmoil of
the country, following the National Elections in March. *Kashar* groups
among the warring clans took charge and negated any attempts by
Maliks to come to terms with the 'enemy'. The feelings and expressions
of hatred were surprisingly bitter and deep. All communications between
the clans ceased.

The entire resources of both factions were now diverted to the
confrontation. 'Commanders', a term incorporated in Pukhto by the
many ex-soldiers, were appointed. Fully armed old men and young
boys with a day's food rations took daily and fixed turns in manning
the forward lines. If a brother was outside the Agency, then a male
from the house would have to fill in and take the turn twice. Kin in the
Arab Gulf States responded by contributing 100 rials per person for
the war effort and within a week the A'Khel boasted that they had
collected Rs. 200,000 from such remittances. At least four sophisticated
rapid-fire G-3 rifles were in use in the area, each costing about Rs.
40,000, and the Rabia Khel *mashars* talked of buying a cannon.

I realized that it would be impossible for the administration to sit
the affair out and therefore mobilized my resources to restore peace in
the area by firstly moving up with my entire political staff to the actual
area of shooting. After endless hours of hearing and talking about the
dispute in private and public *jirga* sessions, first the A'Khel and then the
Rabia Khel agreed to stop firing 'if the others did not provoke them'.
I was now involved in a direct and, in terms of traditional wisdom,
unorthodox manner and any more deaths would result in the administration being blamed. By now wide coverage was being given to the
affair in the national press (*Khyber Mail, Mashriq, Pakistan Times*,
May 1977). These day-long visits conducted separately with each
faction brought about an informal ceasefire. The clans still refused to
discuss terms with each other and I failed to bring them under one
roof. Once the shooting stopped I mobilized my entire resources to
assemble some fifty to sixty tribal leaders – Maliks, *mashars* and
religious leaders – and sent them in two passenger buses I hired for
the purpose to act as a *jirga* in the disputed area. Left on their own
the *jirga* members may have run into objections such as partiality or

demands for religious leaders to be present and perhaps have taken two to three days to arrive at the disputed area, during which time more lives could have been lost. I had made sure that the *jirga* represented both Gar and Samil factions and also different types of tribal leadership. The presence of the *jirga* in their midst arguing and counselling for six days more or less forced the clans to start negotiations regarding such issues as the disputed land, the cost of the shooting, compensation for the dead, and the fate of prisoners and the wounded.

Perhaps as important as the presence of some of the most distinguished Orakzai grey-beards in their midst in reconciling the parties to negotiate was the increasing cost of the military operations. One bullet for a .303 gun alone cost over Rs. 10. Daily duties on the front line meant neglecting employment or other normal domestic activity. Besides, the cost of maintaining hospitality to the stream of visitors, *jirga* and political officers trying to bring peace to the area was crippling. Cows and sheep had to be slaughtered twice daily, good quality rice and bread cooked so as not to offend the dignity of the visitors. *Jirgas* can break up at such imagined slights as poor hospitality. Individuals from the powerful and inaccessible Ali Khel clan began to arrive in sympathy for the A'Khel. I was told privately by at least a dozen A'Khel Maliks that if the confrontation lasted a week they would be economically crippled: their powerful allies the Ali Khel were eating twenty to thirty cows a day in one area alone.

There are traditionally three ways in which a *jirga* can decide such a case. Religious divines (*alim*) can give a decision based on the Holy Koran and the *shariat*. Second, by *Pukhto lar* (literally meaning the path of Pukhto and derived from *Pukhtunwali*) to be decided by a *jirga* representing both sides equally in numbers. Third, by *wak* (authority) given to any body or group by the disputants. *Wak* may be given to the Political Agent or a *jirga*, who may reach a decision by any means they deem fit. Giving *wak* or requesting the political authorities to oversee a *solla* makes a government truce (*hakomati solla*) more formal than tribal truce (*qami solla*). In this particular case both factions agreed on the last possibility, to give *wak* for three months to the *jirga* to announce their decision. In the meantime hostility of any kind would be punished by fines imposed by the *jirga* and the status quo of *Mullah patay* would be maintained. Any individual or group breaking the truce would be fined Rs. 50,000 or have his property destroyed in lieu thereof and the ten .303 rifles given by the clan as security to the *jirga mashars* be forfeited. A strong deterrent indeed. A *teega* is thus effected between the parties (Appendix).

The crisis was over as abruptly as it had begun. I had noted the sense of comradeship and kinship among wounded Rabia and A'Khel youths in the Hangu hospital as they lay side by side during the conflict. When I chided them for fighting in the Agency and sharing meals, cigarettes and a radio in the hospital they looked sheepish and had no answer except what they did was Pukhto. After the truce elders of the three clans would still not talk to each other in public. So, to finally and symbolically close the chapter of events, I organized what is called in the Tribal Areas a 'grand tribal *Jirga*' at Samana, the ridge famous for some sharp encounters in the 1897 campaigns, followed by lunch to which elders from the three combatant clans, along with other clan elders and the *jirga* members, were invited. Elders met, laughed and joked across the dining table for the first time since the shooting began a month ago. Seeing them I was made aware that here was a homologous situation to the working of agnatic rivalry in Pukhtun society, intimacy and warmth in kinship that shared the same womb but was divided by a thin line from hatred and bitterness.

I shall conclude by briefly restating three key and interconnected points raised in the chapter. Firstly, political hegemony is expressed and acknowledged internally by a voice in the tribal *jirga* and externally in dealings on behalf of the sub-section with other sub-sections or with the administration. In any case leadership in the *jirga* or out of it is restricted to those on the tribal charter. Secondly, the basic causes of conflict are usually neither land nor wealth. They are summed up in intangible concepts involved in *tarboorwali* and Pukhto. Finally, leadership cannot be transmitted. Shahzada Malik's sons and grandsons are all uneducated and derive current status from his personality and political status. In sharp contrast, Abdullah's sons are educated and are now doing well in government service. The junior Shati lineage Malok have turned to business successfully. The future is obviously theirs, a fact tacitly recognized by the actors including Shahzada. Leadership cannot be transmitted and is inherent in the individual. Tribal society remains democratic to the end. The good and great qualities of a leader are buried with him in his grave.

The discussion of unilineal descent and its importance for lineage and leadership organization above has supported my thesis. Pukhtun genealogical consciousness, ideology and structure and the proliferation in numbers of Maliks have combined to restrain and diminish the importance of the Malik. Pukhtun egalitarianism, a cardinal principle of *Pukhtunwali*, is thus maintained as I hope I have illustrated above. In cases of lineage and leadership organization TAM largely and SAM partly approximate to the ideal-type model as the case-studies illustrate. Deviance in SAM is explained directly as a result of its encapsulated condition. For instance the role of the *jirga* in SAM is affected by the presence of alternative and legal institutions of the state to redress wrong. Placement on the tribal charter among the Mohmand acts as a diacritical factor to distinguish Mohmand from non-Mohmand with far-reaching social and political ramifications. I shall discuss the role of non-Mohmand groups, religious and occupational, in society in the next chapter.

6 Non-Pukhtun groups: patron and client relationships

'They do not carry guns and exist to serve us' (*diw topak na garzai aw zamong khidmatgaran di*) — common Mohmand saying.

In this chapter I shall explain the integral situation of the religious and occupational groups within Pukhtun social structure and the functioning of their rights and duties in society. However, in spite of their integration, or perhaps because of it, the role of the non-Mohmand groups in society is clearly demarcated through the social mechanism of the tribal charter and its lineage ramifications. The differentiation of roles which results in discrete spheres of activity is part of my study. I have furnished arguments in the last chapter and will continue the argument in this chapter to illustrate how non-Mohmand groups function in an ideal situation (TAM) and how, and to what extent, changes in their role appear in encapsulated situations (SAM).

At the outset let me state that the majoritarian ideology and population are Pukhtun in the Tribal Areas. Of a total population of 1,463 in Shati Khel and Bela Mohmandan, only 117 or about 8 per cent were non-Mohmand, that is, they belong to religious or occupational groups. In Shati Khel itself there were only 40 in a population of 1,031, that is less than 4 per cent, whereas in Bela there were 77 out of 432 and about 18 per cent. My data is borne out by another survey of 19,254 Musa Khel (Upper Mohmands) in which 96 per cent of the population were Mohmands and the rest non-Mohmand groups (Mohmand, 1966). None the less it is the paradox of society that men generally believe in the principle of equality but encounter and accept the presence of inequality.

The important point I wish to make is that both the Pukhtuns and these groups view themselves as interrelated. I also assume that the existence of a patron–client relationship presupposes mutual interdependence and a certain monopoly of patronage on the one hand and of services on the other within the societal whole. Although marginal to traditional Pukhtun activity such as agnatic rivalry, these groups are integral parts of society and are involved in the entire range of *rites de passage*. They view themselves as essential social appendices to the clan they are attached to. In certain cases they have created fictitious lineage links to their patron clans. Such links are fictitious within society but for purposes of outsiders, defined in geographical or tribal phyletic terms, they imply a tacit admission of filiation by society including the patron clan. I refer to both religious and occupational groups as non-Mohmand in the study since technically neither feature on the tribal charter, a fact that excludes them from certain attendant privileges such as rations, *khassadaries*, etc., and duties, such as those of the *khassadars* or being liable to pay collective fines for an arrant Pukhtun member of the lineage.

I Sayyeds, Mians and Mullahs: 'saintly' model

(a) *Mians*

The Prophet's saying that 'there are no genealogies in Islam' has theological and social implications. It implies the equality of believers before the omnipotence of God and that of man in relation to man in society. Koranic verses repeat the equality of man. However, the political sociology of Islam indicates the unique importance of descent in legitimizing or succeeding in political activity.[1] The descendants of the Prophet, the Sayyeds, provide the basis for social stratification in Islamic society and are generally considered a superior group.[2] Ideally there is no social division within a Muslim community but a hierarchy is conceptualized and partly explained, as indeed is social mobility, through economic differentiation as quoted in the proverb common to the Muslims of Pakistan and north India: 'Last year I was a *jolaha* (weaver), this year I am a *sheikh* (disciple of the Prophet) and next year if the prices rise I will be a *Sayyed*.' The saying is reflected in societies with forms of stratification (Béteille, 1977: 143) and embodies the concept of upward mobility and 'Sanskritization' (Srinivas, 1966).

There are no Sayyeds among the Mohmands. None the less Mohmand religious groups generally assume the name, and with it the status, of the next senior ranked group in the idealized Islamic hierarchy. For instance, the ignorance among Mohmands in differentiating a Sayyed from a Mian presumes two facts: a general ignorance of fine and fundamental religious matters and the limited importance attached to religious

status. Apart from some *mashars* like Shahzada and Shamshudin few
people in TAM and SAM could distinguish a Sayyed from a Mian. Mians
therefore get away by describing themselves as Sayyeds and unless
pressed for a specific definition, when he is confused, the tribesman
describes them thus. A member of the religious group is generally
defined by the Pukhtun as 'a Mian or Mullah man' (*Mian Mullah saray*).
It is as much a definition of a role as it is the delineating of status
groups and social boundaries of action. Religious groups may also be
called *stanadar* and respected for a negative reason.

Their curses (*khayray*) are said to be effective. Mohmands often
explain the fall of the Ranra lineage and the rise of the Musa by the
cursing of the former when they incurred the displeasure of the Mians
almost 100 years ago (Chapter 7). So while Pukhtuns may not show
Mians undue deference they will also not molest or insult them. Although
there are no Sayyeds in Shati Khel or Bela Mohmandan the Mian of
Bela calls himself and is called a Sayyed. For this reason I am wary of
accepting a Sayyed category among the Mohmands as most Mians prefer
to be called *badshah* (king), a title given to Sayyeds among Pukhtuns.
Over the generations the descendants of Mians have assumed Sayyed
status.

The role and position of the religious groups among Pukhtun society
clearly raise interesting questions. The Mian is aware that he is of
superior social status to a member of the occupational group (*qasabgar*).
In private he would even argue that as he bears the torch of faith and
because of his putative genealogical links with the Prophet (as a Sayyed)
he is the equal, if not the superior, of the Pukhtun. Mian Jalil would
say: 'We think we are socially higher, they think they are higher'.

The Mians, a community of about 100 people in the Gandab, live in
three small hamlets which have split from the main Mian village of Mian
Kassai (Map 5, iii). Segmentary fissures and agnatic jealousy are not
a monopoly of the Pukhtuns. The present social position of the
Mians is largely a consequence of their ownership and organization of
the only and most central market among the Mohmand, Mian Mandi.
They are a self-contained social unit and do not keep *hamsayas* or
qasabgars. There are some examples, beginning in the 1960s, of Mians
giving to and taking daughters from Pukhtuns, the latter being from
affiliated lineages such as the Ghunda Khel. Previously Mians were an
entirely endogamous group often going to Afghanistan to their kin
in Laghman to arrange marriages. Mians are generally educated in
the Holy Koran and Islamic learning and, compared to the Shati

Maliks, appear softer, plumper, cleaner, darker and physically better groomed. The senior Mian of Kassai, universally called Mian Kassai, has had five wives and innumerable descendants. His eldest son, Mian Abdul Hakim, has nineteen sons, and traces his descent, three generations removed, to Arabia. It is significant that in the formal questionnaires the Mians traced their descent to Arabia and not, as do almost all Pukhtuns, to Kabul. Mian Jalil, a cousin of Mian Hakim, is a fine example of Mian virtues. He explained ideal Mian role and behaviour among Pukhtun society. The Mian is soft-spoken, never loses his temper, never quarrels, never takes sides in Pukhtun factions and never carries a gun. The primary characteristic of the Mian is his pacifism; he is an almost ideal prototype Christian figure. The Mian normally dresses in white, the colour of peace, and comports himself with deliberate dignity. He is acutely aware of the predicament imposed on him by his position in society. If he deviates from the expected ideal by repeated quarrelsome behaviour or is seen to be drinking and debauching or manipulating people for political power, his neutrality and status are compromised and the respect and privileges withdrawn. For all their putative social influence the Mians remain uncomfortable in Pukhtun areas and whenever they accompanied me to Shati Khel they did so most reluctantly and with a dozen excuses. They repeated that they had no business to be there and did not wish to run the risk of being insulted. The TAM Mian provides the ideal-type model of correct social behaviour, moral propriety and studied disinterest in political matters.

The Mian cannot compete in a game and its arena into which he is not allowed by the rules or participants of that game. In spite of their social airs the Mians do not receive any of the privileges of the Pukhtuns in the Tribal Areas such as allowances, *lungis, muajibs* or rations, which has always been a sore point with them. The local sub-section or section would resent the thought of including even the handful of eminent Mians among *lungi*-holders or *muajib*-takers. If the Mians are given political allowances, this is done secretly and the clan is assured that in no way are their interests diverted or diminished. Fourteen Mians who belong to Gandab are on the Mohmand Agency electoral list (pp. 46-7). The inclusion of the Mians is a deviance in the Tribal Areas for usually they are not included on such voting lists since they do not share Pukhtun rights or duties. For instance, Akhundzada Saeed, son of the respected Akhundzada Mahmud involved in the famous case of the kidnapping of Miss Ellis in 1923, could not stand for elections in 1977 in the Orakzai Agency as he was categorized as an Akhundzada, an eminent religious leader. This was in spite of the fact that he was the recipient of various secret governmental favours originating from the role of his father in the recovery of the girl.

In anthropological literature the social role of the Mian might be structurally likened to the *agurram* among the Berbers (Gellner, 1969a). This would be a mistake. The role of the *igurramen* and the Mians is conceptually and empirically very different. The Mians do not supervise the election of the Pukhtun chiefs or provide leadership against outside aggression; nor can they claim to perform miracles (ibid.: 78). The single attribute the Mians and the *igurramen* share is pacifism. However, on the surface, the ideal Mian is defined, as indeed is the *agurram*, as one descended from the Prophet, mediating between man and God, between man and man, dispensing blessing, a good and pious man, uncalculatingly generous and hospitable and one who does not fight or engage in feuds (ibid.: 74). This in the ideal is very much how the Mians would like to see themselves. If the Malik, discussed in the last chapter, may be said to conform to a 'chiefly' model then the Mian conforms to a 'saintly' model in Pukhtun society; with the added and important clause that the latter are in no way pretenders to political authority unlike religious groups in complex *qalang* societies such as Swat (Barth, 1972). To the saintly model of the Mian, knowledge (*ilm*) is the central feature just as the gun is to the Pukhtun model. The Mian contrasts himself and his *ilm* with the diametrically opposed model of the Pukhtun and 'the gun he carries'. 'The work of the gun' (*the topak kar*) is the Pukhtun's, he will explain, and is seen as diacritical in determining social categories. This too is why he is an impotent judge or arbiter in disputes as he has no force to back his decisions, unlike the Pukhtun *jirga*.

In certain Islamic tribal societies like the Somalis there is a clear-cut distinction between men of God (*wadaad*) and men of the spear or warriors (*waranleh*) but 'in practice warriors and priests rub shoulders together in the same lineage' (Lewis, I. M., 1969a: 263) and both groups belong to the *dia*-paying group. Among the Mohmand the Mians, the men of God and the Pukhtuns, the men of the gun, do not rub shoulders in lineages, marriages or settlements. Both remain distinct groups with distinct functions. How then do the Mians, representing Islamic tradition and custom, and the Pukhtuns tribal custom, accommodate each other and at what point do they clash or come together? The Mian consciously inflates and exaggerates Islamic symbols within society to maintain his position and importance as interpreter of religion, although painfully aware that in many ways he is outside the Pukhtun social world.

They see themselves as 'middle people' between the Pukhtuns, men of the world (*dunya*), and esoteric Sufi figures who have renounced it for religion (*din*). Their primary functions as viewed by them are: to arbitrate between warring factions; to provide religious blessing for medicinal purposes; and to remind Pukhtuns of Islam and their duties as Muslims. They may sometimes perform the more routine functions of the *rites de passage* normally reserved for the Mullah. Unlike the Mullahs they are paid neither in cash nor kind by Pukhtun groups. Conceptually and ideally the functions of the Mians are to act as a neutral or buffer group or zone between two or more tribal segments. Their physical location and village is symbolic of this neutral position being situated at the boundary where two or three sections or sub-clans meet. For example, in the Gandab the Mians of Kassai are placed between the Yusuf Khel and Shati Khel, the Hamza Khel and the Kadai Khel. In practice their role in affecting a cease-fire or even an agreement is limited as they are not backed by any physical or coercive force. They, however, play a useful role in keeping the lines of communication open between two fighting factions to evacuate the wounded, the sick, the women and children. Mian Jalil described how the Mians would wear white clothes and carrying a white flag visit and talk to both parties whenever there was shooting in Shati Khel between factions. In cases of death they would remove the corpse during the cease-fire. In the 1973 shooting when Yad Gul, the Ranra *mashar*, died, four Mians, including Jalil, negotiated between Mazullah on the one side and Major Sultan Jan and Shahzada on the other for a cease-fire. Mian Jalil's car was used to convey and announce the news of the agreement and request people to go home and later to take the wounded to hospital. In normal times they attempt to live lives that would ideally depict the saintly model. But as Mian Jalil himself admitted the recent economic activities and involvements of the Mians especially in their market, Mian Mandi, have not only decreased their prestige in the eyes of the Pukhtuns but have made the Mians themselves more worldly and correspondingly less spiritual. Today they own flour mills, cars, buses and, of course, the most lucrative property in the Agency, the Mian Mandi (Chapter 9).

So we may come to the conclusion that although the Mians claim social equality with Pukhtuns they can in no way attempt to appropriate or legitimate political power, for which they have neither the guns, the men, nor the economic resources. When I questioned the Shati Khel Maliks whether a Wali of Swat could have emerged among the Mohmand, they simply answered with rather rude references to the 'manliness' of Swatis. Shahzada explained the typical *nang* social structure which would never permit the emergence of local Pukhtun or non-Pukhtun leadership among the Mohmand to the status of ruler. His explanation is corroborated by the difficulties such famous religious leaders as Chaknawar and the Haji of Turangzai faced in attempting to compose even a temporary united front of the Mohmand clans against the British (Chapter 3).

(b) *Mullahs*

The role of the Mullah is clearly defined and involves him fully in the *rites de passage* (Table 4 at the end of this chapter). At birth he is to recite the *azan* in the ear of the new born within twenty-four hours of birth. He reads the prayer (*doa*) after the circumcision of the boy. He 'ties the marriage knot' (*nikah tari*) which formalizes and legalizes the ceremony. He prepares the corpse and performs the death rites (*janaza*) by wrapping it in a white sheet about ten yards long on which he writes the *kalima* and then outside the village, in an open space, with the corpse lying in front, leads the congregation in a special prayer. On such occasions Mullahs often gather from neighbouring villages and items such as soap and a little money are distributed among them. The Mullah then accompanies the body to the cemetery with the male members of the community, the females visiting the grave later. He performs the final funeral rites by praying on a handful of mud and spreading it on the grave.

Apart from rites the Mullah also tends to the mosque and calls the *azan* five times a day and leads the congregation in prayer. Depending on his powers of persuasion and medicinal knowledge he distributes talismans (*tawez*) for curing diseases especially of children and cattle, or for keeping the evil eye away from them, for which he charges one or two rupees. Mohmand *mashars* believe that *tawez* given by a religious person, like Mian Kassai or the Imam of Bela, can cure diseases especially in women, children and cattle. Hamesh Gul assured me that the Bela Imam had been giving him a talisman, for a small fee, which worked in removing worms from his cattle and increasing the output of their milk. Fever and headaches are commonly believed to be cured by the Imam,

who says a prayer and usually gives a talisman with some Arabic writing
on it. His payment is called 'payment in thanks' (*shokrana*).

Just as the Mian upgrades himself to Sayyed status, so the Mullah in
a similar self-imposed upgrading, and usually after migration to a new
locality, calls himself a Mian. The ignorance and indifference of the
Pukhtuns ratifies this upward mobility and in time the new status is
accepted, genealogical fiction being converted to social legitimization.
The Mullah or Imam of Bela prefers to be called a Mian.

The TAM Mullah, in contrast to the Mian who has a legitimate place
and influence in the Pukhtun world, is usually a complete outsider,
often brought in from the Settled Districts for fixed periods, usually
during the month of fasting on a contractual basis. He may receive Rs.
150 to 200 monthly from the patriarch and, when animals are sacrificed
in the month of the big Eed, their skins as added payment. His role is
strictly limited to activities around the mosque such as conducting
prayers and perhaps teaching children the Holy Koran. There is no
doubt in his mind as to his client status. His terms and conditions and
period of stay depend entirely on his patron, the Malik of the household. Shahzada Malik keeps a Mullah for longer periods than do most
Maliks. Most Shati settlements do without a Mullah. Some, like Ranra,
provide the services of a Mullah locally – Zardullah, Malik Mazullah's
son, in this case.

Shati Khel Mullahs such as Mullah Ahmad, who came to Chino some
three decades ago, are so named and considered because of their relative
Islamic education but are often fugitives from the law and criminals
(*mujrims*). Taj Mohammad and Abdullah, two other Shati Khel Mullahs,
also arrived seeking shelter from the arms of the law. Very rarely do
Mullahs have enough money to buy land and as temporary employees
would not be permitted to do so in Shati Khel or the Gandab. The
Mullah's is an itinerant profession in Shati Khel but the family of the
present Imam of Bela is said to have come to the village some three
generations ago. The Imam himself is too old and infirm to conduct his
duties which have devolved on his grandson, Ibrahim. The Imam's son
prefers to till his fields as an agriculturalist and has given up any claim
to religiosity. The Bela Mullah is called Imam as a sign of respect for his
age. He was given one and a half acres by the village, but then he has
been serving Belawals for almost seventy years. The Mullah in Bela
receives no regular cash payments but is given the tenth part of every
crop of maize from every household head. The Bela Mian, called a
Sayyed, was presented about one and a half acres of land and is paid

nominally in kind (a quarter of a seer[3] per household) after every crop.

In *hujra* conversations Pukhtun *mashars* would question the role of the Mullah: 'He is illiterate. What does he know of Islam? Why should he intercede between us and God?' Pukhtun Islam may be perhaps equated to the 'muscular Christianity' of the Victorian era: it is a laic, uncomplicated, surface reaction to an inherited tradition that is suspicious of dogmas, debates and formalized priesthood. Mohmand *mashars* would express their opinion of the religious groups just as Khushal Khan Khattak did centuries ago, though perhaps with less eloquence:

> I have observed the disposition
> Of present-day divines;
> An hour spent in their company
> And I'm filled with disgust (Mackenzie, 1965: 79).

They would reflect equal cynicism regarding traditional claims to payment by the religious groups:

> The plunder these *sheikhs* carry off
> While chanting God's great name (ibid.).

The duties of the Mullah have been briefly enumerated. Primarily he attends to the demands in society regarding religious functions in the *rites de passage*. His behaviour and personality determine the respect he can command in the community. I shall now consider the role of the occupational groups in society.

II Occupational groups

In the traditional and ideal Pukhtun schema, occupational groups are 'those who pursue a craft or profession' (*qasabgars*) and 'those who serve the Pukhtuns' (*khidmatgars*). Shahzada or Mazullah would describe a *qasabgar* as 'one who is a servant or underling' (*qasabgar mohtaj de. Khidmatgar de*). Others like Haji Umar of the junior Malok lineage would be gentler: 'They are good people. They work and earn their living. They are weak.' These descriptions contrast with the definition of the Pukhtun of himself as a man who 'carries a gun'. The occupational groups, conceptually neutral between lineage groups and in their political rivalries, travel unarmed and serve them impartially and equally. Similar occupational groups with no clan alignment are attached to other tribal segmentary societies called the *foquaha* among the Berbers (Gellner, 1969a: 298) and the *sab* among the Somali (Lewis, I. M., 1962b: 381). Professionally they may be equated to the *kamin* in Indian villages (Mayer, A. C., 1970: 63-74) who are also paid in kind with so many pounds of the crop 'per plough' (ibid.: 67) and *kammis* in Pakistani villages (Ahmad, S., 1977).

Clearly it would be a mistake to categorize *qasabgars* as down-trodden groups such as serfs or manumitted slaves. It is important to point out the dyadic and voluntary nature of the association between the *qasabgar* and the Pukhtun. The relationship has no memory of slavery as among groups attached to other Islamic tribes like the Baluch (Pehrson, 1966: 30) or the Kababish Arabs (Asad, 1970: 190-3). The *qasabgar* may even trace descent from mythical religious ancestors (Barth, 1972: 21). *Qasabgars* can and do insult or humiliate Pukhtuns in their own way and get away with it. The late Hakim Khan, a SAM carpenter, when offered a small sum of money at a wedding would throw it on the ground and make a scene saying: 'This is too little, it is an insult, what sort of a Pukhtun are you?' The acutely embarrassed host would immediately placate him by offering more money.

The *qasabgar* may be considered socially inferior in the traditional Pukhtun schema but in social life, along with the Mullahs, they are referred to by Pukhtuns of all ages as teachers (*ustaz*). So just as Arsal the barber visiting Shati Khel is called *ustaz*, so is the Imam of Bela Mohmandan. Pukhtuns, especially *kashar* and those belonging to junior lineages with ignorance of or indifference to their own hegemony, often refer to religious and occupational groups as *qasabgars* much to the chagrin of the former who, in private, uphold their social superiority over all other groups. Arsal, the Sangar barber, who attends to Shati Khel, would also dispassionately argue with me that, apart from the Pukhtuns who were socially superior because it was traditionally their land, the *qasabgar* and Mians or Mullahs were in the same category.

The barbers or carpenters of the Gandab valley, living in Sangar, are adamant regarding their Halimzai affiliation. 'Of course we are Halimzai. Who denies this?' they would indignantly query. Indeed, the Bela carpenters who migrated from the Gandab three generations ago call themselves Halimzai Mohmands with no tribal genealogical charts to substantiate the claim, a claim which is universally but privately rejected within the Pukhtun community. However, for outsiders non-Mohmand groups are part of the local tribal community so the carpenters in the

Gandab valley and those of Bela may be accepted as Halimzais. In more complex *qalang* societies, occupational groups like 'carpenter, black-smith and potter' claim 'spurious' descent from the king and prophet David, of the Old Testament (Barth, 1972: 21), but the Mohmand groups have no such genealogical memory or pretensions. Fictitious links to the patron clan provide a basis for social equality which is supported by two independent factors: firstly, being Muslim there are ideally no religious, ritual or commensal barriers between groups and no rigid caste-like stratification that distinguishes groups in Indian society (Béteille, 1974, 1977; Dumont, 1970; Dube, 1965; Mayer, A. C., 1970). There are even examples of inter-marriages between Pukhtun and non-Pukhtun groups and perhaps the most dramatic is that of Anmir's marriage to the daughter of Gul Mohammad, the father of Aziz Ingar.[4] Secondly, general economic poverty in TAM and SAM allows the occupational groups to manipulate their position as suppliers of monopoly services into those of economic equality and indeed superiority, as in Bela, with the Pukhtuns (Chapter 9). It is political power and prestige based on the descent charter and the laws of *Pukhtun-wali*, specifically centring around *tarboorwali*, that distinguish Pukhtun and non-Pukhtun groups and place the former in the role of patron. Otherwise in dress, food, domestic and agricultural modes of living they are identical to Pukhtun groups. Sitting in the *hujra* it would be diffi-cult to separate the Mohmand from non-Mohmand groups.

The tribal groups that I am examining are, of course, part of what I refer to as *nang* Pukhtun society but *qalang* society, of which as I have argued earlier Swat is a good example, presents a complex structure of ranked social groups and sub-divisions with wide-ranging ramifications (Barth, 1972). The classic simplicity of *nang* structure is perhaps best reflected in the Shati Khel which is inhabited only by Pukhtuns and two other groups, Mullahs temporarily engaged usually for the month of fasting and brought from the Settled Districts, and the family of Aziz. This contrasts with the complexity and stratification of life in Swat. TAM simplicity denotes as much the material poverty of *nang* society and its relatively fewer needs, and therefore fewer groups offering specialized services, as it does the purity of ideal-type Pukhtun life. For instance, there are no Gujars, a distinctly non-Pukhtun ethnic group. Gujars live in groups along the Yusufzai belt between Swat and Mardan to act as lowly herders of cattle and sheep for the Khans in the *qalang* areas. As the economic unit is atomistic among the Mohmand, women tend domestic cattle and sheep.

Barth has listed twenty-seven social groups which he has called 'castes' in Swat society; I reproduce them below in Table 3 to illustrate the development and incorporation of such groups into traditional Pukhtun social organization (Barth, 1972: 17). The fact that there are only two of the twenty-six non-Pukhtun groups in Shati Khel may be misleading. As we know, nine other social groups on the list provide services to Shati Khel Pukhtuns, but they live in Sangar and Ghazi Kor a few miles south of Shati Khel. Sangar and, near it, Ghazi Kor with a population of about 1,500 form a service pool for the Gandab Halimzais. The families of some twelve barbers and ten carpenter/blacksmiths live here, numbering about 100 each. They divide their weekly schedule according to the sub-clans, sections and sub-sections living in the Gandab and visit them on appointed days. For instance, Arsal will visit Shati Khel twice a week to shave the faces and heads of his clients. Paradoxically, and in the context of the study, these clients are his patrons. In Bela it is the patron Pukhtun who visits the client *qasabgar*, like Ihsanullah who visits the barber every Friday for a shave. An examination of the relationships between Pukhtun and *qasabgar* in TAM and SAM helps illuminate the shift from pure tribal structure where the Pukhtun does not depend solely on agriculture for his livelihood (he is also raider, smuggler, receiver of political allowances, etc.) to that of agriculturalist in the Settled Area and, consequent to his new role, to an almost total dependence on the *qasabgar*. To cite one example, he cannot work his land without the plough made by the carpenter. Ideally he is patron to the *qasabgar* clients by virtue of being member of the Pukhtun group as in TAM. In SAM he may be patron by Pukhtun custom *de jure* but *de facto* he has to visit and humour the busy *qasabgar* to extract work. He is a patron with little patronage just as the *qasabgar* is a client in possession of indispensable goods and services.

Bela Mohmandan shows a more complex social situation than Shati Khel. Nine of the social groups enumerated by Barth are present in the village itself as well as others not mentioned by him. I would like to emphasize again that these are neither economically depressed nor socially inferior groups. They may migrate, sell or buy land and refuse to work. I do not agree with the use of the word 'caste' to describe *qasabgar* among the Pukhtuns. It creates more problems than it solves. I also disagree that 'caste membership merely limits the range of positions to which a man can aspire' (ibid.: 22). Among the Mohmand, 'caste membership' has not prevented non-Mohmands such as Akbar

TABLE 3   Mohmand and non-Mohmand groups

		Shati Khel	Bela Mohmandan
1 descendants of the Prophet	Sayyed		Yes
2 descendants of Saints	Sahibzada		
3 various orders of	Mian*		
4 Sainthood	Akhundzada		
5	Pirzada		
6 traditionally landholding tribesmen	Pukhtun	Yes	Yes
7 priest	Mullah	(temporary)	Yes
8 shopkeeper	Dukandar		
9 muleteer	Paracha		
10 farmer	Zamindar		Yes
11 goldsmith	Zargar		
12 tailor	Sarkhamar*		
13 carpenter	Tarkan*		Yes
14 smith	Ingar	Yes	Yes
15 potter	Kulal		
16 oil-presser	Tili		
17 cotton-carder	Nandap*		
18 butcher	Qasaab*		
19 leather worker	Mochi/chamyar*		
20 weaver	Jola		
21 agricultural labourer	Dehqan		Yes
22 herdsman (in part non-Pukhto speaking)	Gujar		
23 ferryman	Jalawan/mangay		Yes
24 musician and dancer	Dam		
25 barber	Nai*		Yes
26 washerman	Dobi*		
27 tong- and sieve-maker and dancer	Shah Khel/kashkol*		

*Those living in the Gandab valley provide services to Shati Khel.

Khan, a trader, from twice representing them in the Provincial and National Assemblies. Therefore the word caste for such groups, being value-loaded in the anthropological literature of the subcontinent, may be usefully eschewed.

There are five notable omissions in Table 3. Firstly, a group, which is not on Barth's caste-list, called *tatarian* (tinkers), visit the area once a month charging Rs. 1 or half to fix broken pots and crockery. The *tatarian* serving Bela live near Chalghaezi, the Bela cemetery, but there is no such group or family living in the Michni area. Shati Mohmands rely on Shabkadar for the services of the *tatarian* as there are none in the Gandab. The second omission on the list is that of the *banjari*, usually an Afridi, who roams the area by bicycle according to his monthly schedule with a box containing cheap cosmetics, bangles, clips and rings. He usually sells on credit, which is invariably respected. The profession is called *banjaritob*. The third omission is the *manjawar* who cleans the shrine (*ziarat*) of the local saint and lives in or by it. The *baghwan*, form the fourth omitted group, visits Bela five times a week carrying fruit and fresh vegetables in a basket on his head. He accepts payment in cash or kind. A family of *baghwans* lives in Zarif Kor.

The fifth omission from the list is the *hamsaya*, a direct client of a *mashar* or Malik. In heart-land Pukhto areas like Tirah, *hamsayas* are usually non-Muslim groups like Hindus and Sikhs attached to patron Maliks called *naik* in this relationship (Ahmed, 1977a). There are, for instance, Sikhs and Hindus living in Buner in Swat (Government of Pakistan, 1975: 9). There are and never were Christian or Jewish groups in the Tribal Areas. Hindus traditionally acted as 'bankers, accountants and shopkeepers' among the Mohmand and were well treated (General Staff, 1926: 30; Merk, 1898). Patron-client honour is inextricably tied together and I have case-studies from present-day Orakzai Tirah of Maliks using the most drastic measures, including death, to uphold the honour of their *hamsaya*. Among the Halimzai and Tarakzai most non-Muslim groups left for India in 1947 although some remained behind among the Upper Mohmands like the Khwaezai. Siva Singh, a Hindu, living in Bela Mohmandan, but not as a *hamsaya*, owned and ran the village shop but left after 1947 with his family. He is still remembered by the elders of the village. Bela's only shop remained closed until the 1970s. In my field-work areas the name *hamsaya* has assumed a different meaning and implies any person or group who takes temporary shelter with a patron Malik escaping from his own area due to economic or political reasons. A *hamsaya* may be a Proclaimed Offender escaping from the laws of the Settled District, as is the person called 'Criminal Khan' (*Mujrim Khan*) in the Ranra village. The patriarch is responsible for his good behaviour and in turn gives him protection. His duties are those of helper (*khidmatgar*). He serves the guest of the Malik in the *hujra*, bringing tea or pillows for the cots, helps in the harvest, will fight for his patron and is generally visible as a symbol of his patron's strength and influence. Such Proclaimed Offenders are common in the Tribal Areas and are not seen as criminals since they usually commit crimes based on the Pukhto Code. None the less their client status is apparent: 'They are like servants' (*da nawkar pe hisab*), Mazullah the patron explained.

The most important *qasabgar* living among the Mohmands are traditionally carpenter (*tarkan*), barber (*nai* – also called *dam*) and blacksmith (*ingar*). The last sometimes performs the duties of the *tarkan* as in Bela Mohmandan. Their functions in relation to society and its *rites de passage* will be seen at the end of the chapter in Table 4, and I shall briefly recapitulate their role in·social life.

The *tarkans* are functionally important to social life and no *rites de passage* are complete without their presence and duties. In return the *tarkans* are paid in kind and in addition on specific occasions such as marriages. Increasingly in SAM they are paid in cash. Though living in Bela the carpenters and barbers serve other neighbouring Mohmand villages like Kas and Kodo on fixed dates. The typical duties of a carpenter may be divided into agricultural, social and domestic. He is as indispensable to agricultural life as the barber is to the social life of the village. He makes and repairs the farmers' agricultural implements such as the plough (*ewa*). In Bela he also repairs and tends to the sugar-cane pressing machines (*ganrey*). Socially, for the marriage rites, he makes the cot (*palang*) on which the groom is seated and displayed during the marriage ceremony. In death it is the duty of the carpenter to prepare the wooden plank on which the corpse is taken to the grave and also to prepare the grave for the burial. Domestically, the doors and windows of the houses are made by him. The main wood-beam in a new house is made and placed by him. He will charge extra for additional work such as making doors and windows. Today his labour alone could cost up to Rs. 20 a day. In Bela the demand for his work is great and reflected in the complaint that is often voiced that one can jump the queue if his palm is appropriately greased: 'The carpenter takes bribes' (*tarkan rishwat khori*). His is the most important of the occupational groups and it is not surprising that the average carpenter owns more land than

the average Bela Pukhtun. He is also the best paia ˎ
groups. Every Bela carpenter is paid in kind with twent₎
and twenty seers of wheat twice annually, after the sumnᵪ
and winter (*rabi*) crops have been harvested, per plough (*de quᵢ*
sar) by members of the village who utilize his facilities. Double tnᵪ
amount is expected from those people owning two *qulbas* of which
there are only four or five at any given time. In Shati Khel he receives
similar payment in kind but instead of maize, which is not cultivated,
receives barley.

The barber's functions are as manifold as they are versatile. He
shaves the face and head of his clients and clips their nails, circumcises
their male offspring, carries invitations during the *rites de passage*,
registers and records money paid during the rites (*nindara*) and may
even substitute as the cook if the professional *kulal* is not available
during the rites. The *nai*'s wife is called a *naiganra* but she does not
perform the duties of her husband. Mohmand women cut their own
hair and clip their own nails.

The barber is often called *dam* in the Tribal Areas which does not
connote a prostitute as it does in the Settled Areas or musician and
dancer as in Swat (Barth, 1972: 17). *Dam* derives from drum (*damama*)
and the verb to drum (*damamay wahal*). The barber is called *dam*
because he traditionally performed his function at circumcision and
marriages and proclaimed the occasion by beating on a drum. A few
generations ago he would beat on the drum as the Pukhtun *lakhkar*
gathered and marched into battle.

Like the carpenter, the Bela barber expects payment in kind and
cash. He makes his rounds after the harvests twice a year and receives
four seers of wheat and four seers of maize calculated per male 'head'
(*sari pe sar*). In Shati he is given the same quantity but barley in place
of maize. As mentioned, his fixed income in kind is supplemented by
tips given at the rites. The son of Haji Gul, the barber, is one of the three
Bela Mohmands in the Tarakzai platoon no.241 of the Frontier Constabulary and posted at Bara. Amin (Do Khel) and Shahdad (Sabah Khel),
the son-in-law of Hamesh, are the other two. According to Frontier
Constabulary tradition Pukhtun society retains its structure in service.
Haji Gul's son is professionally recruited as a barber and does not
parade or accompany the platoon on raids. He only shaves the platoon
and cuts their hair. In addition to his normal pay he receives from every
person who uses his services half a rupee monthly for soap.

The potter (*kulal*) is usually paid one bag of wheat after the crop and not money. For this he provides two or three earthenware pots (*mangi*) and one earthenware flask (*kuza*). The *kulal* brings his wares on a donkey and also cooks at marriages, for which he charges Rs. 3 per dish.

Lal Sher, seventy, a Qulamat Khel, is the ferryman of Bela. The ferryman is called *mangay* unlike Swat where he is called *jalawan*, and is employed for about four months every year. He is given four seers of wheat, maize and *gur* after every crop per household. He does not receive any tips during the rites although he may be given a rupee or two when ferrying people across the channel. When Lal Sher is unwell, which is often, his son Ziar Sher, twenty-five, acts as *mangay* in his absence. The Shers are a good example of deviant Pukhtun behaviour. Although of a junior lineage, they none the less could be technically classified as *qasabgars*.

In contrast to the highest paid client group among the Mohmands, the carpenters, the Mians, like Mashad of Bela, are the least well paid of the non-Pukhtun groups. They receive one-fourth of a seer of the wheat and maize crop annually.

Non-Mohmand groups, like the *qasabgar*, neither feel politically subjugated nor economically depressed because they are not dependent on a single person, or even a single group or family, for their income. They belong to the community. For instance the Mians, barbers and blacksmiths in Gandab are affiliated to the three major sub-clans of the Halimzai. No one settlement would think of insulting or short-changing them. If they did so they would be the losers because the *qasabgar* command monopoly services. The situation is reversed in the *qalang* areas where the *qasabgar* are entirely dependent on the mercy of one Khan on whose demesne they live.

In concluding, I would like to point out that the *qasabgar* enjoy a privilege denied to the Pukhtuns: that of migration. The *qasabgar* have no mystical or ancestral attachment to the land and can and do migrate when they are offered better employment opportunities. They can also indulge in patterns of behaviour that are excluded from the normative behaviour expected of Pukhtuns. The freedom of choice this implies was indulged by two non-Mohmands both living in SAM, one who was divorced and one who committed suicide — the only such examples in my entire field-work area. As I argued earlier, the Pukhtun free in his Tribal Areas is a prisoner to his Code and customs.

Table 4 relates the activities of the entire community and its groups and reflects their interrelationships and interdependence marking each

1. Tarakzai country in the Agency

2. Frontier Constabulary post at Michni

3. The colonial encounter and the Mohmand, 1897 (from National Army Museum)

4. Mohmand attack on Shabkadar Fort, 10 August 1897 (from National Army Museum)

5. Mohmand tower in Gandab blown up by No. 1 Company Mohmand Field Force, 1908 (from National Army Museum)

6. Shahzada and Shah Khan (Musa) in former's *hujra*

7. Mazullah (Ranra) in his *hujra*   **8.** Shahmat (Musa)

10. Hassan, son and grandson
(Ganjian)

9. Shahzada and his cannon

11. Shamshudin (Kado) at Bela

12. Hamesh (Madar) in his courtyard

13. Hussain (Jano)

14. Amin (Do) *kashar* of Bela

15. Author as Political Agent with *jirga* during inter-clan conflict, Chapter 5 (courtesy of *Mashriq* newspaper)

16. Mian Jalil outside his house

17. Shahzada and Mullah in former's mosque

18. Imam of Bela

19. Bela mosque with cot for dead

20. Eed prayers in Bela mosque

21. Grandsons of Hussain in Bela with sacrificial sheep at Eed

22. Arsal (barber) shaving Amirzada

23. *Tatari* visiting Bela

24. *Baghwan* visiting Bela

25. Shamshudin's kitchen

26. Kado girl carrying fuel in main Bela lane

27. Bela children

28. Shahzada's *bruj*

29. Malok well and village

30. Entrance to Malok village

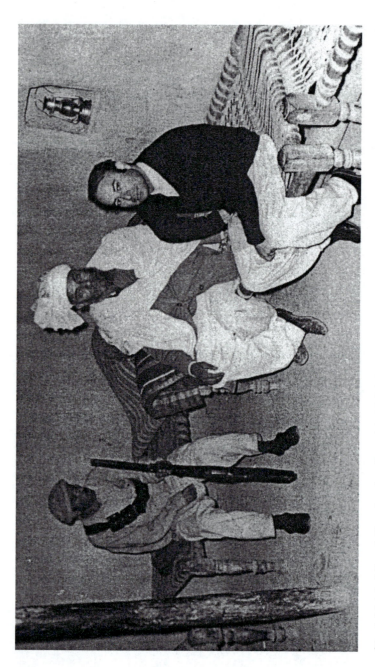

31. A Malok, Miam Jalil and author (l. to r.) in Malok *hujra*

40. Bela shop and owner

41. Bela canal number 3

42. Akbar Jan outside Lakhkar village

43. Ihsanullah at home

44. Deputy Commissioner, Peshawar, in Bela *hujra*

45. Bela school

46. Shati Khel school

47. Entrance to Mohmand Agency, Ekka Ghund

48. Construction at new headquarters, Ghalanay

stage of a person's life in the *rites de passage*. The close functional interdependence of groups is apparent at a glance. Birth (*padaish*), circumcision (*sunnat*), marriage (*wada*) and death (*marg*) are summed up by
Pukhtuns as *gham-khadi* (literally 'sad-happy' occasions) and attendance
or absence from them indicates political alliance and social status.
Expenditures on *rites de passage* based on case-studies selected from
senior and junior lineages and non-Mohmand groups are discussed in
Chapter 9.

   This chapter has attempted to define broadly two non-Mohmand
social categories, the religious groups, Mians and Mullahs, and the
qasabgars, mainly the carpenters and barbers. While the *qasabgar* has no
social pretensions, the Mian is not prepared to accept Pukhtun social
superiority. In his own ideal-type model he approximates to the 'saintly'
model among Mohmands, a definition which precludes political activity.
Conceptually the highest point of his 'saintliness' coincides with the
lowest point of political activity. The presence of the Mian and the
Mullah in Pukhtun society is a visible and self-conscious reminder of
Islamic values. Their presence acts as social mechanism to sustain Islamic
symmetry in Pukhtun society and correct cases of assymmetry. However in the ideal-type Pukhtun situation of Shati Khel both groups are
clearly seen as clients through the eyes of the Pukhtun and subordinate
to his political authority. The Pukhtun casts himself in the role and
status of patron. The Pukhtun world is still largely undisturbed in its
traditional symmetry in 1975-6. However, the role and importance of
the religious groups *vis-à-vis* administration has undergone a significant
change since the departure of the British. From a position of hostility
to an infidel government the Mians and Mullahs are now generally
favourable to what they consider a Muslim government (Ahmed,
1977a).

   Clear deviances emerge, however, in the encapsulated tribal village of
Bela Mohmandan. The social importance of non-Mohmand groups
grows in inverse proportion to the diminishing importance of the
Pukhtun lineage and its Code. This newly emerging relationship is
further complicated for the Pukhtuns by their shift from traditional
occupations to an agricultural livelihood. They are now inextricably
bound to the specialized and monopolistic talents of non-Mohmand
groups like the carpenters. The Mullah is no longer client of the household head but a central and, because of his personal qualities, respected
figure of the village community. In a sense he has risen above the status
of client to the Pukhtun and become pivotal in the village *rites de*

TABLE 4   Rites: functions of sexes and groups

| | *Family* | | *Religious groups* | *Occupational groups* | |
	Men	Women	Mian, Mullah	Barber	Carpenter
1 Birth (*padaish*)	Entire *kor* celebrates the birth of a son, and the women are busy preparing food and tea for the stream of visitors come to congratulate the father; birth of a daughter passes unnoticed and if it is the third or fourth consecutive daughter there is general mourning		says the *azan*, the call to prayer, in the right ear of the child within 24 hours of birth to symbolize his Muslimness. During the usual illnesses of a child, supplies talismans and suggests herbs	shaves the child's head ceremonially and collects money (*zairay*)	
2 Circumcision (*sunnat*)	usually performed between 3 to 5 years. Men and women of the house celebrate and pray. The boy is now considered 'fully' Muslim		prays informally after the circumcision	performs operation, usually with a razor	
3 Marriage (*wada*)	arrive at the bride's house with the groom, are feasted by noon and return with the bride by dusk. The formal marriage ceremony is performed. The custom is changing	dress in red and receive groom's party. A male 'the father for the marriage' (*de nikah plar*), usually a paternal uncle, represents the girl and on her behalf gives	is essential to the ceremony according to Islamic Law and tradition and binds the couple in marriage after receiving the consent of both the contracting parties	exceedingly busy in his role as conveyor of invitations to near and far and as the person who counts, and records, sums of money given to the boy when they go to bring the bride, so	if the couple move to a new house within the parental compound or outside it, makes the doors, windows and lays the roof, for which he charges

and *nikah* is performed in certain SAM cases at the girl's house. Men fire guns to celebrate	consent to the Mullah for the formal marriage ceremony. The boy's father is 'the husband of the marriage' (*de wada khawand*)			these may be reciprocated on a similar occasion
4 Death (*marg*) men remain dignified and composed. If the death is of a man then only males will wash his corpse preparatory to burial rites, and vice-versa if a woman dies	general wailing of women (*weer*) and reciting of the Holy Koran in the house. No food is cooked and neighbours provide food. Women do not accompany corpse to grave but visit it later	Mullah helps bath the body, leads the village in a congregational prayer before the corpse, wrapped in a shroud he has blessed with writings from the Holy Koran, and then escorts the funeral procession to the grave, where he reads final prayers over the mud of the grave after burial. Mullahs gather for this occasion and the agnatic kin of the deceased distribute small sums of money, rice, soap and *gur*, called *skhat* among them	shaves the corpse and cuts its nails	makes the wooden plank on which the corpse is placed and buried
Death provisions are called *gor-kapan* (literally, coffin) and include payments for services to all groups. The corpse is buried before noon and rarely kept for more than a few hours. On the third (*drayma*) and fortieth (*salwekhtama*) days, and after one year (*tlin*), according to Islamic tradition food is cooked for distribution to the poor and neighbours by the household of the deceased				

passage. These shifting relationships pose the dilemmas of encapsulation to SAM anew and within society. The Pukhtun is now confronted by the economic not political facts of his new situation and he is stripped of his own symbolic possession of Pukhtunness, his gun. As a small land-holding agriculturalist he is increasingly at the mercy of tradition-ally client groups. The traditional patron and client roles may not have been reversed in SAM but they are now in the process of being re-defined and, apart from the certain fading mystique of Pukhtun lineage, non-Mohmand groups are asserting themselves. The fading mystique of Mohmand lineages is a consequence of encapsulation and clearly that part of my thesis suggesting the continuation of the traditional schema of ideal Pukhtun society stands disproved in the SAM situation. Ideal society conceptualizes a hierarchy of ranked groups within a recognized social schema at the top of which is the Pukhtun, which as I have illus-trated exists in TAM. My thesis that the ideal model exists in TAM is thus upheld by the arguments in this chapter.

I will discuss in the next chapter the core features of *Pukhtunwali, tarboorwali* and *tor*, through extended case-studies, and illustrate how both TAM and SAM tend to approximate in their behaviour to the ideal-type model, thereby substantiating a major part of the thesis contained in the study.

7 Pukhto paradigm

'Do Pukhto if you are a Pukhtoon
Many are the sorrows I have endured through Pukhto' -- popular
Pukhto folk song (Enevoldsen, n.d.:71).

In Chapter 4 I had argued that the two essential features of the *Pukhtun-wali* model as locally interpreted (and which coincide largely with the foreign model) are *tarboorwali* and *tor*. I shall argue in this chapter that though other features, such as hospitality, may be emphasized in *Pukhtunwali*, observed frequencies of normative behaviour and cultural values in society lead me to the conclusion that it is actually translated to mean *tarboorwali* and *tor*. I will illustrate how TAM data approximate closely to the ideal model and thus prove that an ideal model of society does exist. More importantly, I shall utilize SAM data to substantiate my thesis. SAM, in spite of the severe constraints of encapsulation, also adheres to the ideal although signals, however faint, may be recognized of increasing internal and external pressure to accommodate and compromise. That SAM social behaviour after encapsulation still so closely approximates to *Pukhtunwali* substantiates the major part of my thesis, that is, *Pukhtunwali* survives encapsulation.

I Tarboorwali: agnatic rivalry as expression of the nang principle

The two case-studies I analyse in this chapter, one from TAM and one from SAM, stretch over four to five decades and involve three to four generations of ascendants of many of my respondents. In the background and often intruding with their own complex patterns are the differing regional frameworks in colonial and independent periods. An understanding of the relationships of the actors to each other, which may be seen in Figures 6 (TAM) and 10 (SAM), will clarify why people acted as they did in the context of the operative lineage and agnatic rivalry. Figure 10 in this section specifically depicts the relationships of the main actors in the case-study from the Kado Khel.

As we saw in Chapter 5 *tarboor*, the kin term for Father's Brother's Son, denoted enmity in Pukhto custom and tradition (Barth, 1959; Morgenstierne, 1927). *Tarboorwali* thus carries the meaning of agnatic rivalry. The network of consanguineal and affinal relationships within which ego functions is visualized in Figure 8; it depicts a discrete sphere of hostility regarding male agnates which also invariably involves female kin. Although the *tarboor* may grow up as the childhood companion, in time he becomes the chief rival for status and political leadership within the lineage: 'When he is little play with him: when he is grown up he is a cousin; fight him' (Ibbetson, 1883: 219). Mohmands are acutely aware of the *tarboor* and what he has come to mean in society and I have heard them say: 'If the *tarboor* is good he kills others, if he is bad he kills us.' Another common saying is: 'Tolerate any one but the *tarboor.*' *Tarboorwali*, deriving from agnatic competition, includes the rivalry of paternal uncles: 'God knows that the uncle is a *kafir*' (Ahmed, 1975: 35). This relationship may contrast with other tribal societies where hostility is reserved for the 'outsider' and 'non-kin ... is the synonym for "enemy" or "stranger"' (Sahlins, 1969: 150).

Tarboorwali cannot be explained in terms of a man-to-man duel after which the board is wiped clean and a new relationship may emerge. It is neither chivalric nor romantic. It does not occur at an appointed place and time with selected weapons and roughly equal chances of victory but may be a shot in the back at the least expected time. As the case-studies will show no place is sacrosanct, mosque or *hujra*, no age immune, infant or ancient. The *tarboor* 'waits for the moment', Mohmands will state. It is only a means to an end. The end is revenge (*badal*) itself. At all and any cost. That is why *badal* implies such an awesome and ineluctable sequence of social action and counter-action. It is a highly complex socio-psychological relationship rooted in social history.[1] *Tarboorwali* as it operates socially can best be understood as rivalry revolving around two male collaterals, usually of the same generation, representing closely related but different lineages within the sub-section and often involving similar series of rivalries on similar depths of the clan genealogy.

As I have mentioned earlier, the political situation is not a two-bloc system representing the major groups on an Agency or tribal level as in Swat (Barth, 1972). However, it may be said to be a two-bloc system in the sense that there are two blocs on every level of segmentation within the lineage formed around two opposed agnates. The system is replicated within every sub-section and could be considered a multi-bloc one at the sub-sectional level, where tribal lineages are operative, if seen horizontally at that level of segmentation. Thus two major groupings led by two or more patriarchs, usually of the senior lineage, traditionally divide every sub-section among the Mohmands. On another level of the genealogical charter, the section, similar blocs may crystallize. As Shahzada and Abdullah oppose each other on the sectional level in the Halimzai, Afzal Khan and Said Qahar oppose each other among the Tarakzai (in the Michni area) and on this level in the Baezai, Mir Azam is opposed by Amin and in the Khwaezai, Haji Asghar opposes Mir Akbar. Needless to say the rivals are lineage cousins. The first group in each sub-clan support Shahzada because their rival groups are with Abdullah in enmities stretching over decades. We have seen how Amin's father Muhasil (Baezai) had fought against Shahzada's father Anmir in 1915 (Chapter 3). Active rivalry and the major arena of agnatic competition is, however, restricted to the sub-section. Although there will be sympathy cross-cutting lineage boundaries, there is little consciousness of belonging to larger homologous blocs or factions in the Agency. The loose identification with one or other group may assume the form of vocal sympathy but beyond the sectional level on the genealogy very little else. Lineage foreign policy is shifting and strictly based on the dictum that 'my cousin's enemy is my friend'.

Extra-clan support is restricted to sympathy and does not include men for fighting. Religious or occupational groups under mutually agreed and honoured tradition do not participate in the front-line shooting. In the most literal sense, the killing is restricted to and done by members sharing close unilineal descent.

(a) *Case-study: TAM*

The key words and motivation in *tarboorwali*: *nang*, shame (*ghairat*), prestige (*izzat*) and Pukhto recur in the following case-study. No political beliefs or economic arguments are involved, neither are women (*zan*), gold (*zar*) and land (*zamin*), the three traditional bases of most Pukhtun conflict (Ali, 1966; Coen, 1971; Spain, 1962, 1963; Swinson, 1967). Conflict is based on the notion of cousin enmity and the desire to maintain honour in relation to him. The rules of *tarboorwali* conflict are known and respected by the concerned parties. Geographical and segmentary boundaries, that often correspond, delimit the arena of conflict. The limits of fighting and the arena are physically restricted to the Shati Khel within sub-sectional conflict, and to the Gandab valley where sectional or sub-clan allies are involved, and within the clan except for stray incidents in Shabkadar. Actual front-line shooting in the trenches which involves the risk of being wounded or killed is done by members of the particular sub-section only. Supporters (such as occupational groups) may assist in a variety of other indirect ways such as organizing a courier service. Leaders of groups provide ammunition, food and even snuff to their supporters in the trenches.[2]

The agnatic blocs in TAM as seen through the eyes of Shahzada Malik, and those of his father Anmir, and as personified by the rivals, are on three genealogical levels of varying and deepening depths: firstly, Atta Khan of the same patrilineage Musa Khel, second Mazullah of the same sub-section Ranra (both living in Shati Khel) and third, Abdullah of the same section Wali Beg (Figure 6) living in Sangar (Maps 2 and 4). In the foreground of the case-study is the bitter and tenacious struggle of Atta Khan over five decades against the increasingly greater odds mobilized by his agnatic rival Shahzada. The three levels of seg- mentation interweave and interact at various stages in the story, some- times in alliance, sometimes in conflict, sometimes active and some- times dormant.

Within the Halimzai in the Gandab valley the other two sub-clans, Hamza and Kadai, maintain a diplomatic balance between the two major enemies, Abdullah and Shahzada in the third sub-clan, the Wali Beg. Within Abdullah's sub-section, the Inkay Khel, his rivalry with his cousin Rasul of Khwajang Khel and Dost Mohammad of Shahgul Khel is as intense and on the same genealogical depth as that of Shahzada's with Atta and the Ranra Khel. It is also as long-standing. Around 1905 Abdullah's father had Dost's father killed. When Shahzada increases pressure on Abdullah by aiding Rasul or Dost Mohammad, Abdullah retaliates by supporting Atta or Mazullah. None the less it is important to conceptualize the operative lineage, the sub-section, as the main arena of rivalry and leadership. How and to what extent these ally with each other or transgress each other's boundaries will be made clear by the case-study in this section. Factions are easily deserted and alliances constantly shift but the two-bloc structure at every level of the sub- section remains.

The TAM case-study has its origins in the middle of the last century when Saida Mir (Musa), the grandfather of Anmir, was under constant pressure from his cousins the Ranra Khel, the senior Shati lineage, who were then politically supreme in the area. They destroyed Saida Mir's following and physically hounded him out of Shati Khel. The Musa in Shati Khel were expelled. They were a finished force. However, Saida Mir sought the help of Kadai kin and managed to stay on in the Gandab valley.

It is at this stage in the case-study, at the ebb of Musa fortunes, that a frequently described incident took place. The Ranra Khel robbed a group of holy Mians passing through Gandab and in addition heaped insults on them. Saida Mir helped them recover their goods and provided them with hospitality. The Mians are said to have cursed the Ranra: 'May the Ranra Khel be destroyed by Saida Mir'. Saida Mir would have had good reasons to be sceptical about the prophecy at that stage. Until then the Musa had few male offspring whereas Ranras were producing males in profusion. Saida Mir who died in the 1870s had eight male members against the Ranra's 240 (these figures are part of Shati oral history now). However, the prophecy, though it took almost four generations, did come true. Except for one small settlement in Shati Khel, Mazullah village, allowed by courtesy of Shahzada, the Ranra[3] have been expelled from their ancestral homes (Map 5i, ii, iii).

In the closing years of the last century Said Hassan, the patriarchal senior of the Ranra who was to be ejected from Shati early this century by Anmir, hired a Kabuli assassin to murder Anmir's father Gul Amir, then an old man, while he was at prayer in Shabkadar. The attempt failed and Anmir's cousins tracked the assassin to Lalpura in Afghanistan a few months later and shot him. As revenge three nephews of Said Hassan were gunned down near Mian Mandi. The Ranra retaliated by killing Gul Amir in 1895 while he performed ablutions for prayers in Shabkadar. Anmir, his son, took revenge by chasing the killer and shooting him on the spot. Said Hassan was ejected from Shati Khel as a result of the concerted effort of the Musa Khel. Over the next decades, as I will show, the considerable property the Ranra owned in Shati was occupied by the Musa, for instance the land Shahzada sold to the government for the hospital and school. This branch of the Ranra was too exhausted to participate in the Shati struggle and to this day Samar Khan, the affluent descendant of Said Hassan, and living in Shabkadar, cannot construct a settlement in Shati Khel without the permission of the Musa. Ranra leadership devolved on Mazullah descended from a junior Ranra lineage.

On the deeper level of the genealogy, Saida Mir's grandson, Anmir and his rival Inayatullah, and later his son Abdullah, continued their rivalry. In 1898 Inayatullah was honourably received in Kabul and awarded official robes of honour (*khilat*) and *lungi*. Given the alternative choices available in such agnatic rivalries Anmir contacted the British. These loyalties were generally maintained by the two parties and their descendants until the departure of the British in 1947. As a result Atta, the Ranra and Abdullah's group opposing the British, dubbed Shahzada and his family as British agents and non-believers, a charge of the utmost seriousness in the Tribal Areas where Mullahs waited for just such an excuse to declare *jihad*, burn houses and impose fines (Chapter 3).

The results of their rivalry within the context of events on the larger canvas were discussed in Chapter 3. In 1918 Anmir, against general Pukhtun tradition, brought Aziz's grandfather, a blacksmith, from Peshawar to live in Shati and make guns and ammunition for him. He consolidated the contract by marrying the blacksmith's daughter by his second wife, a Dawezai Mohmand, and gave him a site captured from the Ranra to build his home. This alliance secured Anmir's munition sources and the blacksmith's family became part of Shati social structure. To this day Aziz and his village are called 'blacksmith' (*ingar*).

The tradition of rivalry between the Musa and their sub-sectional cousins Malok and Ranra continued into the 1920s. In the early 1920s almost twenty people died in a clash between Malok and Musa. In the background was the rivalry between Inayatullah and Anmir. However, a temporary truce among the Shati cousins and a formal truce with Abdullah in 1928 by Anmir brought hope of peace to the Gandab valley. This peace was soon to be shattered by a debilitating conflict lasting over four decades which had its origins in a trivial incident.

Anmir's sons were passing a summer afternoon trapping quail on the fields of the Ganjian, allied to their lineage, when some Malok elders and later Atta Khan (Musa) interfered. There was an altercation between the women of the sub-section and the next day a Ganjian group fired and wounded Atta Khan. Fazaldin, the father of Atta with his other son, Shah Khan, realized the matter could escalate beyond control and sought out Anmir to clear up any misunderstanding he might harbour. Atta, however, refused to go to Anmir and expressed his desire for revenge. Tension remained in the area and shortly afterwards in a similar trivial quarrel some of Anmir's sons caught and disrobed the son of Pasham Gul, the grandson of Said Mir (Malok). The women of the house were up in arms and pressed Said Mir for revenge. In retaliation for this grave insult of Pasham Gul's son, Atta and a Malok party with

35. Malok mosque and *hujra* with tower in background

36. Malok children in front of village

32. Destroyed Malok village facing Shahzada village

33. Lakhkar's tower

34. Lakhkar village

37. Shati Khel cemetery

38. Mian Mandi

39. Bela sugar-cane *ganrey*

feeling of *déjà vu* and the Assistant Political Agent, Mohmands, wrote
to government, summing up the situation:

> The present state of affairs demand that all warring factions should
> unite together in the common cause of serving the Government and
> in fighting the Upper Mohmands.
> (1) It would be impolitic for us to create any discontentment
> amongst the majority of Gandab Halimzai at the present juncture.
> What we need is a temporary truce for the duration of the period
> during which Government forces stay in Mohmand country.
> (2) I recommend that Anmir should be given an assurance that his
> case would be fully gone into after the achievement of the purpose
> for which the troops have entered Gandab and he should be told this
> was not the time in which he should press for redress.
> (3) I have not much experience of the Mohmand affairs, but to my
> mind the solution lies in referring the matter to a strong and im-
> partial *jirga* from outside. If the *jirga* consider that Anmir has any
> claim whatsoever on these villages then the villages should be com-
> pletely demolished in accordance with the terms of condition 6 of the
> truce dated 10-6-1928. This would bring the parties back to status
> quo (ibid.).

The Governor of the Province supported these recommendations
which underlined non-interference with the status quo in tribal affairs.
It is important to understand that status quo in the eyes of the administration invariably involved tilting in favour of loyal Maliks and meant,
in effect, loss of status quo in internal tribal affairs. To shore up their
position the British threw their weight behind Anmir and Shahzada.
They were given added allowances, irrigated lands in Shabkadar and,
when the Upper Mohmands burned their Shati property (as in 1932),
compensation. Most important of all, Shahzada was allowed to import a
small cannon[6] in the 1930s which altered the balance of arms power in
Shati Khel. Shahzada, as *quid pro quo*, risked his life and property in
the 1935 campaign led by General Auchinleck by supporting the British.
He was damned as a *kafir* by the Upper Mohmands who fought the
British and his settlements along with those of his supporters in Shati
were burnt.

However, the British, firmly committed to the classic imperial
dictum, *divide et impera*, were not prepared to create tribal chiefs with
unchecked power and balanced Shahzada, in spite of his unwavering
loyalty, with Abdullah who was apparently always in opposition to

them as far as their policies allowed. Although whenever Abdullah proved too strong for Shahzada to contain, the British restored the status quo by arresting him, none the less he was granted generous allowances. His personal *lungi* allowance was similar to that of Shahzada, Rs. 500 per year. Their sectional *muajib* allowances were identical, Rs. 288 per year, and he was permitted to recommend almost as many *khassadars*, about twelve, for employment from his section as Shahzada. Nor was siding with the British such a simple choice for Anmir and Shahzada in the face of the intense tribal pressure. They may have thrown in their lot with the British yet they maintained a certain independence on certain issues. In 1935 both father and son were banned from entering the Gandab valley and were placed virtually under house-arrest in Shabkadar as they opposed the building of the ill-fated Mohmand road.

Between 1933 and 1940 when another truce (*teega*) was signed by Abdullah and Shahzada,[7] twenty-nine people had been killed in Shati alone, seventeen from Atta's faction.[8] The *teega* was followed by a period of relative calm in the land especially as both groups had lost their leaders, Inayatullah in 1930 and Anmir in 1938, and needed a respite to regroup. After Malik Anmir's death his Musa sub-sectional brothers and nephews began to split into separate settlements clustered around their ancestral home at Chino, the furthest and most strategic point in Shati. The present small Musa settlements of Murtaza, Saz, Machoray, Khanewar, Sarfaraz and Shahmat date from this period and are a typical illustration of segmental fissures in tribal society (Map 5, iii). Shahzada himself shifted from his father's village onto the present site and built a new settlement for his immediate kin, since called 'new village' (*nawa kilay*) or Shahzada Malik village. Shahzada inherited his father's Maliki but his paternal uncle, Major Sultan Jan, remained a main voice and leader of the Musa.

Said Mir, a major Malok rival of Shahzada, died in 1940. Fazaldin and Shah Khan, the father and brother of Atta, had crossed over to Shahzada's side bringing some Malok elders with them. This was a period of consolidation for the Musa and by 1946 Shahzada felt strong enough to lead his party in a successful attack on Sangar, Abdullah's village. Abdullah had gone to Shabkadar to collect the *muajib* leaving his village unguarded. Shahzada handed over the village to Abdullah's arch-enemy and sub-sectional cousin Rasul. Three of Abdullah's men were killed and his son, Rahim, taken prisoner and kept in Shati Khel for six months. Abdullah found himself expelled to Shabkadar but was soon back.

Shahzada and Abdullah finally agreed not to interfere in each other's sub-sectional rivalry in 1953. Shahzada would not support the Rasul Khel against Abdullah who in turn would withdraw his support from Atta. Shahzada's main rival Atta Khan was now isolated. Shahzada mounted a dawn attack led by Major Sultan with some 200 supporters and finally captured Atta Khan's village. Atta himself was in Shabkadar. The village walls and structures were blown up, the cattle and cots allowed to Atta's family but the main wood beams of the roof were taken by the victors as spoils of war. Atta's village remains in its demolished condition to this day as a symbol to the hatred *tarboorwali* can generate. Atta refused to bow to Shahzada's group and lodged an official complaint with the political authorities that Shahzada had violated the *solla*. After considerable deliberation the authorities agreed and Shahzada was fined Rs. 12,000.

In the same year Dilawar Khan, a Malok, allied himself with Abdullah through a series of marriages. Dilawar married Abdullah's daughter, his son was married to Abdullah's granddaughter and his daughter to Abdullah's grandson. Dilawar's grandfather, Gulzamir, had been killed by a cousin, Sar Gul, another Malok, at Shahzada's behest. Dilawar's father, Itbar Jan, and paternal uncle, Qadir Jan, were expelled from Shati Khel in 1917 and their village reduced to rubble (Figure 6). Dilawar was born in the Swabi Subdivision of Peshawar and after making his fortune growing tobacco returned to take revenge on behalf of his ascendants a quarter of a century later. His wealth, loyalty and energy were to prove an asset to Abdullah.

Atta Khan counter-attacked in 1960 by capturing Mazullah's village through Kadir Khan, a Ghunda Khel, who lived as Mazullah's *hamsaya* and acted as a fifth columnist. Mazullah and the Ranra had by then entered into a surface truce with Shahzada. Shahzada attacked in force, recaptured the village and returned it to Mazullah. To strengthen his party Shahzada arranged for a disputed area of about sixty acres,[9] in nearby Yusuf Khel, to be given to Malik Lakhkar. Lakhkar had been residing for a generation in Mardan District where he was born and until then had supported Atta Khan as his own cousin was in Shahzada's camp. Lakhkar suddenly found himself in the middle of Shati Khel politics. Shahzada consolidated the alliance by marrying his son, Amirzada, to Lakhkar's daughter. Four other intermarriages between the families of Shahzada and Lakhkar followed.[10]

The only village which Atta Khan could now seek shelter in was Shabana where his brothers, including Shah Khan, and nephews lived with their Malok host, Buchay. In 1963 Atta's nephews, Bahram and Wahabudin, in connivance with his brother Shah Khan, approached Amirzada secretly and promised to kill Buchay and hand over the village to Shahzada. This they did. Atta was in Shabkadar and horrified. To his mind the killing of a host was the grossest violation of hospitality and Pukhto custom. Atta's brothers requested him to compromise with Shahzada to which he replied in what has now become a common saying among the Mohmands: 'You are without shame for a Pukhtun does not bow before a *tarboor*.'

None the less the incident shook Atta Khan. His last base in Shati Khel was lost. Two years later another incident was to break his spirit altogether. His favourite and eldest son, Hazrat Khan, was shot from the top of a bus outside Mian Mandi near Shati Khel by Murtaza, the son of Zarin, one of the six men killed by Atta in 1933. Although Murtaza was only three years old at the time, his mother, Atta's own sister, had promised to take revenge and had not forgotten the thought for a moment. She kept Zarin's bullet-riddled waistcoat and over the years showed it to Murtaza as a symbol of *Pukhtunwali*. People lauded the act and said of her, 'After all the mother was also a real Pukhtuna'. She herself explained her obsession: 'I kept my husband's torn waistcoat and vowed that when Murtaza grew to be a man I would take my husband's *badal* from my brother.' Zarin was avenged by the primary law of *badal* thirty-two years after his death. 'The Pukhtun who took revenge after a hundred years said I took it quickly' is a well-known proverb (Ahmed, 1975: xvii).

Atta protested to the political authorities that Shahzada's men had broken the truce, and Shahzada was fined Rs. 12,000 for the murder as it was committed on the road and another Rs. 3,000 for breaking the *solla* agreement. The total was later reviewed and reduced to Rs. 8,000 which was deducted on a monthly basis from the pay that Shahzada's *khassadars* received.

Maddened with grief at the loss of his son, Atta made a clumsy and abortive attempt to kill Major Sultan Jan, the Musa king-pin, in Shabkadar. He then promised his daughter in marriage to his nephew Bahadur if he killed the Major. In 1966 Bahadur, using a double-barrelled gun, fired twice at the Major in Shabkadar but missed. The Major, in retaliation, emptied his revolver into Bahadur. Shortly afterwards, in 1967, Atta died, broken in health and spirit. Of the three major enemies of Shahzada he alone had refused to come to terms with him. In the end he stood alone against Shahzada but 'refused to bow his head to his cousin'. He felt he was betrayed by his father Fazaldin, his brothers and his nephews. His progeny was dead. The village that carried his name lay in rubble. His very name was obliterated in Shati Khel.

Although politically defeated, Atta's obduracy and courage in the face of overwhelming odds have won him renown and admiration among TAM and SAM alike. In the Weberian sense, Atta Khan's behaviour approximates to the ideal-type Pukhtun model and he himself to the ideal-type Pukhtun. What is important to emphasize is that this behaviour approximates to the 'home-model' or 'native model' (Ward, 1969) and its comprehension and cognition of the ideal-type. Among the Mohmand Atta symbolizes courage against odds, pursuit of revenge and refusal to submit to the supremacy of another's will. It is commonly said of him: 'He tolerated every affliction but did not bow his head to his *tarboor*.' In discussions about ideal Pukhtun behaviour Atta's example is quoted among the Mohmand as the perfect illustration of *Pukhtunwali*. In society he embodies the Pukhto saying 'Pukhto is half-madness' (*Pukhto nim liwantob day*). His behaviour is quoted as the finest example of *nang* and *ghairat* in *Pukhtunwali* and he is mentioned universally as an example of a 'real Pukhtun man' (*Pukhtun saray*).

In a moment of rash miscalculation Mazullah provoked Shahzada into a conflict in 1973, was attacked and roundly defeated. Mazullah's Kadai Khel allies had melted into the night. His supporters and those of Dilawar, Abdullah's son-in-law and Shahzada's cousin from the Settled Districts, were no match for Shahzada's Shati relatives. Shahzada's tower (*bruj*),[11] the only one of its kind in Shati, constructed at the mouth of the Shati Khel, blocked Mazullah's supplies. The cannon fired from Shahzada's village played havoc with Mazullah's mud walls only some 500 yards away, and the twenty-one cannon balls fired next day convinced Mazullah that the game was up.[12] Mazullah's relative, Yad Gul, lost his life and another *solla* was agreed upon. Shahzada also agreed to a *solla* with Dilawar who was willing to come to terms with him. As a result Shahzada returned about five acres of land captured from Itbar Jan, Dilawar's father, in 1917, to Dilawar.

The next year Abdullah and Major Sultan Jan died symbolizing the end of a period in Shati history. The same year new development schemes penetrated into the Agency diverting energies into economic activity. The Gandab valley was finally becoming safe for the Mohmands to travel around in without danger of being attacked, wounded or killed on the road by hostile agnates.

Between 1933 and 1973 a total of about sixty cousins killed each

other. The choices can be acutely painful for a sensitive young man in
such a highly integrated and endogamous society in the complex
patterns of agnatic rivalry. The mother of Feroz is Atta Khan's sister
who was given in exchange marriage when Feroz's father's sister married
Atta's brother. Atta is therefore doubly related to Feroz. On the other
hand Feroz's father Usman is the son of Shahzada's paternal uncle
while he himself is married to the granddaughter of Shahzada Malik.
Shahzada too is therefore doubly related to Feroz (Figure 9).

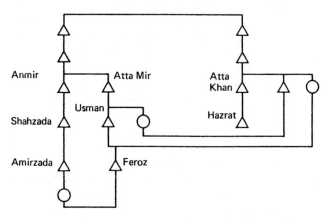

FIGURE 9 *Agnatic rivalry and its dilemmas for Feroz*

Where, he would ask me, did that place him? His voice betrayed the
intense conflict of emotions he must undergo when contemplating the
situation:

> My mother still cries when she talks of those terrible days. Men
> would not spare their closest relatives. They ate each other's flesh.
> Pukhtunness is really madness. She loved her brother Atta intensely.
> I admire Atta Khan as he was a real Pukhtun. On the other hand
> Shahzada is both my uncle and wife's grandfather and I must show
> him loyalty. He is strong. Neither I nor my father can afford to
> oppose him. He is our elder. He has the qualities of Pukhtun leader-
> ship being generous and brave. So I sleep in his *hujra* at least twice a
> week to show my support. But my maternal uncle Atta was a real
> Pukhtun in every respect of the word.

Many others like Feroz faced similar dilemmas created by the intense
agnatic rivalry within highly endogamous lineages.

Ganjian, supposedly with Shahzada, managed to maintain a sort of neutrality through the latter half of the affair. Earlier, Haji Hassan had tilted towards Atta but after being shot in the body twice and having his settlement blown up by Anmir retired at an early stage of the conflict. Such groups with the occupational and religious groups were neutral throughout and not trusted altogether by either side. Their social status is, as we know, determined by the fact that they are not allowed by Pukhtun tradition to 'carry a gun'. Haji Hassan, the Ganjian elder, reflected the views of the non-Mohmand groups on the entire affair and form of Pukhto: 'They were mad (*liwani woo*); those were non-religious acts and they were of weak minds – they killed one another.' None the less, he agreed with society that Atta was 'a real Pukhtun man'.

Three villages, those of Itbar Jan, Atta Khan and Ranra Khel, still lie in ruins to testify to the strength of the victor and the fate of the victims (Map 5, iii). The major cause of Shahzada's ultimate emergence was the combination of a powerful patriarchal personality backed by a large band of loyal and courageous Musa male kin. Shahzada, including his sons and grandsons, has eighteen males to 'carry' guns for him and in a fight he can muster a total fighting strength of fifty to sixty people at short notice which include his brothers, living in the Chino settlements, and their sons. This is one of the primary reasons of his success. As the Musa explain themselves, 'we pushed ourselves forward' (*mong zan makhkay ko*). The final, possibly the deciding, factor was access to the infinite resources of an administration which saw in him a dependent and reliable Malik among turbulent and hostile clans.

If the impression emerges that Shahzada is a powerful tyrant or a towering figure in the Gandab valley or Shati Khel it is a wrong one. The enmity of his lineage cousins, the Ranra, the Malok, Abdullah and the opposition of the *kashar* more than balance him politically. As we saw, Atta Khan did not give in to the end. Nor was he the only one with a cannon;[13] Abdullah had acquired one and so had his Kamali cousins. In the early 1960s Abdullah's son, Khanzada, procured a bren-gun, the only one in the Gandab. Constant 're-emergences' of played-out lineages like Lakhkar and Dilawar continued to check his authority. Finally, he is acutely aware that his sons and grandsons will not be able to maintain his Pukhtun standards. The arena is shifting from the politics of courage and loyalty to that of education and business. In neither of these fields do his progeny match up to his stature. Being completely illiterate but still proud, they have failed in contrast with

the Malok, who are now becoming involved in non-Pukhtun activity
and are successful business men and traders, and with Abdullah's sons,
who are educated and in government service. Any further rounds
belong to the sons of Abdullah or Malok Khel and it is significant that
the Halimzai candidate for the Mohmand National Assembly seat in
1977 was Khanzada, the son of Abdullah. Besides, affiliated groups
always resentful of Shati domination in Shati Khel await their turn to
emerge or at least witness the downfall of the traditional senior lineages.
The doctor in charge of the Shati hospital recounted to me how the
Ghunda Khel would often block his path to the main road as they said
his hospital was built on Shahzada's land. Their indirect rejection
reflected latent hostility to Shahzada's hegemony. Shahzada, in turn,
saw to it that when government brought electricity to Gandab in late
1973 his Musa kin villages received connections but ensured it was not
given to the Ghunda Khel and the Ranra.

(b) *Case-study: SAM*

I would like to illustrate *tarboorwali* affecting my SAM respondents
of the Kado lineage through a similar case-study. As the case-study is
almost identical to the TAM case in its patterns of agnatic rivalry
involving three generations over two decades and the same depth of
genealogical kin, I will merely recount the bare skeleton of the story.
On the sub-clan level the Kasim Khel (of which Kado are a sub-section)
and the Dadu Khel are led by Malik Afzal and Said Qahar respectively
whose own rivalry resembles that of Abdullah and Shahzada. Because
Afzal supports Shahzada, his cousin Said Qahar has thrown in his lot
with Abdullah. That is, both TAM and SAM took part in the same set
of cleavages.

The significant point I wish to illustrate by this case-study is that
until the division of TAM and SAM in 1951 (and even later) both
groups approximated to the ideal-type model of *Pukhtunwali* regarding
its major operative principle of *tarboorwali*. Therefore both case-
studies, in TAM and SAM, conform and approximate to the *Pukhtunwali* model I constructed in Chapter 4. *Pukhtunwali* is maintained
regardless of cost to life and property. The conclusion is not difficult
to reach and supports the thrust of my thesis: changes in Pukhtun
social behaviour begin only after encapsulation of SAM groups after
1951. After 1951 SAM though willing and, as the example shows,

recently involved in upholding Pukhto to its extreme and logical conclusion, cannot but deviate from the *nang* ideal-type model. For example, guns, the symbols of Pukhtunness and a diacritical feature in the Agency between Pukhtun and non-Pukhtun, are illegal without licences which are the privileged possession of a few and difficult to obtain. An important emergent difference in the continued generational rivalry in Shati Khel is the involvement of the younger generation. For instance Lakhkar's, Dilawar's or Shahzada's sons would be and are fully involved in the feuds of their fathers which they will inherit as part of their legacy. This contrasts sharply with SAM where the mild tussle among the *mashar* is a matter that does not overly involve or interest the young generation. I discovered this in private conversations with Bela youngsters. For instance Farman, a younger son of Shamshudin, said his three best friends were the sons of Khushal (Do Khel), Halim Said (Zarif Khel) and Sawbat (Kado Khel) respectively.

In the early 1930s the female cousin of Bahadar, a Kado Khel of Bela and a retired Scouts Subedar, was engaged to a cousin Sadat when the latter died of illness. Said Noor's cousin Raz Mohammad, another Scouts soldier, wished to marry the girl, now called a widow (*kunda*). Said Noor was Shamshudin's mother's brother and there was intense agnatic rivalry between Bahadur and his cousin Raz. This affair acted as a catalyst to their hate. Bahadur sought the support of his cousin Shamshudin's father, and together with other cousins they attempted to frustrate Raz and Said Noor. As a result Iranai's cousins, led by Roghan Mohammad, elder brother of Baz Mohammad, shot Said Noor. Some eight years later Rahmat and his Father's Brother's Son, Kher Mohammad, took revenge by shooting Gulaney, son of Durrani, and a nephew of Iranai (Figure 10).

A few years later Ala Mohammad, younger brother of Roghan, and Noor Rahman, the father of my Kado assistant Shamshur Rahman, shot Rahmat in revenge during the holy month of Ramadan. Noor's sister had planned with her brother and his group to bring her brother-in-law, Rahmat, to them for this purpose to avenge the death of her other brother, Gulaney. Shortly afterwards Raz Mohammad's son by his first wife was shot. The entire sub-section was fined Rs. 3,000 by the Political Agent as the murders took place in the Agency. Four deaths had resulted and this affair prepared the ground for the following sequel. The brother of the murdered Rahmat prepared Saz to take revenge for his dead brother and uncle Said Noor by constantly suggesting that Roghan and his group were determined to kill him. Saz was already having problems with his cousin Lal Zir who was backed by Roghan, his own brother.

Saz like Lal, his Father's Brother's Son, was a retired soldier of the Frontier Scouts and about the same age. There was no particular dispute between them but *tarboorwali*; both claimed 'I am the *man* of this village' (*ze the de kili saray yam*) and the deep cousin hatred festered. Following a petty quarrel begun by the women of the family Saz, married to Shamshudin's sister, killed Lal, father-in-law of Habibur Rahman, as he slept in the *hujra* of Bela Mohmandan; he then fled to Afghanistan. Saz's brother agreed that he was now outlawed from their area (*koshinda*). As the murder was committed in the Settled Area Saz became an official Proclaimed Offender (*mafroor*). The rest of the killings now shifted in the 1940s again across the border into the Michni area where *rogha* or *badal* are private matters concerning the family only (*khpal karona*). However, Saz returned some years later and lived in hiding with his brother Roghan, Shamshudin's father-in-law. Lal's son Aslam shot at Saz in the fields but missed. Fearing that Roghan was planning with Mohammad Aslam to kill him, Saz gunned down his brother Roghan and chased and killed his son Mir Mohammad who had climbed onto a roof to defend himself. Saz again escaped to Kabul but returned some years later. Saz beat and bullied Mir Mohammad's young sons when they were out grazing cattle, fearing that when they grew to manhood they would avenge their father's and grandfather's death. He threatened to kill them before they could kill him. The mother quietly disappeared to her father's village with her sons for their protection. In 1952 Saz's brother Baz Mohammad and his son Inayat Khan shot Saz down in the fields.

Shahzar, Saz's only son, swore revenge and promised to continue the vendetta but was finally persuaded to bury the hatchet by his uncle and cousins. The Kado lineage was debilitated and males and females unanimously asked: 'Why should we pluck our own feathers?' (*khpaley benrey da zan na waley obaso*). Saz's son agreed to give his sister to Baz's son in marriage and the daughter of Baz Mohammad was married to Mir Mohammad's son, patrilateral parallel cousins, to terminate the intra-sub-sectional killings. Earlier Daulat, a wise *mashar* and son of Said Noor, the first casualty in the episode, had waived his right to take *badal* by forgiving the murderers: 'He had forgiven his father's murderers' (*de plar marg ye obakho*). This act terminates the law of *badal*. Daulat's magnanimity is partly explained by the costs of *badal*, the encapsulation of the groups and the example of senior Maliks. Malik

Afzal had earlier forgiven his Father's Brother's Son, Rahman, who had treacherously murdered his father, Aziz, in spite of receiving various favours from him. In the earlier TAM study we saw the personal agony of agnatic killing through the eyes of Feroz. In SAM, deaths as seen through the eyes of Ihsanullah involve close male kin and are equally agonizing: he lost a maternal grandfather, two granduncles, his mother's brother, and four senior male kin. His mother's eyes still fill with tears when she talks of her murdered father and brother.

Figure 10 depicts the lineage relationships. Blocked triangles signify males killed specifically in the case-study. Marriages contracted after the deaths occurred and in order to bring peace between kin groups are numbered a and b. I have numbered the deaths to provide a sequence, of point and counterpoint, in the ineluctable logic of *badal*.

The case-studies described in this section support my thesis: if the practice of *nang*, understood through the eyes of the actors as *tarboorwali* and *badal*, were sociologically dysfunctional they would have tended to disappear. This leads to two sociologically relevant questions: what social purpose does *tarboorwali* serve in Pukhtun society? what advantages accrue from it to ensure its perpetuation and what form do they take? Firstly, and most important, *tarboorwali* provides diacritical social behaviour distinguishing Pukhtun and non-Pukhtun. Only the Pukhtun carries a gun: 'a gun is part of the dress of the land' (*topak de watan jama da*). Only the Pukhtun follows the laws of *tarboorwali* to their extremity. At the moment of enactment *tarboorwali* separates non-Pukhtun from ideal Pukhtun behaviour and confers superior and inferior status in society. He is thus confirming by expected outward social behaviour what is already a genealogical fact, his Pukhtunness. Pukhtun agnates descended from a common ancestor only are involved in *tarboorwali*. Khanzada told me that when he was Superintendent of Police in Bannu District he was approached by a murderer who promised to kill Major Sultan Jan for Rs. 10,000. Khanzada refused saying 'it was our affair as we are the descendants of one father.'

Secondly, and following from the above point, Pukhtunness carries with it various social and political advantages and implications. Political authority and leadership in society are seen as a monopoly of Pukhtuns. In external matters it is the Pukhtun who represents his lineage group to the administration and is able to extract favours confined to his kin or section (Chapter 5).

Having concluded that *tarboorwali* defines and distinguishes Pukhtun

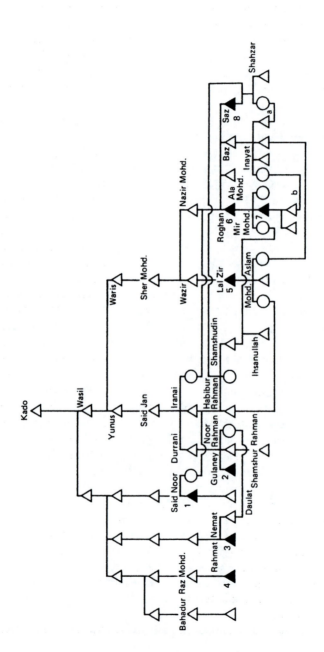

FIGURE 10 *Kado Khel agnatic rivalry and intermarriages*

from non-Pukhtun social behaviour we may begin to answer the second question: what is the prize or the goal? It is not land: there is a limited quantity available which, because of its barrenness, is economically unattractive; or access to water – there are no lakes and rivers in the Agency; or minerals and mines; or women – genealogically all Pukhtun women are related and their honour is therefore of universal concern. My contention is that the prize or goal cannot be defined in material terms. Yet what are the compulsions that drive men with such intensity that they are prepared to kill each other? The answers lie in the concepts of the *tarboorwali* cousin syndrome – concepts that are intangible, non-material and based on notions of honour: *saritob, ghairat* and *sharm*. Pukhtuns freely equate Pukhto practice to madness or 'heathen behaviour'. And who is the victor? No one is really the winner and every enemy death extracts as much sorrow as it does jubilation from within the circle of contestants, all close cognatic kin. The prize is negligible, the price is exorbitant. It is a systematic cannibalistic devouring of the innards of the sectional unit. Feroz's comment was a literal translation of the metaphor: 'Cousins eat each other's flesh.'

In concluding this section I shall make three general points that emerge from the argument above. Firstly, seen from a certain view *tarboorwali* contains a negative logic for society: the deaths and expulsion of defeated groups from Shati Khel maintain a crude Malthusian balance between population expansion and the available land that can support a population. The operation of *tarboorwali*, and the intergenerational and cyclical family movements as a consequence of it (Figure 14), require diachronic analysis as methodology in studying society. Second, the intensity with which *tarboorwali* is practised checks political power, curbs individual ambitions, and in a bloody and dramatic manner underwrites the principles of Pukhtun democracy. Such exceptional men as Abdullah, Atta and Shahzada, who in other places and at other times may have left their mark on local history, are opposed and balanced by equally exceptional cousins. Weberian-type charismatic leaders possessing 'superhuman' and 'exceptional powers' (Bendix, 1960; Weber, 1961) are reduced and negated within the tribal structure functioning through the mechanics of *tarboorwali*. In Pukhtun *nang* structure *tarboorwali* acts as an in-built check to 'eruption' of charismatic leadership.

Finally, it may be argued that the consequence of agnatic conflict is not dissonance or disharmony in society but, on the contrary, and as seen through the eyes of the *involved groups in society*, a confirmation and perpetuation of the key concepts of social behaviour and social organization. The saga of murder and revenge may be seen from outside as anarchic and symptomatic of a breakdown of the entire system. In fact it is not seen as such through native eyes. It is seen as upholding and supporting the principles of *Pukhtunwali* that approximate closest to the ideal-type model. It is no coincidence that the social mechanism terminating violent agnatic rivalry is the giving and taking of women in marriage from enemy groups, as in the marriages sealing the peace agreements in the TAM and SAM cases cited above. Paradoxically both the murders and marriages underline the close kin relationships of the actors and in one sense symbolize this unity. The case-studies illustrate that *tarboorwali* is practised in TAM and SAM society as it is socially understood and therefore tends to support my argument which I shall further support with reference to the other key feature of *Pukhtunwali*, *tor*, discussed in the following section.

II Tor: **female chastity as expression of the** nang **principle**

The chastity and good name of a woman are the most sensitive points of honour in Pukhtun society. Genealogically violation of a woman's honour is tantamount to classificatory incest in a society related on the tribal charter. Socially a woman's acts reflect her husband's status and honour. The male Pukhtun is most vulnerable through the behaviour of the women of his house. It is important to underline that the only killing in society that does not invoke the laws of revenge is when a man and woman are believed to have had an illicit liaison. They are then said to be *tor*, the colour black and opposite to that depicting purity, white (*spin*).[14] No person is beyond the law of purity and no price too high to uphold it. Such couples, whether involving mother, father, daughter or son of ego, are immediately and by unanimous social agreement killed. The act of death alone atones for this greatest of blots on Pukhtun character. The severity of punishment among Pukhtuns for adultery is in contrast to other Islamic tribes, for instance, the Berbers (Hart, 1976: 166-7) or among the Kababish Arabs where 'a wife is never killed for adultery, only severely beaten' (Asad, 1970: 58). The onus of punishment lies on the immediate agnatic kin of the guilty couple — father, uncles and brothers. Fathers and mothers acknowledge the deaths of their *tor* offspring by agreeing 'Pukhto has been done'. The 'vengeance group' which in some societies like the Bedouin is the 'tertiary segment' with a span up to five generations (Lewis, I. M.,

1969a, b; Peters, 1960) is restricted among Pukhtuns to the immediate male kin.

The ideal Pukhtun woman is a model of virtue, chastity and loyalty.[15] Opposed to the model of women involved in the disgrace of *tor* is the other female model of *mor*, the mother. *Mor* is the symbol of exalted status and emotion in Pukhtun society. She symbolizes *Pukhtunwali* as, for instance, Murtaza's mother in the preceding section. If the *tor* model is to be wiped out by death, the *mor* model is enshrined in song and proverb as the personification of Pukhto virtue. 'Heaven lies at the feet of the mother' is a common Pukhto saying, derived from an exhortation of the Prophet of Islam. Although *tor* cases empirically almost always approximate to the ideal and the two lovers, but especially the woman, are killed as the case-studies will show, the actual *mor* model deviates considerably from the ideal. Life for women is physically hard and monotonous as the unchanging time-tables for Mohmand women both in TAM and SAM illustrate in Chapter 9. Perhaps their lot is best summed up in the proverb that normatively places them through life's span either in the house or grave (*gor*): 'For a woman either the house or the grave' (Ahmed, 1975: 47). Males, especially educated ones like Feroz, admitted 'the lot of women is miserable, they are helpless' (Ahmed, A. S. and Z., forthcoming).

Evocation of shame (*peghor*) through constant pressure on women at the water tank or well and men in the *hujra*, is a powerful social mechanism for conformity. As I shall show through the following cases, the girl is usually shot by her own father or brother and the boy, unless he can manage to escape from the Tribal Areas, by his father or uncles. In one case quoted below the son shot his own father. Death alone atones for guilt. Honour is thus vindicated and Pukhto upheld; *tor* has been converted to *spin*. The impure has been cleansed and made pure. In cases where an illicit union cannot be proved, *tor* may be converted to *spin* by ceremonial offerings of a lamb or sheep cooked at a feast by the boy's family. A girl who elopes is called *mateza*. *Tor* cases are referred to as 'shaming' (*sharmawal*) by, and of, the group. Shame is associated directly with the action as honour is with the reaction. If the boy can escape and cross into the Settled Districts he will be declared *koshinda* whereby his own immediate family declare him *persona non grata* and accept the verdict that he may be liable to be shot whenever he returns or wherever he is found. Such severity of punishment and unanimity between involved groups, representing the boy and girl, act as a social mechanism to ensure continuity within the system of certain moral standards and social behaviour. The whole is kept greater than the individual.

Not surprisingly there is little glamour or romance in Romeo and Juliet stories in the Tribal Areas. The fate of the lovers is sealed from the moment of love. However, in an area often torn by agnatic rivalry and conflict the honour of women is universally respected. Genealogically every woman is a female sibling and dishonouring her would be tantamount to classificatory incest. Women may graze sheep alone or help in reaping the harvest unarmed and unescorted since rape or abduction of Pukhtun women is unknown in the Tribal Areas. *Tor* cases imply consent and, as will be seen below, usually involve unmarried couples. The concept of Pukhto as 'word of honour' is significant in understanding that an 'engaged' girl is considered as good as married. The 'word' has been given. If she elopes and marries another man her fiancé and society will consider them *tor*. The fiancé from the moment of engagement, often a spoken commitment at the girl's birth, is considered the 'husband' of the girl.

The *tor* cases below are from my field-work areas. Some are recent but they have all occurred in the last two decades. As they involve the honour of known people I shall present them in brief form and keep the names and dates anonymous so as to minimize the possibility of identification. I have similar case-studies for the Orakzai tribe but will restrict myself to selected cases from my Mohmand field-work groups. I have deliberately chosen cases involving different groups to illustrate the underlying principles and the reaction of the kin around ego to differing situations, thereby illuminating confirmation or deviance and its forms from the ideal. The cases will illustrate the principle that Pukhto practice in TAM and SAM groups still largely approximates to the Pukhto ideal-type. However, recent SAM cases reveal a tendency towards softening of attitudes, especially by mothers where marriage may follow *tor*, and also a tendency towards exoneration in cases where non-Mohmand actors are involved. TAM *tor* cases up to my field-work period invariably end in the death of both boy and girl, blocked in black in the following figures.

FIGURE 11 Tor *cases (TAM). Case no. 1*

A Pukhtun married couple, D and E, arrive at Malik A's village as *hamsayas* seeking political refuge from *tarboorwali.* B, A's son, begins a quiet affair with E. D reports the matter to A who arranges a feast, at the end of which he asks all present to pray. He then pulls out his revolver and empties six shots into his son B. Pukhto has been done. After the forty days of Islamic mourning for his son's death, A calls D and gives him the same revolver and asks him to also do Pukhto by shooting his own wife E. D shoots E. A then declares in public that as of now D is his legal son and marries him to his dead son's wife C.

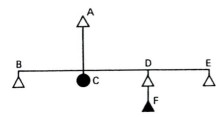

Case no. 2

F and C, nephew and aunt, have an affair and run away to Karachi. The family of A is subject to intense *peghor.* C and F are lured back and while B shoots his sister, E shoots his nephew with the blessing of and in the presence of A.

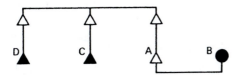

Case no. 3

D and C, cousins of A, make suggestive signs to A's wife B while she is on the roof of her house drying clothes. Realizing their error D and C run away to the Settled Area in Shabkadar. A returns to hear his neighbour's *peghor.* He kills his wife B and then follows D and C to Shabkadar and kills them there.

Non-Mohmand religious and occupational groups follow an equally rigid Code of behaviour regarding the honour of women. There is thus no difference in the practice of the Code between Mohmand and non-Mohmand groups in *tor* cases as the following cases show:

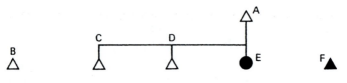

Case no. 4

Case 4 involves a member of a religious group and illustrates that they are subject to the same laws applicable to Pukhtuns in such cases. E, engaged to B, runs away with F, a member of the local religious group, to Peshawar where they are married. Some time later they are lured back by false promises and A, B, C and D shoot both E and F.

Case no. 5

This case involves an affiliated group. C's husband B is dead and C has an affair with D. A, brother of B, shoots C while D escapes to the Settled Area and is declared *koshinda*.

SAM, in spite of their encapsulated situation, do not permit compromise in *tor* cases. The legal attitude in court, embodied in the Pakistan Penal Code and the Criminal Procedure Code, and especially where applicable in the Frontier Crimes Regulation, makes allowances for such crimes of passion involving *tor* particularly among tribal groups. For instance, in the following cases police and judicial officers, through intermediary kin, make it clear that if the murderer returns from the Tribal Areas, where he invariably escapes after committing the crime, he would be leniently dealt with. Such assurances are always honoured.

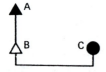

FIGURE 12 Tor *cases (SAM). Case no. 1*

A has an affair with C, his son's wife. B is employed outside the village.

Son returns to hear hints of *peghor* in the village and shoots his father A and wife C.

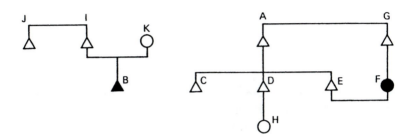

Case no. 2

E, the husband of F, a patrilateral parallel cousin has been employed abroad for the last three years. B is engaged to H but people spread the rumour that he is having an affair with F. A and G, the elders, face *peghor* of the community and decide that A's sons C and D will shoot B and F. B and F are shot. According to the condition he had imposed on his family after he had heard of the affair, only then does E return from abroad. B's father I and uncle J are satisfied 'Pukhto has been done'. J regrets he did not personally shoot B. But K, B's mother, breaks down and hits her head with stones and claims people made mischief and that her son was innocent.

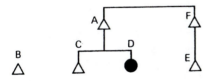

Case no. 3

D engaged to B was picking maize in the field when E, a young cousin and son of F, chanced on her. While he talked to her, B happened along and accused them of being *tor*. B complained to A who, with his son C, shot his daughter D. E ran away from the area and went into hiding. The elders arranged *uzar* worth Rs. 1,500 so as not to split the group. E was later allowed to return.

The following four SAM cases suggest mild forms of deviance in normative Pukhtun behaviour regarding *tor* but may be suggestive signals of future attitudes. However, it is essential to point out that two cases involve non-Mohmand groups.

Case no. 4

A non-Pukhtun boy B, from a religious group, is suspected of having had an illicit relationship with a girl C, also a non-Pukhtun. Nothing is proved but the village community refuse to pray with the boy standing in front of them to lead the prayers. A *jirga* of *mashars* from the village and Maliks from the Agency decide that the case is weak and in deference to A impose a nominal fine of Rs. 200 and the ceremonial *uzar* of one lamb after which the case is considered closed. The laxity in this case may be contrasted with the severity in TAM of case no. 3 where an entirely blameless wife is murdered, or of case no. 4 involving a religious group where an unmarried but engaged woman eloped with and married a member of her group but was shot with her husband.

Case no. 5

B, married son of *mashar* A, elder of Pukhtun lineage, is caught in *flagrante delicto* by an old half-blind Pukhtun with married woman C, from an occupational group, during the day-time in the fields in summer when the crops afford protection from prying eyes. As the witness is almost blind, the girl from a weak (*kamzor*) group and the Pukhtun *mashar* prepared to pay *uzar* to patch up the matter, it is over-looked as one of misunderstanding and dropped.

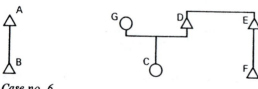

Case no. 6

Case no. 6 illustrates changing attitudes to *tor* cases in SAM especially where the women of the house are involved. No one is killed in this or the next case in spite of attempts at shooting and murder. C is F's patrilateral parallel cousin engaged to him but has an affair with B, a soldier, and on the plea of seeing a doctor spends the day with him in Peshawar. B wants to marry C and his intentions are honourable. However, as mentioned above, an engaged girl in Pukhtun society is considered 'given' to the boy and the breaking of an engagement is a serious violation of honour. D beats C and breaks her arm and with E plans to kill her and her paramour B who runs off to join his unit in the army. C on the secret advice of her mother G runs to the house of A, her lover's father. *Jirgas* and Maliks gather to prevent bloodshed and proclaim a fine of Rs. 30,000 for anyone committing murder. G, the mother of C, then connives with some *mashars* for C to be taken to where B is posted and the couple get married. F, still seeking vengeance, now has to accept the *fait accompli*. The happy ending is a rare one.

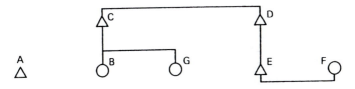

Case no. 7

B, engaged to A, runs away to Peshawar with her cousin E already married and becomes *mateza*. Both B and E are declared *tor* although they marry. *Jirgas* and Maliks attempt to reconcile the parties and after five years D, father of E, accepts his guilt for not being able to prevent his son, E, from dishonouring A and pays *uzar* to the tune of Rs. 2,000. The *uzar* converts *tor* to *spin* but A, still called, like all fiancés, *khawand* of B, refuses to accept the decision of the *jirga* and on two occasions shoots at E hitting him in the arm once. As E is involved in a *tor* case and on the defensive he cannot shoot back for *badal*. To appease A, the father of B offers her sister G in marriage but A refuses. However, he feels his honour vindicated in this act of refusal and the case ends with A marrying outside the family.

The case-studies above illustrate that where actual illicit sexual relationships are contracted between two parties they face the extreme penalty of death enforced by their own male closest kin. Under no condition do groups in TAM overlook sexual scandal even if extenuating circumstances are present as the case-studies show. The studies from SAM illustrate the effects of three decades of encapsulation. There is a perceptible softening in attitude especially where it is possible to compromise due to insufficient evidence as in cases no. 4 and no. 5, or where the girl is unmarried and the intentions of the boy are honourable and the affair ends in marriage as in case no. 6. But these deviances occur only where extenuating circumstances exist and actual cases of adultery are dealt with as severely as in TAM. In *tor* cases Mohmand social behaviour in TAM and SAM approximates to the Pukhtun ideal-type model.

It is in this sense that the blood and thunder of *tarboorwali* and *tor* paradoxically emphasize continuity and stability in society and structure. As illustrated by the case-studies, *tarboorwali* is simply another mechanism that underlines the importance of lineage structures and opposed segmentary groups and with *tor* ensures the perpetuation over generations of *Pukhtunwali*.

Status and honour are allocated to individuals, male or female, who through certain actions have lived up to the central concepts of *Pukhtunwali* at high personal costs. Atta, in the earlier case-study, has won high status for himself and is universally quoted as an example of Pukhtun manhood and behaviour; so are women like Murtaza's mother in TAM or Noor's sister in SAM, who continue agnatic rivalry even at the cost of killing male siblings. Similarly, the ideal woman in *tor* cases does not mind being killed in order to establish her innocence. Perhaps this explains why women in a man's world are such staunch upholders of Pukhto.

In concluding this chapter I wish to point out that the case-studies have been pieced together from accounts garnered from various sources and groups including women. Dates were always somewhat vague and I have had to rely on extensive counter-checking and, where possible, archival material to ensure maximum accuracy. The case-studies illustrate three important points, one methodological and two theoretical. Methodologically, I have accepted informants' statements and accounts as value judgments but it is clear that ideal and actual social behaviour have closely coincided *through their eyes* in the case-studies described above. The 'conscious' or 'home-made' model (Ward, 1969) though representing a wide temporal and spatial span has been successfully maintained.

From a theoretical point of view I see social encounter in tribal society not as isolated incidents but as related sequences in a long and connected process of social relations. The larger historical framework is thus of direct relevance in understanding tribal social structure. The emergence of certain leaders and the resultant imbalance in agnatic equilibrium may be seen as one result of the interests and intervention of larger conterminous state systems. Social structure can be conceived of as an aggregate of formal and continuing sets of relationships of related groups within a social system. Thus analysis of such systems is possible only through 'sociological history' or 'diachronic sociology'. In short, I am advocating demands for method and theory that rest on extensive use of diachronic case-study material, what anthropologists have called 'the extended-case method' (Gluckman, 1961) and 'situational analysis' (Velsen, 1964, 1969) for 'a synchronic analysis' of society within a theoretical frame that allows for 'diachronic analysis' (Velsen, 1969: 149).

I have stated earlier that man is not a reified concept in abstract theoretical models. He is not externalized to society or independent of it. He is born into a pre-existing matrix of social configurations which determine his social being. The same social groups may be plausibly analysed within different frames of reference (holist or individualist) at different periods of social history and in different geographical and administrative areas (Ahmed, 1976).

Simplistically put, man, in this case the Pukhtun, is free to and does maximize life's chances by manipulating society and its symbols around him. He is man analysed in the individualist frame. However, once he activates the key principles that order his society and are meaningful to him, such as *tarboorwali* and *tor*, he is almost mechanistically locked to a pre-determined pattern of social action and interaction that has all the inevitability of a geometrical equation. He is caught inexorably within social laws from which there is no escape even if he wished it. Society in general and in particular in the form of his closest kin, his mother (as in the case of Murtaza in TAM avenging his dead father) or sister (as in the case of Noor Rahman in SAM helping him to avenge their dead brother Gulaney), compel him to conform to expected normative behaviour. Every important symbol to the Pukhtun revolving around *Pukhtunwali* is activated. In rejecting these symbols he runs the risk of rejecting his very 'Pukhtunness'. He is now man to be analysed within the holist frame. The case-studies above are illustrations in support of the argument in the social sciences for the need to synthesize the frames of reference as tools in social analysis (Alavi, 1973).

Aggregates of social behavioural sequences create patterns that the anthropologist may analyse as social reality and conversely, from the instances of irregularity from normative behaviour, he may illuminate that reality and help it to be understood. The examples quoted in this chapter approximate as closely as is empirically possible to ideal Pukhtun behaviour. What is remarkable is that there is so little deviance from the ideal. Obviously *Pukhtunwali* continues to be idealized and practised. The important distinguishing factor between TAM and SAM is the creation of the political and administrative boundary in 1951. After this date although TAM continue to maintain traditional behaviour regarding *tarboorwali* and *tor*, SAM find it increasingly difficult to do so. In terms of my study they are confronting the hard facts of encapsulation that partly inhibit them from following traditional and ideal behaviour. They are thus under pressure to deviate. There are still cases of agnatic murder based on *saritob*, like the one that occurred during my field-work and mentioned earlier, but these involve complications with the law and are therefore becoming relatively rare. However, this is not to say that SAM have abandoned the principles of *Pukhtunwali*. Deviance is a relative not absolute social condition. It must be underlined that the only examples of fratricide and patricide I have come across were from SAM, the former involving *tarboorwali* and the latter *tor*, the cardinal principles of *Pukhtunwali*.

In this chapter I hope I have effectively deployed my data in substantiating my argument that in the two cardinal features that Mohmands see as comprising the *Pukhtunwali* model, *tarboorwali* and *tor*, actual social behaviour approximates to the ideal in the main. The conflation of the two sets of models is the major point in the chapter as indeed it is in the study. It may be stated unequivocally that TAM act in accordance with normative ideal behaviour and SAM, although encapsulated, and under various strains, also largely attempt to live by the two essential features of *Pukhtunwali*.

Having illustrated the high degree of similarity between the actual and the ideal in social behaviour I now turn to a discussion in the next chapter of matters related to Pukhtun social organization such as settlements and marriage patterns. I hope to shore up my argument further by illustrating that both in settlements and marriage patterns Pukhtun actual practice largely approximates to the ideal model.

8 Settlement and domestic structure

'With the strong one, either keep your distance or your peace' —
common Pukhto proverb (Ahmed, 1975: 44).

Settlement arrangements and, following from them, marriage patterns,
two significant and inter-related aspects of social organization among
the Mohmands, provide further evidence in support of my argument.
This I shall illustrate, in the present chapter, with the extensive use of
figures and data. I will be arguing that in TAM ideal Pukhtun deployment of settlements based on Pukhtun hierarchy and the current dominant lineage is closely adhered to. In SAM palpable deviances from the
ideal are perceptible but the contours of the ideal may be identified.
The fourth section of the chapter, on marriage, wholly corroborates my
thesis. Figures from both groups reveal the very high rate of endogamy
in spite of the often blurred genealogical and social lines in SAM. In this
situation encapsulation does not affect the basic Pukhtun values regarding the giving and, indeed, taking of women.

Within shifting settlement arrangements there is always one factor
assumed constant. The boundaries of the sub-section, identified in the last
chapters as the operative lineage which correspond to marked geographical areas usually with prominent natural boundaries, are universally
honoured. However successful one sub-section is against the other, it cannot annex or occupy the land of the defeated sub-section. While other
Halimzai groups may assist and ally with one or other faction and, in the
extreme and rare situations, invade Shati Khel to punish groups of the
sub-section by burning their houses, as the Upper Mohmands did in 1932
(Chapters 3 and 7), universal tribal custom would not permit occupation.
The ideal Pukhtun settlement pattern is also apparent in the case of the
Tarakzai sub-sections to which the people of Bela Mohmandan belong.
Map 3 illustrated the areas of the two major sub-clans of the Tarakzai,
the Kasim Khel and the Dadu Khel, separated by marked geographical
features such as deep and dry stream beds (*khwar*) or hill ranges.

As I shall show below the three major lineages in Shati Khel, descended from a common ancestor, arrange and rearrange their village situations within the Shati Khel area as a consequence of the agnatic rivalry discussed in the last chapter. However, non-Shati groups, like the affiliated Ghunda Khel and Ganjian, remain outside and across the dry stream bed, Tor Gat Khwar, that separates them and the size of their land ownership remains fixed and unchanging. Map 5 below illustrates both points. The boundaries of the Yusuf Khel, Kadai Khel and Shati Khel have remained unchanged over the last century as have the peripheral lands occupied by the Ghunda Khel and Ganjian within Shati Khel. It is however within the core area of the Shati Khel, between the Tor Gat Khwar that divides the descendants of Shati from the affiliated Ghunda Khel and Ganjian groups, and the southern and eastern boundaries along the watershed of the mountain range encircling Shati Khel, that the drama of agnatic rivalry is enacted resulting in emergent or destroyed settlements. As the proverb quoted above suggests defeated or weaker lineages either keep their 'distance', as do the Ranra, or their 'peace', like the Malok in relation to the dominant or 'strong' lineage, in Shati Khel, the Musa.

I Ethno-dynamics of tribal settlements: spatial mobility and lineage politics

The changing settlement arrangements of the three lineages in the maps[1] of Shati Khel below illustrate the principles of sub-sectional rivalry; in addition, by the unchanging boundaries of the affiliated groups, they illustrate ideal Pukhtun settlement patterns. Shati Khel is defined by the watershed on the mountain ranges on its three sides and a dry stream bed on its fourth, in the west, along which the new road now runs. The western stream bed demarcates the Shati Khel from the Yusuf Khel and the Kadai Khel areas. The highest point is at Khazana Sar, 4,910 feet, forming part of the Nahakki range and overlooking Shati Khel. The fresh-water springs at the end of the Shati Khel area in the east are of vital importance to the settlements, especially in view of the scant rainfall, and it is no coincidence that the Musa, the dominant Shati lineage, live by the springs and their main settlement is still called after the water springs, Chino.

An analysis of Shati Khel's twenty settlements and population tends to support my thesis in three significant features. Roughly half of the total population of 1,031 is of the Musa lineage. This figure would illustrate the principle that success in agnatic competition results in political domination and is expressed in the number of settlements. Secondly, the non-Pukhtun settlement, that of Aziz, constitutes 4 per cent of the Shati Khel population. Pukhtun purity is thus maintained in the settlement arrangements. Third, tribal democracy is strengthened by the average number of people, just over fifty, in each settlement. Most of the settlements are small and fort-like and fall readily into three distinct categories which will be discussed below.

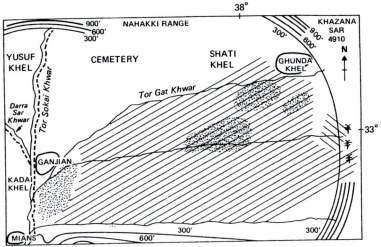

MAP 5 *Shati Khel: shifting settlements and lineage politics.* (i) *Shati Khel: 1900*

Certain features in the maps require elaboration. Firstly, the affiliated lineages, Ghunda Khel and Ganjian, remain across the Tor Gat Khwar that separates them from the descendants of the Shati Khel. The land north of the *khwar* is rocky, uncultivable and derives no benefits from the Shati springs. It is in this barren area that the Shati Khel also bury their dead in a sprawling cemetery at the foot of the mountain range. Aziz's father, who as we saw earlier was brought to Shati Khel by Malik Anmir as a munitions specialist, was given land to build a house across the Tor Gat Khwar. The Mians remain within the defined area of Kassai except that they too exhibit fissures in their settlements (Maps 5(i) and (iii)) as do the Ghunda Khel and Ganjian. In Map 5(iii) there are four Ghunda Khel and four Ganjian settlements in 1976 originating from one each in 1900 (Map 5(i)). As mentioned earlier, no occupational

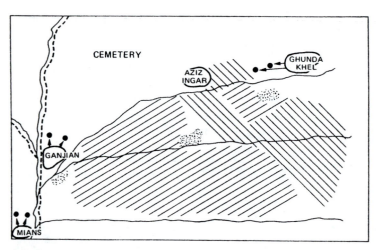

(ii) *Shati Khel: 1935*

groups of any kind live in Shati Khel but visit it to ply their trades on fixed days of the week from the mixed village of Sangar.

Second, within the core area of Shati Khel, Musa lineage history begins with Saida Mir, the great-grandfather of Shahzada, being driven out of Shati Khel, lock, stock and barrel, by the Ranra in the last century and having to seek refuge among the Kadai (Chapter 7). Maps 5 (i), (ii) and (iii) illustrate how the rise in the fortunes of the Musa corresponds in inverse proportion to the decline in the fortunes of the other two cousin lineages, Ranra and Malok. As we saw in Chapter 3, between 1915 and 1935 the British were involved in Mohmand politics against the hostile Upper Mohmand clans and the shoring up of the power of Anmir and his son Shahzada, power which they manipulated with consummate skill to consolidate their own position in Shati Khel *vis-à-vis* cousin lineages.

Third, after the death of the Musa patriarch, Anmir, in 1938, a series of fissures took place among the segmentary group resulting in seven Musa settlements from their single village, Chino (Map 5(iii)). Map 5 (iii) also illustrates how the Musa now command the Shati Khel area. They monopolize access to water and because of their higher situation, by 200-300 feet on the foot-hills of the mountain range, they are placed in a militarily strategic position. As a consequence, and because of its association with the dominant lineage, this area is socially the most prestigious and its land therefore the most expensive in Shati Khel.

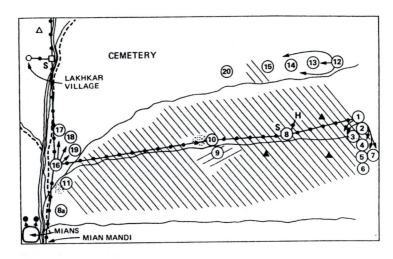

(iii) *Shati Khel: 1976*

KEY TO MAP 5 (i), (ii) and (iii)

Not to scale
Sectional boundary -----
Sectional fissure ⟶
Stream bed (*Khwar*) ～～
Spring ⚥
Road ══
School S
Hospital H
Frontier Scouts camp △
Community centre ▢
Electricity •-•-•
Destroyed settlements ▲

N.B. Geographical features
in Map (i) are assumed
constant for Maps (ii) and (iii)

Settlements: Shati Khel lineages

Musa ⟍⟍⟍ Ranra ⟋⟋⟋ Malok ░░░

1 Chino   9 Ranra/Mazullah   10 Malok/Sar Gul
2 Saz   11 Shabana
3 Murtaza
4 Khanawar
5 Sarfaraz
6 Machoray
7 Shahmat
8 Shahzada/new village (tower 8a)

non-Shati Khel settlements
affiliated groups

Ghunda Khel   Ganjian
12 Said Malal   16 Hassan
13 Mir Ahmad   17 Mian Khan
14 Said Hakim   18 Hazrat noor
15 Sheradad   19 Sawtar

occupational groups
20 Aziz Ingar

The Ranra who began by dominating the Shati Khel (Map 5(i)) are in 1976 restricted to one village (Map 5(iii)). In a typical example of tribal legerdemain Shahzada donated Ranra and Malok lands, acquired by force, to the government for a school and a hospital (Map 5(iii)). A grateful government, in turn, gave Shahzada various favours including electricity connections in 1973, extensions which he ensured reached his Musa kin and the now subdued Malok but not the Ranra. The destroyed villages of Atta Khan, Malok and Ranra, each built on about half an acre, remain as rubble and are symbolic of the victory and hegemony of the Musa; no clearing of the site for cultivation or construction is allowed by the Musa.

Map 5(iii) indicates the appearance of institutions with social and economic ramifications for Shati Khel and the Mohmand: the Mohmand road, linking Peshawar to Nawagai and Malakand; the new settlement of Malik Lakhkar; and the growth of the first market common to the Mohmand clans, the Mian Mandi.

The settlement arrangements of Shati Khel represent empirical reality approximating to the idealized Pukhtun model: concentric circles moving outside from the core circle, which is inhabited by the dominant lineage and descendants of a common ancestor and successively representing groups of lesser social importance. The correlation between the core circle and the dominant lineage is obvious. We may conceptualize four such concentric circles. The first circle, inhabited by the dominant lineage, the Musa, represents political power and social status. Its physical elevation over the other settlements symbolizes its higher situation. The second circle is also inhabited by the descendants of the common ancestor Shati, the Malok and Ranra, sub-sections now politically subdued. This circle corresponds geographically to the Tor Gat Khwar in the north that separates the descendants of Shati from the non-Shati, and the geographical limits of Shati Khel in the east and south. The third concentric circle is still within the Shati Khel area but north of the Tor Gat Khwar and inhabited by the non-Shati Khel groups of Ghunda Khel, Ganjian and Aziz. The population of the first three circles is exclusively *nang* Pukhtuns (with the notable exception of Aziz). The fourth and final circle may be conceptualized as one containing non-Shati but Halimzai groups, like Yusuf Khel and Kadai, and non-Mohmand groups like religious groups, the Mians of Kassai, and the occupational groups at Sangar. Figure 13 depicts the conceptualization of lineage domination and settlement arrangements in Shati Khel.

An interesting feature of settlement arrangements, explained paradoxically by both success and failure in the political life of tribal groups, is their tendency to be pushed out of the Agency and pulled to the Settled Areas often creating the *dwa-kora* settlements discussed in the next section. The *nang* migrations to *qalang* areas are not seen as a diaspora or a dispersal of clans but as a sloughing off process among groups with commitments and intentions of retaining contacts with the original home and eventually returning once their position is financially secure.

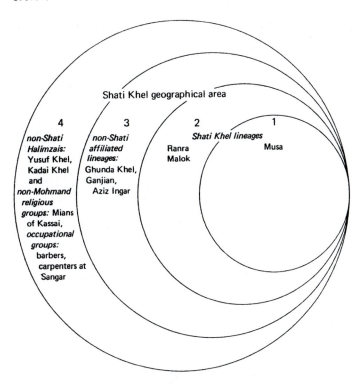

FIGURE 13 *Lineage domination and settlement arrangements*

II Dwa-kora: the concept of dual residence

Islamic tribes have been analysed in terms of 'nomadic' groups (Asad, 1970; Barth, 1961, 1968; Lewis, I. M., 1961; Pehrson, 1966; Tapper, 1971, 1974a, b) or 'sedentary' groups (Barth, 1953; Gellner, 1969a; Inayatullah and Shafi, 1964; Leach, 1940; Stirling, 1965). The Mohmands are neither 'nomadic' nor 'sedentary'. They do not live in microcosmic, largely self-sufficient, largely isolable village units as groups do on the rest of the subcontinent in India (Bailey, 1960; Dube, 1965; Lewis, O., 1958; Marriott, 1955; Mayer, A. C., 1970) or Pakistan

(Ahmad, S., 1973, 1977; Alavi, 1971; Eglar, 1960). This section will attempt to define a third category, that of the *dwa-kora* tribal group. Mohmands usually own two homes, often at considerable distance from one another, and are therefore called *dwa-kora*. Even so, the second home is spatially within the same sub-section or group as the first and is either managed by close agnatic kin, brothers or sons, as joint property or owned outright in certain cases. Unlike other tribal groups in the area, for instance the Baluchis (Pehrson, 1966: 4) Pukhtuns do not prefer nomadic camp life. They prefer permanent dwellings in spite of the *dwa-kora* system; both houses, although of mud, are fixed places of residence.

It is important at the outset to state that the concept of *dwa-kora* is to be understood in a literal and figurative sense. The *dwa-kora* category is as much a state of mind as a spatial or physical arrangement. Houses are made of mud and the only valuable part is the main wood-beam of the roof as in the houses of the Kurds (Leach, 1940: 49). They may thus be abandoned with ease and reconstructed with equal ease. Life is spartan and possessions limited. The Mohmands shift from one to the other house not like nomads in response to seasonal change but when and how lineage politics and/or economic compulsion dictate. The two houses are fully functional and interchangeable. *Dwa-kora* therefore describes a critical component of the character of the Mohmands and has a direct bearing on socio-political behaviour.

Successful tribesmen like Inayatullah and his son Abdullah, Anmir and Major Sultan Jan, his brother, made houses for themselves in Shabkadar, the town from where the Mohmands were administered, largely to be in contact with officials. Shahzada bought himself some rooms in the early 1920s. Failure in Shati also created a similar process of migration to Shabkadar. Defeated groups like the Ranra found their way to Shabkadar after being expelled from Shati Khel. Other defeated groups, like Dilawar's father Itbar Jan or Lakhkar's father, moved further into the Settled Areas to work as farm labourers and then eventually as independent farmers.[2] The point I wish to make is that through all these generational population shifts contact in varying degrees was maintained with Shati Khel, a factor crucial in understanding the nature of the intergenerational agnatic rivalry in Shati Khel. Thus Dilawar and Lakhkar, born in Mardan District, are aware of their place on the genealogical charter which would legitimize activation of claims to land their fathers may have lost two or three generations ago (Figure 14). The loser invariably shifts to the Settled

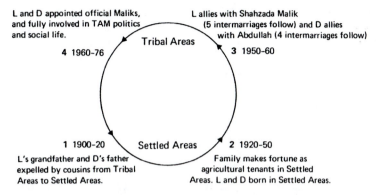

FIGURE 14 *Cyclical and intergenerational movements of Malik Lakhkar and Malik Dilawar*

Area and becomes one *kora*, but in his mind is the other *kor* lost in TAM which he hopes to regain in his life-time or that of his sons. This does happen frequently as in the cases of Malik Lakhkar and Malik Dilawar.

We questioned all household heads about migration: when they migrated, which relation migrated, where from and to and why? In an analysis of the *dwa-kora* houses in a random and stratified analysis of migration from Shati Khel to Shabkadar, I discovered that the major movement took place in the 1950s when the Agency Mohmands were in a position to exploit their situation in the Agency and could still farm in Shabkadar on irrigated land and thereby supplement their income. As a result many of the household heads in Shati Khel have a few acres of irrigated land around Shabkadar and one or two small rooms in the town itself. This rather large exodus is distinct from the movement necessitated by agnatic rivalry discussed in the previous paragraph. The people of Bela migrated 150 to 200 years ago and took most of the land which was unclaimed (*shamilat*)[3] and largely uncultivable more or less freely. In those days Bela must have appeared more attractive agriculturally than the Michni area as there was no water in the latter. Shamshudin and his brother Habibur Rahman had divided their lands before the death of their father, Iranai, and as the former was in SAM and the latter in TAM they could together claim to be *dwa-kora*. In such cases the concept remains to sustain the system and its memory as in practice the barriers between the Agency and District grow. Perhaps it is significant that junior lineages of the Kado left their homeland, Kado Korona, to settle in Bela. Habibur Rahman, the elder son of Iranai, remained in the Agency.

It is important to point out that the identification with and emphasis on land, the earth (leading to the concept of Mother Earth, chthonic deities), etc., in agricultural peasant societies does not exist among the Mohmand. There is no mystique attached to land or the earth. One may lose land in Shati and be ousted from TAM areas but retain one's position and rights in the tribal charter. Emphasis is thus on descent groups and filiation in the lineage structure.

III Types of tribal settlements

Names of villages specifically derive from the senior-most living agnate in TAM, for example the village of Shahzada Malik (*Shahzada Malik kilay*) or generally from the sub-section, Ranra or Malok villages. Villages may even have temporary and dual names. Ranra village is also known by the name of its living senior Malik, Mazullah Khan, as is Malok by its senior Malik, Sar Gul. SAM villages have permanent and generalized names, for example, Bela Mohmandan, village of the Mohmands. Even so, Bela's 'sister' village a mile away and in the Tribal Areas is still called after the dominant sub-section of the clan, Kado Korona, providing both with an opportunity to refer to themselves as *dwa-kora*. TAM villages are small and little more than nuclear settlements exclusively inhabited by the descendants of a common ascendant. The average population of a hamlet may be about a dozen people consisting of an elementary, nuclear family as in Lakhkar village (Figure 15 (i)) or about sixty people forming a compound family if the senior is a polygynist as in Shahzada Malik village (Figure 15(ii)). Larger settlements like Ranra or Sar Gul villages, ranging from 100 to 150, are inhabited by the families of several married brothers living clustered together in a joint family (Figure 15(iii)). Bela houses are largely inhabited by nuclear families (Figure 16(i)), although there are still examples of the extended family household (Figure 16(iii)).[4]

Statistics gathered from the formal questionnaires indicate differentiated demographic patterns in the two areas. In Shati Khel the average number of people per household (not per settlement) is fifteen whereas it is seven in Bela. Equally indicative of nuclear familial arrangements in SAM are the significant statistics regarding single and joint families. In Shati there are 75 per cent joint families and 25 per cent single whereas in Bela the situation is reversed: 72 per cent people live as single families and only 28 per cent as joint families, indicating a trend towards peasantization of tribal demographic arrangements and permanent fissure in the lineage. Births in both areas are largely local: 77 per cent of TAM and 85 per cent of SAM people were born in their villages. The average age of household heads is older in TAM than SAM, 55 in Shati and 51 in Bela.

(a) *TAM settlements*

In the figures below I shall illustrate the main features of the three types of settlements in TAM. The first settlement is called after the household head, Malik Lakhkar, and is an example of a nuclear family village. This village was begun in the late 1960s. The second example is of a typical compound family village in which the patriarch of the family is the dominant and central figure. The village is named after the patriarch, Shahzada, but is also called 'new village', a name given to it when it was begun in the late 1930s. The third example is of a typical joint family village called after the lineage which inhabits it, the Malok, or sometimes after the old and infirm senior-most agnate, Sar Gul.

Lakhkar's village, as indeed do the other TAM settlements, illustrates the underlying structural principles of Pukhtun domestic arrangements reflecting the Code and its principal features. The village is in the shape of a square and guarded at the two diagonal ends by towers. A clear division, which I have indicated by double lines, separates the strictly private life of a Pukhtun household from public life. The former symbolizing the primary law of seclusion (*parda* or *satar*) for women is differentiated from the other half containing the guest rooms symbolizing political prestige and the other vital aspect of Pukhtun social activity, agnatic rivalry. Within the private domain are housed four distinct and important items: the women, the cattle, the grain stores (usually in the base of the tower) and the water well. The importance of the well in supplying water to the village can only be emphasized in terms of it still remaining the first and major target of an attacking force. Once the well is captured there is little resistance from the village. The *parda* of women is maintained ever for toilet facilities which are available only to their sex within the village. Men answer the call of nature often before sunrise and in previously allocated areas by the village usually in a dry stream bed or ravine. They, however, bath in the village. The household head occupies the main room with his wife and daughters and the other room is occupied by the sons of the household head. As marriages are entirely virilocal sons, after marriage, invariably have a separate room made for themselves and as these are of mud it is neither an expensive nor a time-consuming proposition.

There are no cupboards or tables in the rooms as there are no chairs in the *hujras*. The only possession in the rooms are cots (usually shared by children) and for the adult a tin box containing his prized possessions and in which the household head locks his money. Unlike other Islamic groups such as the Kababish Arabs where women own the tents (Asad, 1970), among the Pukhtuns the house and everything in it belongs to the male.

The total population of the village is thirteen, including three labourers and seasonal employees. Apart from Malik Lakhkar and his daughter, who is married to Amirzada, no other person is married. Akbar Jan, Lakhkar's eldest son, is engaged to be married to Amirzada's daughter from his first marriage.

In the *hujra* there is always a fixed place for prayers and ablutions. A dozen cots, of dwarf palm, and quilts (for winter) are always at hand. The greater the number of guests the greater the prestige and importance of the household head. The main entrance leads into the *hujra* and is a large wood and iron gate, 12 feet high by 10 feet wide.[5] There is also a smaller entrance by the south-eastern tower for the use of the family only.

The total settlement looks like a square and is almost 40 yards by 40 yards in length and breadth except where a wall of 2 yards has been added on the south side to protect the well which is still under construction. The walls to the north and east face the Nahakki range and are 18 feet high to prevent the possibility of sniping from the dominating hills. The walls on the west and south side are 3 to 4 feet lower. The thickness of the walls is about three feet and as they are made of mud and stone they are calculated to prevent bullets and even cannon balls from penetrating. The towers are 27 feet high and 16 square yards in area. Inside the house the room of the household head is 21 feet in length and 15 feet in width. The other living room is smaller in size and the one for cattle even smaller.

Lakhkar's village, built in the late 1960s at the foot of the Nahakki range, and by the side of the Mohmand road, was of critical importance in the crossing of the Nahakki Pass and the subsequent penetration from 1973 onwards.[6] Lakhkar's hospitality and cooperation elicited official patronage from the political authorities, including the construction of the only cement rooms in his village, the two guest rooms, and the promise for finances to dig a well. As we saw earlier Lakhkar's moments of glory with the administration, when he basked in their patronage, resulted in Shahzada's antagonism. Once the political authorities became involved with wooing the Safis in the north Lakhkar's demands for a well fell on deaf ears after an initial grant of Rs. 4,000. He has dug 186 feet in vain for water through the expensive and dangerous device of exploding dynamite underground.[7] None the less Lakhkar must continue digging until he finds water if he is to establish his new-found settlement as a permanent and viable social and economic unit.

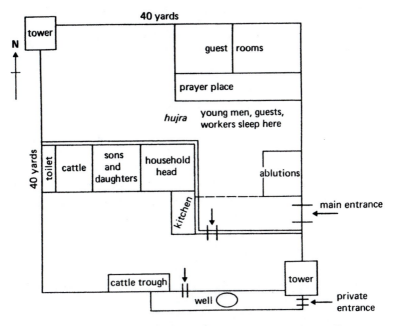

FIGURE 15 *TAM settlements.* (i) *Nuclear family: Lakhkar village*

Malik Shahzada's settlement[8] represents that of a typical tribal compound family (Figure 15(ii)). As mentioned earlier, Anmir's death in 1938 triggered off fissures among the Musa living in their traditional village at Chino. The six villages at Chino were built in the 1940s and are structurally similar to Shahzada's village. They are dominated by living patriarchs after whom they are named. In such villages, as in Shahzada's village, a clear division (double lines in the figure) demarcates private and public domains. The three sons of Shahzada by his first wife live in the western half of the village. The elder son, Amirzada, has a larger courtyard area than his brothers. However, all these rooms are of mud and the favoured status of the second wife and her sons is reflected in the five rooms to the east of the village which in 1976 are in the process of being constructed with cement. So far the household head has lived in one room with his second wife and her sons in an adjacent room. These two rooms had cement ceilings and were built in the 1960s.

Shahzada's village houses between fifty to sixty people at any given time which includes Shahzada's two wives, eight sons, of whom four are married with their own children, and seven unmarried daughters. Shahzada, his sons and grandsons number eighteen. Only these are allowed inside the private area of Shahzada's village. Cousins and poor relatives, who often act as helpers or servants, are never allowed to cross the double line in Figure 15(ii) and sleep in the *hujra*. Thus at any given time, at least a dozen sons, grandsons or relatives occupy the *hujra*. Guns are prominently hung on pegs driven in the wall of the *hujra* and indicate a state of alertness.[9]

A private entrance in the south ensures privacy for the females of the village. The main gate in the east wall of the village is 12 feet high and 10 feet wide and of corrugated iron and steel. Shahzada, no doubt aware of the impression such shibboleths make upon visiting officials, has inscribed the following legend in multi-coloured calligraphy in cement on the ceiling of his *hujra*: *'Pakistan zindabad, ya Allah, Bismillah ir Rahman ir Rahem, ya Mohammad. Haza min Fazal Rabi Nawab Shahzada Mohmand 25-9-1973.'* Roughly translated it means 'In the name of Allah the Merciful and His Prophet Muhammad'. The date of the completion of the *hujra* and Shahzada's self-elevation as Nawab is also indicated in the calligraphy. The Pakistan flag is engraved on the roof of the *hujra* correctly coloured green. Shahzada repeated to me several times that he worked not for officials but for the flag, pointing to it each time he said this. In return for permission to construct the first primary school in the Gandab valley at Shati Khel a grateful government provided the village, among other facilities, with a well operated by a diesel pump costing Rs. 16,000 in the 1960s which successfully provides water at all times. Water is at a depth of about 240 feet. Shahzada's village is 100 yards in length running east to west and 60 yards from north to south. The walls are 18 feet high and between 3 to 4 feet thick. The north-west tower points towards the Malok settlement and the other tower allows Shahzada to keep an eye on the third Shati lineage, the Ranra, across the *khwar*. A separate tower situated at the entrance to Shati Khel is strategically placed to block Ranra or Malok ingress and egress into their villages in times of trouble. This tower is called Shahzada's tower (*de Shahzada bruj*).

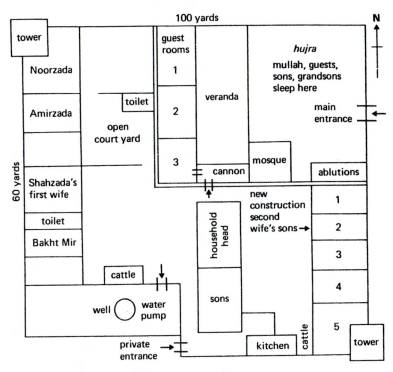

(ii) *Compound family: Shahzada Malik village*

The Malok village is typical of the tribal joint family village and there are structural parallels across the *khwar* in the Ranra village or among the major Ganjian villages. The village is divided into five clearly demarcated sections inhabited by the five sons of Said Mir,[10] the grandfather of Sar Gul, the village elder. The arrangement of the village is almost classic in its symmetry in depicting lineage seniority and relationships (Figure 15(iii)). The twenty-four houses (often one or two mud rooms) of the village are so arranged as to conceptualize an inner circle inhabited by the elder sons of Said Mir and an outer circle by his junior sons. The sons of the elder son, Sar Gul, and the second son, Umar Gul, possess the central section of the village running north to south. The offspring of the next two sons, Saad Gul and Rahim, live to the east and west side of the village and those of Za Gul, the youngest son of Said Mir, live in the eastern section of the village. Za Gul's situation is symbolic of junior status in its distance from the *jumat* and *hujra*, the focus of the village, and also in directly facing Shahzada Malik's village to the east. Three of Sar Gul's sons have exhibited further fissure by starting their own houses in the northern rim of the village. The population of the village is 127.

There is no doubt that the economic and social unit is the nuclear household, to which all things are finally reduced and equated, while budgets are strictly organized within its boundaries. So although on the surface TAM might present a picture of joint family groups living together as in Sar Gul or Ranra villages, in fact each house is a separate and distinct unit. A room or two, a small store for the grain, and a shed for cattle with perhaps a pocket-handkerchief courtyard make up the house. Cattle are locked up within the household, however small and cramped it may be. The poverty of material life is immediately visible in the bare mud rooms and their meagre possessions, usually one cot and one tin box per male adult.

As in all tribal villages, every inhabitant traces direct descent to a common ancestor. There are no outsiders in the village and visitors are only allowed in from the main door in the north to the *hujra* by the mosque. The *hujra* is a single mud-walled room about 18 feet in length and 14 feet in breadth and the low mud roof with its wood beams is supported by two main wood logs in the centre. About twelve cots lie in the *hujra*. Guns may be hung on the wooden pegs in the wall. Two or three Islamic calendars with the name of Allah or His Prophet or posters of popular Arab leaders, usually those of the late King Faisal of Saudi Arabia, hang on the rough mud walls. A single naked electric bulb represents the twentieth century through the courtesy of Shahzada Malik and his influence with the administration.[11]

The mosque is bare. It is almost the same size as the *hujra* with which it shares a wall and is in the same compound. The floor is slightly higher than the *hujra* by about 4 to 6 inches. A line from the Holy Koran and the name of God and His Prophet are written inside in ordinary chalk or coal on the mud wall as in Shahzada Malik's mosque.[12] In the main and only praying room of the mosque the mud floor is covered with a variety of dried elephant grass to enable worshippers to sit on the floor without slippers or shoes. In winter the grass prevents the cold and in summer has a cooling effect. The village Malik in the

Tribal Areas regulates the affairs of the mosque through his choice of Mullah to conduct prayers who might even be, as in Mazullah's village, his own son.

The village well is connected to the village by a direct and private door used by women. The well itself has been dug in a depression and therefore the height of the tower overlooking it appears exaggerated at 25 feet. The well is surrounded by an embankment almost 15 feet high to afford access to water during shooting. It is 240 feet deep and an unending source of excellent potable water. The area of the village is about 120 yards east to west and 100 yards north to south. The walls vary in height from 12 feet in the north to 10 feet in the south, as the southern end overlooks the *khwar* which is itself àlmost 6 feet deep it is therefore given added height. To the north-west and outside the village is the flat circular area (called *ghobal*) for communal threshing of wheat and towards the west is a large man-made depression to collect rainwater, the traditional manner of storing and supplying water before the installation of the well. Sar Gul village was initially built as a tower to contain Shahzada and later many Malok shifted to it from Shabana, further to the west.

The Malok have successfully diverted their energies from political to economic activity over the last few years, especially finding employment as contractors and labourers in the new Agency development schemes like the headquarters in Ghalanay begun in 1974. They have thus consciously adopted employment which is traditionally non-Pukhtun and which, for instance, neither Shahzada nor the Ranra would take. Some economic results are already apparent. A large cement garage built last year to the north-west of the village is the only concrete structure in the village and houses the passenger bus and truck of Sar Gul. The general poverty of the Malok village contrasts with the other two settlements especially in terms of accommodation. None the less the economic future of the Malok appears more secure than that of the other Shati lineages, although it may be some years before tangible results are achieved and visible to offset their initial disadvantages of belonging to the weakest lineage in Shati Khel.

The important principles of the TAM settlement and village model are:
(1) the household is the average unit of consumption and cooperation typified by Lakhkar's village. The molecular level or hearth is called *kor*.[13] The *kor* is the centre of multicentric social and economic functions although there may be three or four generations represented in it;

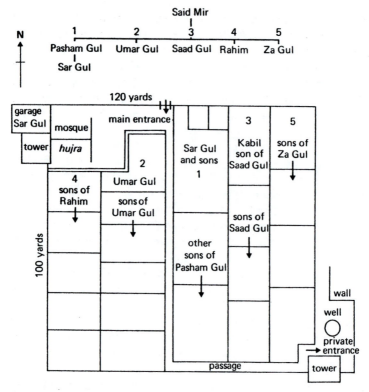

(iii) *Joint family: Sar Gul/Malok village*

(2) moreover, if there is a compound family household with married sons living in it, and if the patriarch is politically and economically in a position to do so, the budget remains unitary as in Shahzada village; and finally

(3) if there is a joint family settlement then budgets are independent and relate to the income of the owner of the house.

(b) *SAM households*

Having examined typical examples of the three different categories of tribal villages among the TAM I shall now turn to consider the household arrangements among SAM. Simple or nuclear families (like Lakhkar's), polygynist or compound families (like Shahzada's) and joint families (like Malok) find their corresponding equivalent categories among Belawals. But three interconnected and important differences are immediately apparent between TAM and SAM villages. Firstly, and of the utmost importance, are the genealogical links with the direct ascendants of the inhabitants of a village in TAM which provide its lineage identity and its name. No outsiders, including cousins, live as owners of rooms in the village. The second point leads from the first, in that there is a clear division in every TAM village demarcating the private domain, symbolizing the seclusion and chastity of women, and the public domain, represented by the *hujra*, symbolizing political activity. In SAM villages, although there are recognizable and defined areas corresponding to lineages, the village represents a composite unit of sub-sectional and even sectional members of the clan, non-Mohmand Pukhtuns, religious and occupational groups. The purity of the unilineal descent in determining settlement arrangements is compromised. Although the concept of the seclusion of women remains developed it is now translated in relationship to people from outside the village. The entire village which includes every group is theoretically conceived of as one social unit and its men and women conceptualized as fictitious siblings. Men will generally refer to Bela women as either sister (*khor*) or, if older, aunt (*tror*) and women will call Bela men brother (*ror*) or uncle (*kaka*). *Parda* is strictly observed in the presence of strangers or visitors. Similarly, the role of the *hujra* has shifted from the household to a common point in the village and is maintained communally. It is no longer the *hujra* of a Malik or patriarch but the joint property of the community. The village mosque and *hujra*, sharing a wall, act as the focal social point for Bela villagers whether of dominant Pukhtun lineages or occupational groups. The balance has shifted from the patriarch to a group of village elders with little coercive economic or political authority to support them.

Third, TAM villages are constructed as both social and military units. As such the high and thick surrounding walls and towers serve a specifically military purpose. This need does not arise in SAM, which is not to say that walls have disappeared altogether. Most houses are surrounded by walls between 5 to 8 feet high and are about a foot thick. As these are made of mud and as their purpose is really more symbolic than practical, they are often in a state of disrepair for months on end, usually following the spring rains. An interesting difference reflecting the greater sense of security is the fact that most walls around houses in SAM do not have doors. There may be a gap of 10 to 15 feet in the wall which generally acts as the main entrance to the compound of the house. Doors are redundant as there is no possibility of either forcible occupation of households as in TAM, or of theft or dacoity as in and around the urban areas of Peshawar. I was curious regarding the lack of theft and was always given the same answer: 'Who would steal from us and where would the thief hide? We are all relatives and every one knows each other for miles around.'

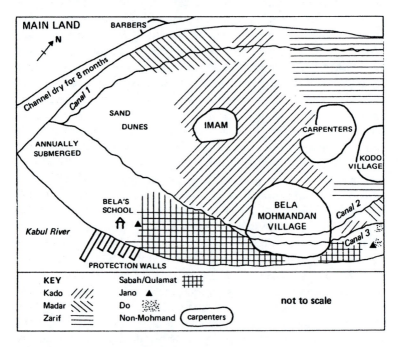

MAP 6 *Fields of Bela Mohmandan: lineages and lands*

Bela lands are divided in three broad categories corresponding to their exposure to the river (Map 6). The poorest quality of lands, which are annually submerged, are to the extreme south-west of the village and are communally owned property. When the river has receded, the land remains agriculturally barren as it is of a rocky nature and covered with stones brought in by the river. Dividing this unproductive land from the next two categories are natural sand-dunes lying roughly west to east. The second category of land to the south-east of the village mainly belongs to members of the junior lineage, the Sabah Khel and Jano Khel, and because of its exposed position runs the risk of flooding.

Five spurs of varying lengths, and in varying stages of disrepair, have been constructed over the last ten years by government to prevent flooding. The third category, and the best lands, are spread from the north-west of Bela to the east of the village and belong to the senior lineages such as the Kado and Madar Khel. Non-Mohmand groups like the Imam of the mosque and carpenters also own land here. The barbers have acquired land across and on the banks of the western channel following domestic problems. To the north-east lie the fields of the neighbouring village of Kodo largely inhabited by the Zarif Khel. Map 6 also shows the three irrigation canals that water the fields of Bela. Canal number 3 exclusively and 2 on Fridays only provide water to Bela. Canal number 1 carries water to Kodo and the other villages north of Bela. The water is diverted near the Michni rest house. As the river is 20 to 30 feet below the land surface during most of the year the village has not solved the problem of lifting water from it. The village has neither decided to acquire a diesel pump nor has it electricity to operate an irrigation pump.

The sixty households of the village Bela Mohmandan may be conceptualized as three concentric circles which divide the sub-sections of the Khalil Khel, the two houses of the Zarif Khel and those of the religious and occupational groups (Map 7). The core circle is housed by Kado Khel, the senior sub-section; the second circle housed by the Madar, the Imam of the mosque and the Sayyed of the village. The third circle consists of occupational groups, the barbers and carpenters, and the junior and weakest lineages of the village, the Sabah Khel and the Zarif Khel. It is not difficult to correlate the residence of the senior lineages, Kado Khel and Madar Khel north of the main water canals (numbers 2 and 3) running through the centre of the village and that of the Sabah and Jano, the weaker and junior lineages south of the canals. This schema may help to conceptualize traditional tribal ethnic settlement arrangements. But Map 7 of the village shows there is a tendency to deviance, for example, Kado households situated south of the central village canals.

The central point of the village is the mosque and the *hujra* where *mashars*, *kashars* and guests sit and while away the hours when not working on their fields. Recently some *kashars* led by Amin (Do Khel) of a junior lineage have built a mud room as their *hujra*. Like all Mohmands, Belawals say their prayers regularly and most of the elders manage to say the prescribed five daily prayers. The mosque has a well, and water is found at about 12 feet, which is common to the village.

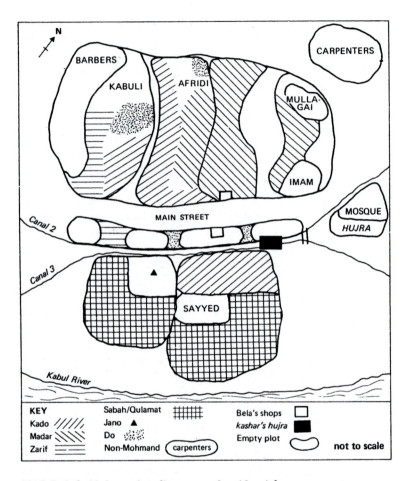

MAP 7 *Bela Mohmandan: lineages and residential arrangements*

There is no cement building or room in Bela. No walls or fortifications run around the village for reasons I have explained above. There is a relaxed and easy-going atmosphere in the *hujra* with respect for elders but little of the formality that marks the presence of younger people in the presence of the TAM patriarchs.

I have drawn up a lineage ownership list of houses based on the vague seniority generally accepted in the village and by no means the equivalent of caste either in a commensal, social or religious sense.

TABLE 5 Population, houses and lands of Bela Mohmandan

		Houses	*Population*	*Fields* *(in acres)*	*Average land* *(per person)*
1	Tarakzai				
a.	Khalil Khel:				
	i Kado	15	88	32	0.36
	ii Madar	11	58	6	0.1
	iii Do	4	27	1	0.04
	iv Jano	1	26	8.5	0.33
	v Qulamat/Sabah	15	114	9.25	0.08
b.	Zarif Khel	2	16		
2	Religious groups				
a.	Sayyed	1	4	2.5	0.63
b.	Imam	1	12	3.75	0.31
c.	Mullagai	1	6		
3	Non-Mohmand Pukhtun groups				
a.	Afridi	1	10		
b.	Kabuli	1	16		
4	Occupational groups				
a.	carpenters	5	34	16	0.47
b.	barbers	2	21		
	Total	(17 acres) 60	432	79	average 0.22

The descendants of Khalil, including affiliated lineages such as Sabah Khel, constitute about 72 per cent of the village population of 432. The Kado, the senior lineage, constitute 20 per cent of the village population and about 28 per cent of the Khalil Khel population. However, it is the junior-most and poorest lineage, the Sabah and Qulamat, who have the largest population in terms of figures and their 114 constitute 26 per cent of the Bela total. The Zarif Khel account for almost 4 per cent and the Pukhtun total percentage of Bela is about 82 per cent or 355 people. Non-Pukhtuns constitute almost 18 per cent of the total figure, in marked contrast to Shati Khel.

The sixty houses of Bela are built on a total area of 17 acres, giving the average house an area of about a quarter acre. The only four houses occupying an area of about half an acre are Hussain Khan's, whose house occupies one and a half acres while the families of the Imam, Shamshudin and the carpenters have about half an acre each.

The Kado Khel with a population of eighty-eight are the largest land-owners in Bela owning almost 32 acres, 0.36 acre per person. The Jano average 0.33 per person while the Sabah with the largest single lineage population of 114 own only 9.25 acres and average 0.08 acre per person. The Do Khel have the worst average, for a population of twenty-seven of almost 0.04 per person. As I explained earlier the Do, Sabah and Jano are the junior lineages of Bela with fictitious lineage links forged to Kado Khel (Figure 7). The economic position of Jano is better than that of Do and Sabah largely due to the hard work and economic acumen of its *mashar* Hussain Khan. Hussain is probably the biggest landowner, owing 9 acres followed by Shamshudin who has 6½ acres. The carpenters emerge with an average of almost half an acre per individual in the group which is over twice the average land ownership of 0.22 per person in the village.

Of the total cultivable fields around Bela Mohmandan only 79 acres are owned by Belawals, the rest having been lost through sale, bad debts, mortgages, etc., mostly to Zarif Khel owners living in neighbour-ing traditional Zarif Khel villages. Another 20 unirrigated acres are owned in bits and pieces by Belawals. The average land ownership per household in Bela is 1.3 acres of irrigated and 0.6 unirrigated land as compared to 0.9 irrigated and 3.7 unirrigated land in Shati Khel (including built areas).

Figures 16(i), (ii) and (iii) illustrate three different types of house-holds among SAM: the nuclear family, the joint family and the extended family. While military strategy partly explained the positioning of the Musa village at an elevation in the east of Shati Khel, economic strategy partly explains the better located houses in Bela which are north of the canals running through the village. The first example of a household, the nuclear family, belongs to Shamshudin consisting of his wife, their son, Ihsanullah and his wife, and three young sons and one unmarried daughter (Figure 16(i)). The two married daughters of Shamshudin, living with their husbands in Kado Korona, often come and spend the night at their father's place. Shamshudin's house is situated in the north-west of the village in what is probably considered the best site determined by its distance from the Kabul river and the threat of floods. The house itself structurally approximates to the ideal prototype and is designed as a simple square. The walls around the house are five feet high and about a foot thick at the base but crumbling and narrowing at the top. In fact, half the eastern wall which fell during the rains two years ago is still to be rebuilt. The area is 50 yards north to south and 40 yards east to west and covers about half an acre of land.

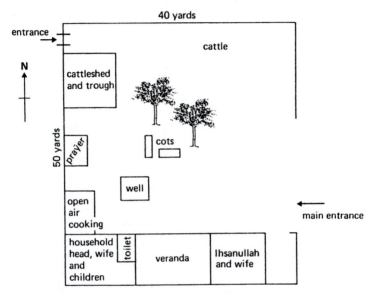

FIGURE 16 *SAM households.* (i) *Nuclear family: Shamshudin (Kado Khel)*

There are only two rooms, one of which is used by the household head and his wife and unmarried children. There is a toilet provided for the females of the house in the main room. Ihsanullah and his wife have been given the other room which is also used as the guest room in which case the regular occupants shift to the main bedroom. Both the rooms are 24 feet in length and 12 feet in width and in between them is a veranda which is used for cooking when it rains and as reserve area for guests and spare luggage such as cots, etc. There is an open cooking area by the main room and adjacent to that an area five feet in length and three feet in width for prayers, facing the west, the Kaaba in Arabia. In the northern corner there is a cattle-shed (*ghojal*) although most of the cattle stand outside their shed in the courtyard or are out in the fields during the day. As with most Bela houses there are a few mulberry trees in the centre of the courtyard to provide shade under which lie a few cots. These trees provide the only green in the otherwise starkly brown mud houses and their grassless courtyards. Shamshudin's house is one of the few in Bela with its own well and water is found between 12 to 15 feet. Like all houses in the village it is entirely constructed of mud and the women of the house keep the rooms spotlessly clean, in spite of the dung dropped from cattle who share the courtyard, which brings into relief the stark poverty and meagreness of material possessions in them. The only valuable part of the SAM rooms are the wood-beams used in the roof and those to hold it up. The roofs are about 10 feet high and plastered with fresh mud-clay twice annually after the rainy season. There are no windows in the rooms. Although Shamshudin's house may be structurally similar to the other SAM houses it is still slightly bigger in area as Shamshudin, a *mashar* of the dominant Kado lineage and the son of a respected and well-known Kado Malik, began life with relatively more advantages than his fellow villagers; however, as we shall see, the differences are merely of degree rather than kind. Shamshudin's inherited superior lineage position allows him a plot only a few yards larger than the average Bela house.

The next example is that of a joint family household and selected from the weakest and poorest lineage, the Sabah Khel, and is situated on the south side of the Bela water canals in the less prestigious area of the village (Figure 16(ii)). The house is owned by Mehr Gul and has an area of 40 yards east to west and 30 yards north to south and covers about one fourth of an acre of land. The walls are about six feet high and about a foot thick. There are only two rooms in the house both 18 feet by 15 feet in size. One is occupied by Mehr Gul along with his mother, his wife, three daughters and three sons. Mehr Gul has five other sons who are employed, four in various parts of Pakistan, and who provide him with his main income. The cattle are kept in a shed adjacent to the room. In the other room of the house lives Sher, Mehr's son-in-law and the son of his late brother, with his family. Between Sher Alam's and Mehr Gul's room is the cattle shed for the former's cattle. The cooking is done in the north-west corner of the house and in an open area. There is a third shed-like room by the southern wall in which the sons of the two owners or their guests may sit and sleep. By this shed is a pen for sheep. In the centre of the courtyard stand some mulberry trees. The entrance is in the east wall.

The third example of a SAM house represents the extended family and belongs to Morcha Khel, the village carpenter, and a member of the occupational group (Figure 16(iii)). Along with Morcha and his unmarried children live the families of three of his other brothers. It is important

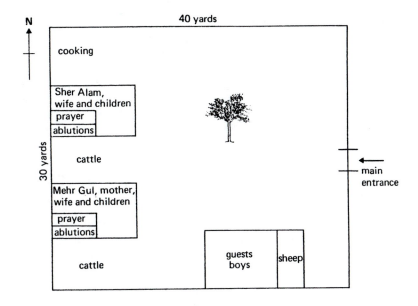

(ii) *Joint family: Mehr Gul (Sabah Khel)*

to emphasize the point made earlier in this chapter when discussing extended families in TAM that each family operates as a separate economic unit cooking and earning for itself. There is a direct correlation between segmentary fissure and political strength in Pukhtun society. Morcha Khel's house is 55 yards from north to south and 35 yards east to west and because it is, along with the other houses of the carpenters, somewhat isolated at a distance of a few hundred yards to the north of the village, it is protected by walls that are four feet higher than the average Bela walls. The ten foot walls have two doors which are eight feet high and usually closed at night. The area covers about half an acre of land. The houses are arranged in the typical SAM manner with one family separated from another usually by cattle-sheds: Morcha, Abdul Hakim, Hakim Khan and Khan Khel (brothers) and their sons Zar Taj and Akhtar. Mir lives in the place of his late father, Hakim.

The elder of the family, Morcha Khel, has two rooms. Morcha himself shares the main room with his wife and two daughters and his other room is shared by his sons. Except for Morcha every other married family has one room each. The size of the rooms varies from a large size for senior members like Morcha, 24 feet by 15 feet in dimension, to a small

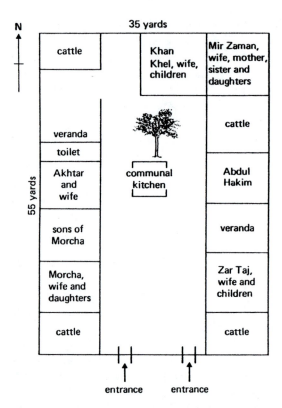

(iii) *Extended family: Morcha Khel (carpenter)*

size, as for the sons of Morcha, 7 feet by 15 feet. The communal kitchen is in the centre of the courtyard by the mulberry trees. Abdul Hakim's married son Zar, dependent on him, lives separately. His single sons, like most young males, either sleep in the main courtyard or in the village *hujra* or usually in groups by the river bank on hot summer nights.

The total population of Morcha's house comes to thirty-four but it is important to point out that the cramped living conditions of the occupational groups should not be mistaken for poorer economic status in comparison to the Mohmand lineages. The carpenters have decided as a matter of policy to invest their money in buying some of the best land in the north-west areas of the village, have a higher average income and own more than double the average land compared to the average Belawal.

In concluding this section I would like to make four general points: firstly, socially significant change ideally operates within the sub-sectional operative lineage of the clan. Within the geographical zone corresponding to the area of the sub-section, settlement arrangements may be conceptualized as concentric circles with the most important and dominant Pukhtun group in the centre and the non-Pukhtun occupational groups in the outmost circle. Residential groupings from this perspective appear as a structure of a hierarchy of levels of integration which, from inside and on the ground, appear as a series of concentric circles: the nuclear family, the extended family, the sub-section, the section and so on. However, for practical purposes the primary and effective social and economic unit is the immediate nuclear family, whereas the boundaries of the wider universe, the operative lineage, are largely confined to the sub-section. Both in TAM and SAM, household structures are the combined results of several deeper structural levels of a hierarchy of causes of which the most important are military strategy, access to water, access to the road and the social prestige associated with certain areas.

Secondly, each settlement is a microcosm of the world to its lineage head; it is his house, his village, his fort, reflecting his honour and his strength. He is called 'the husband of the house' (*de kor khawand*). One of the youngest and earliest English soldiers to penetrate the Mohmand interior came to the correct conclusion: 'every man's house is his castle. The villages are the fortifications, the fortifications are the villages. Every house is loopholed, and whether it has a tower or not depends on its owner's wealth' (Churchill, 1972: 18). Although the settlements in TAM are inhabited by descendants from a common ancestor there is a recognized boundary beyond which strangers, and even kin not belonging to the house, cannot cross. Inside this private domain are the four most important possessions of the household head on which depend his social prestige and economic situation: his women, his cattle, his store of grain and his water tank. In Bela although *parda* is of equal importance in society, the face-to-face village situation and the demands of agricultural cropping prevent any boundaries being drawn between private and public areas. Within and between villagers there is no *parda* and if I were sitting in Shamshudin's house Hussain Khan or any other Belawal would walk in addressing Mrs Shamshudin: 'Good morning sister, how are you?' This informality would be unthinkable in the TAM situation. SAM deviance in social behaviour is compensated by equally strict *parda* when confronted by outsiders, that is non-Belawals.

Thirdly, the stark poverty of material life is reflected in the living arrangements. The average main room is usually used by the household head, his wife, his daughters and often his parents if they are alive and the second room usually houses the sons, whatever their number.

Finally, the names of villages either change with the name of the lineage patriarch or have dual names, unless named after geographical features such as Chino (springs) or Sangar (breast-work) in which case they do not change. Shahzada Malik's and Malik Lakhkar's villages, the prototype of the newer villages, are named after the household head and are known as such around the region. Fathers, if old and infirm, may transfer the name of the village to their eldest son as Sher Jang of the Musa lineage did to Sarfaraz. In other cases, like Shahmat's another Musa, the younger brother makes the village and names it after himself if the older brother prefers to live elsewhere, in this case in Shabkadar. Villages in which extended families live like the Malok and the Ranra villages have dual names after the recognized elder of the lineage. Thus the Malok village is called after Pasham Gul's son, Sar Gul, who is now the Malok senior. The same village was called after Sar Gul's grandfather Said Mir and then his father Pasham Gul. Similarly the Ranra village is also called after the Ranra senior Mazullah.

To conclude: I have illustrated that Pukhtun household arrangements and domestic structure thus confirm, and conform to, the ideal. Their internal structure reflects the two most vital aspects of social organization, agnatic rivalry through the *hujra* and the concept of *parda* through the seclusion of women. Leading from a discussion of household patterns, I shall discuss marriage patterns in the next section and attempt to argue that the high rate of endogamy approximates to and maintains ideal Pukhtun social organization.

IV Pukhtun marriages

I shall now discuss what I see as the most important of the *rites de passage* in Pukhtun society, marriage. Through marriage we may analyse: 1 the structural principles of society involving rules of endogamy and patterns of hypo- or hypergamy that reflect lineage status; 2 the manner in which status is expressed through marriage expenditure; and 3 the most critical stage in the development of the household. As marriages are virilocal, it is usually after marriage that the son is given an independent house or room. The seeds for segmentary fissure are thus sown. I now turn to an examination of the data concerning the genealogical and physical patterns of Mohmand marriages which determine domestic structure. The discussion will provide a link with the previous section on settlement and household patterns and illustrate how the former relates to the latter. The traditional rites largely approximate to the ideal-type model. They are stark, simple and functional. The internal structure of the family presupposes from the first the existence of social rules regulating forms of marriage, filiation and residence which are required for the legitimate existence of any family and which determine some aspects of the 'developmental cycle' (Fortes, 1958; Goody, 1972: 22, 28). Marriage is strongly endogamous and the preferred form is to the patrilateral parallel cousin. I agree with Barth's material on the Swat Pukhtuns that it is possible to list six characteristics of the rites: 1 food and services are reciprocated; 2 ceremonies are public and well attended; 3 the scale of the ceremonies is commensurate with wealth and rank; 4 there is a moral compulsion to attend; 5 those who dodge this expectation advertise their enmity; 6 the ceremonies give men a chance to establish political ties (Barth, 1972). I also agree with Barth that marriage is seen as the most significant rite in society as, for instance, funerals are among the Giriama (Parkin, 1972: 77).

Marriages, through hypo- or hypergamy, as I shall show in the table below, are important as an index of political status and in making political alliances. In the latter case, marriages may be exogamous to section or sub-clan but are seldom contracted outside the clan. There is a direct correlation between high traditional Pukhtun political activity in TAM and political marriages indicating sub-sectional exogamy as I shall illustrate below. Of the 350 marriages recorded a tribal endogamy figure of almost 100 per cent was observed except in the notable exceptions of the Imam of Bela and Aziz Ingar in Shati Khel who intermarried with Pukhtuns. Marriages to Father's Brother's Sons are preferred but as we see from the figures not prescribed. Marriages are almost always virilocal. Uxorilocal marriage may be a consequence of a feud which may force the husband to the wife's residence as in the case of Tiladar Jan (Kadai) living in his wife's village, the Malok.

Tables 6(i) and (ii) are on tribal endogamy and reflect vertices in society. A1 to A5 represent levels of Mohmand segmentation from the sub-section to the tribe, B the affiliated Pukhtun groups, C the religious groups and D the occupational groups. The percentages illustrate endogamy at that level of segmentation, for instance, in A1, representing the sub-section, 148 or 53 per cent of the total Pukhtun marriages of 280 are endogamous to the sub-section. In the next category, representing the sectional level of segmentation, another twenty-four marriages are con+ acted of which twenty-four are endogamous and the total of 148 plus twenty-four makes 61 per cent endogamous marriages of the total number of 280 Pukhtun marriages. In category C a relatively high percentage of marriages (47 per cent) have been contracted exogamous to group; the percentage is somewhat inflated through the six marriages with Pukhtun lineages by the descendants of the Bela Imam. D, representing occupational groups, illustrates an entirely endogamous situation, except, of course, in the exceptional case of the family of Aziz Ingar. For purposes of clarification I repeat the classifications I am employing at the various tribal segmentary levels in a footnote.[14]

TABLE 6 (i) Tribal endogamy: universe

	TAM		SAM			
	Endog.	*Exog.*	*Endog.*	*Exog.*	*Endogamous marriages*	*Total*
		Pukhtun				
A1	47	2	101	6	148 (53%)	156
A2	4		20		148 + 24 (61%)	24
A3	57		13		172 + 70 (86%)	70
A4	10		5		242 + 15 (92%)	15
A5	8		7		257 + 15 (97%)	15
	126	2	146	6	272 (97%)	280
		Affiliated lineages				
B	8	14			8 (36%)	22
		Religious groups				
C	6	1	2	6	8 (53%)	15
		Occupational groups				
D	5	6	22		27 (82%)	33
Total:	145		170		315 (90%)	350

Certain points stand out immediately. The endogamy percentages within group A become higher as the marriages contracted reach the tribal boundary of Pukhtunness. As mentioned above the only example of Pukhtun girls marrying non-Pukhtuns, that is a case of hypogamy, was of the sons of the Bela Imam who acquired Pukhtun wives. There is no such example in TAM although non-Pukhtun wives may have been married from the family of Aziz Ingar. Pukhtun lineage endogamy contrasts with Baluchistan society where 'approximately 70% of the unions are between non-kin' (Pastner, 1971; Pastner and Pastner, 1972: 132). Second, there is a notably high endogamous incidence of Pukhtun marriages in the sub-section, for purposes of analysis in this study, the operative lineage, 53 per cent or 148 of the total 280 marriages. However, a significant number of endogamous marriages are made in A3, the sub-clan, where giving and taking of cousins in marriages illustrate the pattern and intensity of agnatic and political rivalry, seventy in number, and added to those in A1 and A2 make up 86 per cent of the entire total. In TAM this would include the parties of Abdullah in Sangar, Shahzada in Shati and Lakhkar in Yusuf Khel. This is the level that helps contain enemies and build alliances. Various political marriages cementing alliances such as between Lakhkar and Shahzada or Dilawar and Abdullah have already been mentioned in previous chapters. In SAM the sub-clan spreads largely in the Michni area and includes Kasim and Dadu Khel.

Finally, a marked difference in marriage patterns emerges between TAM and SAM, if we break down the above figures further for a closer analysis, which is partly explained by the emphasis on political activity in TAM. The majority of marriages in SAM, 66 per cent, are contracted within the sub-section A1, whereas the TAM figure is 37 per cent. In TAM the majority of marriages, 44 per cent, are within A3. It is the total of TAM and SAM in A1 which give it the high final percentage of 53 per cent. A4 and A5 are almost identical in both areas emphasizing Pukhtun endogamy in general.

Table 6(ii) further subdivides TAM and SAM marriage figures to indicate extent of endogamy.

The marriage figures make the following points explicitly: Mohmand Pukhtuns are entirely endogamous. The only exceptions are the marriages contracted in Shati Khel by the blacksmiths and the Imam in Bela. Pukhtun marriages in their ideal-type situation in TAM concentrate largely on sub-clan marriage alliances and the highest number of marriages, fifty-seven out of 128 marriages, are within this level of

TABLE 6 (ii) Tribal endogamy: TAM and SAM (percentages in brackets)

	A1	A2	A3	A4	A5	Endog. marriages	Total
TAM	47 (37)	4 (3)	57 (44)	10 (8)	8 (6)	126 (98)	128
SAM	101 (66)	20 (13)	13 (9)	5 (3)	7 (5)	146 (96)	152

segmentation. Such marriages are contracted outside the immediate sub-section or even geographical area for political reasons such as those involving Shahzada Malik, Malik Lakhkar and Dilawar Khan, which involve a deeper span of the genealogy and far-ranging geographical areas that include distant parts of Mardan District. In this regard in general my TAM findings corroborate those for the Swat Pukhtuns:

> In contrast to what is found in some other lineage-based societies in the Middle East (e.g. Barth, 1953), marriages are rarely sought with close agnatic collaterals. Several Pathan chiefs volunteered reasons for this: Fa Br Da marriage, they said, is known as a device for preventing conflict between agnatic cousins, but it is never very successful.... It is better to use the marriage of daughters and sisters to establish contacts or reaffirm alliances with persons of similar political interests to one's own; then one will be strong in the inevitable conflicts with close agnates (Barth, 1972: 40).

However, it is important to point out that Pukhtun girls are seldom, if ever, given to non-Pukhtuns although non-Pukhtun women may be taken in marriage by Pukhtuns. There are no examples of Shati women marrying into religious or occupational groups although there is a rather exceptional example of Shati men taking women in marriage from an occupational group (Aziz Ingar's). My concern is to illustrate the pattern of movement of women through marriages and thereby argue that Mohmand marriages are almost entirely endogamous and conform to their concept of social exclusivity and superiority.

In spite of the often bitter enmity and latent hostility between the three sub-sections in Shati Khel there is some intermarriage among them. Out of a total of thirty marriages among the Musa Khel only two were exogamous to tribe, to Yusufzai and therefore hypergamous, reflecting their dominant position and attempt to create political alliances. Thirty per cent of the Musa married within the Musa Khel and 42 per cent of the Ranra married within the Ranra Khel, while 36 per cent of the Malok married among themselves. The Shati Khel sub-sections indicate a tendency to contract alliances outside their immediate lineage for political reasons but none the less they marry within the tribe.

TABLE 7 Shati Khel endogamy

	endogamy		hypergamy	hypogamy	total
	sub-section	tribe			
Musa	9	19	2		30
Ranra	18	25			43
Malok	20	35			55
	47	79			128

The Ganjian show an interesting hypergamous and exogamous trend which would indicate a consolidation of their affiliated position. Out of twenty-two marriages nine were hypergamous with junior lineages of the Halimzai clan (four Ranra and five Malok) and only eight within their own household (Table 6(i)). The remaining marriages were homogamous with other affiliated lineages like the Ghunda Khel.

In contrast to the highest number of marriages that took place on the sub-clan level in Shati Khel (44 per cent) reflecting a wider range of political activity and alliances, Bela Mohmandan marriages on this level (9 per cent) reflect significantly no such signs of political ambitions (Table 6(ii)). The maximum number of marriages in Bela were contracted within the sub-section and mainly with neighbouring village groups 66 per cent as compared to 37 per cent of marriages endogamous to sub-section in Shati Khel. There are no examples of intermarriages with occupational groups in Bela. The six marriages of the Imam's family in Bela with Pukhtun women (there are no such Pukhtun marriages in Shati with religious groups) and the six marriages of Aziz Ingar's women with Pukhtun's (there are no such Pukhtun marriages in Bela with occupational groups), skewed the symmetry of the ideal-type position somewhat but also illuminated two interconnected points as they explained the deviance: the importance of the social status of the Imam in SAM and that of political alliances and activity in marriages with Aziz, the expert and manufacturer of munitions, in TAM.

Analysis has shown that marriages in other Muslim tribal societies are generally contracted within the political system and universe compared with non-tribal marriages (Barth, 1953: 68, Table III). Endogamous family marriages of tribals were as high as 71 per cent and contrasted with 37 per cent for non-tribal families. Similarly figures for non-tribal village endogamy were 78 per cent, almost as high as those for tribal village endogamy, 80 per cent (ibid.: 68). These figures illuminate the significance of the highly endogamous nature of the Mohmand where marriages are entirely endogamous to the tribe. Although Barth makes a valid point – that as there is a political emphasis in contracting marriages in tribal groups, in non-tribal groups there is an economic emphasis on marriage – my own data do not testify to this. TAM and SAM remain highly endogamous in spite of the latter's encapsulated condition and dependence on agriculture. TAM marriages may emphasize political alliances that cover a wider geographical and genealogical span but none the less remain highly endogamous.

The following four customs, embodying Pukhto concepts and illustrating the strength of the native model even where it clashes with an Islamic one, are tacitly maintained although widely condemned. Men in formal and informal interviews are aware of these deviances from Islamic customs and condemn such practices. Yet they admit they are helpless to change them as 'this is Pukhto *riwaj*'. Firstly, an un-Islamic custom that is condemned by *mashars* and *kashars* alike and slowly but steadily losing hold is that of 'money for the head' (*sar paisey*) or bride-price for the girl. Evans-Pritchard suggested 'bride-wealth' as an alternative term to bride-price as the latter was crudely put and suggested buying and selling. In the Tribal Areas the more appropriate term would still be 'bride-price' because daughters are literally bought and sold. I shall therefore not use the neologism or euphemism. The bride's father may take anything between Rs. 2,000 to 20,000 for the girl from the groom's family, usually the father, either as a lump sum or in instalments. The father is ideally supposed to reinvest the money as part of the dowry but rarely does so. The price depends on a variety of factors such as the girl's beauty, age, lineage, status and whether she has been previously married. The re-marriage of widows does not involve bride-price. This custom is held to be odious by almost everyone I talked to. Bride-prices were low a century ago and 'a man wanting a hard working, useful wife can easily procure an Afridi or Orakzai woman for a sum varying from Rs. 150 to Rs. 200' (Gazetteer, Kohat 1883-4: 63). Cash and material items flow from the groom's to the bride's family in far larger amounts than what the bride brings as her dowry which is minimal. This contrasts with other societies on the subcontinent where the dowry may be considerable consisting of jewellery, furniture and cash (Goody and Tambiah, 1973; Lewis, O., 1958; Mayer, A. C., 1970).

Although society disapproves of keeping a daughter at home after she is fifteen or sixteen, status is an important factor in marrying daughters. Senior lineage Pukhtuns are reluctant to give their daughters in hypogamous marriages to members of junior lineages. The point supports my argument that concepts of status over-ride economics even in SAM. For instance Zaidullah (Madar) has two unmarried daughters over twenty-one and awaits suitable suitors in spite of the attractions of bride-price. Hamesh, too, has an unmarried daughter of twenty-one and will not marry her off to 'anyone' as he feels, belonging to a senior lineage, he has not found a suitor of her status. Meraj Gul, thirty years old, Do Khel of the junior lineage and the son of Khairaz Gul who is blind, poor and about seventy years old, cannot find a bride as he has no money. Meraj's sister is married to Hussain Khan's son but no father is prepared to give away his daughter 'free' to him.

Khanzada Khan of TAM related an anecdote that illustrates why *sar paisey* is expected and taken among Mohmands. A father married his daughter without *sar paisey* and when the bridal party was returning home a stream had to be crossed. The husband made his new bride wade across it. The girl was furious and rebuked the groom saying he had no respect for her. The husband agreed. He said, 'You were given free to me. You cost me nothing.' So she returned home promptly to her father who then charged bride-price. This time the husband arranged for her to be carried in a litter (*dolai*) over the stream.

Secondly, as I explained earlier, 'Pukhto' can literally mean 'word' (of honour). Most Mohmand marriages highly endogamous to lineage in any case result from a mother 'booking' a girl at birth. The word is given and accepted as such by the community. The booking by the boy's mother of a new-born girl is tantamount to the formal engagement (*koidan*) often and, not unnaturally, of little importance in *nang* society.[15] Henceforth the girl is considered engaged and as good as married to the boy. Violation of this verbal and informal agreement involves the entire *badal* and *tor* sequence on the assumption that the girl is considered married. This explains why the fiancé in some of the *tor* cases mentioned in Chapter 7 took it upon himself to take revenge; his fiancée was conceptualized as his wife both by him and the community. Her elopement or abduction meant dishonour for him.

Thirdly, the agreed rights of a woman under Islamic law in the event of divorce (*haq mehr*)[16] are not mentioned by either party, let alone claimed. The general illiteracy reinforces ignorance of female rights. *Haq mehr* would not be given either in TAM or SAM for divorce, involving the honour of a Pukhtun, is theoretically impossible in Pukhtun society. Although a woman has the right to divorce her husband under Islamic law, this is a social impossibility among Pukhtuns. If divorced legally and married to another man she would be considered as having become *tor* and both would run the risk of being shot. The question of rights in divorce cases therefore remains hypothetical. As mentioned, to my knowledge no case has ever been recorded of a Pukhtun divorce. The two cases of deviance regarding inheritance are both from SAM. Shahtota, now sixty years old, was left a widow when her husband (Madar Khel) died thirty years ago, leaving a son and daughter as babies. He had written in her name the house in which she is now living. She is one example of an unmarried widow. Chapter 9 discusses a case-study regarding a woman inheriting land in SAM.

Finally, another deviance from Islamic tradition may be mentioned. The formal marriage ceremony, the *nikah*, is performed after the bride is brought from her natal home to the groom's house. Why is the girl brought to the boy's house for *nikah*? Firstly, it implicitly reflects the lower status of the girl-giver and second it explicitly reflects the general status of women. Once at the groom's house the bride is in no position to refuse consent to the marriage. Almost all Mohmands, *mashars* and *kashars*, are so married.

The family is highly conscious that 'a female belongs to another' (her husband) and is therefore a 'temporary visitor'. Most patriarchs, like Shahzada, could remember neither the names nor the numbers of female descendants of their married daughters. In an apt categorization, various Mohmand *mashars* described women as *khidmatgaray*, a term generally used for the occupational groups.

Empirically it would appear that women are crammed into the interstices of tribal structure with little apparent scope for roles of social importance and as victims of considerable social injustice. This is not entirely a correct picture. Many women exert considerable influence on, and even dominate, their men. Women in theory stand in low status but in practice they are often close and valued companions directly affecting the lives of their men. Towards the end of my field-work I saw how Hussain Khan, otherwise tough and invulnerable, became a broken man when his wife died. For days on end he would not eat and began to cry like a child at the slightest provocation. Sitting in the Bela *hujra* he would repeat that his life was 'over' and those around him, representing various lineages and groups, agreed that the late Mrs Hussain was like a mother to all of them. The cause of her death heightened the sense of tragedy. Hussain's son had brought pesticides for the sugar-cane crop from the Agricultural Department and his mother, thinking it was medicine for her as she was ill at the time, drank it and died within an hour. The village elders, including Shamshudin, rushed her to the dispensary in Michni and then hoped to save her life by taking her to the hospital in Peshawar but she died in the bus. Hussain Khan was inconsolable. He constantly said 'I'm ruined' (*ghark shom*) and that until this time at eighty he could work 'harder and better' than his sons but now had no more will-power to carry on. He said he had married his wife, who was some fifteen years younger than him, about fifty years ago and she was like a friend, adviser and comrade. In a similar situation, and again during my field-work, Shahmat's wife, an old and trusted companion, died in Shati Khel in 1976. Shahmat suddenly seemed to have lost the will to live and died within two weeks of her death.

A man may re-marry for a variety of reasons but mainly because his wife is barren. The incidence of polygamy is low among the Mohmands being 0.4 per cent for my entire field-work area. Of the total Shati Khel males 0.6 per cent and of the Bela males 0.2 per cent were polygynist with two, or in very rare cases more, living wives. We may conclude that Mohmand society is largely monogamous. For instance, Mazullah has been married thrice, because his wives died but has never had more than one wife at a time. One of his wives was his dead brother's widow. Similarly, Amirzada married Lakhkar's daughter after the death of his first wife. Almost all second marriages are contracted after the death of the first wife. Wives tend to die earlier in TAM, perhaps due to the stress and strain to which they are subjected. There are only three people in Bela Mohmandan who have two wives, Mohammad Aslam, Faqir Jan and Amin (Jano). Each one of them married because their first wives were issueless and with the consent of their wives. Other males, like Hamesh, married a second time when their first wives were long dead. Not all widowers re-marry, as we saw earlier. Hussain Khan who was quite shattered by the loss of his spouse had no intention of marrying again. In Shati Khel, too, among the entire twenty villages the incidence of polygamy was rare. Senior lineage Maliks, like Haji Abbas, often married a second time to provide a home for a dead brother's widow. One of the few exceptions is Shahzada Malik who has two wives, the second a Kamali Halimzai, bringing him political contacts in the *maira* and in turn leading to further exogamous marriages outside the sub-section.

The most popular season for marriages is spring when the weather is pleasant and more important, money from sale of crops has come in. Marriages never take place in the months of *Rabi-ul-awal*, in which the Prophet died, *Moharram* in which his grandsons were martyred and Ramadan the month of fasting.

Marriages involving the offspring of senior Maliks are beginning to show signs of change that herald a new order for traditional occasions. Cooks, coloured tents (*shamianas*) and varieties of sweetmeats and fruit are brought from Shabkadar or Peshawar. Recently dowry has been acquired in shopping sprees in Peshawar. An exogenous custom creeping into marriages is the hiring of dancing girls from Peshawar to entertain guests late into the night. Traditionally, Mullahs would recite from the Holy Koran and relate events from the life of the Prophet. Habibur Rahman, Shamshudin's brother in the Agency, and Haji Gul, the Bela barber, refused to have such women at their sons' marriages recently. When they were brought, Habibur Rahman stood on the roof with a gun, and declared that he would shoot at anyone approaching his house and insisted that the Mullahs recite religious verses. However, once the singing of the women commenced a furlong away the audience began to thin out and soon the Mullahs discovered that they had all but lost their audience.

Haji Hassan, Umar and Shahmat, elders of Shati, talked of the days when marriages were very simple affairs. No clothes or any kind of jewellery were given and the bride came virtually with little else than a few pairs of *kames-partog* and a *sadar*. They emphasized that not even tea was served and in the 1920s and 1930s the entire function including *sar paisey* would cost between Rs. 300 and 500. The boy did not go to his future father-in-law's house. The bride was seated in a small simple wooden structure made of mulberry branches, called *dolai*, covered with a shawl or veil, which was lifted by four agnatic kin of the groom and was brought home without much ado. Today they may expect to be given necklaces (*amail*) and other items of jewellery (*tika, pata, qulay*).

The following are two examples of typical Mohmand marriages and the expenditures incurred. Fawzoon's future father-in-law, Sobat, took Rs. 2,000 for the girl but spent most of it on her future domestic needs such as crockery and quilts. Arabistan paid no *sar paisey* but it was understood that he would be compensating by excessive expenditure on gold, furniture, etc., for the girl. In theory, the *sar paisey* is to be spent by the father on the girl's material needs in her future home. The expenditure on engagement, which is traditionally a simple affair, has been included in the list. Item 2 of Table 8 below would typically include six to eight (unstitched) pairs of *kames-partog*, vests, socks, slippers, mirror, combs, soap, bangles, towels, cots, quilts, a tin box and perhaps a cupboard. Nowadays cosmetics like lipstick and powder may also be expected. Item 3 would be a standard meal of rice. If the groom is poor as in Fawzoon's case, rice would be of low quality, round grain (*ghat*) – Rs. 70-80 a maund -- but if he is better off as in Arabistan's case then a better variety of rice, long grain (*narai*) – Rs. 170-200 a maund – would be cooked in vegetable oil. Chicken and meat are cooked by senior Maliks and few people can afford such items. There is no custom of serving sweetmeats or fruit following the simple meal of rice and vegetable oil. Guests may number between 500 and 2,000 and take turns to eat in groups at the groom's house.

TABLE 8 Marriage expenditure: 1976 (in Rs.)

	Fawzoon (Kado)	*Arabistan (barber)*
1 *sar paisey*:	2,000	–
2 groom provides:	2 ounces gold: 2,460 clothes, etc.: 1,000	2½ ounces gold: 3,355 3,500
3 food (*dodai*):	1,185	3,680
4 extras: relatives and occupational groups:	200	1,200
5 transport:	–	560
total:	6,845	12,295

These examples illustrate two points, one social and the other economic. Marriages, like the other social rites of all social groups, follow an identical pattern and, second, the average economic standard of the occupational groups *vis-à-vis* Pukhtun groups is reflected in the comparative expenditures above. Although this should not be taken as an absolute comparison, the barber's expenditure is almost double that of a member of the Kado senior lineage. Haji Gul, the father of Arabistan,

had just returned from employment in Iran and is said to have brought
back some Rs. 40,000 with him.

The generalized and traditional movement of connubial investments
is depicted graphically in Figure 17 and the numbers relate to items in
Table 8.

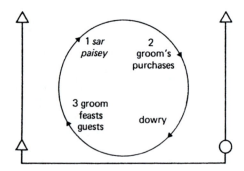

FIGURE 17 *Bride-wealth patterns*

Items 1 and 2 may be utilized as dowry by the girl's father. In TAM the
father usually keeps almost the entire *sar paisey* and sends his daughter
with very little to her future home. Expenditure is almost entirely
borne by the groom's family. Of all the *rites de passage* marriage is the
most expensive and elaborate. Birth, circumcision and death involve a
certain amount of expenditure on food cooked for guests and payments
made to members of occupational groups but these come nowhere near
marriage expenditure. Marriage is the best illustration of Veblerian conspicuous consumption and show of status among the Mohmand.
Needless to say, economic and social strength and the desire to display
them determine the quality of the feast and number of guests involved
in the rites and vary from individual to individual.

There is a high frequency of *badal*[17] marriages between close agnatic
kin, usually brothers (Figure 18). A sister or daughter is 'given' and a
sister or daughter 'taken' simultaneously. In such *badal* marriages the
father of the bride does not take money for his daughter as the *sar
paisey* cancels out. When no money is taken for *badal* marriage it is
literally termed 'head for head' (*sar pa sar*). Sororate, though practised,
is uncommon while levirate is more common (Figures 19 and 20). A
brother usually marries his dead brother's wife; it keeps the woman in
the family as it does the property. There is an example of deviance in

SAM of a widow living alone, which would be unthinkable in TAM, as in the case of Shahtota. *Swara* is a marriage arranged among kin to conciliate, or bind fighting agnatic groups, usually after murder has been committed, and is common among Pukhtuns (Barth, 1972: 96).

FIGURE 18 (i–v) *Exchange (*badal*) marriages*

(i)

Badal marriages are common among collaterals within the operative lineage in TAM and there are examples of two or three in each Shati settlement. For instance, Abbas married his patrilateral parallel cousin and in return 'gave' his sister to his father's brother's son.

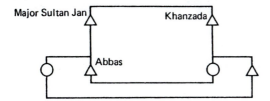

(ii)

In this example local marriages are contracted exogamous to clan but are socially homogamous. Major Sultan Jan, the paternal uncle of Shahzada, married his son and daughter to Tarakzai kin in the 1960s. As a result an important political alliance was forged as Yusuf Mohmand, once a Member of Parliament, is an important political figure. In turn it gave the Tarakzai family a foothold in Shati Khel and contracts for various development schemes such as the hospital.

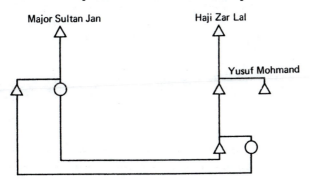

(iii)

As in case no. i above in another typical example of a simple *badal* marriage two brothers exchange sons and daughters in SAM. No *sar paisey* or other elaborate costs are involved. As Ihsanullah was marrying his father's brother's daughter, and as part of a *badal* marriage, there was no bride-price. None the less, each father still spent about Rs. 10,000 to 12,000 on the marriage feast, and the crockery, cots, quilts, etc., for the couple. *Badal* marriages, like Ihsanullah's, usually take place on the same day.

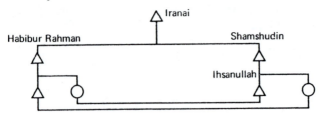

(iv)

In the following example Saz marries Shamshudin's sister who, in exchange, marries his brother's daughter. These intermarriages can be acutely awkward in complicated cases of agnatic rivalry, as in the case of Roghan and Saz illustrated in the extended case-study on agnatic rivalry in Chapter 7.

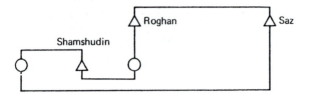

(v)

A more complex pattern of four *badal* marriages involving three sub-sections in Bela, one senior and two junior lineages, is illustrated below:

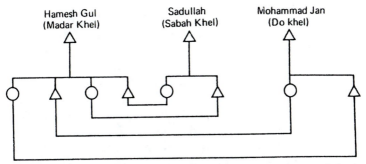

Levirate is more common in TAM than SAM and one of the only two examples of it in SAM was when Dawai Khan married the wife, who already had two little daughters, of his father's dead brother Munawar Khan. Such a marriage is considered socially homogamous. The *nikah* is performed, without ceremony or guests, in the evening, and the marriage passes quietly and unnoticed. It is considered entirely a family affair.

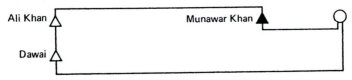

FIGURE 19 *Levirate marriage*

In TAM levirate marriages are more common. For instance Haji Abbas, the son of Sultan Jan, married his dead brother's wife who had two children from her first husband Karim.

Although there was no example of sororate marriage in Bela itself there were a few in Kado Korona, one involving Shamshudin's first cousin, Saida Jan, who married his dead wife's sister, both patrilateral parallel cousins. Another example of sororate marriage is taken from Shati Khel involving Shahmat of the Musa lineage:

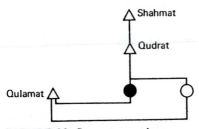

FIGURE 20 *Sororate marriage*

In this chapter I have attempted to relate settlement and domestic structure to the larger thesis of the study: how tribal groups adjust to changing administrative situations and what structural changes this presumes and creates. Through the use of detailed documentation of fundamental organizational criteria like domestic structure and marriage statistics, I have attempted to illustrate the extent and quality of differentiation in social life and organization between the groups since they were administratively severed almost three decades ago. I have argued, and indeed I hope have conclusively illustrated, how in the two important features of social organization, settlement and marriage patterns, Mohmand life largely approximates to its ideal model. There is a significant homology between TAM and SAM patterns. In this chapter I have attempted to depict the underlying structural principles of the two key domestic features of society, household settlements and marriage. The correlation between physical settlements and lineage organization and marriage patterns has been indicated. Settlement deployment in TAM strictly adheres to the schematized and symmetrical conceptualization of the Pukhtun model. Deviance in SAM, by the blurring of genealogical and social lines in settlement patterns, partly refutes my thesis that *Pukhtunwali* can survive encapsulation. Evidently in the SAM settlement patterns the ideal model, although discernible, cannot maintain its purity. However, it is in the marriage figures that my arguments are borne out. TAM and SAM continue to remain almost entirely endogamous. The marriage figures are conclusive evidence that the phyletic and social boundaries of Pukhtunness have been maintained in both groups; all the more remarkable in SAM, exposed as it is to the vicissitudes of encapsulation. In the next chapter I shall illustrate how the economic situation based on case-studies of income and expenditure further corroborates my arguments.

9 Economic structure and lineage ideology

Whatever other means tribesmen devise to elevate a man above his fellows, and they are several, this one (the appropriation of critical productive means by some few) history's most compelling, is not open to them (Sahlins, 1968: 76).

A chapter on economic structure presupposes a primary occupation with economic questions such as modes of production. I have been arguing that in the ideal economic activity remains secondary to political activity, and shall continue to do so in the present chapter through the use of extended case-studies. My concern will be to support the set of premises related to my thesis: that TAM behaviour approximates to the ideal Pukhtun model as indeed does that of certain SAM senior lineages. A clear correlation between conspicuous consumption based on certain laws of *Pukhtunwali* such as hospitality and those groups living up to the ideal emerges. Irrational social expenditure thus often predominates over rational economic expenditure and husbanding of resources.

TAM organize their lives around their ideal model by living on unirrigated, low-production lands and supplementing their income by non-agricultural sources such as smuggling, in itself a consequence of their political situation. Economic investment and government employment are often directed towards continuing political agnatic rivalries. As will be seen, junior lineages and non-Mohmand groups, especially in SAM, prefer to concentrate on economic activity at the risk of deviating from the traditional ideal model. Simultaneously they are abandoning some of the precepts of *Pukhtunwali*. Part of my thesis is refuted as I shall show how and why SAM have adopted economic activity rather than politics as their major concern. Although there is undoubtedly an element of simplification in this analysis it largely supports my thesis while pointing to the differentiation in social behaviour and organization that encapsulation has brought about among the Mohmands.

In a Marxist sense, tribal society appears to have arrived at the final Marxist stage without having gone through the prescribed orthodox schema. It is almost a Marxist situation in its ideal form, stateless and egalitarian. There are no opposed classes of merchants and creditors, landlords and tenants, factory owners and factory workers; no classes of exploiters and exploited and therefore no surplus value or alienation of labour. Tribal society in its ideal form has been conceptualized as a state of 'pure communism' in a significant Marxist analysis (Engels, 1970: 266–317).

Polanyi (1968b) made his major contribution to economic anthropology by distinguishing three main categories of economic relationships in society: reciprocity, redistribution and exchange. Briefly, reciprocity denotes movements between correlative points and symmetrical groupings while redistribution designates movements towards the centre and out of it again and exchange refers to vice-versa movements taking place under a market system. Sahlins usefully further analysed reciprocity (Sahlins, 1969). Although I find this theoretical categorization of economic relationships within tribal structure an interesting starting point for a discussion on economic interaction within tribal groups, I cannot sustain it with my own data. In its simple form reciprocity is a 'between' relationship, the action and response of two parties, whereas redistribution is a 'within' relationship, the collective action of a group with a defined socio-centre where goods are concentrated and thence flow outward, 'redistribution is chieftainship said in economics' (Sahlins, 1968: 95). In terms of Sahlins's categories of reciprocity Mohmand lineage cousins would be involved in relationships of 'negative reciprocity', while in keeping with chiefly tradition, patriarchs would invest in 'generalized reciprocity' especially when dealing with outsiders. However, decreasing productivity on barren land makes inter-lineage and intra-lineage hierarchization a problematic affair. As chiefs cannot maintain a focal position in redistributive function they cannot sustain large conical domains. Surplus is thus diverted into horizontal rather than vertical circuits in TAM and SAM.

In terms of my taxonomy of Pukhtun groups, just as economic relationships and functions are largely based on reciprocal rather than on redistributive economic systems in *nang* society, *qalang* Khans may appropriate crops which in turn they may redistribute in various forms to their tenants, symbolizing a ranked society and their political power. Among the Mohmands the household head, especially after the death of his father, inherits his own small piece of land. We have seen how small average land holdings are: 4½ acres in TAM and 2 acres in SAM per household. Inheritance is often egalitarian in the extreme. No one man owns so much land as to be able to convert it into the redistributive economic pattern which may in turn be reconverted into political authority. Among TAM and SAM groups therefore the entire structure of economic relationships is reciprocal and converts easily into tribal democracy which it reinforces.

Without wishing to become involved in a Substantivist versus Formalist debate in economic anthropology on which there is a flourishing and sophisticated literature[1] I think that few anthropologists or economists would today deny that there exists the closest possible relationship between social groups and their economic environment and activity which determine social organization in tribal society. I will assume the relationship and start from this simple statement and hope to support it by the organization of my data.

Recognition that kinship relations dominate the organizations of tribes is almost as old as anthropology (Morgan, 1871), a relationship Marxist anthropologists recognize (Godelier, 1967: 112). I am arguing that among the Mohmand kinship lineage politics dominates economic considerations. For example, the Mian Mandi, the key economic market and site in the Gandab, indeed the Mohmand Agency, has been allowed unchallenged to the Mians. The primary interest of the Pukhtun remains political not economic activity. The Mohmand idealize the concept 'that those who press the trigger do not press the hoe'.

What implications does ideal Pukhtun behaviour, centring around agnatic rivalry, have for economic activity such as the accumulation of wealth, production and exchange of resources? Conceptually, serious Pukhtun activity by any aspiring political pretender or group of pretenders must subordinate economic to political interests. A large part of this political activity is totally sterile in economic terms. The examples of Malik Lakhkar and Dilawar diverting their hard-earned economic resources over a generation into political activity in Shati Khel have been given above. Khanzada, the son of Abdullah, repeated the complaint of factional leaders that supporters tended to steal and embezzle expensive items such as ammunition during the long nights of factional fighting; feuds are an expensive investment.

A second point follows from the above relating to the economic activity of junior lineages and non-Mohmand groups. Because junior lineages (Malok) and affiliated lineages (Ganjian) in Shati Khel have consciously opted out of political activity as they are politically debilitated they are free to concentrate on economic activity. Such economic activity only underlines the social reality of their political situation. Needless to say, in a changing situation, their economic resources are beginning to pay dividends and may eventually bring them more satisfaction than the activities of the Musa and Ranra who still largely adhere to the ideal Pukhtun model. The younger elements of the senior groups are also showing signs of abandoning traditional political activity for chances of economic betterment: Abdul Wahid, the grandson of Shahzada, and Bahadar, the eldest brother of Feroz, left for Saudi Arabia in 1976 to take up jobs as manual labourers.

SAM presents no such dilemmas between political and economic choices of behaviour for Pukhtun activity. The hospitality of *mashars* like Shamshudin and the vocabulary of *Pukhtunwali* that they employ appear somewhat unreal in Bela while the talk of Hussain Khan, about acquisition of land and debts, is in harmony with the social and economic environment. In this sense, as I shall show below, the Bela situation with its emphasis on agricultural economics, in the main, points to deviance from ideal Pukhtun behaviour.

1 The agricultural cycle

This section discusses the annual agricultural cycle and related characteristics of TAM and SAM. There are no sugar-cane or maize crops in Shati Khel. One crop of poor quality wheat and barley, depending entirely on the scant rainfall, grows in Shati Khel. Sugar-cane forms the major cash crop in Bela and is planted on almost three-fourths of its land, providing its main source of income. Categories of sugar-cane are divided into native (*watani* or *desi ganey*) and farm (*faramay*) – a 'foreign' induced variety. The former is of little commercial value and consumed locally while the latter is used for extracting sugar-cane syrup, and is commercially valuable. Belawals converted to producing the second variety in the 1960s. Wheat and maize are also divided into *watani* and recent popular varieties such as Mexi-Pak. No rice or fruit are cultivated due to scarcity of water. Land in SAM is often called by distinguishing characteristics such as its proximity to a canal (*nehar-wand*); near or producing figs (*inzar-wand*); near water (*dand-wand*) and near or producing mulberry trees (*toot-wand*). No such divisions obtain in TAM as land is uniformly barren and unirrigated.

Few people in Shati or Bela can afford a *qulba* and the number fluctuates. In the entire Shati Khel area there were said to be only eight *qulbas,* six with the Musa and two with the Malok. People were selling *qulbas* to invest in alternative and new activities such as transport. Just as the dominant lineage, the Musa, own the maximum number of *qulbas* in TAM, the *mashars* of each group in SAM own *qulbas*: Shamshudin (Kado), Hamesh (Madar), Hussain (Jano), Majeed and Mehr Gul (Sabah/Qulamat) and Mashad (the Bela Sayyed). The carpenters are the only group with two sets of *qulbas*. One *qulba* is reckoned as being able to work on half an acre per day. Land is locally reckoned according to this measure; 'I have one *qulba*' would mean 'I have half an acre of land'.

The four flour machines, run by diesel oil, serving TAM, and the four sugar-cane pressing machines turned by buffaloes in SAM reflect the economic and social interrelationship between groups. In TAM one flour machine, bought in 1965, is owned by Shahzada and services the settlements in Shati. It is housed and operated by Aziz Ingar. The Mians own three machines of which two are owned by Mian Jalil. These service assorted groups, including those like Ranra who would rather not use Shahzada's machine. Mian Jalil was the first to introduce the machine in the Gandab in 1958. Mian Karim bought his in 1960. Charges are uniform and in kind, one-sixteenth of the ground flour. The machine is capable of grinding six maunds in one hour.

The owners of the *ganrey* of Bela Mohmandan are rather apt illustrations of emerging and declining lineage groups of the village: Hamesh Gul (Madar) – the second-senior lineage, Hussain Khan (Jano) – junior lineage, Majeed (Sabah) – another junior lineage, and Morcha (occupational group) own the four machines. Shamshudin shared the ownership with Hamesh Gul when they bought it together some fifteen years ago for Rs. 1,500 but sold his rights recently to Hamesh Gul. Today it is worth about Rs. 3,500. The oldest *ganrey* belongs to the carpenter who bought it almost twenty years ago. *Ganrey* are loaned to the user who books it in advance often with two or three people and arranges for its operation for a charge of one rupee per maund of *gur* extracted. The three men who operate it are usually Kohistanis, escaping the northern winter, and they sleep by the *ganrey* if hired; if the owner cannot afford labourers he and his male kin operate the *ganrey* themselves.

I made a study of the canals that provide water to the fields of Bela (Maps 6 and 7). Water canals are communally cleaned and maintained and the distribution of water which is meticulously organized reflects the democracy of Bela. Although there is no written schedule or committee to supervise and organize actual distribution of water, it is done by the Bela *mashars* on a mathematical basis depending on the needs of the crops, seasonal requirements and the amount of land owned by the farmer. An average of just over an hour per acre per week is allowed irrespective of the lineage or group of the landowner. The operation involves the owner, his brother or son, who supervises the diversion of water to his fields at the appointed time and for the fixed period. If anyone tries to divert, or tamper with, the canals the entire village would take action and either beat up the person or punish him by stopping his water altogether. No such case was brought to my notice for the last few years. Perhaps the harmony is partly explained by the fact that the entire operation is organized by the villagers and no officials of the Irrigation Department are involved. The canals are full of a steady supply of water diverted near the Michni rest house in spring when the snows have melted and the Kabul is reaching its fullest flow. Canal number 1 is mainly for the villages of the Zarif Khel and Kodo neighbouring Bela. Canal number 2 is also mainly for Zarif and Kodo but on Fridays water is given to Bela. Canal number 3 is exclusively reserved for Bela.

Among TAM agricultural activity is given neither much social nor economic importance in the ideal; rather, other more unorthodox and certainly more imaginative sources of income are tapped, like smuggling, dacoity, international trade and allowances from the political authorities. The uncertainty of rainfall diminishes the value of land as a reliable source of income and agriculture is shrugged off thus: 'if it rains the crops will grow.' This increases cynicism about agricultural pursuits and agriculturalists are looked down on. Land, placed in bits and pieces of one or two acres on sides of mountains and *khwars*, is treated more as a political factor in laying a claim to the tribal charter than as a source of agricultural income. Land in Bela sustains and feeds the family whereas in TAM it may identify the individual on the tribal charter and strengthen membership to it but can rarely feed him. He has to supplement his income by other means.

In contrast to TAM, Belawals are acutely aware of Pukhto months and their properties, tied up as they are with the agricultural cycle. In TAM most young men and many elders could not recount the sequence of Pukhto months to me, indicating the lack of importance they attach to them, and broadly divided the year into its four seasons. Table 9 depicts the agricultural cycle for the Mohmand:

TABLE 9 The agricultural cycle.

	sugar-cane (ganey) (*occupies three-fourths of Bela land*)	wheat (ghanam)	maize (jwar)	barley (orbashay)
			(these three crops are usually grown in rotation on the same plot)	
January (*Mah*)	6 inches high	water every fortnight		
February (*Chetar*)		fertilizers		sowing
March (*Pagan*) water in Kabul river as snows start to melt; main rainfall				
April (*Isaq*)		harvest, thresh (*ghobal*)		
May (*Jet*)	3–4 feet high dung/ urea		sow, plough (*qulba*)	harvest (in 3 months)
June (*Har*)	fertilizers (*sara*)			
July (*Pashakal*) rain, Kabul cuts off Bela into island for 4 months				
August (*Badro*)	5–6 feet high, re- quires much water every 7 days			
September (*Aso*)			harvest (in 3–4 months)	
October (*Katak*)	10–15 feet cutting begins next 3–4 months during which *ganrey* busy		wheat planted on same plot after maize harvest	
November (*Magan*)				
December (*Poh*) Kabul river at driest	sugar-cane cut annually but sown in four- year cycles (rationing); in fourth year wheat and maize are cultivated	seeds (*tokham*) plough cultivation begins		

The mode of production, defined as the totality that relates to economic activity, is clearly differentiated in the TAM and SAM situations. With relatively less importance given to agricultural activity the dominant economic institutions of TAM are political and unorthodox such as smuggling, secret allowances, etc., centring around and dependent on kinship and lineage position. In SAM the dominant institutions may be said to be agricultural with discernible characteristic patterns. Economic activity depends on permanent residence, cash crops and declining influence of lineage, that is, organization of labour and economic relationships depend less on kin ties than in TAM. These statements are borne out by my case-studies quoted in previous chapters and will be supported by data in this chapter.

The situation raises an interesting theoretical question central to my thesis. How can two such structurally similar groups deriving their socio-cultural values from one model exhibit such marked differences? The differentiation can be shown in the 'indifference curves' of preferences which stem from the following problem. Given a choice between sitting in a *hujra* ostensibly to indicate political support or spending an extra hour in the field, or doing business at Mian Mandi where money may accrue, there is little doubt that the former choice, expressing the domination of political institutions, would prevail for TAM. The Mohmand diaries that I discuss below show that, however active economically, and junior lineages like the Malok have of late become very active in this field, TAM males would still visit the *hujra* at least twice a day. They would usually round off the day's work with a couple of hours at the *hujra* in the evening, including visits to more important Maliks like Shahzada. Feroz, the *kashar* who is *dwa-kora* with his main house at Shabkadar, prefers to be seen at the *hujra* of Shahzada where he sleeps at least two or three nights a week. Such choices are not difficult to understand in TAM where unirrigated lands severely inhibit the attractions of diverting energies into economic activity. Put in another way — what are the choices and alternatives open to TAM for the utilization of his time? And what forms do they take? The answers lie in what is locally known and understood as political activity with its focus on agnatic rivalry and expressed through various forms such as time spent in the *hujra* or with the administration.

In contrast to the indifference with which TAM tend to their fields, SAM generally invest every available resource of time and goods in their fields. If a similar choice of utilizing an extra unit of time in the field or the *hujra* were offered to SAM, the chances are that they would choose to spend that unit in agricultural activity. Hussain Khan would often deliver long lectures to me on the virtues of hard work and the useless-ness of idling away time in the *hujra*. The Bela *mashars* have common sayings like 'an agriculturalist cannot sit idle. If he sits he will lose'. The important point here is that this Protestant ethic and nascent spirit of capitalism is not entirely activated by agnatic rivalry. The conclusions have ramifications for my thesis. Hussain Khan chooses to spend the extra unit in his field or with his cattle simply because he believes in this form of activity as more meaningful in moral terms and more pro-ductive in economic ones. Hussain now faces the dilemmas of Economic Man. He is faced by problems of choices between scarce means and alternative ends. He must learn to balance his income resources and consumption expenditures if he is to maximize or optimize. If agnatic rivalry also provokes him, then it is at a subconscious and not social level. However, the diary of Sial Khan (Kado) discussed below clearly illustrates that visits to the *hujra* as typical Pukhtun activity have not been completely terminated in SAM. Sial prefers chatting in the *hujra* to working in the fields. None the less, the over-all picture in SAM gathered from the annual agricultural cycle and the weekly diaries illustrates the tendency for economic activity to dominate political activity.

In the ideal exchanges among the Mohmands are related to: 1 con-sumption goods such as primary needs, wheat, oil, soap, etc. Barley is mainly eaten by animals in SAM but until a few years ago was the main staple diet of adults in TAM; 2 production resources such as blades for ploughs, closely followed by 3 weapons. Guns, either bought, inherited or stolen formerly from British India symbolized a man's courage and resources and also reflected his status.[2] A gun costs anywhere between Rs. 10,000 and 20,000 today depending on its quality and make. Finally, and more recently, 4 luxury goods like televisions, radios, cassette tape-recorders and even cars. These barely existed until 1974 but today they are highly visible status symbols. SAM's general economic situation in comparison to TAM may be gauged from the fact that there are only eight radios in the village for sixty houses as distinct from one for each household in TAM (except where TAM elders, like Haji Hassan, disallow them on religious grounds).

The argument I am trying to sustain in this chapter may be summed up by two examples, one from TAM and the other from SAM. They concern the acquisition of land by men, their attitudes to it and their plans for it. It is important to note that the two examples exemplify the ideal-type in TAM and deviant Pukhtun behaviour in SAM. First, Shahzada has acquired three plots of land by force, which itself is a symbolic exhibition of political status in the tribal section. The fact that he does not permit the clearing of the three destroyed hamlets on this land and cultivation or construction on their sites is similarly symbolic. Shahzada's seventeen sons and grandsons symbolize traditional tribal activity. They do not work and spend their time idling in the *hujra* and act as 'muscle' to Shahzada's political status by 'carrying guns'. When and where they can, they make quick money through smuggling, etc. (see Amirzada's income statement below in the next section). In contrast, Hussain, SAM of a junior lineage, began life with almost no economic resources but through shrewd non-Pukhtun activity, such as loaning money, has built up a position where he is the biggest Bela landlord and possesses one of its four *ganrey*. Following a deliberate policy of employment, there are seven government employees in his house (Figure 21). In Bela he has emerged in the 1970s as a man of astute business acumen and economic wealth who exemplifies a tacit rejection of TAM behaviour.

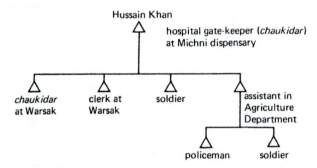

FIGURE 21 *Hussain Khan: employment and status*

Employment of seven members of Hussain Khan's family not only augments earnings but also represents a wide spread of government departments and concomitant authority. The employment of his sons, his own shrewd investment in agricultural land and the credit he gives for mortgaged lands (often defaulted to him) has given weight to his junior lineage and made him a serious contender for social and political status. Similarly, Mehr Gul (Sabah) has five employed sons who augment his meagre income from agriculture and increase his junior lineage status. Shamshudin and Hamesh Gul, the *mashars* of the two senior lineages of Bela, on the other hand, are not employed and nor are their sons. In contrast to Hussain's accumulation of land they are inclined to mortgage or sell it to keep up the demands of hospitality, expenditure on *rites de passage*, etc., which they feel their traditional status demands of them. Hussain may not be in a position to become the village elder but he has successfully blocked and curtailed the authority of the Kado *mashars* as in the examples regarding the Basic Democracy Elections or the Bela Cooperative Society (Part Three).

Qalang societies, like Swat, produce a complex variety of landlord and tenant relationships and categories (Barth, 1972: 44-5). Of the four major categories of farm labour distinguished in Swat (ibid.) the *dehqan*[3] or agricultural labourer is the most socially and economically depressed. He has no rights in land whatsoever. There are no *dehqans* in TAM and SAM. Certain elders like Shamshudin may hire a seasonal labourer to help harvest a crop or help in the *ganrey* but the general rule is one of domestic self-sufficiency. Among the Mohmand the most common category of labour contract and one not listed for Swat is *nim-kara* (literally, half-the-share). The *nim-kara* is more a mechanism to accommodate credit dealings within the community than a contract with outside labour with fixed terms and rules. It is a typical Mohmand arrangement. *Nim-kara* implies cultivation of one's own land. The debtor borrows money and agrees to pay the creditor half his crop until the debt is paid off. These categories are not labour contracts and we may conclude that apart from drifting or seasonal labour employed by a few households TAM and SAM do not engage agricultural labour as happens in Swat (Asad, 1972; Barth, 1972). The unity of ownership and work-ing of agricultural land prevents the growth of complex and bitter relationships resulting in the alienation of labour and the confrontation of classes in Pukhtun society (Asad, 1972). On the other hand it is the Mohmand *dehqan* or *ijargar* (the latter renting a plot and perhaps sub-infeudating it) who has established a foothold in Mardan and Peshawar Districts since the turn of the century and is today a middle-class land-owner. For instance, Lakhkar took 45 acres with four brothers on *ijara* a generation ago at Rs. 200 per acre paid annually. The five brothers and their sons could muster up to eighteen 'fighting' men, excluding sons-in-law, who were available in times of crisis, in the Settled Areas against their landlords. They soon translated physical strength into economic demands and insisted that the *ijara* be reduced to Rs. 120 a year. In time they bought the 45 acres which were divided between the brothers.

Below is a table depicting the relative economic situation and assets in TAM and SAM from household averages based on the formal question-naires:

TABLE 10 Economic situation of TAM/SAM: 1976

		TAM		*SAM*	
Land (per household) (in acres)					
irrigated land		0.9		1.3	
unirrigated land		3.7		0.6	
Crops (rupees per maund)		produce (in maunds)	sold (in rupees)	produce (in maunds)	sold (in rupees)
sugar-cane	100/md	16.2	32	40.2	3,198
wheat	80/md	28.7	12.9	15	35
maize	70/md	6	–	8	9
barley	40/md	5.7	16	0.1	–
Animals (rupees per animal)					
buffalo	1,500	0.4		1.9	
cow	1,000	2.7		2.1	
goat	200	5.3		0.4	
sheep	300	2		2.7	
Total universe					
Transport		3 cars 6 buses 3 trucks		1 bus	
Employment: local		44		33	
abroad		4		6	

On the face of it, SAM households with an average of 1.3 irrigated and 0.6 unirrigated acres of land to TAM's 0.9 irrigated acres (all around Shabkadar in the District) and 3.7 unirrigated acres of land depict a picture of relative self-sufficiency. Sugar-cane brings in good money for SAM and they ought to be better off than TAM whose lands are barren. The average household in TAM produces almost twice as much wheat as SAM, as the latter concentrate on sugar-cane. TAM earn less than half of what SAM earn in selling wheat, as the former eat most of the wheat while SAM have enough left over to sell. TAM produce and sell barley which is eaten by cattle and humans alike. Younger Mohmands like Feroz complain that their stomachs ache whenever they eat bread made of barley (*rota*). Barley is grown in SAM to feed animals. In TAM those cattle that actually work in the field are fed barley; otherwise they are given chaff (*bhoos*). The figures in Table 10 above on ownership of animals display no major differences. A higher percentage of buffaloes are expected in SAM due to their employment in agriculture, whereas the greater number of goats in TAM is explained by their being easier to look after in the rough mountainous terrain. The startling discrepancies emerge in the ownership of vehicles. In fact, TAM own buses and trucks and even cars that cannot be explained in conventional terms of agricultural cash crops, income or activity (TAM transport is discussed in Chapter 11).

In TAM work is intermittent and sporadic, ceasing when not required for the moment. To this ordinary irregularity a neolithic economy adds long periods of seasonal unemployment following the harvest, or at least a depressed level of activity implying a concealed unemployment. It is no coincidence that during such periods trade, involving extensive networks across international borders, is fully activated or that after the harvesting seasons dacoity in the Settled Districts increases as tribesmen come down to add to their incomes (Dichter, 1967; Elliott, 1968). In contrast SAM are fully involved with, and tied to the rhythm of, the agricultural seasons.

Constraints of technology and limited land dictate that in order to preserve the rate of production in relation to consumption one of two alternative strategies is adopted, either territorial expansion, which is not possible, or population shifts to prevent over-saturated population. Hence the movements since the last century to the *maira* among TAM. Political defeat means expulsion from Gandab, TAM's crude way of settling the Malthusian problem. The end-product is a simple transitive ordering or regrouping of lineages. Such shifts tend to reinforce rather than weaken Mohmand ideology for the principal levels of agnatic interaction remain invariant through the intergenerational oscillation. In the next section I shall specifically discuss income, consumption and expenditure based on specific TAM and SAM case-studies.

II Income, consumption and expenditure

Income, consumption and expenditure patterns based on fine-grained case-studies will be examined in this section. The second half of the section will examine expenses incurred on *rites de passage*. Within the framework of my thesis I will be correlating the relatively higher

expenditure of senior groups on hospitality, etc., as part of their concept of *Pukhtunwali*, and the more careful budgeting of junior and
non-Mohmand groups. The weighting, in terms of income and consumption units per household members, indicates the latter groups are not
economically depressed. The weighting will thus provide an accurate
picture of the income/consumption expenditures of TAM and SAM
groups and also support the point I have made above.

(a) *Income, consumption and expenditure*

The case-studies are based on the detailed monthly and annual budgets
of seven households randomly selected from various groups in TAM and
SAM, three are from TAM and four from SAM. I have selected the
extra budget from SAM as it gives me the opportunity to illustrate the
mode of living of a widow on her own, in itself a deviant situation and
one not represented in TAM. The three TAM studies depict budgets of
average tribesmen representing the three different lineages of Shati Khel
and the four SAM studies represent a member of a senior lineage
(Kado), a junior lineage (Sabah), a woman and an occupational group
(carpenter). I felt the selection of a member of the occupational group
only from SAM justified as Aziz Ingar of TAM, with his two Bedford
buses and special political relationship with the dominant Musa lineage,
would not be a typical example of a member of the occupational group.
Four of the following seven cases selected have had their diaries recorded
and, therefore, read with their budgets, fairly accurate conclusions can
be drawn of how they organize their social and economic life and what
constraints and choices they face and how they solve them. The domestic arrangements of the seven households may be examined through the
household structures graphically illustrated in Chapter 8.

Income has been recorded annually and not monthly for it is so
calculated among the Mohmands, depending as it does on annual crops
or irregular business deals rather than monthly wages. Expenditure,
however, has been divided both into recurring monthly household
expenditure and annual expenditure to enable a clear picture of the
year's total expenditure to emerge. These details will allow a realistic
weighting of income and consumption according to household members
and a calculation of income and consumption units per person so that
accurate comparisons of actual standards of income and consumption
among the Mohmands may be made.

The number at the head of columns in each of the next three tables corresponds to the name of the household head, his age, his sub-section, land ownership and the population of his household thus:

1 Amirzada, 53, Musa, household no. 15
2 Saida Khan, 26, Ranra, 4 acres, household no. 5
3 Kabil Khan, 40, Malok, 5 acres, household no. 8
4 Shamshudin, 50, Kado, 6½ acres, household no. 8
5 Mehr Gul, 60, Sabah, 2 acres, household no. 9
6 Morcha Khel, 50, carpenter, 5 acres, household no. 8
7 Shahtota, 60, Madar widow, half an acre, household no. 1

How accurate or representative are the budget figures below? Apart from certain unspecified items I would argue they add up to a fairly accurate economic picture confirmed by the diaries and my own observations. It is important to point out that TAM and SAM economies are functioning on two slightly different levels. For instance, there are no unspecified incomes in SAM. Conversely, because of the barren nature of the TAM areas prices of such commodities as vegetables, *gur*, etc., are higher by half or one rupee per seer than in SAM. Those items not easily available to SAM and reflecting the special administrative situation of the Agency, such as ammunition (illegal in SAM) and green tea (smuggled from Afghanistan), are cheaper in TAM. The unspecified income derives from various sources such as political allowances, international and national smuggling euphemistically called trading (*tijarat*), and perhaps even dacoity. The Mohmands traditionally used their strategic geo-political situation to tap these sources: 'nothing was easier than to reconnoitre and plan an attack on some unsuspecting village, swoop down, and skip back across the border the richer by a couple of Hindus for ransom, a bag of rupees and forty or fifty head of cattle' (Elliott, 1968: 162). The details have been left out of the analysis so as not to embarrass my respondents. Although non-quantifiable, it is important to mention this sphere of activity for any economic calculations in the Tribal Areas.

Examining the economic structure of typical Mohmand households two immediate conclusions are formed: material life is poor and austere but, and this is the second point, life has not sunk below the bread-line or to the famine level. Here I would refer to the pertinent observation made by an anthropologist and quoted earlier regarding the correlation between starvation and the evolution of cultures (Sahlins, 1974: 36). There are no cases of starvation in TAM or SAM.

Certain points emerge from the figures below which fit in with my larger thesis depicting the importance of *Pukhtunwali* in society — in

TABLE 11 Annual income: 1975–6 (in Rs.)

Item	1	2	3	4	5	6	7
sugar-cane				8,000	2,000	5,000	village 300 brother 100 in-laws 100
wheat		2,400	2,400	3,200	400	800	village 240 brother 80 in-laws 80
maize			400		300	560	village 210 brother 70 in-laws 70
barley						1,500	
buffaloes						1,900	
cows					380		
sheep							
poultry						24	40
eggs						30	16
carpenter						wheat 4,800 maize 4,200 (Bela and neighbouring villages)	
transport bus/truck			12,000 (shares with Malok cousins)		recently acquired		
ganrey business (including smuggling, etc.)	20,000	8,000	12,000			800	

			contractor (started this year)	1 son abroad 24,000 4 local 7,200	tips rites 150 extra jobs 3,000	
wood/timber						
transport employment		9,600				
others (unspecified political allowances)	3,000					
Total:	23,000	20,000	26,800	11,200	34,280	22,764	1,306

TABLE 12 Recurring monthly expenditure: 1975–6

Item	price in rupees	1	2	3	4	5	6	7
maize	70/md			140		40	40	
wheat	80/md	560	320	420	300	160	160	40
rice	5/sr	50	50	25	25		5	2.50
potatoes	2/sr	30	30	16	6	6	4	1.50
turnips	1.50/sr	12	4	13	6	6	5	0.50
onions	4/sr	12	4	8	18	8	2	1
garlic	3/sr	3	1	3	2	1	1	0.25
semolina	4/sr	16	8	12	3	3	3	1
gur	4/sr	50	60	80	40	30	33	2.50
sugar	7/sr	84	21	56	36	12	6	1.50
black tea	24/sr	24	18	24	36	24	18	6.50
green tea	20/sr	10	5	10	20	5	5	0.50
lentils	2.50/sr	20	20	50	12	4.50	5	2.50
milk	3/sr	150	45	45				
mutton	14/sr	70	42	56				
beef	8/sr	64	40	64	56	28	7	
fish	16/sr			16	catch			
eggs	6/doz.	66	12	12				
veg. oil	12/sr	204	120	190	78	39	26	9
red chilli	10/sr	2	2	2	1	2	1	0.50
salt	0.75/sr	2	2	3	2	1	1	0.50
coriander	3/sr	6	8	6	4	4	1	0.25
turmeric	6/sr	2	2		2	2		
cardamom	144/sr	6	4	6		3		
snuff	12/sr	12	12	12	12	12	12	
soap	6/sr	36	18	24	6	12	12	1.50
mustard oil	40/sr	10	10	10	5	5	5	1.50
matches	4/doz.	6	4	4	4	2	2	1
kerosene	2/sr	24	17	20	6	6	4	2.50
ammunition	10/bullet	220	100	100				
fodder		40	40	40	200			
sweetmeats					5			
rites de passage		100	30	50	50	20	10	10
Total:		1,891	1,049	1,517	935	435.50	368	87

this particular case, shown as expenditure on hospitality, *rites de passage*, etc., by senior lineages. The fact that the only two people financially running into yearly losses belong to senior lineages supports my contention. It is because of the desire to live up to certain standards that Amirzada's accounts do not balance; he is in the red by Rs. 4,909. He spent Rs. 1,200 buying new clothes for the family and Rs. 1,200 on rites in both cases far more than other TAM. The TAM figures reflect the pitfalls of indulging in such statistical exercises. On the face of it Amirzada, the eldest son of Shahzada, widely accepted as one of the

TABLE 13 Annual expenditure: 1975–6

Item	price in rupees	1	2	3	4	5	6	7
marrow	1.50/sr	12	5	10	10	4		
aubergine	3/sr	30	30	30	18	4	4	1.50
lady's finger	3/sr	15	12	12	7	6	5	3
cucumber	1/sr	4	2	4	4	2		
radish	.50/sr	5	1	2	2	2		
carrots	1/sr	2		2	2	1		
spinach	1/sr	15	5	10	4	2	3	1
oranges	3/doz.	90	36	12	6			
bananas	4/doz.	8	40	20				
persimmon	4/doz.	8		24				
pears	3/doz.	32		18	2		4	
guava	4/sr	30	30	32	4			
tomatoes	4/sr	36					6	
other vegetables		100	50	50	30	20	20	10
dried fruit	10/sr	60	20					
fertilizer					520			
			100 per suit			*30–50 per suit*		
clothes	5–15/ yard	1,200	300	600	640	180	240	30
shoes	20–50/ pair	250	150	200	200	75	100	30
crockery		300	200	200	200	100	150	20
barber		160	120	160	360	60	80	
carpenter		160	80	100	160	60	self	
doctor		1,000	600	2,000	480	480	240	80
Eeds		1,500	1,000	500	640	400	200	30
hotel		200	90	400				
transport			60	80			20	
Imam			80	200	80	60	80	
children's school					1,000			
farm labour					30			
Total:		5,217	2,911	4,666	4,399	1,456	1,152	205.50
Grand Total mon X 12 + yearly:		27,909	15,499	22,870	15,619	6,682	5,568	1,249.50
yearly saving:			4,501	3,930		27,598	17,196	56.50
yearly loss:		4,909			4,419			

most prominent *mashars* of Shati Khel, has no fixed source of income. His father's 7 acres are still undivided and in any case Amirzada will only inherit perhaps half an acre of unirrigated land. In a successful business deal involving tribal trade across international boundaries Amirzada may make Rs. 20,000 in one year, but on the other hand he may run into financial loss the next year. Similarly Kabil may earn a large sum this year but run into a deficit next year. Allowances from the political authorities largely depend on the good will of Amirzada's father and have therefore been substantially reduced and in danger of being altogether cut as he remains out of grace with his father. He has a large family of fifteen, almost double that of Kabil, and three times that of Saida. The economic position of the Malok, traditionally the third and junior-most Shati sub-section, reflects their involvement with the new development schemes of the Agency. Almost every Malok household is either contracting or labouring in one scheme or the other. Their economic position will radically alter for the better in the next few years. Agnatic rivalry has been channelled by the Malok into an outlook which drives them with the intensity of the Protestant ethic and the spirit of capitalism (Weber, 1962). There is an almost exact mirror-image of the Protestant ethic translated into Islamic idiom emerging among the Malok. They say of themselves: 'We are not opium-eaters, gamblers, loafers or adulterers. We do business. We work hard and pray regularly. There are seven *hajis* in Malok. We make money and we reinvest it. We do not relax.' The implication is that 'we' have specific attributes which 'others' so conspicuously lack. It is not difficult to guess who the others are.

Shamshudin, too, spent proportionately more on clothes and rites than other SAM, and had a budget deficit of Rs. 4,419. Shamshudin, owning three times more land than Mehr Gul of the junior lineage, nevertheless runs a deficit budget most of it accounted for by expenditure on guests. In contrast, neither Mehr Gul nor Morcha Khel feels the Kado compulsion to uphold hospitality. Shamshudin spends almost Rs. 600 on payments for *rites de passage* annually whereas Mehr Gul and Morcha spend about Rs. 240 and Rs. 120 respectively.

An even more significant point is the emergence of employment as a major source of income. Mehr Gul's income is almost three times as much as Shamshudin's although we have just seen that the latter owns three times more land than the former. Mehr Gul's income figure is inflated because of five employed sons, one of whom earns over Rs. 24,000 a year in the Arab states, a large part of which he sends home. Mehr Gul has invested most of this income recently in a passenger bus which is yet to break even economically and bring in profits. This is the only vehicle owned by a Belawal. Mehr Gul's other sons earn an average of Rs. 250 to 350 in government service and may send home as much as

Rs. 150 to 200 monthly. The trend has clear ramifications for traditional social structure based on land and lineage as a source of income and status. Shamshudin and Hamesh Gul, the two *mashars* of the senior lineages, have no employed sons in contrast to the seven employed people in Hussain Khan's house and five in Mehr Gul's house both representing junior lineages. In an almost similar situation in TAM no sons or grandsons of Shahzada Malik or Mazullah work whereas the junior and affiliated Shati lineages are economically active.

Morcha, the SAM carpenter, annually earns over twice as much as Shamshudin. As we saw above the income of Mehr Gul of the junior lineage is three times that of Shamshudin. Such economic figures underline my thesis that Pukhtun political status is not entirely dependent on economic positions of superiority. Morcha Khel's annual income is almost twice that of Shamshudin's as he receives income from 1 five acres of land which is situated in the best area of Bela (Map 6); 2 traditional payment in kind from agriculturalists who use his services to make and repair agricultural implements; 3 payment during *rites de passage* in cash; 4 cash payments for extra work such as making windows and doors; and 5 about Rs. 800 a year from renting out his *ganrey*. In sharp contrast Shamshudin and Hamesh Gul, the elders of the senior lineages, depena entirely on land for their income and have no other sources of income. Their unemployed sons are an economic liability. For instance Shamshudin spends about Rs. 1,000 annually on books, transport, etc., for the education of Ihsanullah and his other two sons.

Shahtota presents an interesting development and deviance from Pukhtun household arrangements of which there are and can be no examples in TAM. She is the widow of a Madar Khel and has been allowed to live in his house by his relatives until her death. After her death the house will revert to the nearest male kin.

A glance at the expenditure figures would show the importance of doctors and medicines in Mohmand life. Women's diseases are often unidentifiable, lengthy and costly, treated as they usually are by incompetent dispensers or orderlies at the Michni dispensary standing in for doctors who are not easily available for posting in remote areas. Even Shahtota, who lives on the charity of the village, and whose monthly expenditure comes to less than Rs. 90, spends Rs. 80 a year on medicine. Medicines are of poor quality and a visit to the doctor has more therapeutic than actual medicinal value.

In spite of Bela representing certain characteristics associated with peasant societies and villages, the economic idiom is still influenced by Pukhtun tradition, even among junior lineages. When I asked the Jano Khel who recently began to grow bananas in their house why they did not sell them, the indignant reply was 'We are Pukhtuns and not *baghwans*' (the latter, as we saw in Chapter 6, cultivate and sell vegetables and fruits). Khan Ali (Kado) who has a house by the canals running through the middle of Bela also planted bananas for domestic consumption but does not think of selling them as 'it is not Pukhto'. The exception is Badshah Gul (Sabah) who grows a bitter variety of grapes and sells them although people laugh at him and scorn him for it. Belawals feel that selling wheat, maize or *gur* is the work of agriculturalists and there is no shame attached to it, but selling fruit is the work of the *baghwan* and deviance from Pukhtun activity as understood in SAM.

Anthropologists often find themselves handling economic data in other than monetary units even in societies where the economy is partially monetized. Bailey in his study of Bisipara employed units of paddy (Bailey, 1957: 279); Salisbury employed the concept of 'time-budgets' among the Siane (Salisbury, 1962: 106); and in her study in south India Epstein allocated twelve points for one acre of wet land and four points for one acre of dry (Epstein, 1962: 42). Anthropologists thus handled the problem and concept of 'opportunity cost' by which is meant the 'cost' in the final analysis of a rejected alternative. 'Opportunity costs' thus involve choices and foregone alternatives in an endeavour to optimize usage of scarce means (Benham, 1948: 6).

An empirical selection of the yardstick allowing measurement of economic data relating to household income within the social and regional framework of the community was then related to the concept of the 'consumption unit' of the household to enable a realistic picture of income and expenditure to emerge. Since the size and age composition of households vary considerably it was found necessary to introduce the concept of the consumption unit which weighted household members according to their sex and age. Different and complex coefficients have been employed (Bailey, 1957: 277; Epstein, 1969: 160) but I shall adopt the simple index used by Salisbury in which he estimates that children eat half of what an adult eats (Salisbury, 1962: 79). The consumption unit assumes that male and female adults consume equal amounts as do children after the age of twelve as they are usually involved in active forms of manual labour. My wife and I came to this conclusion after watching, analysing and participating in dietary sequences. We will therefore allocate one unit to an adult male or female over the age of twelve, and half to anyone under twelve.

In her study Epstein divided the number of allocated points per household obtained through land ownership (bearing in mind that one acre of wet land equals three dry) by the number of consumption units and arrived at a points allocated per consumption unit per household. I had made a similar suggestion in my Field-work Proposals (Ahmed, SOAS, 1975) and had assumed that one unit of irrigated land in SAM would be equal to three units of unirrigated land in TAM based on current prices. I then proposed to divide the points allocated for income from land by consumption units derived from the number of people in the household. Once in the field I discovered that there were so many variables at work, particularly in a TAM/SAM comparison, that a scientific or statistically valid statement along the above lines would be difficult to sustain. Most of these variables were a condition of the unencapsulated nature of TAM and certain emerging variables which reflected the penetration of development schemes in TAM. For instance, on paper and in the field, one irrigated acre of land in Bela producing sugar-cane, a valuable cash crop, should be about three times the price of an acre in Shati Khel where there is no irrigation water and little rainfall. This should have made the Epstein formula of one equals three logical and applicable. But with the development schemes launched in 1974 in the Mohmand Agency, and with government buying property for headquarters, schools, etc., prices in the Agency rose rapidly. By 1976 an average acre cost about Rs. 15,000 in Shati Khel which was a slightly higher price than an average Bela acre. Another problem in quantifying income also arose out of the political situation in which TAM find themselves and which does not apply to SAM. Land in TAM is considered, as is agriculture, a secondary if not a tertiary source of income. As Table 11 shows, incomes are derived from unorthodox activities (trade, dacoity, smuggling, etc.) which are difficult to tabulate. To this list of incomes was added that of contracts and labour involved in the development schemes begun in 1974. Considering the rather unorthodox nature of economic activity involved in TAM, I appreciated the difficulties in drawing up an accurate opportunity cost chart and explanatory figures without compromising my informants. For these reasons I abandoned Epstein's formula and fell back on one in which I decided to utilize monetary units of income. I will therefore divide the annual income in rupees per household. In a second and related table I shall divide the actual consumption expenditure by the consumption

units per household. Together the tables will provide weighted income
and expenditure figures per household consumption unit and a realistic
basis for economic comparison of TAM and SAM.

The same seven households as in Tables 11-13, representing fifty-
four people (about 8 per cent of my TAM and SAM universe[4]), produce
the following picture:

TABLE 14 (i) Weighted income per consumption unit

	annual income (Rs.)	household population number	no. of con- sumption units in household	household member consumption unit (Rs.)	
				monthly	yearly
TAM					
Amirzada					
(Musa)	23,000	15	11½	167	2,000
Saida					
(Ranra)	20,000	5	3½	476	5,714
Kabil					
(Malok)	26,800	8	5½	406	4,873
SAM					
Shamshudin					
(Kado)	11,200	8	6½	144	1,723
Mehr Gul					
(Sabah)	34,280	9	8	357	4,285
Morcha					
(carpenter)	22,764	8	7	271	3,252
Shahtota					
(Madar)	1,306	1	1	109	1,306

The weighted income per consumption unit supports my argument:
the incomes of senior lineages are noticeably at the bottom of the
economic ladder, apart from the widow who lives by herself and on
charity. Mehr Gul emerges with the highest monthly household member consumption unit in SAM, 357, Morcha is second with 271, and
Shamshudin has 144. Shahtota, a widow, is not too far behind Shamshudin with 109. So in SAM we have a situation where lineage seniority does not imply economic superiority.[5]

Amirzada's monthly weighted income per household member consumption unit is 167 compared to that of 476 of Saida and 406 of Kabil.
However, his position is not as grave as it appears for Shahzada ensures
that he is provided for through regular gifts in cash and kind. The

traditional upholders of *Pukhtunwali* are not equipped to change with the times by assuming the role of contractors and labourers.

On the face of it, it would appear that someone like Shahzada with a political income calculated around Rs. 100,000 annually in comparison to Kabil Khan with a political income of almost zero would be far superior in economic wealth to the latter, but this is not so on a weighted scale. Shahzada's monthly income unit is 333,[6] lower than that of Kabil and Saida. This is accounted for by his large number of dependents and non-income-earning sons and grandsons and the demands of hospitality.

Table 14 (i) indicated the weighted incomes per household consumption unit of various groups: Table 14 (ii) below indicates their weighted expenditure per household consumption unit. With the caveat sounded above regarding incomes, I have drawn up another related table of weighted expenditure per consumption unit. In this table the actual household expenditure is divided by the consumption unit per household accounting for savings and debts. The results of Tables 14 (i) and 14 (ii) read together confirm my general thesis correlating senior lineages and excessive spending. Both Amirzada and Shamshudin of the senior lineages have incurred debts in an attempt to live up to expected standards, whereas junior lineages and occupational groups such as Mehr Gul and Morcha save considerable sums. As a result weighted expenditure of the latter per consumption unit is considerably lower than their weighted income per consumption unit; in short they prefer to risk being labelled miserly rather than spend. Mehr Gul's

TABLE 14 (ii) Weighted expenditure per consumption unit

	annual expenditure (Rs.)	annual saving/ debt	household population number	no. of consumption units in household	household member consumption unit (Rs.)	
					monthly	yearly
TAM						
Amirzada	27,909	−4,909	15	11½	202	2,427
Saida	15,499	+4,501	5	3½	369	4,428
Kabil	22,870	+3,930	8	5½	347	4,158
SAM						
Shamshudin	15,619	−4,419	8	6½	200	2,403
Mehr Gul	6,682	+27,598	9	8	69	835
Morcha	5,568	+17,196	8	7	66	795
Shahtota	1,249.50	+56.50	1	1	104	1,249.50

weighted expenditure per consumption unit is one-fifth that of his weighted income unit whereas Morcha's is one-fourth of his weighted income. The three remaining households reflect roughly a similar expenditure and income consumption per unit pattern. They are neither saving nor borrowing excessively to meet their needs.

The figures in Table 14 reflect the underlying difference between *nang* and *qalang* systems and partly explain how and why the two perpetuate themselves. In Swat prominent chiefs had approximate incomes of Rs. 50,000, twenty years ago, from the sale of grain alone when the average villager's income was Rs. 300 (Barth, 1972: 79). These wide discrepancies may be compared to the highest and lowest income figures in TAM and SAM where, if anything the weighted economic situation of the prominent political figures does not match up to those of some members of junior lineages and occupational groups.

Figure 22 depicts how goods and services flow in the ideal Mohmand model, what form of activity they are invested in, what the goals of this activity are and how the circle is completed by the reinvestments accruing from the achieved goals. The traditional cycle and flow are represented by cycle A in the figure. Concretely, the circle illustrates how the flow of goods and services is patterned in discrete spheres and demonstrates the nature of the unity within, and barriers between, the spheres. Cycle B represents deviances from the traditional model. The figure is based on questionnaires and the data above. The normative

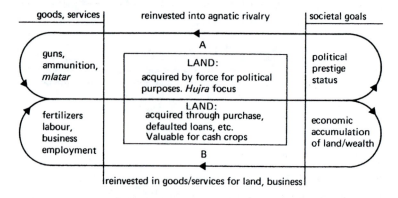

A: Mohmand model (TAM including senior lineages in SAM)
B: deviances (post-1951 SAM and including junior lineages
   in TAM in the 1970s)

FIGURE 22 *Mohmand economic activity: input and output ratios*

values implicit in the discrete spheres are corroborated by the day-to-day diaries that I have recorded of average Mohmand daily activity.

Goods and services in cycle A constitute the labour of the factional fighting force (*mlatar*) and their supplies of guns and ammunition. These goods and services are invested in land often acquired by force and primarily to establish and exhibit political status. The *hujra* is the central physical index of political status and activity of the leader who must maintain a reasonable standard of hospitality to maintain the sympathy of his followers. The goal is not to convert acquired land into an agricultural asset but to demonstrate political status. Local political emergence brings with it recognition and contact with the political administration, which, in turn, implies patronage. Such patronage is then reinvested into continuing factional/agnatic rivalry by further expanding goods and services, in our case, the social institutional complexes such as the *hujra* and *mlatar*, which further increase prestige. And so the cycle is complete. This model may be taken as a contemporary Mohmand model of TAM and would approximate to certain behaviour patterns of the senior lineages in SAM.

Cycle B illustrates deviances from the Mohmand model, especially marked after 1951 in SAM when traditional Pukhtun activity centring around agnatic rivalry is restricted. Goods and services are translated to mean fertilizers and labour to be invested in land which is acquired through purchase or against defaulting loans. Traditional crops such as wheat and maize give way to cash crops such as sugar-cane which are transported to the markets of Shabkadar and Peshawar. The goal and cyclical movement of economic activity are the accumulation of land and wealth which, in turn, are reinvested in improving the quality of the goods and services used as inputs in land. An important and emergent factor in both areas is the diversion from agricultural activity to investing time and labour in traditionally non-Pukhtun activity such as employment, business and trade.

(b) *Expenditure on* rites de passage

This sub-section supports the major thrust of my thesis argument sustained in the preceding pages. The detailed expenditure for *rites de passage* of TAM and SAM groups has been randomly selected from various groups to provide us with case-studies. These groups are already familiar through their income and expenditure patterns discussed above. The rites have occurred in the last four years and involved a member of

TABLE 15 *Rites de passage* expenditure (1972–6) (in Rs.)

Rites		Amir-zada (Musa)	Saida (Ranra)	Kabil (Malok)	Sham-shudin (Kado)	Mehr Gul (Sabah)	Haji Gul (bar-ber)
1 birth:	A1	45	40	40	25	20	20
(*padaish*)	A2		20				
	A3						
	B	400	300	400	500	400	300
	C	90	100	180			
	D						
	E	300		300			
	F		400		100	80	80
	G	100		100	80	40	
	Total:	935	860	1,020	705	540	400
2 circum-	A1	60	50	60	20	15	20
cision:	A2	100	80	100	80	60	
(*sunnat*)	A3	50		50	50	40	
	B	840	400	1,200	600	280	
	C	350	320	540	160	120	
	D						240
	E	1,760	1,000	1,400	300	500	500
	F	1,500	400	1,200	250	200	300
	G			300	40		100
	H	500	150	376			100
	Total:	5,160	2,400	5,226	1,500	1,215	1,260
3 marriage:	A1	50	50	50	50	30	
(*wada*)	A2	250	100	180	240	150	
	A3	100	80	100	100	75	
	A4				200	100	
	B	1,800	360	360	2,000	1,000	340
	C	420	60	48	320	170	1,000
	D		140	240			
	E	2,000	1,760	2,000	2,000		
	F	6,500	2,000	4,400	5,000	3,000	500
	G	600	700	400	1,000	1,100	600
	H	370		100	300		
	I		6,000	1,000			
	Total:	12,090	11,250	8,878	11,210	5,625	2,440
4 death:	A1						
(*marg*)	A2						
	A3						
	B	500			800	650	
	C	168	320		260	220	

D		600	300			500
E	2,000	2,000	400	1,600	1,000	
coffin cloth	500	200	250	200	150	100
charity (*skhat*)	2,520	320	600	560	400	80
Total:	5,688	3,440	1,550	3,420	2,420	680
Grand Total:	23,873	17,950	16,674	16,835	9,800	4,780

A1 = Mullah	B = rice	F = cloth and jewellery
A2 = barber	C = vegetable oil	G = fruit, etc.
A3 = carpenter	D = wheat/maize	H = tea and sugar
A4 = *kulal*, worker	E = sheep/cows	I = bride-price

the household.[7] I have selected actual details and breakdown of expenditure in the case-studies selected from different strata to complement the general averages and detailed analysis on income and expenditure of these groups in this chapter. The patterns of expenditure support my main thesis. Social status, measured through conspicuous consumption and as part of Pukhto tradition, is maintained by senior lineages although their incomes may be considerably lower than junior or non-Pukhtun groups. Amirzada, the eldest son of Shahzada, has spent about Rs. 7,000 more than Kabil of the junior Malok lineage in his grand total for the rites, although the latter is on his way to becoming a prosperous government contractor and the former has no fixed or regular source of income. Similarly, Shamshudin in Bela has spent almost four times as much as the barber. It is not surprising that senior lineages, like the Kado, are often in debt and gradually lose their lands through debt default and mortgages to junior lineages. Conspicuous consumption, however, is not restricted to senior lineages. It is interesting to compare the marriage expenditure of Haji Gul, the barber, in Table 15 above with what he spent on another marriage in 1976, after his return from Iran when he is said to have brought back a small fortune. He spent five times more on the marriage organized for his son and discussed in the previous chapter (Table 8). Another aspect of my thesis is also supported by comparison of total expenditures between TAM and SAM. TAM expenditures are consistently higher, reflecting more economic activity and flexibility of sources. SAM on the other hand depend entirely on agriculture for their income. In an economic sense they are fully encapsulated and their sources of income quantifiable, known and static.

Marriage, as discussed in the last chapter, is the main occasion for conspicuous consumption, where senior lineages tend to exhibit their status by excessive spending. The second highest expenditure is claimed by funeral rites. Birth and circumcision expenditures involve only male offspring. Circumcision is compulsory for every male and usually takes place between the ages of three and five. The birth of a daughter is not celebrated and involves no expenditure. Groups of relatives and friends attend the rites as part of the social process of *gham-khadi*, to see and be seen. Attendance or absence indicate political alliances and social status.

Certain general points may be made regarding the above scheme of *rites de passage* which has been culled from numerous functions witnessed and recorded by me and my wife. Firstly, and most significant, is the fact that the pattern of the *rites de passage* is repeated in all groups whether Pukhtun or not. This implies social and cultural equality underwritten by religious tradition. A Mullah or barber will order each sequence of the rites exactly in the manner of the senior lineage Pukhtun. The marked adherence to traditional Islamic custom during *rites de passage* needs to be underlined (Chapter 6).

Secondly, preference for a boy at birth and for 'losing' an unimportant ancestor by death reflect the fundamental principles of a patrilineal tribal society. Women explained why a boy was preferred to a girl: he would uphold *Pukhtunwali* and *tarboorwali* and therefore the house would be respected; the house would be 'complete' as girls are born to leave the house after marriage; he would earn money; he would inherit land and keep the property in the family; he would work in the fields and finally, he would perpetuate the family's name. People in general believe that 'the more the children', meaning sons, 'the greater the happiness'. In TAM they point to Shahzada and in Bela to Mehr Gul and Hussain Khan as examples.

Death invariably tests the importance of an ancestor. Graves are made of mud and no writing or marmoreal slabs mark the spot; therefore if the ancestor is unimportant he is easily 'lost' or 'forgotten' in time. There is no ancestor worship and little importance is given to cemeteries and shrines. Often a piece of the dead person's clothing is used as a flag to hang over the grave for a short while. *Shahid* (a person dying specifically in the cause of Islam) is commonly and wrongly used when death takes place by an accident such as drowning or in agnatic rivalry. Shati graves are sometimes marked with coloured stones. Perhaps a slab of rough-hewn stone or granite marks the grave as a headstone. Such headstones are exactly the same for men and women except that, for women, the stone at the feet is at a right angle in relation to the stone at the head, while for men both stones are parallel. Major Sultan Jan, Malik Anmir, the Musa elders, as indeed all Shati lineages, are buried in the Shati cemetery. They are buried in traditional Islamic manner, head to north, feet to south and face pointed towards Mecca in the west. In SAM it is socially significant that the dead of Kado, the senior lineage, are buried in their own traditional cemetery in the Michni area near Kado Korona while those of junior lineages, including Sabah, and non-Mohmand groups like the religious and occupational ones, are buried in the Chalghaezi Baba cemetery some three miles from Bela towards Peshawar. Kado thus maintain a barrier that even the Shati Khel do not. In this regard SAM approximate to the ideal in maintaining social lineage discrimination in death if they cannot do so successfully in life.

Thirdly, there is a qualitative difference in the ceremonies organized by a poor or better-off person regardless of lineage. I hasten to add that no correlation exists between economic well-being and Pukhtun groups. Various ceremonies organized by the Mians of Kassai or junior lineages like the Malok exhibit similar extravagance as that of senior lineages like Musa. However, there is a difference between TAM and SAM functions. SAM are generally poorer and can rarely muster the funds from the wide and versatile range of resources that TAM appear to be capable of mobilizing, especially as they translate agnatic competition into forms of conspicuous consumption for such occasions.

Finally, perceptible social changes and deviance from traditional behaviour, in a qualitative and quantitative sense, are emerging as I have shown in the discussion on marriages in the last chapter. They indicate the influence of the larger Pukhtun civilization in the Settled Districts, and even the world beyond. These changes have wide ramifications both for the status of groups, including that of women, and the structure of society.

III Mohmand daily diaries

With the help of my assistants I was able to record an intensive two-week diary of three couples each in TAM and SAM in early February 1976. The activities of the males and females were recorded from the time they rose to the time they slept. I was aware of the danger of a possible bias towards senior lineages and Maliki activity and, as I wished to obtain information regarding average Mohmand activity, I decided to exclude the handful of more important Maliks, like Shahzada, and then select the diarists at random. I am therefore in a position to represent the activities of a busy contractor, Kabil Khan (Malok), Rustam (Malok) also attempting to establish some form of business for himself, and Saida (Ranra) and their women in TAM. The Bela diaries are based on the activities of a poor agriculturalist, Mehr Gul (Sabah), an average agriculturalist Sial (Kado) and an above-average agriculturalist Morcha (carpenter) and their women. Figures illustrating the houses of four of the six couples featured in the diary have been shown in Chapter 8 on settlements and may be consulted to relate them to their neighbours and other distinguishing features. Similarly detailed case-studies of income and expenditure of four couples have been discussed earlier in the chapter.

Due to their length and considerations of space I have omitted the diaries themselves although I shall discuss their salient features. The diaries clearly illustrate the rhythm of life among the Mohmands and the activities of the various discrete groups that constitute it such as senior lineages, junior lineages and occupational groups and the discrete sphere of activities of women. The average day of the Mohmand is generally divided into five parts, roughly corresponding to the timings of the five obligatory Islamic prayers. The Pukhto names of the parts of the day are used interchangeably with the Islamic names of the five prayers. The day begins early, usually before sunrise, by answering the call of nature outside the settlement or village, ablutions, prayers and then tea. In summer the day begins even earlier and ends later but is broken by a period of afternoon rest for two to three hours. There are clear and demarcated boundaries for the social and economic activities of males and females.

Conclusions regarding the relationship between the various groups involved in the social universe and their emergent attitudes to economic activity relevant to my thesis are discussed below:

(1) It appears that TAM rise somewhat earlier and sleep later than SAM and this partly explains their higher mobility. TAM economic activities do not centre around their lands but rather around new and non-traditional spheres such as trade and building contracts. The new economic activity has certain social ramifications as it ignores, by-passes and overrides traditional agnatic rivalries; for instance, Kabil Khan is a contractor at the Ghalanay Agency headquarters in a business alliance not only with Dilawar (Malok), a traditional enemy of Shahzada, but also with Murtaza (Musa), a cousin and supporter of Shahzada.

Kabil, whose father was killed by the Musa (Chapter 7), makes a point of visiting the *hujra* of Shahzada at least once a week so as to register his acknowledgment of the former's status. TAM mobility is high and spans an area ranging from Nawagai in the north, some twenty-four miles from Shati Khel, to Peshawar and almost forty miles away, in the course of a day. However, it is important to point out that the high TAM mobility involves adults between twenty and fifty years of age. Older *mashars* lead a regular life around an unchanging schedule. Haji Hassan's routine is that of a typical mashar. He wakes at 6 a.m., says his prayers, has tea, visits the *hujra* for a chat, eats lunch by 11 a.m., again visits the *hujra* and then goes home to rest until 1 p.m. when he rises for prayers. He has tea around 2.30 p.m., dinner by 6.30 and is at the *hujra* until he returns home to sleep by 10–10.30 p.m. The burden of conducting active business falls on his sons. In contrast, Bela economic activity is restricted to the confines of the village boundary or, as in the case of Sial who shares land with his brother, in the neighbouring area of Michni. SAM show a more regular rhythm of daily life that follows the larger rhythm of the sowing and harvesting of crops and that of the seasons. The rhythm of daily life is subordinated to that of agriculture; for example, if it is the individual's turn at the *ganrey* he may have to be up at 2 a.m. with his buffaloes to start work, which may take the entire day and most of the night, and there will be a queue waiting behind him. Similarly, when it is his turn to water his fields, from the Bela canals, he may be up early or late to comply with the scheduled distribution of village water.

(2) Women rise earlier and sleep earlier than men and have a tight schedule of daily chores to perform. The rhythm of life for women repeats itself with unending monotony. As the men are distinctly the bread-winners of the family the women are expected to care for the children, maintain the house, cook the meals, etc. Women are even more regular in saying their daily five prayers than the men. Apart from their daily and essential duties they may also have to look after elderly in-laws like the mother-in-law of Mrs Mehr Gul who is about 80 years old. The monotony of their daily rhythm is broken for short spells when they gather at the village well or when a female neighbouring relative visits or is visited before or after lunch. Under no condition and because of the strict laws of *parda* may women visit outside the settlement or village without the consent of their husbands and especially after the late afternoon. The laws of *parda* prevent TAM women from doing their own shopping and it is the man who purchases vegetables

or meat from Mian Miandi. Feroz told me of the exasperation he experienced when buying his wife new slippers. He had to visit the market four times before he obtained the right size.

(3) Meal times are as regular as is the menu. Tea is served for breakfast with half or a full *dodai* (literally bread, but commonly used to mean a full meal, lunch or dinner). Only with some economic wealth and recently can people afford *paratay* (similar bread cooked in vegetable oil). Eggs are seldom, if ever, eaten with breakfast. Lunch between eleven and twelve o'clock usually consists of one or two *dodai* and a simple vegetable curry. Meat, sweetmeats or fruit are rarely eaten. Feroz confirms what TAM *mashars* told me that during his childhood in the 1950s sweetmeats and fruit were an unknown commodity in Shati Khel and a father wishing to spoil his child would bring a few walnuts from Peshawar. A similar situation exists in SAM. Tea, without *dodai*, is drunk again between 3 and 4 p.m. and the evening meal at sunset is similar to lunch.

However, as the diaries reflect, Pukhtun laws of hospitality override economic constraints and a host will entertain his guest with tea, *paratay* and even eggs. There is a social gradation defining the importance of guests which is correlated to the fare served. If he is of some importance a chicken will invariably be served to the guest. In case of a visit by a *jirga*, a marriage party or even a political officer, a goat or sheep will be cooked. If the Political Agent or some other senior official is expected, then a cow will be slaughtered as a gesture of hospitality and deference to the status of the guest.

(4) The importance of praying in the village mosque and attending the village *hujra* as social expression are apparent from a glance at TAM diaries. No matter how tired or how long a TAM has travelled that day he invariably visits the village *hujra* after dinner, which he almost always eats at home with his family. Travel after dusk is rare and most people return home by sunset. SAM visit the *hujra* less frequently and usually to chat with their own group whether along lineage, age or occupational lines. Sial (Kado) visits the *hujra* almost every evening before dinner. It must be mentioned that four of the six men maintained the obligatory prayers five times a day, often under difficult conditions while travelling, and the other two say at least two to three prayers; women say their prayers in their houses as they can neither visit the mosque nor the *hujra*.

(5) The diaries reflect both the humdrum and trivial daily social activities of normal people but also the spill-over effects of larger developmental

activities in the Mohmand Agency which will be discussed in Chapters
10 and 11. For instance, Kabil Khan is busy as a contractor building a
school at Yusuf Khel, near Lakhkar's village, and office buildings at the
new Ghalanay colony. Saida and Rustam too attempt to secure a foothold in the development activities of the Agency. In contrast to SAM,
their attitude towards their own land is indifferent and casual. They
visit their land to 'see what is happening on it', almost as if it ought to
fend for itself without their aid. In Bela the attitude to land involves
taking care of the needs of the crop including timings of water, fertilizers
etc. For Bela this is the period of cutting and processing sugar-cane into
gur and the preoccupation can be seen in the activities of Sial and
Morcha. The rhythm of the trivia of daily life is broken only by the
four defined *rites de passage*. Acts of omission are most seriously
viewed and, as the diaries show, births and deaths are immediately
acknowledged by social visits.

The main economic activities of men, women and children may be
summarized as below:

Male	*Female*	*Children* (3–4 years onwards)
plough, sow, cultivate and harvest all crops. General economic activity, includ- ing trade. TAM mobile and SAM involved in agricultural pursuits. Organize and procure domestic needs, including food.	cooking for and cleaning the household, washing clothes, feeding animals, keeping the roof and walls of the house in repair, helping cut and carry crops and also sifting wheat and maize grains. Before the coming of flour milling machines in the 1950s, women ground corn and wheat under a mill-stone called *maichan* in TAM and SAM.	as limited number, and that only recently, attend school, the tradi- tional occupation, depending on age, concerns grazing of cattle during the day and generally help- ing parents when required.

I would hope that the rhythm of the daily routine and its humdrum
nature tend to correct or even dispel the impression of anarchic tribal
life which may perhaps have emerged as a result of the case-studies on

agnatic rivalry in Chapter 7. I will consider inheritance in TAM and SAM in the next section.

IV Inheritance

In this brief section I shall show how in the critical factor of ownership and transmission of land, Pukhto custom has survived intact in TAM and SAM in spite of the encapsulation of the latter and the laws of the state it implies. Actual practice approximates to the ideal Pukhtun model and supports my thesis. However, through a case-study I shall illustrate the single instance of deviance in SAM and the social mechanism involved. The section discusses inheritance of property and not succession to the Maliki which has already been discussed in Chapter 5.

Inheritance is based on two fundamental concepts in society. Land is divided as inheritance only in the male line and on the basis of equality. Inheritance among male siblings is egalitarian in the extreme. The elder brother, with the concurrence of his brothers, is usually given an extra share as *masharana* for the upkeep of the family *hujra*, etc. Inheritance of land carries the seeds of rivalry between male agnates and is the first step towards fissure in the segment and therefore tends to emphasize political rivalry between cousins.

The laws of inheritance in cases where no male issue is alive are established by tradition. When a man dies without male issue and his father has predeceased him his full brothers inherit equally; second, the property may revert to the father's brothers, and third to the father's brother's sons. If none of these are alive the sub-section shares the inheritance. The dramatic manner in which Lakhkar inherited land in Yusuf Khel due to a series of fatal mishaps to the line of male kin, and was propelled into Shati Khel politics, has been discussed earlier. His example is a good illustration of the customary laws of inheritance. He happened to be the nearest living male claimant to the property although removed in time and space.

During his lifetime inheritance is decided by the owner who by tradition includes his sons and may include his grandsons in a share of the property. He also decides when to distribute his property. For instance Shahzada has not divided his property or hinted at the shares. He is still the sole owner of the property and this is usually the case with patriarchs, especially in TAM. Feroz explained his own position. His father Usman, who has not divided the property with his brothers, owns 16½ acres of which 2½ are in Shati Khel and the rest in Shabkadar.

Usman has three brothers and will therefore inherit about 4⅛ acres. Feroz has five brothers and will inherit less than an acre himself. On the other hand, Hamesh Gul in Bela has divided his 6 acres of land equally between his sons in his lifetime leaving about 2 acres for himself.

In any case and contrary to Islamic law neither women nor their daughters inherit property, a practice it would appear is common in other Islamic tribal societies (Asad, 1970: 69-70). If the deceased has a son by a mistress[8] the boy cannot claim his father's land. If the husband dies without a son both his wife and daughters are subject to the mercy of his brothers who may marry them, eject them or, as until the 1960s among the Burhan Khel living east of Shati Khel, sell them. Property reverts to the living brothers or, if there are none, to the nearest agnatic kin in case no male heirs are born. I recorded various examples of property reverting to brothers or nearest agnatic kin when a woman's husband dies and she is either issueless or has produced only girls (her condition is called *mirata*, as explained earlier, from *miras*, meaning inheritance in Arabic). A woman whose husband is deceased can only keep his land and house if she has a son and in the name of that son. In some cases, as that of Ali Khan's widow below, she may even marry her dead husband's brother in spite of having a son, as her position is none too secure unless the boy is old enough to 'carry a gun'. I came across no cases of a *mirata* inheriting land in TAM. However, I did record one exception to the rule in SAM which became something of a *cause*

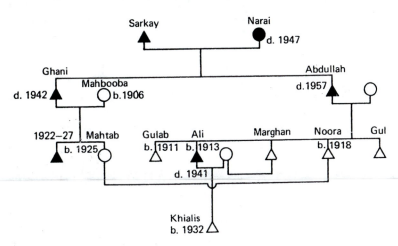

FIGURE 23 *Inheritance: a deviant case*

célèbre when it occurred and which was concluded during my field-work. It shows that a break from a fundamental concept of Pukhto *riwaj* has been made in SAM, although after three decades of encapsulation.

Abdul Ghani and Abdullah, sons of Sarkay (Sabah Khel), shared 25 acres of unirrigated land just outside Bela. Ghani, the elder brother, died in 1942 and his wife Mahbooba, who is still alive, lived with her son-in-law Noora, the son of Abdullah. Ghani and Mahbooba had one son who died at the age of five and one daughter Mahtab who was married to one of Abdullah's five sons in 1949. When Ghani died there were three women representing three generations dependent on him; Narai, his mother, Mahbooba, his wife and Mahtab, his daughter. Abdullah, who inherited half of the 25 acres, decided to break with Pukhto tradition and give 4½ acres, 1½ each to the three women, and keep the rest − 8 acres − of Ghani's share for himself. By taking his brother's land he was following traditional Pukhto *riwaj* but by giving 4½ acres to his mother, sister-in-law and his niece, who was also his daughter-in-law, he was acting against it. The transference of rights of the 4½ acres remained a promise and *de facto* possession was with the sons of Abdullah. One of the three female claimants, Narai, died in 1947. Shortly before his death in 1957 Abdullah ordered that 1½ acres be given to his daughter-in-law Mahtab.

When Abdullah's land was being divided Gulab Khan, the eldest brother, received an extra half an acre as *masharana*. When his brother Ali Khan died their other brother Marghan, in keeping with Pukhto tradition, married Ali's wife three years after his death. Ali Khan's son Khialis Khan combined with his uncles and cousins to oppose the division of land among women.

Noora, the husband of Mahtab, insisted that the 4½ acres be given to his wife and her mother but his brothers and nephews resisted this demand. After some tension within the family, matters came to a head and authority was given to a *jirga* of ten *mashars* who decided that 1½ acres were to be given to Mahbooba and the rest divided between the sons of Abdullah. Noora, risking the Rs. 10,000 fine of the *jirga*, challenged this decision and insisted that his wife Mahtab should also be given 1½ acres according to the wishes of his father Abdullah. The *jirga* was placed on the horns of a dilemma. On the one hand the dictates of justice demanded that the wishes of Abdullah be honoured, and on the other hand traditional Pukhto *riwaj* had to be maintained as best it could. The brothers of Noora were, however, conciliatory and persuaded the *jirga* to overlook Noora's repudiation of its decision. A larger *jirga* of twenty *mashars* was held on 18 April 1977 and after hearing each party in detail moved to an isolated spot where they discussed the matter for an hour. Firstly they announced that any party refusing to abide by their decision would be fined Rs. 20,000. Then the *jirga* announced its decision. One and a half acres were to be given to Mahbooba and the same to Mahtab. The *jirga* emphasized that their decision was based on truth or right (*haq*) and not *riwaj*. Their decision was received with considerable interest and aroused general controversy. People commonly said 'they have stamped on *riwaj*'. They argued that such a decision and attitude towards women and a serious break from *riwaj* could only have been possible by members of the junior lineage, and that senior lineages like Kado would have never allowed it.

This is a unique case of its kind in that women were allowed to inherit property in the face of such strong opposition and Pukhto custom. Had this not happened, Ghani's entire property of 12½ acres would have been distributed among the sons of Abdullah according to Pukhto custom. This particular case is partly explained by the fact that it involved Noora, a son of Abdullah, and meant that the property would, in any case, remain within the family of Abdullah. Had Mahtab not been married to her first cousin Noora but outside the family, there would have been very little hope of her inheriting any property at all.

V Market function in the tribal economy

As I have shown in earlier sections, ideal Pukhtun settlement arrangements do not make allowances for markets, as ideal Pukhtun behaviour discourages trade. In terms of the model I would like to emphasize that the discouragement does not derive from religious sanction but from the very nature and quality of the ideal Pukhtun model. A flourishing market implies connection with trading networks and larger systems and the opening of formerly closed systems. It also implies a certain dependence on external systems. The Pukhtun model thus consciously rejects the presence of a focal and central market place with its socio-economic ramifications. By remaining closed it remains self-sufficient and therefore can perpetuate its unencapsulated condition.

In this brief section I shall show the functions of marketing in the tribal economy. Three typical situations may be summarized: 1 societies which lack market places and in which the market principle, if it appears at all, is weak. Such societies have 'multicentric economies' (Herskovits,

1962: viii); 2 societies with peripheral markets where the institution of the market place is present but the market principle does not determine acquisition or subsistence or the allocation of land or labour resources; and 3 societies dominated by the 'market principle' and the 'price mechanism' (Belshaw, 1965; Bohannan and Dalton, 1962: 2, 3; Meilla-soux, 1971). For TAM the Mian Mandi: 1 provides a social focal point for exchange of ideas between clans including non-Mohmands; 2 is an economic focus for the Agency; 3 is central to transport routes in the Agency; and 4 maintains a myth of religious sanctity and hence supports the position of the Mians in society. The market location is fixed and money is the system of exchange.

(a) *TAM market*

There are no shops in Shati Khel and the nearest market is Mian Mandi about two miles to the south-west. Mian Mandi is an area of some 10 acres owned entirely by the Mians of Kassai and managed by them though they neither sit nor sell in the shops. The 300 small rooms or shops are made of mud and rented by the Mians on a Rs. 30 monthly basis to groups from the three Halimzai sub-clans, Hamza, Kadai and Wali Beg. Halimzai involvement reflects changing Pukhtun attitudes to non-Pukhtun activity by 'sitting and selling' in shops in their own areas. The Halimzai have devised a mechanism to minimize loss of face through involvement in the market: either junior lineages or non-local 'partners' from neighbouring clans actually operate the shops. Before 1947 non-Muslims organized trade and marketing among the Mohmand, and Ram Singh who migrated that year with his kin is still remembered as the main trader of Ali Mandi, the small shops near Yusuf Khel by the main road. Mian Mandi did not exist even as a dot on the most detailed ordnance and survey maps of 1933 and 1935 but is today the most important and, in fact, the only market centre in the Mohmand Agency. The growth of the market was thus not a product of the colonial situation as in other societies (Belshaw, 1965; Bohannan and Dalton, 1962). In fact among the Mohmand colonialism only helped seal the borders between the Settled and Tribal Areas, and Mian Mandi, as indeed the other market towns in the Agencies, is a recent phenomenon.

The area was 'given' to the Mians by the three sub-clans of the Halim-zai whose borders meet at the Mandi area which now acts as a buffer and neutral zone between them. Because of its ownership by the Mians a kind of political and religious sanctity has developed in the Mandi precincts supported by near-mythical stories. No feuding is allowed in the Mandi and the most bitter enemies must wait to leave its area before they may start shooting at each other. Religious beliefs have grown up among the Mohmand about Mian Mandi and it is commonly held that magical powers prevent murder in the Mandi. Many examples are quoted in support of this belief. A recent and popular one is that of Mazullah Khan who was shot at point-blank range by the sons and grandsons of Shahzada. He escaped unscratched, it is claimed due to the magical attributes of the Mandi. As mentioned earlier, in deference to religious sentiments, radios, which may be sold, are never played at the Mandi. A large mud building at the southern entrance acts as the dominating feature and is the mosque organized by the Mians for travellers. Two boys have been hired to supply water for ablutions, keep the mosque clean, etc., and bus owners make a charity payment of a quarter or half a rupee each for its upkeep. The principle of seclusion of women in Pukhtun society is strictly observed and there are no women traders as there are in other tribal societies (Bohannan and Dalton, 1962: 1-3, 23). On Friday the market remains closed as it is a holy day.

Most of the smuggling to and from Afghanistan across the international borders of the Agency begins and ends at the Mandi and long trails of camels are seen entering and leaving the Mandi daily. The differences in prices, which are almost 10 to 20 per cent higher in Afghanistan for items such as wheat, rice, sugar and vegetable oil, make this a lucrative business. From Afghanistan mainly timber and certain foreign items, such as cloth, tyres, engine parts and electrical goods, are brought in return. Timber is the major import and a standard log 9 feet in length and 1½ foot in diameter increases in value from Rs. 140 at the Nawa Pass on the border to Rs. 190 at the Mandi to Rs. 250 by the time it reaches Peshawar. There is a direct and regular caravan traffic between Mian Mandi and Chagha Serai and Lalpura in Afghanistan.

Since the developmental activities that began in 1974 Mian Mandi has begun to take on the shape of a bustling market centre. Qualitative and quantitative changes are apparent. Some sixty to seventy buses arrive and depart full of passengers from Peshawar daily and about ten buses ply the northern road to Lakaro. Two or three medical centres, the first in the Agency, have recently opened with quack doctors selling and administering medicines. Items new to the Tribal Areas such as sets of crockery, transistors and, with the coming of electricity in the Mandi in 1975, electrical goods are now displayed and marketed. Japanese cloth is another popular item smuggled from Afghanistan. Commodities smuggled from Afghanistan are cheaper in the Mandi than in Peshawar where the costs are higher due to the extra transport and to the risk factor associated with having to cross Customs/Constabulary check-posts. In Table 16 items brought from Afghanistan such as green tea are Rs. 5 (per seer) and crockery Rs. 50 (per set) more expensive in Pesha-war. On the other hand, items brought from Peshawar are more expensive in the Mandi, particularly consumer goods such as sugar and salt and perishable commodities like fruit and vegetables.

TABLE 16 Mian Mandi/Peshawar prices: 1976

Items (price in Rs.)	Mandi	Peshawar
eggs/dozen	6	6.50
beef/seer	8	8
lamb/seer	14	14.50
potatoes/seer	2	2
wheat/maund	80	75
sugar/seer	7	6
salt/seer	0.75	0.50
kerosene oil/seer	2	1.50
crockery/set of six	400	450
green tea/seer	20	25
bananas/dozen	4	3

More than an economic centre, Mian Mandi has come to symbolize an important social centre and meeting place for TAM and other clans crossing ethnic and international borders which I shall discuss in a separate paper (Ahmed, forthcoming c). Most TAM in Shati Khel will make a round of the Mandi at least four or five times a week as the diaries discussed above show, and many will go daily simply to chat while sipping green tea. The distinction between 'market place' and the principle of 'market exchange' that is so important in the study of markets, especially of traditional markets, is only now being made (Belshaw, 1965; Bohannan and Dalton, 1962; Meillasoux, 1971). The 'market place' is a specific location where a group of buyers and sellers meet and interact commercially. The 'market price' principle is the determination of prices by the forces of supply and demand regard-less of the site of transactions. Today both 'principle' and 'place' meet in the single major market of the Mohmands at Mian Mandi.

(b) *The shops of Bela Mohmandan*

In contrast to the colour, variety and bustle of the Mandi are the two drab mud rooms, 8 feet by 10 feet in size and 9 feet high, almost opposite each other, that act as part-time shops in Bela (Map 7). The shop of Hazrat Gul (Madar) sports printed posters of the late President of Pakistan, Ayub Khan, the late Prime Minister Zulfiqar Ali Bhutto and a dead war hero, Major Shabir Sharif. Amin (Jano) owns the other shop. The items are restricted and often stale, and prices almost the same as in Peshawar. As one or other member of a Bela household travels to Shabkadar or Peshawar at least once a week or fortnight, Belawals usually prefer to purchase items there. The shops are moribund and usually locked as the owners, both Pukhtuns of less important lineages, may be away involved in more profitable enterprise in the fields. The shops have only recently opened, in the late 1960s, and represent deviance from the ideal Pukhtun behavioural model.

The simplicity and poverty of Mohmand life is reflected in the small range and shoddy nature of the goods available in the Bela village shops, for example there are none of the electrical goods available in Mian Mandi to be found here. The fact that Hazrat Gul is a member of the second senior lineage reflects changing SAM attitudes from traditional prejudice against trade and marketing.

The shop in Bela belonging to Amin Khan is run by his first wife, Baghiram. Not only the shop but the fact that a Pukhtun woman is managing it, even though within and for the village community, is a major deviance from the TAM model. But the owners are aware they are not shop-keepers out of free will. Baghiram explained the position:

> Hussain Khan had 'tricked' his brother Amin out of 1½ acres of irrigated land leaving him 1 or 2 unirrigated acres and therefore forced Amin into this non-Pukhtun activity. Amin has two wives and four children to look after. Hussain Khan said to Amin that he will not give him part of the land and we separated from him empty handed because that time we had no sons. Then, twelve years ago, my husband married again and God blessed us with a son. Now my husband demands his part of the land but Hussain refuses to offer us land. He is very powerful as he has money and men and can force us. Now my husband is cultivating in the field for others and labouring for others and we pass our life with difficulty.

As the Mian Mandi, situated in a neutral zone and outside the Pukhtun area, upholds my thesis that TAM largely approximate to the ideal model so does the opening of shops in Bela by Pukhtuns. Although Shabkadar and Peshawar are visited by Belawals they have none the less

begun their own shops, however haphazardly. The implication is that
they have deviated from the traditional model. Hence my contention
that the ideal-type model has attenuated in SAM, especially where commerce is concerned, is proved correct.

In concluding this chapter on economic structure and lineage ideology
I can do no better than to refer to one of the earliest British political
officers who directly correlated agnatic rivalry and economic stagnation
in the ideal *nang* situation (Howell, 1931: 49). In the main I am arguing
that TAM still approximate to the ideal *nang* Pukhtun model which
inhibits economic growth as it thrives on agnatic rivalry.

Over the last 400 years TAM and SAM functioned within a similar
geo-political situation. Their sources of income were in the main
similar: 1 primitive agriculture; 2 raids into the richer Settled Areas
and robbing caravans; 3 allowances (from Kabul and/or the British); 4
taxes which they claimed either on caravan routes through the Gandab
as did the Halimzai or the Tarakzai on goods brought down the Kabul
river; and 5 migration and money remitted home. Today divergences
between TAM and SAM sources of income have emerged largely as a
consequence of the political division in 1951. In TAM the sources of
income are: 1 primitive agriculture; 2 political allowances, which are
small, and hardly matched by increasing prices and increasing demands;
3 trade, national and international, legal and illegal; and finally 4 government employment. SAM sources of income, on the other hand, are
largely based on agriculture and their fields. They have neither allowances
nor trade to fall back on although many Belawals have successfully
found government employment. As the daily diaries show, SAM
rhythm of life in comparison to TAM is steady, regular and predictable,
tied as it is to the larger agricultural rhythm of the seasons and the
crops. The relationship with the seasons is reflected in credit dealings in
SAM in comparison to TAM as they are based on longer periods and
involve smaller amounts.

The case-studies of income and expenditure examined in this chapter
illustrate the following points: 1 cash flow in society; 2 the weighted
income–expenditure ratios per consumption units bring into relief the
actual economic situation of the various groups in society; and 3 with
the other data derived from income-expenditure case-studies emphasize
the correlation between senior lineages upholding local notions of
Pukhtunwali and high expenditure on *rites de passage*.

The above data support the general argument of my study. Lineage
politics dominate other forms of activity in the TAM model. TAM

provide a model of ideal Pukhtun behaviour subordinating economic rationality to lineage and agnatic rivalry. The highly egalitarian nature of society is shown by the weighted sources of income and domestic expenditure as is the general poverty which sustains it. The egalitarianism in the economic sphere underwrites the ideal model. My thesis that an ideal model exists is defended by the empirically observed TAM model which largely approximates to it. In SAM deviances from Pukhto ideal behaviour are emerging which imply a partial rejection of my thesis that *Pukhtunwali* survives encapsulation. In the economic sphere deviances are apparent although SAM still use the idiom of *Pukhtunwali* and translate it to their particular situation. Finally, deviance in SAM from the model is examined and explained largely as a result of the political arrangements in 1951 and the differentiated economic modes consequent upon the arrangement. The impact of economic development schemes on social structure and its effect, especially on the TAM model, are discussed in the next two chapters.

Part three

Encapsulating systems, economic development and tribal strategy

10 Encapsulating systems and tribal strategy

The difficulty that faces encapsulated political structures is the difficulty that faces all political structures: how to maintain themselves by finding adjustment with a changed environment (Bailey, 1970: 181).

In this and the next chapter I shall show how encapsulation affects different groups of tribesmen in different ways and how the extent of encapsulation determines their strategy of maximizing various gains with the minimum loss of autonomy and the alternative choices of action available to them. For purposes of my study the data contained in the two following chapters are essential in understanding the current forces affecting the Pukhtun ideal-type model; they partly explain deviance from the model and partly suggest future directions. Encapsulation is an encounter between two different systems implying change. Disjunction is inherent in the situation as, perhaps, integration is in the minds of the encapsulators. We shall be able to perceive the forces and forms of change in the following chapters and assess how *Pukhtunwali*, which is thrown into sharp relief as a consequence, survives, compromises or adjusts in the face of these, proving or disproving parts of my thesis.

From the case-studies and data contained in the following chapters, my hypothesis that TAM allows partial penetration mainly in economic terms while jealously guarding social and political autonomy is apparently proved. However, the problems arising from the engagement of two systems are never so simple or predictable. Economic penetration brings with it certain irrevocable politically integrative mechanisms. More seriously, it generates a debate within society and those who can benefit, like contractors, or disagree with the status quo, like the *kashar*, support change wholeheartedly. As the disjunction between the larger system and TAM is neither wide nor exacerbated by coercion it does not create alarm in society and therefore increases the chances that the ultimate aim of the former, integration, may prevail.

Alavi connects the concept of encapsulation with 'tracing linkages' in the argument between the 'holists' and the 'individualists' (Alavi, 1973: 37-8). Like Bailey (1970), Alavi defines encapsulation in terms of primitive and peasant societies within and confronting larger encapsulating states (Alavi, 1973: 37). For purposes of categorizing SAM, I shall accept this definition and consider it in an encapsulated condition. However, TAM according to the same definition would be unencapsulated as the encapsulating state does not hold either the key to property ownership or patronage (ibid.).

In this chapter, and Chapter 11, I would like to conceptualize encapsulation through physical penetration. Conceptually, an unencapsulated system can be encapsulated physically or politically mainly through superior economic or coercive forces. I wish to explore the alternative strategy of encapsulating systems. The unencapsulated TAM are in the process of being encapsulated through various forms of penetration symbolized by the road, schools, etc. The road brings with it schools, electricity, hospitals and inevitably administration which in the aggregate spell encapsulation; nowhere is there a suggestion implicit or otherwise of the slightest hint of coercive action. Unlike tribesmen elsewhere on the subcontinent who 'feel insecure, baffled by development' (Fürer-Haimendorf, 1977: 7) and bewildered in the face of encapsulating systems (Bailey, 1957, 1960, 1961; Caplan, L., 1970; Caplan, P., 1972; Fürer-Haimendorf, 1939, 1962, 1977; Vitebsky, 1978; Yorke, 1974) Pukhtun tribesmen have learned to manipulate the symbols of encapsulation and manoeuvre them to their own advantage. The questions are why and how? The answers lie mainly in TAM geography and history (Chapters 2 and 3). Most tribes had written treaties with the British in the last century containing clauses which left them and their areas unencapsulated if they agreed to the suzerainty of the British Raj. Pakistan continues to honour these treaties. Part of the answer lies in the descent of the tribesman to the Settled Areas. He learned its ways and then, manipulating his situation in the Tribal Areas and activating tribal networks to maximum advantage, competed successfully (Ahmed, forthcoming a and c). Recent accounts continue to stress the free and unencapsulated nature of the Tribal Areas (Edwards, 1977; Moynahan, 1976; Young, 1977). The Pukhtun ideal-type can only approximate to its ideal model in an unencapsulated condition; encapsulation poses a set of dilemmas for the Pukhtun which are as acute as they are unresolved. Either he deviates from the model or subverts the encapsulating system to approximate to his ideal. Deviance or subversion both are implicit in the situation.

This chapter will briefly describe the authority and functions of the political administration in the Tribal Areas and their ramifications for tribal politics at the lineage level and will illustrate, through case-studies, tribal strategy within encapsulating systems. The first study illustrates TAM's failure to comprehend and come to terms with the larger system which ends in, and is called, prison; the second study illustrates SAM's successful tribal strategy through activation of clan networks in the Settled Areas and ends in, and is called, parliament. The third section discusses education as a factor of encapsulation, and the last section the process of peasantization of tribal groups and their perception of change or deviance from the ideal model. Development schemes, such as roads, as factors in encapsulation will be discussed in Chapter 11.

The importance of tribal groups in the eyes of government depends to a large extent on the latter's long-term plans and strategy to integrate them. For instance SAM, from the moment the Province was created, found themselves in a second-class position *vis-à-vis* the Arbabs who not only knew the police and the revenue officials but also later formed the government in its assemblies. Here the Mohmands were the *outsiders*. They were still in the difficult transitional phase between tribesman and peasant. Worse, they were irrevocably encapsulated economically and politically. In the Agency the Mohmands were the *insiders*. Paradoxically SAM, encapsulated within the Province's primary district, Peshawar, found themselves by-passed by the modernization process and twenty-six years after separation from their Mohmand cousins their village boasted no school, tube-wells, roads, or hospital. TAM, in the meantime, isolated and unencapsulated until the 1970s, found itself showered with every modern amenity it cared to demand, electricity, schools and dispensaries. But even in the Agency, the importance of a Malik and his section depend to a large degree on their geographical location and how and when government wishes to penetrate the region. In the Mohmand Agency penetration, which accompanied various political favours such as schools, allowances and *khassadaries* can be divided into three distinct phases. In the 1950s the focus was on the Tarakzais of the Michni area. In the 1960s it was on the Halimzais when Shahzada Malik and the Shati Khel were the key to the Gandab and the Nahakki, the furthest point of penetration. Finally, in the mid-1970s the focus shifted beyond the Tarakzais and Halimzais to the Safis, north of the Nahakki. Suddenly the Mohmand Halimzai and Tarakzai felt ignored and neglected; but it was too late. Penetration had already assumed a form of encapsulation; the hands of the clock of encapsulation only move forward.

1 The role of the Political Agent in tribal society

The Political Agent in the Tribal Areas is the symbol of government and the focal point of encapsulation. He administers the Agency on behalf of the Federal Government and combines wide-ranging executive powers. His role has been defined as 'half-ambassador and half-governor' (Spain, 1962: 24). His main duties are to ensure general peace in the Agency, specially in headquarters, to protect government roads and buildings and, recently, to supervise development work. His success with the clans and tribes depends to a large degree on his personal rapport with them. It is not surprising therefore that a close relationship and identity develops between the Political Agent and what he calls 'his' tribes, and this identity often leads him to a deep interest and knowledge of tribal organization and customs (Howell in Caroe, 1965: 470).

Political Agents were usually selected from an elite cadre, the Indian Political Service. About two-thirds of the Service were from the Army and one-third from the Indian Civil Service (Coen, 1971). The power, prestige and glamour of the Political Agent's job was unrivalled in the British colonies, including India. However, the vast responsibilities, unceasing tension and external dangers of the job could result in death by assassination or even by suicide (Caroe, 1965; Howell, 1931; Woodruff, 1965). Sometimes the pace of the Frontier was too much even for traditional political officers, as Sir Olaf Caroe recalls when he was Governor of the Province in a case which ended in suicide as the officer 'had found it too much for him' (Allen, 1977: 209).

The policies of the Political Agent, Mohmands, are traditionally based on the use of the carrot and the stick. The carrot takes various forms. The Political Agent is the source of far-reaching patronage and he can: 1 create Maliks and *lungi*-holders; 2 appoint local tribal levies (*khassadars*[1]); 3 recommend students for scholarships to schools, colleges and universities in Pakistan; 4 increase or allot quotas of food rations such as wheat, sugar and rice at special prices to favoured groups; 5 sign chits or permits (incorporated into the Pukhto language as *parmat*) for fixed quantities of timber and rations to an individual or group, which are sold in the market to brokers for small profits. For example, a chit obtained from the Political Agent which sanctions a thirty-five pound tin of vegetable oil at the officially 'controlled' price of Rs. 153 could be sold in the market for Rs. 170. Such chits for sugar are the most valuable as the market price is almost twice that of the controlled price. These informal and often untidy scraps of paper, the *parmat*, carry the same status in the Agency as that of legal tender; 6 as project director of the Rural Works Programme patronize groups by sanctioning various schemes, such as wells, water tanks, schools buildings, community centres and roads. Such development activities bring lucrative contracts with them; finally, 7 grant various and secret financial allowances to those tribesmen he finds politically useful.

The stick of the Political Agent comprises mainly of 1 the Frontier Scouts, represented in the Agency by the Mohmand Rifles and raised in late 1973 under the command of a colonel with headquarters at Yusuf Khel; and 2 the irregular and para-military tribal force called the *khassadars* who work directly under his command, 'a scheme which Sir George [Cunningham] as described thinly disguised black-mail' (Howell, 1931: 26).[2] Apart from the Frontier Scouts and *khassadars*, if the situation demands, the Political Agent may call out the Army and Air Force. However, the use of naked power is a negation of his role as a political officer, and even a tacit admission of failure to solve a problem within the institutional and structural boundaries of tribal society with which he ought to be familiar. Regardless of the great power the Political Agent wields administrative policy in the main rests on the carrot in the 1970s.

The Frontier Crimes Regulation, 1901, validated in 1954 by the Governor-General of Pakistan, allows the Political Agent wide and general judicial authority to fine, blockade, detain, seize hostile tribal groups and confiscate or demolish their property in the Tribal Areas (Sections 21–34). Under Section 40, sub-section i, he may order any person suspected of intended criminal intention 'to execute a bond for good behaviour or for keeping the peace ... with or without sureties ... not exceeding three years'. Although the Frontier Crimes Regulation gives the Political Agent wide legal cover, in practice administration is run with little regard for formal or legal methods.[3]

In his Agency the Political Agent commands great prestige and is universally referred to as *saib* while the Assistant Political Agent is either called *chota saib* (small sahib) as in Waziristan or *depty saib* (deputy sahib) as in the Orakzai and Mohmand Agencies.

Criticism regarding the political administration of the Tribal Areas is growing, particularly from the organization of the *kashar* called

Tehrik-e-Qabail (movement of the tribesmen) who see it in unholy alliance with the Maliks, their arch rivals. An editorial called 'Tribal management' in the *Khyber Mail* pointed out some of the worst features of the system in its conclusion: 'wholesale smuggling, including large-scale trafficking in narcotics, car-thieves, kidnapping etc. are some of the most disquieting features. The downdrift is still without a redeeming feature' (*Khyber Mail*, 23 October 1975).

The intricate pattern of agnatic rivalry with which he must be all too familiar often poses interesting diplomatic problems for the Political Agent. For instance, during my first tour of the remote Mullah Khel, the three sub-sections of the local sub-clan agreed to suspend inter-lineage hostilities for the period of my visit and welcome me only if I had a ceremonial meal with each one of them. As I was in the area for one night I could only schedule lunch and dinner in my programme because breakfast is not counted as a meal. The programme still left out one sub-section. The entire tour was in danger of being cancelled and tension mounted among the sections as to who should host the two meals. We finally hit on a typical tribal solution. I would have two lunches and one dinner. The first lunch began at eleven o'clock and we rose from it, took leave of our hosts, and sat down for the second lunch which began at 12.30 p.m. On both occasions beef and mutton had been cooked for the sumptious and grand lunch served for some 200 guests. Throughout the meals my officials and our hosts kept up the pretence that we were eating our one and main meal of the day. Agnatic jealousy had been averted and honour satisfied. The Political Agent, Mohmands, recounted a similar dilemma and a similar solution in 1977.

Another illuminating illustration of agnatic rivalry involving the administration is an example from Bela Mohmandan during one of the rare visits of the Deputy Commissioner who had come to inspect the damage done by flooding of the Kabul river in summer some ten years previously. In keeping with the Pukhtun tradition of hospitality the Kasim Khel, from which Kado and most of the Bela groups derive their lineage, slaughtered and cooked sheep for their honoured guest. This provided their cousins, the Dadu Khel, the opportunity to convince the Deputy Commissioner that the Belawals were in no need of financial assistance as they could afford such lavish feasts. The Deputy Commissioner agreed with the Dadu Khel, refused to sanction the Belawals any relief funds and left the village somewhat agitated. The Belawals had been pushed between two stools by their adroit cousins: on the one hand attempting to honour their guest by cooking him a meal worthy of his status, and on the other projecting a suitable image of destitution in order to elicit relief funds.

I shall briefly illustrate how and where administrative and tribal structure interact, and the mechanism which provides mutually acceptable solutions in cases where law and order are involved, by two examples, one from my stay in the Orakzai Agency. The Orakzai case received wide publicity as it took an unusual turn and denouement. A member of the rich non-Pukhtun business community (*paracha*) of Kohat was kidnapped in April 1977 from his home by a gang of Afridi Proclaimed Offenders. The outlaws demanded a ransom of Rs. 100,000 from his family. In such cases political authorities traditionally act as mediators and negotiate a scaling-down of the ransom money, though they can often do little else. The outlaws, in this case, turned up at a haunt in Saifur Darra, fifteen miles north of the Oblan Fort, near Kohat, in one of the most geographically and politically inaccessible parts of the Orakzai Agency. The area had never been visited by an official. As I realized that this was a 'test-case' and if unchecked would result in more such incidents, I moved on three levels simultaneously. On the orthodox administrative level the sub-sectional leaders, in whose house the outlaws were harbouring the kidnappee, were arrested. As expected, their relatives immediately applied pressure on the outlaws to negotiate, and so did elders who were mobilized by the administration for this purpose. Secondly, I tapped unorthodox channels and sent Orakzai outlaws to persuade the Afridis to release the *paracha*. Their answer was to reduce the ransom fee. They were prepared to release the *paracha* for Rs. 50,000. Thirdly, I played my trump card, in the somewhat romantic mould of the traditional Political Officer, by mobilizing some 400 Orakzai Levies at my headquarters in Hangu and allowing it to be 'leaked' through Orakzai Levies from the Saifur Darra area that the Political Agent personally planned to lead them on a surprise raid into the Darra. The date and even timing of the surprise raid were deliberately leaked. The ploy worked. Rather than have their sanctuary permanently violated the outlaws decided to release the kidnappee unconditionally. Having brought the *paracha* to the edge of the Settled Areas near Kohat, the outlaws paid him Rs. 50 to hire transport to reach home safely. For the first time in the history of the area a recovery had been made without a shot or a rupee being exchanged and the matter was widely and favourably reported in the press (*Khyber Mail*, 26 April 1977; *Mashriq*, 26 April 1977).

A similar 'kidnap' case involving Shati Khel took place in 1972, the seeds of which were sown a generation ago. Mian Fazle Akbar had contracted out land at Rs. 100 per acre on *ijara* in Hashtnagar to some Ranra from Shati Khel. A brother of Akbar killed Ghazi, a Ranra tenant. Ghazi's son killed Akbar in court in Charsadda as *badal*, and was convicted and hung about twenty years ago. Niaz Mohammad, another son of Ghazi, grew to manhood and with three or four accomplices kidnapped a brother of the Mian with every intention of killing him in the Tribal Areas and kept him in the Ranra *hujra*. Political pressure, mainly through Shahzada, succeeded in averting the Mian's death and he was released after paying ransom money.

I agree with Marxist anthropologists when they criticize Structuralist-Functionalist anthropologists for minimizing or even altogether 'smoothing' out the role of the Deputy Commissioner/Political Agent as an agent of change in tribal society (Asad, 1973). As I argued in Chapter 7 on agnatic rivalry, the involvement and interest of the British helped to consolidate and then create the position of the Musa and Shahzada Malik among the Shati Khel in the 1930s and 1940s. Similarly, there is evidence that in the next three decades some attempts were made by the administration, with its vast resources mentioned above, to cut Shahzada and Abdullah 'down to size'. This would not be difficult in Shati Khel where it is commonly believed that Mazullah's main support and inspiration at one time came from the administration providing him with money and ammunition to challenge and therefore 'balance' Shahzada: a not altogether successful exercise as we saw in Chapter 7. Political administration is clearly in a position to influence politics at the operative lineage in the Tribal Areas. It cannot, however, reorder or restructure society, largely because it remains an external influence due to the geographical and political inaccessibility of the area and to the frequent transfers of the Political Agents which imply changing policies.

My period as Political Agent helped me to see in relief and to contrast it with my recent field-work. The traditional anthropological 'worm's-eye-view' of small social groups was followed and complemented by a 'bird's-eye-view' of society, especially as Orakzai and Mohmand structure are similar. Except for about 15–20 per cent of the Shia area, the Sunni Orakzai clans are segmentary, acephalous, democratic *nang* societies involved in intense agnatic rivalry and living in low production areas. It enabled me to see in action some of the concepts I was interested in purely from an academic point of view, for instance the influence and impact of administration on the operative lineage, the sub-section, of society. Needless to say, whereas I was a neutral and passive 'observer' in the Mohmand Agency, in the Orakzai, because of my position, I became a factor of change.

II Encapsulation: prison and parliament

(a) *Case-study: prison*

The first case-study involves an agnatic murder and is of importance in the history of Mohmand administration as it illustrates two significant and interconnected points: the determination of the administration to preserve law and order in the traditionally agreed and defined protected zone, such as headquarters and roads; and second is a unique and famous case illustrating the entanglement of the tribesman with the lengthy and complicated judicial procedures of the encapsulating system. As we know, the Political Agent moved his headquarters up to Ekka Ghund in 1973 which became his temporary headquarters. A *teega* was signed with the clans of the Agency declaring that a circumference of a mile around Ekka Ghund was protected area and any violation of law and order within it would be punishable by the political authorities. Perhaps had the shifting come a few months later or if the incident had taken place outside Ekka Ghund the case would not even have caused a ripple. As it turned out the case involved every level of administration including the highest, the President of Pakistan.

On 25 June 1973 Saida Jan, a Tarakzai of the Michni area, shot and killed his cousin Salamat Jan with two shots from a .303 rifle in Ekka Ghund. The murder was a typical example of agnatic tension resulting in violence and death. During the previous days the sons of Mohmmada Jan, the brother of Saida Jan, and those of Salamat Jan had been quarrelling with each other. On the day prior to the murder, Salamat Jan had found these two groups of youngsters fighting among themselves and had separated them. The sons of Mohmmada Jan went home to complain to their father and uncle, Saida Jan, that Salamat Jan had manhandled them. The women of the home rebuked the men with *peghor*. Clearly *Pukhtunwali* was involved. Saida Jan reacted by shooting Salamat Jan and proving that not all paternal uncles are *kafirs* and enemies of their nephews (Ahmed, 1975: 35). The son-in-law of Mohmmada Jan, Mohammad Shah, by becoming a prosecution witness similarly illustrated that not all sons-in-law are loyal.

Saida Jan was arrested by the *khassadars* and the Political Agent referred the case under the Frontier Crimes Regulation to a council of

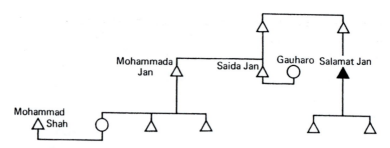

FIGURE 24 *The Saida Jan case*

elders constituted of four *mashars* whose impartiality was guaranteed as they belonged to the Upper Mohmand clans. The council found Saida Jan guilty of murder.

On 4 December 1973 the Political Agent announced the verdict under Section 302 Pakistan Penal Code, read with Section 11 Frontier Crimes Regulation: 1 Saida Jan was found guilty of murder and sentenced to fourteen years Rigorous Imprisonment. 2 He was to be fined Rs. 50,000 as he had violated the *teega* agreement between the administration and the Mohmand clans. Rs. 20,000 of this fine was to be given to the widow of Salamat Jan. One and a half months were allowed for the payment of the fine after which, under the provisions of the Frontier Crimes Regulation, first his property and, failing payment, that of his near relatives, was to be attached and sold. 3 Saida Jan's rifle was to be confiscated by the state.

The case was sent to the Commissioner, Peshawar Division, who took a serious view of the breach of the *teega* in the Agency headquarters. He felt that the case ought to be treated as an example in the Tribal Areas and therefore raised the fine to Rs. 100,000 on 29 December 1973. A review petition was addressed to him on behalf of the convict which he rejected on 1 August 1974.

Saida Jan's wife, Gauharo, and his brother, Mohammada Jan, now moved various mercy petitions to the Provincial Government which triggered off a series of important constitutional questions. For instance, were the normal laws of the land to be applied to the protected areas within the Tribal Areas or should a more traditional tribal decision with its own codes be allowed to influence judicial decisions? In any event, a procedural difficulty arose as to whether the Provincial Government was empowered to hear a mercy petition, as it had done under Section 401 of the Criminal Procedure Code, involving a case that had taken place in the Federally Administered Tribal Areas. The Law Department was of the view that under articles 246 and 247, marginal heading 'Administration of the Tribal Areas' and article 45 of the Pakistan Constitution, the President of Pakistan alone could pardon, remit, suspend or commute the sentence. The Provincial Home Department accepted this opinion and forwarded the case to the States and Frontier Regions Ministry in Islamabad. Mohmand Maliks and *mashars*, especially the Tarakzai like Yusuf Mohmand, Said Qahar and Malik Afzal, petitioned the Government for mercy at all levels. The vigour of the campaign and the publicity it attracted also succeeded in landing Mohammada Jan in the lock-up at Ekka Ghund and Gauharo had now to petition for the release of both brothers. In spite of regular inquiries from the Home Department no decision had been arrived at or news heard about the case at the time of my departure for London in August 1977.

The lesson was not lost on the tribesmen and no further such incident has occurred since the Saida Jan case. None the less the abrupt confrontation of an illiterate tribesman with the bewildering and complex judicial procedures and language (entirely in Victorian English and drafted in the main by Lord Macaulay himself in the last century) illustrates the worst possible encounter on the most unequal terms between the encapsulated and the encapsulators.

(b) *Case-study: parliament*[4]

This diachronic case-study will explain mobilization and articulation of tribal networks and the successful pursuit of power and politics in the Settled Areas by Mohmands. Painda Khan, a Kuga Khel of the Baezai clan, arrived in Takhtbahai near Mardan, landless but determined to make good in the middle of the last century. His son Abdul Mateen, also born in the Kuga Khel area around 1860, worked hard and established a foothold in the area as a tenant-farmer. By the time Mateen's eldest son, Sattar, was born in 1922 in Takhtbahai he owned 60 acres of land. Sattar Khan carried on the family tradition and at the height of his economic powers owned 1,500 acres, most of it subinfeudated to other Baezai Mohmands who were encouraged to migrate to these lands.

The acquisition of land by the Mohmands is an interesting economic phenomenon in Mardan history with clear political and social ramifications. The acquisition was made in the face of severe Yusufzai opposition and through sheer and unremitting hard physical labour initially as farm tenants. Saving every rupee to invest in land, the Mohmands slowly built their economic position.

These Mohmands began to live *dwa-kora* lives and would visit their families in the Baezai area usually for religious festivals such as Eed annually or once in two or three years, sending home remittances 'in cash and kind' (Dichter, 1967: 69). The growing numbers and *nang* values of the Mohmand caused considerable alarm and reaction among the aristocratic Yusufzai of the Mardan area and generated tension between them (which, as we saw in Chapter 3, has historical roots). It was simply the irreconcilability of the *nang* and *qalang* systems operating within one framework.

Sattar Khan was sent to the Government College, Lahore, for his education and was possibly the first Mohmand to obtain a B.A. degree in 1940. He added the tribal name 'Mohmand' to his own, a tradition followed by his family. He advocated a revival of Mohmandness and pride in the name and emerged as the champion of the small Mohmand landowners or tenant farmers against the bigger landlords. As a result he was subject to intense pressure including various assassination attempts. In 1948 he formed the *Tahfuz-e-Kashtkaran* Party (the protection of the rights of tenants party) which in the late 1960s and early 1970s grew into the *Mazdoor Kisan* Party (labourer/tenant party).

I have argued in earlier chapters, as part of my thesis, that *nang* groups leave their traditional land for various reasons, but by keeping regular contact become *dwa-kora* and often complement and feed each other's needs. Sattar Khan, born and bred in Takhtbahai, now diverted his energies and resources to regaining a foothold in the Agency. He finally succeeded when in 1965 his brother Jamshed Khan was elected a member of the Provincial Assembly from the Agency. Sattar had mobilized the Mohmands into an active political force which resulted in his election to the Provincial Parliament in 1951, of which he was the youngest member and of which he remained a member until his death in 1969. Sattar Mohmand was a remarkable man (Spain, 1962) but by the time of his death, at the age of forty-seven, he was financially and physically exhausted with his empire fast disintegrating under the incessant pressure of the local Khans.

Sattar's eldest son, Iftekhar,[5] born in 1950 in Takhtbahai, suddenly found himself in 1969, after his father's death, at the head of the Mohmand community in the Mardan District with wide responsibilities and under extreme political and economic pressure. By now the force-ful economic counter-attack had reduced Iftekhar's property and

financial situation. One method of applying pressure on the small Mohmand cultivators growing sugar-cane by the large sugar-cane mill owners
of Mardan was either not to buy cane and sugar-beet from them or to
delay their contracts or payment. The Mohmands formed themselves
into cooperative societies to sell sugar-cane but these too ran into
serious problems with the large sugar-mills of Mardan, a major problem
which confronted me when I was Registrar of Cooperative Societies of
the Frontier Province (Ahmed, 1973a).

However, Iftekhar, now calling himself Iftekhar Mohmand, in spite
of his youth, reactivated his father's tribal contacts and made his first
visit into the Agency in 1971, two years after his father's death. By
1977 he was politically prepared for the Provincial elections and won
the Takhtbahai seat, polling just over 23,000 of 42,000 votes. Needless
to say the Mohmands voted *en bloc* for him.

The above is an excellent example of tribal strategy, comprehending
and then manipulating the symbols of the encapsulating state to attain
social and economic advancement within the encapsulated framework.
In the process traditional Mohmand values had to be abandoned. For
instance there had to be total commitment to education including
education for women. Another example is the abandoning of the
principle of clan endogamy. Iftekhar's sisters and brothers have intermarried with non-Mohmands, like the Yusufzai. There are examples
of at least three marriages with Swat Pukhtun groups who migrated to
Mansehra as a result of the Yusufzai invasions in the sixteenth century
(Ahmed, 1973b). Finally, and perhaps the most critical deviance from
Pukhto *riwaj* but in keeping with Islamic law, the women of Iftekhar's
family including his mother and sisters have inherited property. The
750 acres which remained to Sattar Khan by the time of his death were
divided between his wife and eight sons and daughters according to
Islamic law.[6]

III Education as a factor of encapsulation

A section on education in the *nang* Tribal Areas could be summed up
by two contradictory but connected conclusions. Firstly, that education
is being slowly but generally accepted and in the areas more exposed to
outside influences, symbolized by the road and proximity to administrative centres, even girls' primary schools have begun to open recently.
Second, and connected to the general penetration of education is a
strong, and I suspect permanent, disenchantment with the actual

benefits that accrue from education. In a highly material and physical society with emphasis on symbols such as masculinity, honour and the gun the teaching profession is looked down on. Conceptually literacy and education imply rejection of the traditional mores rooted in an oral, illiterate and action-orientated society and are often in direct confrontation and contradiction with them. Indeed education may even be seen as a deviance from the ideal model and as the examples in this section illustrate has come to imply just that, sterile investment of time and energy. I shall first discuss the spread of education and subsequently its effects on the Mohmand.

Certain *mashars* who took the initiative in educating their children during the last days of the Raj and early days of Pakistan subsequently reaped high rewards. Haji Abdullah sent his eldest son, Khanzada, who was born in Sangar like his father, all the way to Aligarh in India to obtain his Bachelor of Arts degree in 1940, probably thus becoming the first TAM Bachelor of Arts.[7] Later another son of Abdullah, Hidayatullah, passed the civil service examination after obtaining his law degree from Peshawar. Khanzada in the 1970s was Deputy Inspector-General of Police in the Frontier Province while his younger brother, Hidayatullah, was Secretary to the Commissioner, Peshawar Division. This family set an example to the Halimzai of what could be achieved through education and now carries on the trend by educating the new generation of both sons and daughters in Peshawar. Khanzada's eldest son is a student of Saint Mary's High School, Peshawar, for instance. The comparison with Shahzada's entirely uneducated sons and grandsons, and indeed the entire Shati Khel section, is obvious and one can predict two widely differentiated life styles and patterns in the future. In moments of self-reflection Shahzada assesses the future thus: 'My sons are loafers and useless. They have ruined my reputation. My family will be finished after me.'

Among the Tarakzai, and near Bela Mohmandan, the father of Yusuf Mohmand defied tradition and educated his sons. Yusuf, born in 1924 in the village of Pir Qila and the most talented among his brothers, was selected for the Army, and passed out from the Dehra Dun Academy as a Second Lieutenant in 1944, the first Mohmand officer to be commissioned in the British Army. After the creation of Pakistan he entered politics (adding the name Mohmand to his), became a member of the Provincial Assembly to represent the Mohmands in 1956 and was the first tribesman to become a Deputy Minister in the West Pakistan Government in 1958. His success provided a strong incentive to comprehend and learn the ways of the encapsulating system. Like his father, Yusuf defied tradition by opening the first girls' primary school among the Mohmands. This was in 1957 in his village, Pir Qila, in the face of stiff tribal opposition. Yusuf donated the land free of charge for the school and at first could only find his own daughters and nieces to attend it. The primary school in due course became a middle school and is now a flourishing high school.

Yusuf recalls his own schooling in the early 1930s when he had to walk a couple of miles daily with his brothers to the nearest and only Mohmand middle school at Subhan Khwar on the way to Shabkadar. Shabkadar, as we know, is a Halimzai stronghold and Yusuf and his brothers would be taunted and teased daily for attending schools run by the British *kafirs* and were often physically manhandled. The Halimzai would chant a popular verse deriding English education.[8]

It is not difficult to understand the general opposition of the elders and particularly the religious groups to any form of education sponsored by the British. Yusuf recounts how in the late 1940s the village Mullah dubbed him a *kafir*, not only for having attended school and joined the British Indian Army but also for trivial matters such as drinking water in a glass rather than in the palm of his hand, sitting on English chairs and for committing the final and unforgivable sin of installing a w.c., representing western civilization, in his village home in 1947. Yusuf Mohmand recounted to me how the same Mullah later sent a son to school, who matriculated and now works in the Pakistan Air Force. What is more, the Mullah uses chairs to sit on and glasses to drink from. Today the same Mullah is a staunch supporter of education and backs Yusuf's call for general education among the Mohmand.

Education was possibly the greatest area of failure for British administration and is generally admitted as such (Caroe, 1965: 410). In quantitative terms the post-British growth of schools in the Tribal Areas is impressive (Ahmed, 1977a: 54). In 1947 there was not a single school in the Agency; by 1956 the total number of schools of all categories in the Mohmand Agency was thirty-one and by 1976 it was 128 (ibid.). However their location in the Tarakzai Michni areas reflected the problem of penetration and their male students the strong prejudice against female education.

An intermediate college was opened at Ekka Ghund in 1974. The enthusiasm of the administration for the college was not entirely matched by that of the Mohmand and for the first two years it boasted a staff-student ratio of 1:1, eleven teachers to eleven students. The shifting of the Agency headquarters from Ekka Ghund in the Tarakzai area to Ghalanay in the Halimzai area in 1977 presented a typical tribal problem. The dozen boys belonged to the Tarakzai clan and were reluctant to see, what they saw as, their college shifted to the rowdier Halimzai area. It would also present them with problems of transportation. For instance Ihsanullah, from Bela, travels daily to attend college at Ekka Ghund. In spite of their repeated strikes it was decided to shift the college to Ghalanay.

In an analysis made of the standard Pukhto and Urdu books used in classes and published by the North-West Frontier Province Text Book Board, I identified certain larger national and Islamic themes which in themselves create symbols that are recognizable in the larger encapsulating system. Prose and poetry are largely confined to relating didactic incidents from the lives of Islamic and national figures. The school day begins with a recitation from the Holy Koran, the ceremonial hoisting of the national flag and the singing of the national anthem. Such symbols help pupils to identify their ideas with those of the larger systems. In conversations with TAM and SAM boys, specially those in the senior classes, I discovered that although they had a rudimentary knowledge of Islam, the Holy Koran and the Prophet, they often knew little of wider general historical knowledge. Boys of the seventh class, for instance, had not heard of either Babar or Akbar, the Mughal Emperors. Boys of the fifth and sixth classes had not heard of the great Pukhto poets Rahman Baba and Khushal Khan Khattak. Nor for that matter had elders like Haji Hassan of Shati Khel any idea of who Rahman Baba and Khushal Khan Khattak were.[9]

Education brings with it the language of Pakistan, Urdu,[10] and with it a certain 'Pakistanization' of cultural and political values which emphasize the similarities rather than dissimilarities between local and national, particularly as almost every home in TAM has a radio. I found that most boys above the third and fourth class were fluent in Urdu (and above the eighth class could read English clearly). Urdu songs also, whether Pakistani or Indian, are heard in the most remote parts of the Tribal Areas. During the political crisis following the elections in Pakistan in 1977 tribesmen tuned in to the BBC Urdu news service from London and I was constantly bombarded by the latest information on Pakistan by groups living in the most remote villages and areas of the Tribal Areas.

Shati Khel and Bela Mohmandan have yet to produce a B.A. My TAM assistants, Akbar Jan and Feroz, sat for the exam but failed to clear one paper each. They clearly have little intention of attempting it again. Feroz who had failed the English paper in 1972 could not sit for the exam next year at Shabkadar as he arrived in Shati Khel to support Shahzada in the last encounter against Mazullah. The Ranra and Malok have not even produced a candidate for the B.A. Humayan Sher, the son of Mohabat Sher, a Zarif Khel of Bela, failed his B.A. in 1973. The present Bela candidate for the B.A. is Ihsanullah but he is still in his second year. Apart from these two young men in Bela the two most educated boys are Shamroz Khan, the son of Hussain Khan, and Awal Sher, son of Ghulam Sher, an Afridi living in Bela, who have passed their matriculation examination.

Paradoxically Shati Khel, in the heart of the Mohmand Agency and in its unencapsulated state, had its first primary school almost fourteen years before Bela in 1959, adjacent to and on Shahzada's village land. The school called after Shahzada's village, the Nawa Kilay Primary School, was upgraded to middle status in 1968 and has recently become a high school. The school began as an open-air institution but by the mid-1960s had cement rooms for its students. The school is built on one acre of land and has nine rooms. The staff of thirteen teachers, mostly from the Peshawar District and all without families, live in one room and cook their own food. Most of the staff spend long week-ends away from Shati Khel. This was one of the first schools in the Gandab but the reasons for its acceptance were not entirely academic. Maliks often accept schools for the various and immediate material benefits they bring. Under established tradition, 1 the Malik himself is appointed as the contractor of the building; 2 he also appoints the *chaukidars*; and 3 in many cases uses the building, especially during the vacation, as his *hujra*. In return for permitting this important foothold in the Gandab a thankful administration allowed Shahzada to approve or reject the appointment of the thirteen teachers and appoint three *chaukidars* of the school. It came as no surprise when some of his sons and grandsons found themselves appointed in these capacities – duties which they had neither the time nor the inclination to attend to. However, the sinecure appointments brought prestige and regular monthly income.

Although it is the only school in Shati Khel the enrolment number of eighty is small. Attendance, as at Bela, is irregular and dependent on seasonal and parental demands and classes are rowdy. A teacher who is strict with a pupil is likely to be paid a visit by his father threatening dire consequences. Perhaps as a result of their situation the staff as a matter of policy and gesture of good-will allow students to pass into the higher class whether they are fit for it or not.

About forty children form the fluctuating population which attends the primary school at Bela begun in 1973. Before then those lads desirous of education attended the nearest school at Dab almost three miles away. During four to five months in summer when the channel lying to the north-west of Bela fills up and cuts Bela off from the mainland the boys were exempted from school. The lineage break-down of the Bela school reflects the roughly equal proportion of representation of the Bela lineage groups according to population. In 1976 there were three Kado, nine Madar, five Jano, nine Sabah, six Do Khel, two Zarif, three children from the religious groups and three from the occupational groups at the Bela school. If anything, the figures reflect the reluctance of the senior lineage, the Kado Khel, to encourage education and the support of the junior lineages like the Jano and Sabah Khel in sending their children to school.

The Bela school is nothing more than a thatched roof supported by wooden posts. Inclement weather drenches the children in rain or exposes them to wind storms and during the summer season flooding provides the teacher, who lives down and across the river, a reasonable excuse not to attend. This was one case in which I deliberately abandoned my neutral field-work role as observer and attempted to help the village. In 1976 I requested the Deputy Commissioner, Peshawar,[11] to come to Bela and after visiting the ramshackle and flimsy arrangements for the school he agreed to sanction a cement building for the Bela primary school. In late 1977, after final government approval, Rs. 85,000 were released for the school and tenders were called for the first cement construction of Bela.

The opening of a girls' school has wide-ranging political implications in the Tribal Areas. I was responsible for opening the first two girls' primary schools in the Sunni Orakzai area in 1977 and barely succeeded. Considerable tact, patience and patronage had to be shown to the *mashars* prepared to support and house the school. The problem of lady teachers was acute. Not only were lady teachers, usually from Peshawar, most reluctant to work in the Tribal Areas but the opponents of the school threatened to abduct them. The teachers had to be given an escort, protected and housed with the patriarch supporting the school. Initially only his daughters and nieces would study in the school. Agnatic rivalry was activated and opposing cousins threatened to mobilize tribal support and level down the two settlements and I had to keep the Orakzai Levies on immediate alert in case of such an event. However, matters passed peacefully and the first two girls' schools opened without incident. SAM, in spite of its proximity to Peshawar, still maintains its Pukhto traditions regarding the seclusion of women and as a corollary refuses to educate them. In this regard both Shati Khel and Bela are identical. Shamshudin and the other Bela *mashars* would argue with me for hours, as their wives would with my wife, but refuse to consider accepting a girls' primary school in Bela.

I shall now discuss the second aspect of education and the acute disenchantment it has created among the educated. Three of my assistants were officially enrolled as primary school teachers, Feroz in Nawa Kilay primary school, Shati Khel, Shamshur Rahman at the Kado Korona primary school and Khan Wahid living in the village near Bela, employed at the Lakaro primary school, north of the Nahakki Pass. Their attendance and interest reflected the state and quality of education. Khan Wahid, who had become a teacher after helping me in my field-work, admitted that he could not go to Lakaro, which was almost a full day's journey from Bela, more than twice a week. Feroz who lived most of the time in Shabkadar could not visit Shati Khel for more than a few days of the week and was concentrating on starting an independent business of his own. Shamshur Rahman was desperately looking for an alternative employment. Humayun Sher, of Bela, who we saw earlier failing his B.A., also teaches at Lakaro but admits he cannot make the journey more than twice or thrice a week. During the rest of the week he explores the possibility of alternative employment. The whole business of education lacks motivation and inspiration.

One may well ask why the administration does not take a serious view of the irregular attendance of teachers. The answer is simple. Teachers for the Tribal Areas are hard to come by and, as my own assistants repeatedly complained to me, their low status and pay made the profession an unattractive one. Feroz bitterly compared his pay of about Rs. 300 a month to the thousands made by smuggling and other illegal business by an illiterate Malok cousin of his own age: 'He drives a Toyota car, visits Karachi once a year for pleasure and is totally illiterate. People respect him for his resourcefulness and success. What will education or teaching do for me?' In 1973 Feroz's application for the post of Naib-Tehsildar was, he felt, 'sabotaged by my own lineage elders' who feared his emergence as 'their sons are useless'. Society agrees that education is a futile pastime and quotes Feroz as an example: 'What worlds has he conquered?' In a society that does not make fine distinctions between legal and illegal, smuggling and trading, or even recognize the Durand Frontier it is *what* you have and not *how* you have it that counts. As the .303 gun was a symbol of prestige yesterday, the car and the tractor are the symbols of prestige today. The B.A. has failed to become a symbol of prestige or success in TAM. In Shati Khel and within the rapidly changing values of a traditional society to material symbols of success I found it difficult to convince Feroz that his argument may be erroneous.

The section on education has made two points directly related to, and confirming, my argument. Firstly, the attitudes of TAM and SAM regarding female education are translated to mean the desire to maintain the *parda* of women. Both groups approximate to the ideal in their behaviour. Second, by deviating from ideal Pukhtun behaviour, which brings political prestige and social status, and investing time and resources in education, young Mohmands feel perhaps they have made the wrong choice. A generation ago matters were different when steady government employment carrying status was available through education and made it an attractive proposition. The hold of the traditional ideal model is still strong and the lack of respect education commands or material success it brings is likely to reinforce it further.

IV 'Peasantization' and perception of change in tribal groups

In this section I propose to examine the social processes that are set in motion as a result of encapsulation and affect social organization and behaviour which in turn act as diacritica to distinguish between tribal and peasant modes of social and economic life.

(a) 'Peasantization' of tribal groups

Peasant societies may briefly be described as possessing the following characteristics: 1 the peasant family farm which acts as the basic unit of multidimensional social organization; 2 land husbandry as the main means of livelihood directly providing the major part of the consumption needs; 3 specific traditional culture related to the way of life of small communities, an important aspect of which is community life and lack of privacy (Ayrout, 1963: 87); and 4 the underdog position and the domination of peasantry by outsiders (Dalton, 1971; Gough and Sharma, 1973; Shanin, 1973; Wolf, 1966, 1969a and b, 1971).

Peasant society has been usefully divided into a five-class schema:

1 landlords, 2 rich peasants, 3 middle peasants, 4 poor peasants, and 5 workers (Mao, 1967: 13-59, 137-43). Using the five-class schema Alavi (1971, 1972, 1973) and Ahmad (1973, 1977) analysed Punjab villages in the Districts of Sahiwal and Sargodha respectively. This schema does not serve the purpose for an analysis of SAM. The first two categories, landlords and rich peasants, and the last category of workers are absent and the entire village falls between the categories of poor and middle peasants as we saw in Chapter 9.

Within peasant society coalitions of two kinds are identified, horizontal between peasants and peasants and vertical between peasants and superiors; consensus is implicit in the former as dissensus in the latter. The settled Mohmand villagers are of the former kind for polyadic relations with larger systems have yet to develop and symbols of exploiting classes yet to appear. Although in the process of losing their tribal characteristics and morphologically on their way to becoming 'a vast mass' they still 'do not form a class' in the Marxist sense (Marx, 1951: 302-3). Although they do not form a militant class SAM groups still retain enough of their tribal code and structure, as I am arguing, not to form 'the meek and the miserable' (Gellner, 1969c: 4) that are the base of peasant populist movements (Ionescu and Gellner, 1969).

The confrontation between Mohmand tenants and big landlords in the classic Marxist framework that finds expression in the richer irrigated lands of the Peshawar and Mardan Districts (Bangash, 1972) is outside the scope of the discussion. For our purposes SAM peasantry consists of small landholders, the average household owns less than 2 acres of land, and it is neither in hostile opposition to richer or larger landlords within the community, as there are none, nor in opposition to other non-Mohmand groups.

Administratively Bela Mohmandan is like any other village in the Settled Districts but its proximity and constant socio-cultural reference to Kado Korona prevents it from being fully so. SAM are *in* the settled world but not *of* it.[12] They themselves are aware that as they cannot approximate to the *nang* Pukhtun model they none the less are not part of the *qalang* situation with its ranked hierarchies, large estates and dominant Yusufzai Khans. SAM may not explicitly say so but reflect in their conversation that after 1951 they can speak of doing Pukhto and talk in the idiom of the *nang* model but cannot do Pukhto. Indeed as the SAM case-studies quoted in the last chapters illustrate, the ascendants of SAM could both do and speak Pukhto until that date and after. SAM are aware of deviance and the inexorable drift from the *nang* model and its increasing irrelevance to their administrative situation. For SAM encapsulation is a stage in peasantization just as it is in the 'de-tribalization' process. TAM would often speak of Mohmand groups settled and living in Peshawar as *Pekhawri* or in the Punjab as *Panjabi* suggesting a certain loss of 'Mohmandness' and diminished status. Shahzada or Mazullah would describe the Tarakzai generally as 'half-Peshawaris' (*nim-Pekhawri*) with ill-concealed contempt.

I am in general agreement with Professor Bailey's thesis that stark poverty and material hardship are too often smoothed out in the traditional 'romantic view of rural life' (Bailey, 1973). The peasant's life is uncertain and his individual identity reduced to anonymity. It is partly this fear of anonymity that gives such meaning and relevance to the importance of the tribal genealogical charter in tribal society. In the most profound social sense man belongs to a perceived and defined world and this belonging allocates him a name, lineage and identity. SAM's cumulative pace of 'peasantization' is in direct correspondence to the diminishing importance of sectional lineages. With each decade SAM have moved further towards the irrevocable process making them 'Belawals', villagers, peasants, anonymous groups, and weakening the links that bind them to the ideal-type model. SAM may soon be at the stage of sedentarized tribesmen where the 'last of the important groups in the village is the lineage' (Stirling, 1965: 27).

Indeed, were SAM lineages, especially the senior ones, confronted with their peasantization and its implications they would be most affronted for they see themselves as tribals and use the idiom of the lineage and *Pukhtunwali* derived from the *nang* model. Although I stand in danger of refuting part of my own thesis at a stroke, there is no denying the fundamental and superficial changes that are visible in SAM and distinguish it from TAM. I shall illustrate this point through the eyes of TAM and SAM themselves by drawing up a list of characteristics depicting how they see themselves and each other. The interesting and differentiated models present a crude 'hill' versus 'plain' or 'tribe' versus 'peasant' comparison common to such juxtaposed societies (Bailey, 1957, 1960; Dupree and Albert, 1974; Leach, 1977). The emergent social and cultural differences are a result of almost three decades of administrative separation and in the case of SAM gradual encapsulation into the larger societal whole of the settled region (Table 17).

The TAM impression of SAM as 'soft' and somewhat unworthy of being truly Mohmand is reciprocated by SAM contempt for their illiterate and belligerent life-style. Almost every person I talked to from

TABLE 17 Native apperception of themselves

Pukhtun model	TAM opinions		SAM opinions	
	TAM	SAM	SAM	TAM
revenge (*badal*)	never compromise on *badal* and *tor* cases	in no position to take *badal*, even compromise *tor* cases	acutely aware of deviance from ideal but still talk in *badal* idiom; on occasion do take *badal* especially where it concerns *tor*	wild and unruly, killing not necessarily for *badal*
cousin enmity (*tarboorwali*)	fully involved in agnatic rivalry	too weak to be involved in agnatic rivalry	maintain a form of agnatic rivalry which finds other and milder expressions than killing	motivated not by honour but petty jealousy and uncouth nature
hospitality (*melmastia*)	very hospitable, spendthrift aspects of *potlatch* behaviour	too poor and miserly to be hospitable	hospitable within their meagre means, 'civilized' and 'cultured' in Pukhto lore	calculating in their hospitality, restricted to political officials only
bravery (*tora*)	very brave	meek and even cowardly	consider their ascendants as equal to the bravest of the brave but aware of limitations on themselves	admit TAM bravery but consider it ill-directed, disrespectful and wild
politics	free (*azad*) unencapsulated	under government (*de hokomat paband de*) encapsulated	TAM views are conceded in this regard	

the Halimzai and Tarakzai confirmed the rather stereotyped opinions of each other: Halimzai as tough, belligerent, illiterate smugglers and dacoits but 'real' Pukhtuns and the Tarakzai as soft, more educated, more refined, more encapsulated and less free (less *azad*). The two groups of my field-work area knew of each other but rarely met and on the few occasions when SAM groups accompanied me to Shati Khel they were distinctly uncomfortable, no doubt believing their own version regarding the 'wildness' of their hill cousins. The plaintive comment of Hamesh Gul, the Bela *mashar*, regarding the Halimzai when he visited Ekka Ghund to argue the case of the Madar against the Kado and failed to see even the superintendent of the office, sums up the SAM attitude: 'The Agency people are very rude and uncultured. These Halimzais are real barbarians. I shall never visit them again.' Political officials confirmed that Tarakzai contractors working at the new Ghalanay Agency headquarters would ensure that they were out of the Agency and the area of their Halimzai cousins by dusk.

Social customs reflected in such superficial but illustrative aspects as names and sartorial preferences also indicate differentiation. TAM names reflect what SAM would view as a confirmation of their 'ferocity and wildness': *Lakhkar* (a tribal armed war group), *Ranjak* (gunpowder), *Khanjar* (dagger) and *Rakeeb* (enemy) are traditional TAM names. I met *Pindazey Khan* (literally five-shot rifle Khan) in Shati Khel. In sharp contrast Bela names go beyond the Pukhtun world and reflect other systems: *America* and *Japan* are two young girls of the Sabah Khel and *Rangoon* is a Do Khel male. As mentioned in TAM almost every *mashar* is called Malik *saib* as a matter of courtesy. Any other reference, for instance to trade, would be considered demeaning. In SAM *mashars* are often called after an occupation. Shamshudin is sometimes referred to as *manager saib* because he is the manager of the Bela Cooperative Society. His uncle-in-law, Baz Mohammad, is called contractor sahib (*tekadar saib*) because he is one. Hamesh Gul is popularly called *mimbar saib* from the days when he was a Basic Democratic member over a decade ago.

Over the decades and with poorer diet, SAM are tending to be smaller in size and lighter in weight. I took the average height and weight of 100 Mohmand males, 50 in Shati Khel and 50 in Bela Mohmandan, and selected at random from stratified groups. The average height of the Bela male is 5 feet 4 inches and his average weight is 140 pounds compared to the average TAM height of 5 feet 5 inches and weight of 153 pounds. The heaviest and tallest Belawal is Said Mohammad, the son of a Mullah (*mullagai*) who works in government service, and is 195 pounds and 5 feet 10 inches in height. There are many taller TAM males but the heaviest is Dilawar Khan at 220 pounds. TAM seem healthier and appear to live longer. The oldest man in Bela, Noor Mohammad (Kado Khel) is about ninety years old but is aged, infirm and weary of life. In contrast Umar and Mian Kassai both over a hundred years old appear lively and lucid. TAM elders between seventy and eighty, like Hassan or Shahzada, in no manner exhibit signs of mental or physical senescence. Although superficial, the physical differentiation between TAM and SAM elders fits into the larger framework of this section:

TAM	SAM
clear faces, pinker hues	lined, haggard faces
heavier, taller than SAM	spare bodies, shorter in height
walk straight with head erect	stooped in posture
wear traditional head-dress (*kullah*)	wear worn-out clothes
usually carry gun, and revolver if Malik, sign of Pukhtun manhood	carry no weapons
cultivate beards (usually dyed red with henna)	few days' stubble on face
elders like Shahzada and Mazullah although about 70 look and behave more like 50	elders like Shamshudin and Hamesh Gul although about 50 look and behave over 60
reflect a continuing zest and appetite for life	reflect a state of anorexia towards life

The domestic structure of TAM as we saw earlier reflects the two key principles of society, agnatic activity as expressed by the *hujra* and *parda*, in the structural arrangements of the houses. In SAM there are neither walls around the village nor such internal divisions in the house. Similarly, in TAM about one-fourth of the households contain single families whereas single family atomistic units form three-fourths of the Bela village. A form of deviant behaviour in SAM, unlike TAM, is that few males sleep in the Bela *hujra* and most either sleep at home or in summer by the river bank. Bela reflects a partly peasantized, agricultural-ized village with characteristics which may be recognized in other parts of the subcontinent (Ahmad, S. 1973, 1977; Alavi, 1971, 1972, 1973; Dube, 1965; Mayer, A. C., 1970).

The absence of a clear authority structure is marked in Bela. Deci-sions are arrived at by lobbying and discussion (*pe sawal*) not by force (*zor*). Village affairs therefore often stay unsettled and undecided (a good example is the case of the Bela Society to be discussed in Chapter 11). In contrast the TAM patriarch or Malik is wholly in control of decision making within his household. Pukhto custom and Code ensure a general consensus in society on communal matters that is expressed through the *jirgas*. The authority structure in TAM encourages conflict that may escalate into shooting and death but it discourages the degeneration into frivolous joking or teasing of Maliks or *mashars* by *kashars* as is done in SAM. I have often heard *kashars* like Amin[13] teasing Hussain Khan by calling him a miser, a grave insult in Pukhto, sitting in the *hujra*. Amin would suggest Hussain hoarded his money and never used it to entertain guests according to Pukhto tradition. In retaliation Hussain could do little except look embarrassed. Such a public violation of an elder's honour would be unthinkable on the part of the *kashar* and unforgivable on the part of the *mashar* in TAM.

The TAM Code sustains them in poverty and affliction with a strength and dignity that only such a rigid and defined system can impart. They do not know how to grovel or whine in 'cringing subservience', characteristics of the peasant on the subcontinent (Asad, 1970: xv). Unlike the villager on the subcontinent, TAM has no atavistic weight of mythical social and pseudo-religious traditions to burden him – no Vedas, Ramayanas, or Gitas, no chthonic deities, no mother symbols in cow or land, no anxiety of authority, hierarchy or caste (Addy and Azad, 1973; Béteille, 1974, 1977; Bottomore, 1962; Darling, 1925, 1930, 1934; Dube, 1965; Dumont, 1970; Mayer, A. C., 1970) from which Muslim groups are not immune (Ahmad, I. 1973). In the most profound sense he is an intellectual and cultural nomad. He travels light and carries his social inheritance in his genealogical charter and his political inheritance in his Code and the two, so closely interlinked and interrelated, are always at hand at all times for reference. He is free and being free as no peasant can be he is imprisoned in his Code; he is defined only within its boundaries – outside them he looks the world in the eye and owns no masters or position superior to his.

Belawals often repeat: 'The government is our mother/father (*mor plar*). The government must help us. We are very poor'. This helplessness confirms an aspect of the peasant's view of the bad life (Bailey, 1973) and contrasts with TAM and TAM attitudes to administration, a diacritical factor in differentiating peasant and tribal social behaviour, as I am arguing, and which are diametrically opposed. The peasant avoids officialdom, is often treated with contempt by it and deals with its lowest rungs (Bailey, 1970, 1973). To Belawals the local *patwari*, the most junior official in the administrative hierarchy, is the highest functionary they know. The *patwari* expresses the importance of his duties and that of Bela Mohmandan by making a tour of the village at an average of once a year and lives in Peshawar. The Deputy Commissioner's office is virtually an unattainable zone and level. On the other hand the tribal *mashar*, and especially Maliks, may and do see the head of their administration, the Political Agent, with frequency and the Tehsildar, a senior official to the *patwari*, with even greater frequency. The relationship is always as between equals and friends.

The idiom of *nang* life is used in common parlance in SAM but even this fictitious device to keep alive the tenuous link with the ideal model will probably die with the present generation of *mashars*. The *nang* idiom is as unintelligible as it is untransmittable to those born in the post-1951 SAM world like Ihsanullah. In contrast, the younger generation of TAM born after 1951, though disillusioned with the rhythm of agnatic politics and the machinations of the Maliks, are rediscovering their special unencapsulated status and its concomitant privileges and express no desire to surrender it in any form.

(b) *Perception of change in society*

How do the informants and actors in the areas perceive the extent of change and the rate of its acceleration in society? It is too early to say in TAM. In SAM they may not express it explicitly but they will soon be in a position to speak and not do Pukhto as it is understood in TAM. I have shown there is already suspension, accommodation and alteration of parts of it. By definition SAM is compromised. In informal conversation SAM elders agree: 'Pukhto has gone' (*Pukhto lara*) and 'Today Pukhto means money' (*nan saba Pukhto paisa da*). A common related saying in TAM and SAM is: 'Respect today is in money' (*izat pa lote*[14] *ke day*). The winds of change are also ruffling TAM. Shahmat (Musa), the oldest man in Shati until his death in 1976, complained that '*Pukhto lara*': today Pukhtuns were becoming shopkeepers (*bazaryan shoo*) and traders (*tijarati shoo*). They were even selling eggs. He recalled how some thirty years ago Pasham Gul, at present elder of Malok, took some eggs to Shabkadar and sold them quietly. When the news spread in Shati Khel he had to hide in his house for a full week in shame before he could live down the social opprobrium. Haji Umar of Malok village, at present the oldest man in Shati and said to be over a hundred years old, was more outspoken: 'Pukhtuns feud and kill. Pukhto is a useless word' (*Pukhtun patna aw marg kai, bekara lafz day*). When he talks of '*Pukhto lara*' the Pukhtun is measuring deviance from the ideal-type, mainly in terms of honour regarding women, *tor*, and *badal* in *tarboorwali*. The former is still universally upheld while the diminishing importance of the latter with its capacity to destroy ontire villages and groups is looked on not entirely with disfavour. Similar sentiments may be expressed by TAM but with less conviction and lesser frequency.

The ideal is illusion, what he wants to see in society, and reality is what exists and he cannot see or recognize. *Pukhtunwali* is being reinterpreted, its praxis shifting into the penumbral shades of a changing society. To what extent do these conclusions deduced from an abstract and simplified model apply to the concrete society under consideration? According to the formal questionnaires I conducted among TAM, *melmastia* was considered the foremost feature of *Pukhtunwali*, 67 per cent, *nang* was second, 50 per cent followed closely by *badal*, 46 per cent. In SAM *nang* was number one, 66 per cent, *melmastia* second, 50 per cent, and *badal* third, 34 per cent. As I have illustrated in the cases on agnatic rivalry in Chapter 7, *badal* is an increasingly less important and more difficult activity in SAM than in TAM. On the other hand *nang* is high in SAM as it identifies with ideal Pukhto concepts and at the same time remains intangible and undefinable and therefore undemanding: in short, reduced to a concept and not a social activity. However, there is a reluctance to come to terms with social reality and as cited earlier the entire Mohmand universe believed *Pukhtunwali* was practised in their villages. I do not attach much significance to these quantitative percentages of qualitative features. Social reality derives from frequency patterns in behaviour; what men *do*, not what they say should have been or should be done. It is repeated action that is of significance to us.

Concepts of the pure Pukhto past are as polarized as they are idealized. Shahzada Malik talked of Pukhto as a past equated to dacoity, feuds and no rights for women, whereas Haji Hassan idealized it. For the Haji the Pukhto past meant unity, fidelity, one word, one faith. Both are extreme views and the truth lies somewhere in between. An interview revealed the differences seen in the past and the present through the eyes of an old man:

The old time was very good because the people were simple. They were not jealous of each other. They had a good and friendly love in their hearts for fellow people. The people of this age are very bad.

They quarrel with each other. They steal things like crops from each other and are always fighting with each other.

I have heard similar sentiments expressing concern over social change, especially the materialism and disrespect of the young, from elders of different groups in the most remote villages of the Tribal Areas.

Young men who play cards or roll dice for small sums in secluded places to while away their time are condemned by *mashars* as gamblers (*jawargar*) and loafers (*loparan* — the word is incorporated into Pukhto from the English). In both areas there has grown up a hard core of males between twenty and thirty years old who spend their time thus. The *mashars* are indignant: 'Gambling is forbidden by Islam.' But the younger males answer that there is no other form of pastime or entertainment, no games or sports, not even donkey or quail fights. Feroz recalls that as a boy he played a game in which two teams of between five to ten members each, hopped on one foot and attempted to topple the other team (*skhay*). The game was played in summer under the shade of trees. Hide-and-seek (*pat patonay*) among children and a form of wrestling (*parzawal*) for young boys were also popular once. Girls played no games after the age of seven or eight and by ten or eleven years were segregated. Now Feroz observes even young boys 'earn and chase money and no one has time for games'.

TAM and SAM elders of all groups are concerned at what they see the changing attitudes of youth, their lack of respect (*beadabi*). Although I must confess that in the *hujras* even today in the presence of elders young men, including educated and aware *kashar* like Feroz and Akbar Jan, behaved with impeccable and formal propriety, standing behind the cots rather than sitting on them or sitting on the floor and remaining aloof from the conversation until spoken to.

Until the process is logically complete the Code plays its part: as mentioned earlier, a cold-blooded day-time murder was committed during my field-work period just outside Bela, based on a trivial incident but part of cousin enmity. As this was in the Settled Area the police were involved and the murderer was sent to jail.

I have shown through case-studies how both TAM and SAM, the latter in spite of its encapsulated situation, generally adhere to the Code in the two most important cultural features of Pukhtun society as seen by the actors, *tarboorwali* and *tor*, and thus support my thesis. This is in spite of the fact that revenge-killing is a costly and bothersome affair in the Settled Area involving long jail sentences and heavy debts. The other traditionally important social features are often compromised or dropped and tend to disprove my thesis. For instance *melmastia*, for economic reasons, is another dying institution especially in SAM. In addition, people are away at jobs in Karachi or Kuwait, and many elders simply find it too expensive or a waste of agricultural time looking after guests. In TAM hospitality is still highly regarded. Shahzada's strength derives from his reputation as a generous host, which even his enemies concede. The functions of *jirgas* become redundant with the presence of formal law courts in SAM but the *jirga* still plays an important part in social life. Its loss of prestige and power are the result of its limitations in having its orders carried out. Unlike the situation in TAM, the *jirga* decision is not based on physical coercion and cannot be implemented if the aggrieved party involves the police.

Certain Pukhto words and institutions, *teega*, *badragga*, or *barampta* (recovery of stolen goods through joint tribal action), have been almost obliterated in the memory of Bela, especially among the younger generation, because of its encapsulated situation and the consequent redundancy of the concepts.[15]

In the above chapter I have shown how political administration representing larger state systems (with its two faces, the malevolent: prison, and the benevolent: parliament) and the educational systems derived from the latter are combining to penetrate and encapsulate the hitherto unencapsulated TAM. Clearly, comment is not feasible or valid at this stage of TAM history. The results may be best analysed in another few years, perhaps even decades. On the other hand, the results of encapsulation in SAM over the last three decades are apparent in the peasantization process of this tribal group.

My general argument is here supported in that although TAM continue to view their society as the ideal Pukhtun model they look on SAM as an antithetical form and in a relationship of mutual analytical opposition. None the less the latter still speak the idiom of, and when they can do, Pukhto. How long this situation will last is a question beyond the scope of the study. Granted that encapsulation is neither deterministic nor integration inevitable, the arguments contained above suggest certain directions. *Pukhtunwali* may have to adopt different strategies to survive continued encapsulation if its particularistic values are to withstand the universalistic values of the larger state system. The same theme is continued in the next chapter with an emphasis on economic development schemes and their impact on traditional behaviour and organization in TAM and SAM.

11 Economic development and encapsulation

Economic planners, for instance, not infrequently lack a knowledge of the structure and norms of the community for which they plan. Here the provision of knowledge by anthropologists may be a very important component of the developmental process – though so far as a rule such provision has been conspicuously absent (Firth, 1970: 23).

Having discussed the impact of social and political institutions representing larger state systems on smaller systems in the last chapter, I turn to an examination of economic development schemes as part of the same process in this chapter. The Mohmand road and other development projects along with the effects of labour migration are examined. TAM traditional structure predetermines government patronage. Influential leaders and lineages reap the benefits of modern economic activity discussed in this chapter such as contracts, employment and even visas for working abroad. The SAM situation is altogether different. Encapsulation implies attenuation of traditional behaviour and organization. Pukhtunness may be subordinated in the search for employment and income. The dilemma of choices is not spurious but real. My arguments are partly substantiated in TAM and partly refuted in SAM as I shall make clear in this chapter.

My approach to modern economic development in relation to traditional social structure, as illustrated by the field-work case-studies, will assume the three relevant and fundamental principles generally recognized as interconnected in the field of economic anthropology: 'the questions of interest to anthropologists are answered in part by economists and sociologists, and vice versa. Another is that it must be studied in historical depth. A third is that macro- and micro-development are complementary' (Dalton, 1971: 1). The three principles apply to the methodology of this chapter as indeed they do to the study as a whole. Analysis of modernization will arise from sequences of societal change and an attempt to identify underlying regularities that constitute the core of the ideal-type model. Such analysis will enable us to conclude whether, and at what stage, a society is resistant or receptive to innovation, and how related attitudes are influenced by earlier contacts with alien political systems. Such analysis will partly explain how and why social organization changes when it does and will partly define what is considered successful village or rural development. This leads to an important question: does the view of successful development coincide with that of the administration, representing the larger state, or the people affected in the village? Perhaps to some extent small-scale changes at the village level are in themselves an extension of changes on a macro scale and a result of the 'backwash', 'spread' and 'spill-over effects' of national development (Myrdal, 1967, 1970, 1971). Finally, and from the point of view of the discipline, we can underscore the non-economic sequences of innovation and draw lessons from the failure or success in our case-studies; lessons which may, in turn, be of value to those concerned with planning and executing development programmes for the basic needs of rural and tribal societies. The need to incorporate anthropologists and sociologists when designing rural development programmes is generally recognized (Béteille, 1974; Dalton, 1971; Firth, 1970; Hamnett, 1970; Hunter and Bottrall, 1974; Hunter *et al.*, 1976; Joshi, 1975; Kuper, 1974; Lele, 1975; Myrdal, 1967, 1970, 1971; Oxaal *et al.*, 1975; Pitt, 1976; Srinivas, 1974).

A recent article on the Tribal Areas concluded that 'the customs of the Frontier have scarcely changed since the British arrived in the 1840s' (Moynahan, 1976: 57). I would have tended to agree with this assessment until 1974 but, as the last chapter and the present one argue, the customs of the Frontier are already changing and one can predict further changes in society. Why 1974 and not earlier, or indeed later, is the interesting question. There were various factors working towards this particular period, not least a group of remarkable figures involved in tribal affairs and policy and determined to open up hitherto closed areas. Tribal emigration abroad and contact with the rest of the country were bringing rapid changes in traditional thinking. It was as if the tribesmen had decided finally to lift the curtain that hung over the Tribal Areas and come to terms with the modern world.

I The Mohmand road as a factor of encapsulation

The Mohmand road literally and metaphorically symbolized the penetration of the Agency after 1973. It may be recalled that the last attempts to build a road through the Gandab and up the Nahakki Pass triggered off the 1933 and 1935 campaigns. Under a leader called 'Progress in the Tribal Areas' discussing the fundamental reason for the Mohmand campaign *The Civil and Military Gazette* (23 August 1935) argued that 'launching of road construction projects side by side with plans for the economic development of the country through which the proposed roads passed will give a new orientation to the thoughts of tribesmen of the reasons underlying the road programmes'. But the tribesmen rejected the road totally. The contrast in 1974 was remarkable. Haji Hassan perhaps best summed up local sentiment and exegesis for the change of heart: 'The road was given by the grace of the *kalima* as we are all Muslims. Otherwise we would have never allowed it.'

In late October 1973 the Nahakki Pass, for the first time in history, was crossed by Pakistani officials entering into the Kamali Halimzai area and led by the Political Agent, Mohmands. Until then neither the Pakistan flag nor an officer had been seen north of the Nahakki. I accompanied the Political Agent and the Inspector-General, Frontier Corps, on their first ceremonial drive between Nahakki and Nawagai on 11 January 1974. The latter drove us himself in a jeep through dry stream beds and over flat plains and fields along a rough alignment that was later to become the actual road (Map 2). We were constantly stopped by armed Halimzai and Safi groups who pressed us for tea or *dodai*. As no roads had existed before no vehicle had ever been seen. The joining of the Nahakki road with Nawagai twenty-four miles to the north was accomplished between 1974 and 1975 without a single shot being fired. Buses almost literally followed our first trip to Nawagai and within weeks half a dozen passenger buses were plying the rough route between Lakaro and Mian Mandi.

The two most important and visible signs of penetration that accompanied the road were the Mohmand Rifles and poles for electricity. Together they signified penetration. The combined impact was formidable. Settlements, at least near the road, were enjoying the marvels of electricity for the first time in history. Electricity was still new enough for its properties not to be fully understood. At least two cases of *khassadars* who, bored by their duties, climbed the poles to talk to each other and were electrocuted were reported. The Ekka Ghund–Mian Mandi road was further widened and improved and by 1976 Mian Mandi had become an important commercial and transport centre for the Agency (Chapter 9). Almost sixty buses plied to and from Peshawar daily. Before 1974, perhaps one lorry made this journey daily.

Mohmand roads were allocated a sum of eighteen million rupees in 1974-5, the first year of penetration. What impact did the road, and in its wake the development activities, have on Shati Khel? For one most of the Shati settlements managed to obtain an electricity supply except, of course, Ranra Khel. Many of the Malok and even Musa took up employment either as contractors or manual labourers on the roads, or on schemes like the Ghalanay headquarters which I shall discuss in the next section. Massive sums of money were being poured into road development. Employment was now available almost on the door-step. It heralded social change that would have far-reaching ramifications for lineage politics and organization. The road was truly symbolizing the end of an era and the beginning of a new one (Ahmed, 1977a: 57-60).

In terms of TAM politics it is significant to point out, although not difficult to explain why, the British who attempted to build a road in the Mohmand Gandab valley in the 1930s were supported by certain Maliks but opposed by the clans and *kashar* generally and the religious groups specifically. The British were using the road primarily for purposes of military strategy and the Maliks were playing into their hands in return for increased allowances and other patronage. In the 1970s the position was reversed. The religious groups, the occupational groups and the *kashars* welcomed the road and the employment it brought with it, providing them with avenues of economic mobility. The disturbance of the status quo as symbolized by the developmental activity associated with the road revealed a covert opposition to change by the established Maliks. The Maliks saw in such activities a threat to their hegemony because of the new opportunities they presented. However, some Maliks could do little more than hoist black flags on their towers for the first few weeks as a sign of disapproval. In terms of Shati economic and political structure the results were almost immediately apparent as junior lineages like the Malok, occupational groups like Aziz Ingar and affiliated lineages like the Ganjian, pooled their resources to buy passenger buses and trucks and became fully involved and committed to the new road and the developmental activities it symbolized.

The Malok, Haji Hassan (Ganjian) and Aziz Ingar own five passenger buses between them (Aziz and Hassan own two each). Haji Abbas, of a junior Musa patrilineage, has also bought a bus. One truck is owned by Saz (Musa) and two others by Malok. Shahzada, the Malok and Abdullah Sher (Ganjian) own cars in Shati Khel. In addition, Mian Jalil owns a Bedford wagon which he uses for passenger service and a Chevrolet car bought a few years ago. The only Bela bus belongs to Mehr Gul of the junior Sabah lineage; it was bought last year mainly on the earnings of the son who remits as much as Rs. 2,000 a month from his earnings in Saudi Arabia as a labourer.

Buses and trucks, usually second-hand and which may cost between Rs. 80,000 and 100,000, have been acquired in the last two to three years and registered in Peshawar. In almost all cases profits have yet to start coming in. The driver is usually paid Rs. 25 daily and is accompanied by two cleaners, sons or nephews of the owner. Fares are Rs. 3 to Peshawar and Rs. 2 to Shabkadar from Mian Mandi. The bus returns by dusk to Shati Khel. Haji Abbas, Shahzada's cousin, who owns bus no. PRA 2932, explained the changing attitudes: 'We were mountain animals before, now we are human beings. Now we use tractors instead of the *qulba*, now we talk of trade in the *hujra* and not feuds.' Shahzada disagreed and dismissed the investment of energy and wealth in trade and transport as futile: 'All the buses and trucks are in a mess. All owners are in heavy debt and no profits will be made. They will all be ruined.' In terms of my thesis, it is important to point out that almost all the vehicles are a result of the economic opportunities and activity of the last few years. The notable exception is Shahzada. His cars like his present Dodge Dart and indeed his first car, bought in the late 1940s and the first in the Gandab, are a result of political allowances.

There are almost eighty buses and trucks bought and owned in the last two to three years by Safis alone, who are now fully committed to the idea of keeping the road open. For example when an abortive attempt at a hold-up was made by a local gang in the Safi area, the clans unanimously pressed the authorities for firm action after exposing the culprits. The gang was fined Rs. 15,000 and put into the Ekka Ghund lock-up. The emerging class of bus owners and the increasing number of ordinary daily passengers had no wish to allow the passage of the road to be obstructed. The social implications of the road as a factor of change and its impact on tribal structure and lineage organization involving the emergence of new groups will be discussed at the end of the chapter.

II Economic development: penetration and emigration

This section discusses briefly the two sources of income recently opened to the Mohmand, namely government schemes (Ahmed, 1977a;

Khan, G. J., 1972) and emigration; it outlines their scale and makes a prognosis of their effect on social structure.

(a) *Development schemes*

An examination of the Monthly Progress Reports, Mohmand Agency, prepared by the Executive Engineer's office over the last few years for roads and buildings illustrated the pattern of penetration into the Agency after 1974-5. The entire emphasis shifted after 1974 from the Michni and Tarakzai areas towards first the Halimzai and later the Safi areas. The only previous notable development schemes and those furthest inside the Agency were implemented during the mid-1960s. The veterinary hospital and school at Kassai, the school and hospital at Shati and the water tank and Community Centre at Yusuf Khel date from this period. So does the Michni rest house near Bela and the Community Centre at Ekka Ghund, both buildings used by the Political Agent. A result of accepting the Shati school was the eight-bedded hospital constructed by government in Shati Khel in the mid-1960s. Three acres of land, which belonged to the Ranra but lay in the possession of the Musa, were sold by Shahzada to government. In a generous gesture Shahzada shared the non-technical staff of four sweepers and guards with the Ranra.

In 1974 government acquired 100 acres of land at Ghalanay at the official rate fixed for the entire Agency, Rs. 8,000 per acre. The purchase was made from and divided almost equally by the three sub-clans of the Halimzai, Wali Beg, Hamza Khel and Kadai. Schemes worth ten million rupees including the building of the Political Agent's office and residence and various other departmental offices, schools and hospitals were planned. In all, 175 separate construction units were to be built in 1976. About fifty contractors from the Wali Beg, Kadai and Hamza, who mostly sublet to Tarakzai, were involved. Almost half of the fifty were Wali Beg in accordance with tribal tradition as the headquarters and Ghalanay were in their area.

The Executive Engineer, Buildings and Roads, Mohmand Agency, explained why they never once had labour problems. Work was divided along the basis of sectional and sub-sectional lines of the clan and each contractor was then responsible for the behaviour of his men. Of the total contract 6½ per cent called 'the tribal commission', was distributed among those members of the clan not directly involved in the building through the Political Agent in accordance with the tradition in the

Tribal Areas. The Public Health Engineering Department completed a scheme to supply 5,000 gallons of water from only 5 yards below ground at a point between Ghalanay and Yusuf Khel by 1975. In the same year successful boring of tube-wells was completed in Lakaro in the Safi area as were three of the four sanctioned Basic Health Units.

The glass-making industry, located north of Ghalanay and owned by the Federally Administered Tribal Areas Development Corporation, began operation in 1976. Apart from the economic activity it generated through its buildings on three acres and purchase of land, it employs about 140 people at any given time of whom forty are unskilled and local labour. Local sub-sections also make money from the venture by allowing factory trucks to collect sand for the industry at the rate of Rs. 8 per truck.

The Mohmand Rifles, raised in October 1973, also bought 20 acres for their headquarters at Yusuf Khel. The Yusuf Khel Community Centre temporarily acts as the Officers' Mess. Employment was given to Mohmands interested in joining the Scouts, although of the Mohmand component some 75 per cent were Tarakzai and the Halimzai accounted for only 5 per cent. The latter were still shy of joining government employment and giving up their freedom. Within a year the Mohmand Rifles had grown to a full Scouts Wing Corps. The Mohmand Rifles generated local income by purchases of food supplies, etc., from the Mandi.[1]

Abruptly the Halimzai found themselves flooded with sources of money and contracts which in most cases they subcontracted to the more experienced Tarakzais. The unskilled manual labourer, who according to tradition in the Tribal Areas had to be from the local clan, the Halimzai, was being paid Rs. 8 a day. Skilled labourers like carpenters and masons, brought mainly from Peshawar, earned Rs. 30 a day. Even the donkey owner hired his donkeys for Rs. 5 per day to the contractor to bring water from the Persian wells, 45 feet deep, in Ghalanay. Many Halimzai *kors* now had one or two male members working as labourers daily. Large amounts of money were generated over the year and as we see in the cases of Haji Hassan and the Malok reinvested in buses and trucks.

As Political Agent of the Orakzai Agency I was privileged to help select the location of the future Agency headquarters of the Orakzai Agency, in the Feroz Khel area opposite Kalaya in late 1976, purchase some 100 acres of land and supervise its layout and design. The Governor formally laid the foundation-stone of the future Agency headquarters and the area found itself 'opened' (*Pakistan Times, Khyber Mail, Mashriq*, 31 December 1976). In March I performed the opening ceremony of the first bank in the Orakzai Agency at Kadda in Tirah (*Jihad, Mashriq*, 12 March 1977). Economic forces represented by almost every government department such as at Ghalanay were now released in the interior of the Agency.

I mention the above as examples of the vast scale of the penetration and the equally vast response and involvement of the tribesmen to illustrate the theme of this chapter. For once in their history tribal people were finding easy employment literally within walking distance from their homes. The spread-effects on social structure from the development schemes and economic nodal centres cannot be under-estimated. Similarly, the backwash effects of migration, capital movement and trade have a circular and cumulative causation and process which affects structure. Rural Works Programme officials explain the differences in attitudes in 1973 and 1976: 'Then we begged them to take schemes. Now they chase us for schemes. Now there is less enmity. People want to be better off.' The demonstration effects of cousins living in cement houses, owning cars and, in the Michni area, even air-conditioners (in 1977) are a powerful factor in bringing about changed attitudes. Tractors are now a regular sight on the Agency road and in its fields (mostly Fiats, hired at Rs. 30 per hour less the expense of petrol and driver).

The Annual Development Programme for 1977-8 for the Mohmand Agency comes to 10.9 million rupees. There is a great deal of money circulating in TAM resulting in local inflation and spiralling of prices. For example in 1970 the price of land was between Rs. 1,000 and 2,000 per acre in TAM, in 1974 it was Rs. 6,000 per acre; after the construction of the Agency headquarters started at Ghalanay it rose to between Rs. 8,000 and 10,000 per acre (although officially fixed at Rs. 8,000 per acre). By 1977 prices of land were as high as Rs. 20,000 per acre in certain areas of Shati Khel.[2] The inflation of prices was reflected at every level of society. The price of a dozen eggs in early 1974 was Rs. 1.20, by the middle of 1974 it was Rs. 3 and by 1976 prices were roughly those of Peshawar and a dozen eggs cost Rs. 6. A chicken which cost Rs. 5 in 1974 cost almost Rs. 20 by 1976. Similarly an individual who charged Rs. 4 a day to work on the roads in 1974 was charging double that by 1976.

The situation in SAM remains comparatively static. If these new sources of income were magically removed from TAM, then it would be immediately apparent that the income and expenditure budgets would balance better in SAM than in TAM (Chapter 9). As the situation stands, incomes in many cases may well be higher than expenditure in TAM. An important point I wish to make which differentiates the TAM situation from other tribal groups in similar situations is that development activity has brought no influx of newcomers or outsiders or dominant business and trading groups (Bailey, 1960, 1970, 1973; Caplan, L., 1970; Fürer-Haimendorf, 1977; Yorke, 1974). The monopoly remains entirely with the local section or clan.

(b) *Emigration*

Simultaneous to the sources of income generated by the development activities in the Tribal Areas by government, there was another almost equally important factor at work: employment, largely as manual labour, in the Arab States. The two universal features of the post-war Afro-Asian situation in the most remote societies observed by anthropologists returning to their pre-war fields of study are that men have entered into the external labour market in mass numbers largely to acquire consumer goods (Firth, 1959: 11), and the population explosion (ibid.: 26). The first feature is discussed below and the second will be apparent no doubt when we have comparative and accurate population statistics for the Tribal Areas.

Among the most serious factors affecting tribal population, demography, social structure and political balance are the numerous cases of migration. This process is by no means restricted to tribal groups in the Tribal Areas of Pakistan. It is affecting tribal groups elsewhere, such as the Sherpas in Tibet who are shifting to urban centres and places where manual labour pays high rewards, and are dropping traditions, however martial, for business activities (Fürer-Haimendorf, 1976). During my one-year tenure in the Orakzai Agency I could count six members of my personal staff who left for employment in the Gulf States, including two drivers and two clerks. All six were tribesmen.[3] A similar process is working among the Mohmand. By the time I was doing field-work it was the ambition of almost every young man, whatever his educational or lineage background, to migrate to the Gulf States and be able to return home fabulously rich. Mature, dedicated, and among the Mohmand professionally limited teachers, like Shamshur Rahman, requested me to use my influence to obtain a visa[4] for the Arab States. So did

Feroz who was fed up with teaching at Shati Khel. Although both belonged to senior lineages they were prepared to perform manual

TABLE 18 People working abroad from TAM/SAM
(i) People working abroad from Shati Khel

age	lineage group	date left	money remitted (in Rs.) (1974–7)
30	Musa	2-1-1974	17,000
25	Musa	6-1-1974	10,000
25	Musa	5-3-1976	7,000
30	Musa	3-9-1976	4,300

labour rather than carry on in their present, and what they felt to be dead-end, occupations. Life in the Arab states was pictured as a mixture of Shangri-La and El Dorado which, of course, it is not. From all accounts manual labour is performed under the most severe and gruelling physical conditions. Because of this outflow, adult labour is increasingly difficult to locate in the Tribal Areas and boys between twelve and fourteen are often to be seen working on the roads or buildings.

I made a list of those who have recently left for the Arab States from my field-work areas (reproduced as Table 18). Most of these men are between the ages of twenty-five and thirty and some have sent back sums that may average up to Rs. 2,000 a month per person besides cloth, watches, radios, etc. The actual income from the Gulf States is a secret affair. I was told of examples of youngsters putting away a little bit for themselves by revealing a smaller figure than the actual one for earnings to their elders.

Almost every Mohmand has gone as an unskilled worker to perform manual labour except for Bela *qasabgars* who have a profession to offer. The ten TAM and SAM men are working in either Arabia or the Gulf States except for Haji Gul who went to Iran. Only four people from Shati Khel have left for employment abroad and it is not surprising that they all belong to the dominant Musa lineage. It is not surprising because visas for employment abroad are regulated by the administration and form yet another source of patronage reserved for favoured groups.

Of the six from Bela who have gone abroad four represent non-Pukhtun, religious and occupational groups. Their mobility is perhaps explained by fewer atavistic ties with their geographical areas or less kin status to lose by accepting manual labour. The son of the Imam of

Bela, who traditionally commands respect in his own area equal to that of the Pukhtuns and more than that of the occupational groups, has

(ii) People working abroad from Bela Mohmandan

age	lineage group	date left	money remitted (in Rs.) (1976-7)
35	Kado	18-5-1976	12,000
50	barber	9-6-1976	8,500
32	Sabah	25-6-1976	10,000
28	religious group	15-8-1976	6,000
25	religious group	22-12-1976	-
25	carpenter	24-12-1976	-

also left as an unskilled manual labourer. He, like most others, paid out almost Rs. 4,000 in bribes, etc., for the visa. Only one Kado Khel has left from Bela. However, the Kado Khel in the Michni area of Kado Korona have been more active in seeking employment abroad. In the last three years, fourteen Kado Khel and one carpenter have gone abroad mainly to Libya from Kado Korona.

TABLE 19 People employed by government: TAM/SAM

Shati Khel			Bela Mohmandan	
Musa:	35	(22 khassadars)	Kado:	1
Ranra:	8		Madar:	3
Malok:	1		Sabah:	14
			Do:	5
			Jano:	5
			Zarif:	1
			religious groups:	2
			occupational groups:	2
Total:	44		Total:	33

Apart from Mohmands seeking employment abroad there are also numerous men employed in other parts of Pakistan mainly with military, para-military and police forces. Their wages are comparatively less spectacular and range between Rs. 250 to 350 a month of which they send back, on the average, between Rs. 80 to 100 after deducting monthly expenditures.

The importance of Musa as income-earners among the Shati Khel is apparent from the above figures. Let me qualify both the figures and the statement. While the Ranra and Malok are genuinely 'employed' outside the Agency at least twenty-two of the thirty-five Musa Khel are employed in the Agency as *khassadars*. Of the total thirty-five employed from the Musa Khel eight are employed from Shahzada's village: four *khassadars*, three teachers and one *chaukidar*. All eight are the sons and grandsons of Shahzada. The advantages of connections with the administration and the advantages of belonging to a dominant lineage in TAM are clearly demonstrated by the figures above.

It is not surprising that there is a strong correlation between the Sabah, the junior-most and poorest lineage seeking employment outside the village, and the Kado, the senior lineage staying at home on their lands. It is equally important that government gives no weight to the senior lineage, Kado, for employment or other patronage as it does to the Musa in Shati Khel for political reasons.

Considering the number of Kado Khel abroad from Kado Korona of Michni one would expect a high number employed in the various services such as police and military. The conclusion is obvious: Kado Khel will abandon their traditionally better social and economic positions and geographical areas only if it is worth their while economically as it is in the Arab Gulf States. None of the above are employed as *khassadars* as are many of the Shati Khel.

The cumulative effect of the income generated through employment in development schemes and remittances from abroad will have clear ramifications for social structure in the future. Although outside the scope of my thesis, I have hinted at the effect on the ideal Pukhtun model such income will have. The directions indicated are as varied as the factors involved are complex. Certain changes are predictable. Indubitably, there will be deviation from the prejudice against tradition- ally non-Pukhtun activity as there will be occupational heterogeneity. Junior lineages will emerge from the shadow of their politically more powerful kin, as the Malok in Shati Khel, and perhaps assert themselves. In time the *kashars* will be in a position to manipulate trade and business into openly and successfully challenging the political privileges of the Malik. Their primary demand of adult franchise, if granted, would sound the death-knell of the 'Maliki system'. None the less the picture is not so simple. In spite of the increase in employment opportunities and income I do not foresee a complete surrendering of *Pukhtunwali* by either senior or junior lineages. Perhaps there may be a rephrasing of its idiom or a reordering of its priorities. The advantages of retaining Pukhtunness and guarding unencapsulated status are too many for tribesmen to surrender them easily. By maintaining their discrete Tribal Areas category, TAM can continue to manipulate successfully the resources of the larger state to their advantage; the neglected fate of SAM is a constant reminder of encapsulation.

III The Bela Mohmandan Cooperative Society: lineage politics and development schemes

I shall examine the Bela Mohmandan Cooperative Society as an illustration of the single development or modern endeavour at economic planning in the village and attempt to analyse the causes of its failure. The principal example I have used for elucidating the problems of resolving lineage conflict with modern development projects has been chosen with deliberation as it presents a fine case in point of what I am arguing in the study, namely that *Pukhtunwali* survives encapsulation.[5]

As mentioned earlier Bela Mohmandan, although it is at one rather remote tip of Daudzai Thana, which has its headquarters at Nahakki village, is none the less administratively part of the Thana. Bela therefore formed part of the Daudzai Integrated Rural Development Programme.[6] Of the eighty-nine villages of the Thana eighteen are partly Mohmand villages. Bela Mohmandan was among the twenty-six villages selected in which to start cooperative societies between April 1973 and February 1974 (PARD, vol. 11, no. 2, 1974: 12).

The initial membership of ninety-four of the Bela Cooperative Society on 11 July 1973 reflected the general enthusiasm for the Society.[7] Hamesh Gul was elected as president and Shamshudin as secretary of the Society although for some reason the latter was and is constantly referred to as *manager saib* rather than *secretary saib*. Meetings were regularly held in the *hujra*, under the mulberry trees, after the Friday congregational prayers. Membership reached 126 and cumulative savings Rs. 2,185 by April 1974. Next month, as Registrar of the Cooperative Societies for the Province I visited the Bela Society to register it officially. Accompanying me was Dr Akhtar Hamid Khan, the former director of the Comilla Academy in Bangladesh and an international name in rural development. By June 1975 the Society reached its highest membership number of 136. The major needs of Bela were correctly assessed to be a protection wall or bund to break the impact of the waters of the Kabul river in full spate, and a ferry-boat to ensure communication with the Michni area when Bela was surrounded by water during the summer months. In early 1974 Rs. 64,000 were allocated for the protection wall and a ferry-boat 32 feet long, was completed which cost almost Rs. 5,000 (ibid.: 14).

During this time Bela participated in the Daudzai Project by sending managers and model-farmers for extension training in agriculture to Nahakki and the Academy at Peshawar for short periods. Such candidates were usually of the Kado and Madar Khel or their supporters. The protection wall was completed in late October 1974 and the existing ones partly repaired. The main bund is 540 feet long and the other small ones, almost parallel to it and downstream, are between 30 to 40 feet long (Map 6) and represent the only development work in the village in the last three decades. Perhaps the bunds were completed harmoniously because the threat of floods was a real and recurring danger to the village and also because the project committee represented the major and minor lineages of the village through its elders.

The Society loaned Rs. 13,255 for 270 bags of fertilizers to fifty-three members. The terms were easy. The loan was interest free if returned in three months but increased by 1 per cent every month after that. In 1974 another major problem of drinking water was hoped to be solved by installing a small lift pump by the river near the school. Except for an empty small room completed in early 1975 costing Rs. 5,000 nothing came of this project. Moreover enthusiasm for the Society began to wane as lineage conflict and high expectations frustrated the working of the Society. Junior lineages led by Hussain, representing the Jano Khel, and Amin, the Do Khel, felt the Society was far too much under the influence of Hamesh and Shamshudin, both representing the senior lineages of Bela. When demands for loans requested for non-agricultural purposes were turned down they assumed this to be part of the machinations of the senior lineages. By September 1975 membership had dropped to seventy and was still that number in December 1975 (PARD, 1975-6: Appendix 1). The total capital of the Society remained static for two years and in December 1975 was Rs. 3,063 of which Rs. 1,190 were capital shares and Rs. 1,873 savings. The two most active members of the Society, Shamshudin and Hamesh Gul, saved Rs. 100 each over two years of its existence.

I obtained a copy of the Cooperative Society's Register of Minutes and they revealed that the writing was clearly on the wall after August 1975. Before this date the average meeting attracted an average of thirty members. In any case business transactions such as savings were insignificant and members would contribute no more than a rupee or two as investment.

Rarely if ever did the Cooperative Inspector the 'friend, guide and philosopher' of the movement visit Bela Mohmandan. Apart from the obvious lineage conflicts involving four distinct groups, one of the causes of the failure of the Society was the high expectation, personal and impersonal, which is one of the major problems of Cooperative Societies in the Province (Ahmed, 1973a). Members expected their major village needs such as for a bridge, road and electricity to be solved by government overnight and through the Society, and when they realized that nothing was being done about it soon lost interest in the Society.

By December 1975 it was quite clear that the Bela Cooperative Society was a dying institution and during the first few months of 1976 when I was still doing my field-work no meetings of any kind were held. Membership had almost halved from the maximum average of 1974-5 and the total equity dropped by almost Rs. 1,000 by the end of 1975. Obviously something was seriously wrong with the concept of cooperation in Bela. At probably one of the first meetings of the year in May 1976, which I attended, only some twelve people turned up at the personal request of Shamshudin and contributed a total of Rs. 10 as savings. The meeting summed up the situation of the Society.

Conflict along lineage lines became sharp enough after August 1975 to provoke an open crisis in the affairs of the Society. Shamshudin was the driving force of the Society. He had staked his leadership on its success. Members who had borrowed over Rs. 13,000 for fertilizers from the Nahakki Centre had paid back Rs. 4,000 within the stipulated three months. Another Rs. 2,000 were also paid back after much personal persuasion by Shamshudin. That still left about Rs. 7,000 remaining and debtors simply refused to return the money they felt they had so easily obtained from government.[8] All the while the interest on the money was accumulating and Shamshudin was under intense pressure from the Nahakki Centre. His opponents from the other lineages seized the opportunity and mobilized village support against the Cooperative Society and declared that no loans were to be returned to it. In August 1975 Shamshudin could not convene a single meeting, emergency or ordinary. His sense of honour, rooted in his notions of *Pukhtunwali*, prompted him to pay as much as he could personally muster, about Rs. 4,000, of the outstanding loan to Nahakki from his own pocket.

In January 1976 he resigned from the Society publicly promising never to have anything to do with developmental activity in Bela again. He was bitter after the affair and felt he had been let down by Belawals: 'I am no longer a *mashar*. Do not consider me a *mashar*. Do not come to me with your problems.'

Matters came to a head at a meeting that sounded the death-knell of the Society and brought together the complex lineage politics of the village. Dawai Khan and Amin Khan had mobilized the *kashar* of the Sabah Khel. Amin also mobilized his Do Khel and backed by Hussain Khan prepared to have a showdown with the *mashars* running the Cooperative Society. They argued that Hamesh Gul (Madar Khel) was the president and Shamshudin (Kado Khel) the secretary but that they, the *kashar* and junior lineages, were unrepresented. The first crisis came in a meeting after Friday prayers and in the *hujra* when Morcha Khel, the carpenter, applied for an interest-free loan of Rs. 1,600 to allow his son Sabz Ali to go to Libya. The request was passed by the members and it was agreed that Shamshudin would travel to Nahakki the next day to withdraw the money from the Cooperative Bank for Morcha Khel. At this stage Amin arrived with his group and challenged the proceedings. He threatened to report in writing what he considered an illegal matter to the authorities and also dropped open hints of other illegal financial transactions in the activities of the Society. A serious rift developed and after much argument Morcha Khel's request was reviewed and rejected. The *kashars* had won the day. Morcha Khel then borrowed the money he needed from a Dadu Khel group in the neighbouring village at the rate of 140 per cent interest for six months.

A short time before this Dawai and Amin, with some other *kashars*, had precipitated another crisis that had escalated beyond the sectional level of the lineage. The *mashars* of Bela had decided to loan their ferry-boat, recently constructed by the Bela Cooperative Society, as a gesture of good-will to the Zarif Khel, a few hundred yards down the north-western channel, until the Zarif Khel arranged for their own boat. Dawai and Amin gathered the Bela *kashars* including men from Kado, Madar and Sabah Khel and violated the promise by bringing the Bela ferry-boat back to the village at night. The Kado Khel were particularly annoyed with Haji Gul, the barber, who had helped tow the boat back from the Zarif Khel: 'He is not a Pukhtun and has no right to interfere in the affairs of the Pukhtuns. If we fight among ourselves that is our look out. He is a *qasabgar* and should stick to his own business.'

The honour of the Bela *mashars* was clearly violated. At this point Hussain Khan changed sides and openly supported Amin. Hamesh Gul and Majeed also assumed a neutral posture in the affair. Shamshudin was as much politically isolated as he was personally disgusted and once again washed his hands of the thankless job of village leadership.

The action almost triggered off a sectional clash as the Zarif Khel gathered some fifty men with guns from the Agency and took the boat back by force during the day. Fearing an armed clash for which they would be held responsible, Hussain Khan and Amin backed down and asked for *nanawatee* of the Zarif Khel. By now the matter was beyond their control as it had become a *qam khabara* (common tribal affair). The *mashars* and *kashars* of Bela turned to Shamshudin for advice. After some persuasion Shamshudin agreed and led the *mashars* of Bela to the Nahakki police station. The officer in charge of the police station visited Bela and persuaded the Zarif Khel to return the boat. He also decided that as the Belawals had promised the boat to Zarif Khel they should honour their agreement by allowing them to use the boat for a month until their own was made. The *hujra* conversation agreed that had people listened to Shamshudin in the first place and abided by their agreement with the Zarif Khel the situation would not have come to this pass. None the less, as we saw from the earlier example, Amin Khan was not only to involve himself precipitously once again in village affairs but be instrumental in finally snuffing out the cooperative spirit in Bela. The above two crises involving as they did lineage politics and leadership at various levels killed the Bela Cooperative Society.

Can any general principles be adduced from the failure of the Cooperative Society? On the surface lineage and intergenerational rivalry, the traditional bases of village rivalry, were the causal factors for its failure. However, in terms of my model the Bela Society and its failure brings into relief the dilemmas and problems arising out of SAM's encapsulated situation and raises certain interesting points. The connection with the outside world, however tenuous and ephemeral, indicated SAM's desire to forge links with it. SAM became a recipient of external forces representing change which it initially welcomed. By forming a Society SAM became part of a vast network of such small-scale organizations in the Province (Ahmed, 1973a). In a sense it acknowledged its encapsulation. None the less a discernible ambivalence marks the first tentative dealings with the larger state. For instance the refusal to pay back loans typifies the concept of external as distinct from internal systems in the eyes of SAM. Such liberties may be taken from the external as it is remote and its grasp incomplete. Similarly, the visits to Nahakki and Peshawar monopolized by identifiable groups created resentment against the Society. The Society was seen by members of the community as a base for access to officials and outside bodies manipulated by certain groups for their own advantage. The inherent structural constraints of traditional lineage politics aborted the experiments with development projects. In a sense SAM behaviour lived up to the ideal Pukhtun model and supported my thesis. Considerations of agnatic competition overrode those of mutual economic benefit.

My concluding remarks in this chapter can only be in the form of a prognosis. For the first time large sums of money and numerous sources of employment have suddenly appeared in the midst of the Tribal Areas and with these have come a spread of ideas that herald a change in traditional Pukhto values. In conversations with Pukhtuns in the most remote parts of the Tribal Areas, whether in Waziristan or Tirah, I have heard the new definition of Pukhto: 'nowadays Pukhto means money', and Pukhtuns: 'nowadays we are traders.' In terms of traditional Pukhto values trade or craft, that is *qasab*, are no longer considered socially inferior occupations. A certain failure to transmit successfully social values to the younger generation is already developing which the older generation recognizes. Many youths tend to reject the behaviour patterns of elders which they see as deviating from the ideal and vice versa. In certain cases there is a total breakdown of dialogue between father and son as for example between Shahzada and Amirzada in Shati Khel and Habibur Rahman and his sons in Kado Korona. In some cases it is a straightforward generational gap reinforcing a cultural gap; the young may prefer to be merry and witness the talents of dancing girls at marriages while their elders may wish to hear recitations from the Holy Koran by the Mullahas as in the above case-studies.

The scope of the changes in society and its organization are beyond the charter of my study but the scale and speed with which this will happen is not difficult to envisage.

I shall end this chapter by quoting verbatim similar prognosis but expressed by Akbar Jan, the son of Malik Lakhkar, who symbolizes future TAM and is a lad highly conscious of the finer virtues of *Pukhtun-wali*, such as hospitality, but disgusted with the implications of its bloody interpretation. His rejection of what he sees as 'barbaric' is of significance for the future in terms of values and norms in society and its capacity to transmit them to succeeding generations. In terms of my thesis his sentiments forecast changes in attitudes to the traditional Pukhtun model which would threaten its validity as an ideal form for a society to approximate, emulate or preserve; in short a drastic altera- tion of *Pukhtunwali* as it is understood in TAM in the framework of penetration and the modernization processes now at work:

> People are all backward and there should be education. In this modern time it is ridiculous to carry guns with you all the time. And building forts against each other. Enmities between people should be completely finished. People should be protected by the law, as no poor or powerless man can survive here. This is why all of Pakistan is filled with Mohmands, as all the weak people are driven out. You have always to guard your house or anybody will take it over. This is real barbarism. This state must end. We want peace. We cannot spend our lives killing each other.

As a concluding remark and at the risk of over-simplifying perhaps I can repeat the gist of my thesis point made at the end of the last chapter: up to the middle of the 1970s the Pukhtun ideal-type model has stood the test of time in spite of exposure to various factors of change, especially so in TAM. Despite the severe constraints of encapsu- lation SAM also approximates to the ideal in its behavioural and organiza- tional patterns (especially where the laws of the state are not explicitly challenged such as in marriage patterns, *parda*, etc.). However, the magnitude of penetration and the multiplicity of its schemes forecast change. Until today the world has belonged to Malik Lakhkar but tomorrow it will belong to Akbar Jan, and we have heard his words above. It is difficult to escape the conclusion that certain structural changes may be expected in the coming years, particularly if the present pace of penetration is maintained.

12 Conclusion

In concluding, I wish to draw in the major strands of the argument I have made in the study and point out its salient features as I understand them in order to substantiate my thesis and its related problems. The major concern of the study has been to build an ideal-type model of *Pukhtunwali*, derived from literary, storiological, archival (Pukhtun and non-Pukhtun) but largely field-work data from TAM and SAM. The ideal-type model allows us to examine how the actor perceives social reality and to measure normative and deviant behaviour. It is a device which enables both the social actor and the social analyst to perceive value commensurability and value disjunction; the focus of *Pukhtunwali* remains on *tarboorwali* and *tor*. The high degree of similarity between the ideological model and the immediate model has been illustrated through case-studies. By an exercise in the taxonomy of Pukhtun social organization and a diachronic approach in analysis of data, I have attempted to establish that *Pukhtunwali* approximates to its purest form when tribal groups live outside larger state systems and in low-production geographical zones. I have argued that TAM approximates in the main to the ideal-type.

Having suggested that *Pukhtunwali* forms the central skeleton around which Pukhtun social organization and behaviour are fleshed, I have postulated a thesis: simply put, *Pukhtunwali* approximating to the ideal survives among TAM. I have attempted to defend my thesis by illustrating that *Pukhtunwali* can survive, as in SAM, living within a larger state system. However, though SAM still speak of and often do Pukhto, accommodation and even compromise enforced by the constraints of their situation are clearly apparent both in organization and behaviour. My thesis is thus partly substantiated but partly disproved. Finally, I have suggested that exogenous factors such as numerous development schemes representing penetration by the larger state have been introduced in TAM areas and as a result fundamental changes in social structure and behaviour may be expected in the coming decades.

The ethnographic present generally covers a period from the summer of 1974 and lasts into the summer of 1977 but more specifically it relates to my field-work conducted between August 1975 and August 1976. However, the analysis of TAM and SAM is diachronic. The study implies that a particular social formation is no more than a cross-section of a larger diachronic system, and synchronic models are deducible from the properties of diachronic models, appearing as the various stages in a multilineal system of social trajectories. Diachronic temporal and spatial analyses are combined to produce a picture of social reality as an on-going system and explain the causal factors responsible for its central features. For instance I have attempted to show how the mobility of tribal groups, expressed in the *dwa-kora* system and the cyclical and intergenerational movements of groups from the Tribal to the Settled Areas and vice versa, has implications for the spread of ideas generally and the continuance of *tarboorwali* specifically.

In order to explain my theoretical and methodological framework I have attempted to draw a taxonomy of Pukhtun society, an exercise begun in earlier works (Ahmed, 1976, 1977a) which lends itself to the logical formation of binary and opposed Pukhtun models with far-reaching ramifications: *nang* or Mohmand model, explained in this study (and supplemented by General Staff, 1926; Hamid, n.d.; Merk, 1898; Mohmand, 1966) and *qalang* based on Swat data (Ahmad, M. T., 1962; Ahmed, 1976; Barth, 1959, 1970, 1972; Hay, 1934; Miangul, 1962).

The Mohmand are a *nang* tribe and four interconnected points that I have made in the study in relation to my thesis, which broadly define the parameters of the *nang* system, need to be emphasized. Firstly, the ideal world revolves around the Pukhtun male. He is defined by his patrilineage and his belief in and enacting of *Pukhtunwali* and in turn the two are symbolized by the gun he carries. The gun relates directly to his two major perceptions of *Pukhtunwali*, to *tarboorwali*, competition with the Father's Brother's Son, and to *tor*, as the case-studies illustrate in Chapter 7; members of the group compromising on *tarboorwali* or *tor* are seen to be deviating from Pukhto behaviour and subject to severe social criticism and ostracism. The Pukhtun ideal world is conceptualized as a hierarchy of religious and occupational groups that are organic to society but function to serve the Pukhtun's needs. The population is almost entirely Pukhtun interspersed with families belonging to religious and occupational groups to assist in social functions such as the *rites de passage* and economic functions to support agricultural life (Chapters 6, 8 and 9).

A certain amount of 'mystification' of 'Pukhtunness' conceals the possible contradictions within society between Pukhtun groups legitimizing hegemony with reference to the tribal charter and non-Pukhtun groups who do not find themselves on it. However, I have emphasized the significant point that in the *nang* areas where I conducted my fieldwork there are no landlords and tenants, no masters and slaves, no rulers and ruled. A certain hierarchy and inequality exist in society between men and women, senior and junior lineages and Pukhtun and non-Pukhtun, but they are not based on deterministic economic factors or ritual and commensal ones. Whether Pukhtun or not, every male is the independent head of his household which is the effective unit of economic consumption and distribution functions. Whether he is Malik or not is less important than the fact that he conceives of himself as such in terms of relative status; 'I am the Malik' is the answer that the interviewer will elicit from any household head. The proliferation of official and unofficial Maliks precludes the creation of an elite Malik class substantially superior in economic and political power to other members of their clan. Indeed, it would be difficult to conceive of permanent political domination when the major source of political power, economic resources based on land, is so severely limited and so equally divided (Chapter 9). As we know Shahzada, the most important political figure in Shati Khel and representing the dominant senior Musa lineage, owns some 7 acres of land mainly in Shati Khel and his only other source of income depends on uncertain political allowances from the administration. Similarly, Shamshudin in Bela Mohmandan, representing the senior Kado lineage, owns about 6½ acres of land and has no other source of income. Both Shahzada and Shamshudin have to live up to the Pukhto ideal as imposed on and by themselves, for it is implicit in their lineage position, and continue to maintain a level of hospitality beyond their means.

Second, the pursuit of political power dominates other forms of activity. Politics confers power, prestige and status and is largely limited to agnatic male cousins. Agnatic rivalry may be analysed as a zero-sum situation in which one cousin's gain is another's loss within the lineage where the scarce commodity and source of conflict are personal honour and political status (Barth, 1959). Part of my thesis attempted to illustrate how agnatic rivalry helps to maintain the delicate balance between democracy and stable societal structure on the one hand and emerging despotic leadership and anarchic political conditions on the other. Land or villages, such as Atta, Malok and Ranra in Shati

Khel, are captured as a symbol of prestige and often left deliberately uncultivated to drive home the point, as I have shown in Chapter 7 to substantiate my thesis. There is thus a direct correlation between social activity approximating to ideal-type behaviour and senior Pukhtun lineages in the tribal groups. In contrast, occupational groups at the bottom of the political ladder, such as the carpenters of Bela, theoretically excluded from political activity, not only own more average land per household than the Pukhtuns but also supplement their income by other economic activities related to their trades. In Shati Khel, Aziz the blacksmith is one of the few owners of transport buses, which give him an income far higher than the average Pukhtun's of even the senior lineages. Such groups, like junior Pukhtun lineages, tend to accord less importance to traditional Pukhtun activity, for example hospitality (Chapter 9). Not surprisingly, the weighted average income and expenditure per consumption unit of households reveals a clear correlation: the declining economic position of those senior lineages who, while refusing to indulge in traditionally non-Pukhtun activity like trade, still maintain costly features of the Code such as hospitality, and the emerging position of junior lineages and non-Pukhtun groups who have abandoned such normative practices. The argument has theoretical implications, for clearly political not economic domination is the key factor in understanding the motivating principles that explain behaviour and organization in this tribal society.

Third, I have argued that the operative lineage is defined by the tribal sub-section, usually involving a genealogical depth of three or four ascendants and agnatic lineage within which groups operate and individuals make their major political and social choices such as agnatic rivalry and marriage. The sub-section in its social functions and definition of boundaries is not unlike the 'sub-caste' determining and limiting the effective 'kindred of cooperation' rather than the caste in Indian society (Mayer, A. C., 1970). The important theoretical point is that among the Mohmands it is not the tribe or clan but the sub-section that is the operative lineage.

Fourth, Mohmand society defines itself self-consciously as Islamic and I have examined the existing sociological symbols of religion and their significance in daily social life in Chapter 4 and in a discussion of religious groups and their role in Pukhtun society in Chapter 6. I have argued that just as there is no emergence of a 'chiefly' model among the Mohmands so there is no 'saintly' model or class.

My study attempts to demonstrate how and why a Pukhtun ideal-type model came into being and successfully perpetuated itself over history and that tribal groups in the 1970s can be empirically shown to approximate to the model in their organization and behaviour. Until the late 1940s both my field-work groups, as I have tried to illustrate through case-studies, approximated largely to their own concept of the *Pukhtunwali* model. The two field-work areas, TAM and SAM, were not chosen as two opposing models such as *gumsa-gumlao* (Leach, 1977) but to illustrate the various observable deviances in SAM after encapsulation in 1951. The creation of the Mohmand Agency in 1951 provides a base-line between an encapsulated Bela Mohmandan and a confirmation of the unencapsulated condition of Shati Khel. The field-work situation provides almost laboratory conditions allowing me to test my thesis that *Pukhtunwali* can survive in encapsulated systems. Through various forms of subversion and adaptation of the formal laws of the land, the tribal groups of Bela Mohmandan attempt to minimize their compromise of Pukhto. As case-studies show, murders committed to uphold the two inviolable laws of *Pukhtunwali, tarboorwali* and *tor*, are tacitly accepted by society as having occurred in the Agency so as not to involve the legal procedures of the government. *Tarboorwali* may be translated from actual shooting, as in TAM, to a test of strength without recourse to arms in a village situation, such as the involvement of lineage politics in the Bela Cooperative Society (Chapter 11), or as in cases cited in Chapter 5. My thesis is thus partly sustained. However, it is difficult to escape the conclusion that after three decades of encapsulation ideal Pukhtun behaviour is no longer the only social model. Although the senior lineages like Kado may still uphold hospitality resulting in economic loss, junior lineages while continuing to use the idiom of Pukhto are empirically abandoning it for the accumulation of wealth and land. I have presented evidence of empirically observed cases of deviance in SAM from what is cognitive ideal behaviour in cases regarding inheritance of land by women and their living alone (Chapter 9). However, the difference between TAM and SAM may be more of degree than of kind. In spite of encapsulation SAM can still reflect Pukhto ideal concepts in behaviour: for instance, the only cases of patricide and fratricide in both areas took place in SAM as a result of *tor* and *tarboorwali* respectively. SAM, like TAM, upholding the ideal of *parda* (as related to the concept of *tor*) still refuse to allow a girls' primary school in the village.

Finally, the vast economic development activities that began in 1974 onwards in the Tribal Areas (Ahmed, 1977a) will eventually result in a form of encapsulation of hitherto unencapsulated groups but along a different conceptual route, that of physical penetration. The method and tactics are conciliatory and the symbols of penetration are beneficial and economic: the road followed by electricity, schools and health units. The encapsulation that will ultimately develop from the penetration in the 1970s of the Tribal Areas is not to be seen as a situation where exploiters from different ethnic or economic backgrounds dominate and exploit local groups. As I have shown, the administrators are largely tribesmen and often enlisted from local sections. In a sense these new opportunities have reordered the role of the Malik, the only symbol of exploitation in the Tribal Areas, and his position as that of a broker between his section and government and may soon make him redundant. What long-term effects the development activities will have through the spread of ideas and rapidly changing economic situations on Pukhto values and on Pukhtun social organization is a subject beyond the scope of this thesis. TAM junior lineages and occupational groups have seized the initiative by accepting non-traditional Pukhtun occupations such as manual labour and building contracts as I have shown in Chapters 9, 10 and 11. Nevertheless, as I have illustrated, there are still TAM and SAM groups whose actual observed behaviour through frequency patterns approximates in large measure to ideal Pukhtun behaviour. Whether these will survive the social and economic changes that have been set in motion is difficult to predict and stop short of my thesis charter.

I cannot claim to be entirely value-free in my observations of tribal life. I have been deeply moved by its poverty and illiteracy. Yet without wishing to appear maudlin or romantic, while commenting on the passing of one of the most romantic ways of tribal life that often symbolized nobility and purity in its ideal model to a world that is frequently corrupt and impure, I am not sure the transition to the next phase will be an entirely happy or auspicious one for Pukhtun society. Perhaps one can draw solace from the thought that the intentions are good.

My study has postulated a thesis that a Pukhtun ideal-type model exists based on *Pukhtunwali*. In the ideal *Pukhtunwali* affects the essential aspects of social behaviour and organization. The central features of *Pukhtunwali*, as locally seen, are *tarboorwali* and *tor* and are related to other important facets of social life such as settlement and marriage patterns and income and expenditure figures. I have argued that the ideal model exists given certain conditions and have constructed such a model in TAM. I have thus successfully defended my thesis regarding the construction and functioning of an ideal-type Pukhtun model. I have also tested the connected thesis, that *Pukhtunwali* can survive in spite of encapsulation; in the SAM situation it stands partly rejected but partly verified, especially in the conceptualization of the key features of *Pukhtunwali*, as I have shown above. This is a far more complex hypothesis than the earlier one involving as it does the overlap of two different codes often implying disjunction.

In the end a comment on tribal organization is a statement on the changing relationship between external political systems and local groups that, in turn, affect internal structure and incorporate behavioural variables that may or may not conform to the traditional and the ideal. Although the correlation contains the seeds of an argument that would appear to negate my thesis, it is probably no coincidence that the last agnatic murder in Shati Khel was committed in 1973, the same year the road crossed the Nahakki Pass and electricity came to TAM.

Appendix

TEEGA: formal and written tribal peace agreement

True copy of the deed (TEEGA)*

Malik Abdullah Khan etc., residents of Gandab (first party)

versus

Malik Shahzada Khan etc., residents of Gandab (second party).
Teega deed executed for 15 years from 26-7-1940 to 25-7-1955

Sir,
We both the parties in our mutual interest and with our own free-will execute the following *teega* deed from 26-7-1940 to 25-7-1955 at the political bungalow today. We will abide by the following terms and conditions of the *teega*:

1   We will observe *solla* till the completion of the *teega* period which will conclude on the expiry of 15 years.
2   If during the *teega* period somebody kills the *mashar* of the opposite party he will be liable to a penalty of Rs. 5,000. In case of *kashar* the penalty will be Rs. 2,500. Out of the fine half of the amount will be paid to the government and the other half will be paid to the legal heirs of the deceased.
3   If during the *teega* period somebody causes injury to the *mashar* person of the opposite party with sharp-edged weapon or rifle he will be liable to a fine of Rs. 2,500. If injury is caused to a *kashar* the fine will be Rs. 1,250. Half of the amount of the fine will be paid to the government and the other half to the injured person.
4   If during the *teega* period somebody causes injury to a *mashar* of the opposite party with a blunt weapon he will be liable to a fine of Rs. 100 and in case of *kashar* Rs. 50. Half of the fine will go to the government and the other half to the injured person.
5   In case of murder committed during the night the decision will be based on swearing on the Holy Koran. The complainant party will have the right to choose ten persons to take the oath on the Holy Koran to plead innocence of the accused person. In case of failure to take the oath the accused will be liable to a fine as explained in para. 2.
6   Shahgul Khel, Nasir Khel, i.e. Fazale Ahad, Zulfiqar and Sher Hassan etc.,

* This is an exact translation of a *teega* agreement between Abdullah and Shahzada drawn up in 1940 from a hand-written copy belonging to the latter.

will have the right to construct residential houses on the *arat* of Sher Hassan
during this period. In case of obstruction from the first party, the party will
be liable to a fine of Rs. 5,000. Half of the amount will go to the government and the other half to the above mentioned persons, and force may be
used by political authorities to allow the construction of the residential
houses. The first party will return the occupied property to Shahgul Khel.

7   The Ranra Khel section, i.e. Malik Said Hassan, Mian Jan, Ali Khan, Said
Ahmad, Amir Khan etc., will also have the right to reconstruct their old
ruins of Ranra Khel. Similarly the Ranra Khel section will have the right to
construct their property in the village of Atta Khan Kilay towards the south-
east in the direction of the hills. In case of any obstruction from the opposite party they will be liable to a fine of Rs. 5,000, half of which will be paid
to the government and half to the complainant party. Force will be used to
permit the construction. The second party will return to Ranra Khel their
occupied property.

8   During the *teega* period the parties will decide their disputes of a civil nature,
i.e. recovery of outstanding dues and other such disputes, according to
shariat and in no case will they disobey the *shariat* law. If any party has
made some construction on the landed property before the enforcement of
teega he will exchange suitable land in lieu of the land so constructed and
the issue will be decided by the *jirga*.

9   During the *teega* period no party will attack the village or *bruj* of the other
party. The aggressors will be liable to a fine of Rs. 5,000 in case of a village
and Rs. 500 in case of a *bruj*. Half of the amount of the fine will be paid to
the government and the other half will be paid to the complainant party.
The aggressors will also be pushed back from the village or *bruj* by force. The
damages will be paid by the accused party which will be assessed on oath by
the complainant party.

10   During the *teega* period, if some persons of one party are killed while
burgling the house of the other party, such murder will not be liable to any
fine if ten persons of the village state on oath that the deceased had come to
the village with the intention of burgling, otherwise fine will be levied as
explained in para. 2.

11   No party will commit theft of the cattle of the opposite party. The defaulting party will be liable to pay double the cost of the stolen property which
will be decided on taking the oath on the Holy Koran; the oath will be given
to persons on the basis of one head of cattle, one person. Half of the recovered
amount will be given to the government and the other half to the complainant party.

12   During the *teega* period the parties will not construct any new houses except
constructions made in their own village. They can construct any new rooms
outside the village within the distance of one hundred paces. They will not
exceed this limit in any case. If somebody wants to construct beyond this
limit he will seek the permission of the political officer, Shabkadar, in this
regard. Violators will be liable to a fine of Rs. 500 and the construction will
be demolished. Half of the fine will be paid to the government and the other
half to the complainant party.

13   During the *teega* period no party will kill a member of the other party
through hired assassins. The violators will be dealt with as mentioned in para.
5 and the fine will be recovered as laid down in para. 2. Half of the fine will
go to the government and the other half to the complainant party.

14   During the *teega* period no party will keep or give protection to deserters
from the opposite party. In case of violation the defaulter will be liable to a

fine of Rs. 1,000 and the deserter will be removed with force. Half of the portion of the fine will be paid to the government and the other half to the complainant party.

15 During the *teega* period if some party is required to take oath, the complainant will have a right to choose the person or his collaterals among them for the purpose of taking the oath.

16 The recovery of the fine will be effected from the accused, collaterals or his near relatives. In case the fine cannot be recovered in this way it will be recovered from the property of the entire village situated in the tribal territory or the Settled Area and the persons of the village will be held responsible jointly or severally.

17 In case of the murder of Malik Haji Abdullah Khan of the first party and Malik Shahzada Khan of the second party the fine will be Rs. 10,000. If an injury is caused to the above mentioned persons with sharp-edged weapons, rifle or sword the fine will be Rs. 5,000 and in case of a blunt-edged weapon the fine will be Rs. 500. Half of the fine will be paid to the government and the rest to the complainant party.

18 In case of murder of the sons, uncles or cousins of Malik Shahzada Khan and Malik Haji Abdullah Khan the fine will be Rs. 5,000. In case of the offence mentioned in para. 3 the fine will be Rs. 2,500 and Rs. 100 if the offence is the one mentioned in para. 4, which fines will be borne by the accused party. Half of the amount will be paid to the government and the other half to the complainant party.

19 The parties may fill up the *morchas* prepared in their property for sheltering their *mlatars* and no party will raise any objection to it. No party will have a right to close the paths meant for movement of the opposite party during the *teega* period.

20 Every party will accept the responsibility within their territorial limits which means that no person of any party within these territorial limits will cause damage to the person of the opposite party; in case of default he will be liable to a fine as mentioned in the deed.

21 The *teega* deed executed for 15 years from 26-7-1940 to 25-7-1955 may be duly accepted and enforced on both the parties.

Dated 26-7-1940   Signed and sealed

Glossary

azan: Muslim call to prayers, said five times daily.

badal: primary law of the Pukhtun Code meaning 'revenge' — regardless of cost, time and difficulty. Also means 'exchange' when siblings of opposite sex are married, usually to patrilateral parallel cousins of the same generation.

Eed: Muslim holy festival celebrated twice annually.

ganrey: pressing machine for sugar cane, usually operated by use of bullocks or buffaloes, which produces brown, domestic, noncentrifugal sugar — *gur*.

gasht: reconnaissance exercise on foot by Frontier Scouts in strength and without schedule; main aim to 'show the flag'.

ghair ilaqa: lit. 'foreign or outside areas' meaning Tribal Areas in contrast to *ilaqa sarkar* or Government Areas.

gham-khadi: lit. sorrow-celebration, social acts in the form of *rites de passage*.

gumlao: anarchistic, equalitarian Kachin (Burmese) social organization, *versus*

gumsa: hierarchical, aristocratic organization.

haj: annual pilgrimage to Mecca. One of the five pillars of Islam and therefore obligatory for all Muslims once in their lifetime.

hamsaya: lit. 'one who shares shade'. Used for client or low status groups.

hujra: common village guest-house or rooms, and focal social point for males in the village.

jihad: struggle in the way of Allah.

jirga: assembly of Pukhtun elders to decide various inter- or intra-tribal matters.

jumat: mosque usually adjacent to the *hujra*.

kafir: non-believer, that is non-Muslim.

kalima: the sentence that proclaims 'There is no God but Allah and Muhammad is His Prophet', the essence of Muslimness.

kanrai: (see *teega* below) lit. stone — truce terms.

kashar: lit. young, but used for those with little political standing or weight.

khassadars: semi-official tribal police force under the command of the Political Agent, peculiar to the Tribal Areas, NWFP.

khel: lineage.

khwar: a stream bed, usually dry and a common boundary between tribal sections.

kilay: village — sometimes called *kor* (see below) — usually named after senior living agnate.

kor: house; *korona*: houses; *dwa-kora*: tribal groups with two houses, one in the Agency and one in the Settled Areas.

lakhkar: tribal armed gathering for battle.

lungi: allowances given by government to individuals (see *muajib*).

maira: plain, flat-land. Mohmands generally contrast their mountainous areas with the *maira* of Charsadda and Mardan.

mashar: elder; *masharana*: the extra share usually given to the eldest son when property is being divided between brothers.

melmastia: the law of hospitality, derived from *melma* meaning guest, a primary custom of *Pukhtunwali.*

mlatar: from *mla* (back) and *tar* (to tie); active supporters in factional conflict. Women, religious and occupational groups do not form *mlatar*.

muajib: allowances given by government to tribal section or sub-section (see *lungi*).

nanawatee: from the verb 'to go in'. Once an enemy asks for *nanawatee* he explicitly admits defeat and submission.

nang: honour.

niswar: mild intoxicant commonly used in the NWFP and inserted under the lower lip. Made from ash and tobacco leaves ground together.

parda: lit. veil; seclusion, modesty of women.

peghor: invocation of shame – reminder upon lapse from honour or deviation from the Code of *Pukhtunwali.*

potlatch: means 'give' as a gift: competitive display of lavishness, for example, at a feast to gain social prestige. The 'potlatch' of the Indians of British Columbia is famous.

Pukhto: language of Pukhtuns but also meaning the essence of Pukhtunness and the *Pukhtunwali* Code.

Pukhtun: member of the Pukhtun tribal group, defined by patrilineage and behaviour approximating to the *Pukhtunwali* ideal.

Pukhtunwali: composite of *badal, melmastia, nanawatee, tor,* and *tarboorwali*; the Code of the Pukhtuns.

qalang: rents and taxes among Yusufzai of Mardan and Swat. It also means gifts to religious groups like the Mians in other areas. I am using it in the former sense in this study.

qam: tribe.

qasabgar: from *qasab* (craft) and meaning craftsman, occupational groups like barbers and carpenters.

qulba: a pair of bullocks and a plough.

riwaj: Pukhto custom.

sawab: positive spiritual gain from performing religious or good deeds; the opposite of sin.

Sayyed: descendant of the Prophet.

seer: about two pounds in weight.

shariat: body of Islamic law.

solla: temporary truce for fixed periods during fighting.

spin: lit. white – the process through which guilt in *tor* cases (see below) is exonerated or mitigated.

stanadar: religious person or group, usually entitled to land or other privileges.

tarboorwali: agnatic rivalry involving patrilateral parallel male cousins usually of that generation; *tarboor*: Father's Brother's Son, carrying connotation of 'enemy'.

teega: lit. stone – truce terms (see Appendix).

topak: gun, the 'carrying' of which signifies Pukhtun status in the Tribal Areas. Religious and occupational groups do not carry guns.

tor: lit. black – used in cases where the chastity of women is compromised. Both parties are said to be *tor* and the offence is considered of the utmost seriousness.

wak: mutually agreed authority given by two factions to third party for decision.

Notes

1 Introduction

1 I agree with the reviewers of a previous book (Ahmed, 1976) who criticized me in otherwise favourable reviews for using the term Pathan instead of Pukhtun or Pashtun (Dupree, 1977: 514; Misdaq, 1976: 58). The word Pathan does not exist among Pukhto speakers and the Pukhtuns; it is an Anglo-Indian corruption. I shall therefore use the 'correct' term in this study.

2 Although conceptualized as rivalry directed against the Father's Brother's Sons, *tarboorwali* may extend generally to other male cousins in the patri-lineage, as the case-studies in Chapter 7 illustrate.

3 Including settlements of the three Shati Khel sub-sections, Musa, Ranra and Malok (Chapters 5, 8).

4 Headlines such as 'Kabul moves army units on Pakistan border: officers' leaves cancelled' (*Khyber Mail*, 30 November 1975) were common during this period.

5 I will be using tne terms Malik and *mashar* more or less interchangeably as almost every elder is called Malik, a more formal title, as a matter of courtesy in the Agencies.

6 Mohmands measure land in *jiribs*. Two *jiribs* equal one acre. I shall be using acres for measurement of land in the study.

2 The Mohmand ecological and administrative framework

1 Approximately 18–20 rupees equal 1 pound sterling. I shall use the abbreviation Rs. for rupees.

2 Early in last century the Mohmand tendency to exaggerate population figures was commented upon (Elphinstone, 1972 II: 41).

3 I shall use tribal belt, tract or territory to mean the areas that now correspond to the Tribal Areas (Map 1) administratively created in the 1890s.

4 The Assistant Political Officer belonged to the Provincial Service unlike the Assistant Political Agent who was usually of the Indian Civil or Political Service cadre – an important nuance recognized by tribesmen; the former in British India was native and the latter British.

3 Tribal society and the historical process

1 Controversy among scholars regarding Pukhtun phyletic origins has not yet abated (Caroe, 1965: 3-113). Over the last hundred years scholars have divided into two camps: one camp argued that Pukhtuns were aboriginal inhabitants of the Peshawar valley and supported their thesis by extant

sources from Herodotus, 468–426 B.C. For instance, Bellew argued that Pukhtuns were originally Rajputs and Pukhto a dialect of Sanskrit (1867) and equated the Khattaks with the Sattagudai (1880). Herodotus' Paktues were the progenitors of the Pukhtun, and his Paktuike the Gandhara or Peshawar valley; Ibbetson (1883), Stein (1929) and Morgenstierne (1927) agreed that Herodotus's Aparutai could be eponymous ancestors of Afridis. Tribal migration to and from Kandahar – and indeed the origin of that name – is explained thus: Pukhtun tribes migrated from the Gandhara (Peshawar) valley in the fifth century A.D., giving Kandahar its name, and under pressure from central Asian tribes returned to their original homelands in the fifteenth century (Ibbetson, 1883: 215). The other school of thought, led by Raverty, is closer to putative Pukhtun genealogical charters which trace their ancestry to Afghana, hence the tribal name Afghan, son of Armia, son of Saul, the first King of the Jews (Figure 4). Burnes (1834) supported this theory which categorized the Pukhtuns as the 'Beni Israel' or 'Beni Afganah' – the lost tribe that failed to return to Jerusalem after the Jewish diaspora (Raverty, 1888). For purposes of my study and in the context of this chapter, it is important that all authorities are unanimous in placing Pukhtuns in an Indian–Aryan category in social if not in phyletic terms. In Middle East studies the Pukhtuns find themselves peripheral to the world of Islamic tribes ranging from Morocco to Afghanistan (Coon, 1952).

2   *Baba* is a common appellation of respect for elders.
3   An interesting, if unique, example of complete 'genealogical amnesia' and physical isolation is provided by the Shilmanis whom I visited in an almost totally inaccessible and barren area of the Khyber Agency and south of the Kabul river (Maps 2 and 4). They are Tarakzai Mohmands who migrated to these areas three or four centuries ago and conform to the ideal-type *nang* model: materially poor and highly individualistic, there are no superordinate groups, Maliks, Khans, Sayyeds, Mians or subordinate ones like Gujars, among them. Memory of their Mohmandness has almost faded and they call themselves 'Shilmani' apparently from the number *shal* (meaning 20) signifying either the number of patriarchs or households who initially came to this area and settled it. Shilmanis have one house and are not *dwa-kora*. They find themselves independent but socially in more or less a *hamsaya* status to the Afridis who consider themselves superior within the administrative framework of their (i.e. Afridi) Khyber Agency.
4   The Afridis alone collected Rs. 125,000 a year in the sixteenth century from the Mughals (Spain, 1963: 46). In the seventeenth century a total of Rs. 600,000 was paid by the Mughals to the tribes annually (ibid.: 32).
5   Kabul allowances to the eastern Mohmands in the 1880s were almost Rs. 20,000 (Merk, 1898: 15–17).
6   By 1930 the British were paying subsidies of almost a million rupees to tribes in the Tribal Areas (Kakar, 1968: 329).
7   The grave in Fort Michni was shown to me by the Mohmand Constabulary soldiers early on in my field-work. The plaque on the grave of Lt Boulnois, after a little scrubbing, clearly states: 'Sacred to the memory of Arthur Boulnois who was killed near the fort of Michnee by a band of Momunds on the 12th January 1852 chivalrous accomplished and full of promise this tablet was erected by comrades who esteemed him while living and sorrow at his loss his remains lie buried in the ramparts of Fort Michnee.'
8   Graphically related in official correspondence – Parliamentary Papers, 1898 vol. 2; North-West Frontier, Mohmand Affairs 1903, 1908.

9   Mohmand Affairs, 1908.
10   The billiards room in the Miran Shah Scouts Mess, in North Waziristan, is
     still dominated by the portrait of Captain G. Meynell V.C., Guides Frontier
     Force, 'killed in action Mohmand operations – 29 September 1935'.
11   He was later destined to become C.-in-C. of the Indian Army and a Field-
     Marshal.

4 Segmentary tribes and models of Pukhtun social organization

1   Sections often have similar names. There is an Utman Khel in the Orakzai
     clans, in the Mohmand and in the Bajaur Agencies. There is an Isa Khel
     among the Mohmand and among the Orakzais. Sipaya sections are found
     among the Afridis and the Orakzais. Apart from their names, these sections
     have no other special kin relationships.
2   Pennell, 1909.
3   Bellew, 1864, 1867, 1880; Holland, 1958.
4   Churchill, 1972; Elliott, 1968; Masters, 1965; North, 1946; Pettigrew,
     1965; Raverty, 1860, 1862, 1888; Ridgeway, 1918; Roberts, 1897; Robert-
     son, 1899; Wylly, 1912.
5   Burnes, 1834, 1961; Caroe, 1965; Edwardes, 1851; Elphinstone, 1972;
     Fraser-Tytler, 1969; Goodwin, 1969, n.d.; Howell, 1931; Ibbetson, 1883;
     King, 1900; Merk, 1898; Stein, 1929; Warburton, 1900; Woodruff, 1965,
     1976.
6   Barth, 1959, 1970, 1971b, 1972; Davies, 1975; Dichter, 1967; Spain, 1962,
     1963.
7   Sale, 1843; Starr, 1920, 1924.
8   The *jirga* as a grand concept and design representing a symmetrical seg-
     mentary structure of the Pukhtun tribes (Figure 4) which sends representa-
     tion from the village to the sub-section, to the clan, to the tribe and finally
     to 'the big *jirga*' (*loi jirga*) which can reject or accept the Kings of Kabul,
     has never existed (Elphinstone, 1972).
9   Pukhtun elders explained that the noun 'Pukhtun' is formed from an
     aggregate of those attributes which it symbolizes and as the word is spelled
     in Pukhto:
     '*pey*' for *pat* – comradeship, fellowship
     '*khey*' for *khegara* – doing good to others
     '*tey*' for *tora* – literally sword and meaning bravery
     '*waw*' for *wafa* – fidelity to one's word and cause and
     '*noon*' for *nang* – honour.
     Thus 'Pukhtun', the essence of chivalry, courage, fidelity and honour.
10   Ahmed, 1975; Biddulph, 1890; Caroe, 1965; Enevoldsen, n.d.; Howell and
     Caroe, 1963; Mackenzie, 1960, 1965; Mohmand, 1968; Raverty, 1862.
11   A moment visually immortalized by Lady Butler's famous painting in the
     Tate Gallery, London.
12   There is an interesting and typical account of such a murder in the Wana
     Mess in 1905 witnessed and written by Howell (Caroe, 1965: Appendix D).
13   I shall discuss the growth of saints among the Orakzai Shias in a separate
     paper (Ahmed, forthcoming d).
14   I have had the opportunity of examining four types of Pukhtun
     societies and at close quarters: 1 the pure *nang* Pukhtuns among the
     Mohmands (field-work) and the Orakzais (Ahmed, 1977a); 2 Swat society
     representing the *qalang* form (Ahmed, 1976); 3 those Pukhtuns exposed
     to large non-Pukhtun groups and cultures such as in Mansehra (Ahmed,

1973b) and Hazara (Ahmed, 1977b: 123–48); and finally 4 those Pukhtuns who are assimilated into other cultures and live outside both the *nang* and *qalang* areas like the Rampur Pukhtuns in India.

15 *Qalang* society employs the elite title Khan generally for respectable citizens and specifically for landlords. The term derives from Central Asia meaning 'lord' (Hitti, 1977: 488) or 'ruler' (Caroe, 1965: 82–4). There are no Khans in the *nang* areas and the term indicating hierarchy is virtually unused. As we saw earlier even the term Malik, signifying a petty sectional leader, is disliked. I have heard Mohmands negating the hierarchical implications of the term by saying: 'A Khan does not understand Pukhto' (*khan pa Pukhto na poygee*). To the *nang* Pukhtun, Pukhto and Khan are inherently contradictory; conversely, he will say, when asked, 'every man here is a Khan'.

5 Lineage and leadership organization: alliance and conflict

1 For an illuminating discussion on unilineal descent as organizational principle among four well-known segmentary societies, the Nuer (Evans-Pritchard, 1940, 1970); the Tiv (Bohannan, L., 1952, 1970; Bohannan and Bohannan, 1953); the Cyrenaican Bedouin (Evans-Pritchard, 1973; Peters, 1960); and the Somali (Lewis, I. M., 1961, 1962a, b), see Lewis, I. M., 1969b.

2 None the less in certain individual cases, especially when there is a clear-cut clan or tribal alternative to choose from, the closer kin may be supported. When offered a choice between a Mohmand (Yusuf Mohmand) and a non-Mohmand (Akbar Khan) or a Halimzai (Khanzada) and a Baezai (Baroz Khan) for national elections, Shahzada has stood by the Mohmand clan and candidate. As he puts it, 'they are, after all, kin' (*diw bia hum khpal di*).

3 A story that Mohmand Baba married a Durrani woman who carried the Halimzai ancestor from another husband in her womb (making him *parka-tey*) is popular among the Mohmand. Jurally and genealogically it makes no difference to the Mohmandness of the Halimzai. Halimzais themselves refer to this story with humour and suggest they carry royal Durrani blood in their veins, although Durrani rule in Kabul took place almost 300 years after this incident. In spite of the apocryphal origin of the story but because of the blemish it suggests, it helps the less unruly and less independent Tarakzai to put the Halimzais in their place.

4 The word *khel* itself is common to other Islamic tribes (Barth, 1953: 38).

5 It has been observed that in Indian villages 'nearly all men can recall the name of their father's father, though they seldom remember details beyond this' and the greatest 'generation recall' was limited to four generations of ascendants (Mayer, 1970: 169–70).

6 The Ganjian belong to the Masud clan of the Safi tribe. Haji Umar (Malok) explained the name Ganjian to me. He said their ancestor escaped from the Safi area as a result of a *tor* case and therefore arrived in a disgraced condition. Metaphorically his head was naked in disgrace and he was 'bald-headed' (*ganjay*). The name Ganjian (plural of *ganjay*) has remained with the group since then.

7 The Zarif Khel in Bela, represented by two houses (Table 5, Maps 6, 7), do not involve themselves with village lineage politics.

8 Among certain tribes in Waziristan this arrangement, called *nikkat*, from

grandfather (*nika*), is fixed and unchanging and affects various other aspects of life including politics (Caroe, 1965; Howell, 1931).

9   The origin of the indirect rule system is perhaps based on colonial experience in India during the latter half of the last century. Men like Sandeman, and later his disciple Bruce, in the trans-Indus tracts of Baluchistan were putting into practice the theories of Lyall (1882) and Maine (1861, 1871) which saw sound colonial administration as based on the loyalty of landowning and influential groups in village society (Woodruff, 1965). Lugard, who was appointed Governor of Nigeria in 1914, is wrongly regarded as 'the initiator of Indirect Rule or Native Administration' (Lackner, 1973: 128).

10   Professor of Middle Eastern Studies at the School of Oriental and African Studies, University of London.

11   *Shar* is usually conflict for short periods whereas *patna* stretches over longer periods and is much more serious.

12   *Solla* differs from *rogha* or *teega* in that the latter is a formal and binding truce with agreed clauses for a specific period. *Solla* in comparison is a temporary truce and though it stops shooting it confines the parties to their own areas. *Teega* (literally stone) is the formal agreement in cases of *rogha* and derives from an ancient Rajput custom where details of the dispute were recorded on a stone and placed between the disputed areas (King, 1900). Once an agreement is reached the entire gathering prays for peace and agrees 'the stone has been placed' (*teega kekhodal*). See Appendix.

6 Non-Pukhtun groups: patron and client relationships

1   The caliphs of the early dynasties of Islam, the Umayyads (A.D. 661–750, 929–1031), the Abbasids (A.D. 750–1258) and the Fatimids (A.D. 909–1171) were related to the Prophet on the genealogical charter and traced unilineal descent through agnatic ascendants to their common apical ancestor, Quraysh, and his descendant Abd-Manaf (Hitti, 1977).

2   Studies among Indian Muslims show the emergence of various caste-like groups like the 'high' caste *Ashraf*, the Sayyeds, Sheikhs, Mughals and Pukhtuns and the 'low' caste *Ajlaf*, mostly converts from low-caste Hindus (Ahmad, I., 1973).

3   Forty seers equal one maund and one seer equals two pounds in weight approximately.

4   *Ingar* means blacksmith. Ingar is widely employed as a suffix and part of the family name of this group and their village (Maps 5, i and iii) after they were brought to Shati Khel by the Musa (Chapter 7). Thus Aziz Ingar and Aziz Ingar village (after their present elder, Aziz).

7 Pukhto paradigm

1   *Tarboorwali* perhaps supports Raverty's Beni Israel theory (1888), suggesting that Cain and Abel were the ancestors of the Pukhtuns.

2   I was told by the leaders that there is a good deal of embezzling during prolonged conflict as ammunition and wheat supplied to supporters in trenches at night disappear by daylight and are supposedly used up. The costs of such operations deter leaders from conducting long-drawn-out battles. The swift raid before dawn, ideally organized with forty to sixty men, is preferred.

Cousins facing each other across trenches often joke and playfully abuse each other. Requests may be shouted from across the enemy lines to throw the snuff box across as they have exhausted their supply.

3   The reputation and record of the Ranra survive from the days the Mians cursed them and would prompt Anwar Zeb, one of my assistants, to repeat a local joke that their name should have been 'darkness' (*tiara*) rather than 'light' (*ranra*).

4   Settlements named after three of these may be seen on Map 5, iii.

5   Shah Khan, now a frail old bespectacled man, is universally said to have killed the maximum number of people in Shati Khel, about fifteen, in the last forty years, although neither he nor those who boast about the figures can account for more than ten actual deaths. Shahzada's protection has kept him alive so far in the safety of his *hujra* where Shah Khan spends his last days.

6   With all the mystique that attaches to sophisticated weaponry in primitive society only three men were ever allowed to fathom its intricacies and be allowed the privilege to operate it, Major Sultan Jan (the brother of Anmir), Shahzada and Aziz.

7   I have reproduced as an appendix an exact copy, literally translated, of the truce terms signed in 1940 for a period of fifteen years (but violated before its expiry date in 1955) between Abdullah and Shahzada to illustrate a typical tribal *teega* agreement. Needless to say, little more than lip service was paid to such crucial clauses as those contained in paragraph 7 regarding reconstruction of villages by Atta Khan and the Ranra, which until today remain incomplete. Minute details of arrangements in case of violation of any clause are given. After the formal truce is agreed and announced, revenge for wounded and dead kin cannot be claimed. Such treaties are all the more remarkable when one reflects that they are drafted by formally illiterate tribesmen and without the aid of legal minds.

8   One Malok killed during this period was Kabil Khan's father. Kabil features in Chapter 9.

9   The disputed land had been sold to his cousins by Lakhkar's grandfather before he migrated to Mardan but as they failed to produce male heirs the land, *miras*, therefore reverted legally to the nearest living male relative in the line, in this case Lakhkar (Figure 14).

10 This alliance soured in the 1970s. The point of conflict was typical of the concepts of honour and status (*saritob*) as understood in society. Shahzada took offence when Lakhkar, newly established, gave a dinner for the Political Agent. Shahzada saw this as a personal affront, refused to attend and since then has opposed Lakhkar. Amirzada broke with his father and formed a separate though non-belligerent group with his father-in-law Lakhkar. I have heard many cynical commentaries on this father-son enmity suggesting it is a political ruse to flush out or expose enemies. In any case the tension remains dormant and does not affect the politics of Shati Khel.

11 This two-storeyed tower houses three or four armed men only but is strategically placed at the mouth of the Shati Khel. It is connected to the main road by a ditch, three feet deep and some forty yards long, giving protection from stray bullets to those bringing supplies (Map 5 (iii)).

12 Mazullah later sold the cannon balls for Rs. 20 apiece, not, he assured me, to Shahzada.

13 A cannon cost Rs. 30,000 in the 1960s.

14 I discuss colour symbolism among the Pukhtun in a forthcoming paper (Ahmed, forthcoming b).

15 A famous Pukhto folk song based on a true account of events that occurred
    north of Nahakki commemorates the killing of his virtuous wife, Maimonai,
    by Sher Alam. Sher's was an instinctive response to the accusations of
    shame (*peghor*) hinted at by his neighbours, who wrongly accused his wife
    of flirting with a guest when, in keeping with *melmastia* tradition, she had
    passed him tobacco through a door. Maimonai protested her innocence
    claiming the guest did not even see her face but if her husband wished she
    was ready for death to uphold his and her honour. The song ends: 'God
    ruin you Sher Alam who murdered because of tobacco leaves' (*Khuday dey
    khwar kra Sher Alama de tambaco per panra cha kari margoona*). The
    story symbolizes ideal Pukhtun womanhood: total chastity and total
    loyalty.

8 Settlement and domestic structure

1   The three maps of Shati Khel have been reconstructed thus: the 1900 map
    from interviews, the second from army and government ordnance maps
    circa 1933-5 (note that Mian Mandi, schools, hospitals, etc., do not feature
    on this map). The last map is drawn from my own field-work observations
    in 1976.
2   A similar population thrust at around the same time, and for probably the
    same reasons both economic and historical, was pushing the Orakzais to
    the richer lands around Hangu as tenants of the Hangu Khans. Today the
    Hangu Khans are encircled by Orakzais, once their tenants and now small
    landowners, who have formed political groups and emerged as a power in
    the settled area of Hangu just as the Mohmand have in Charsadda and
    Mardan.
3   The Mohmand elders describe *shamilat* lands as belonging to the most
    powerful (*de zor shay day*).
4   I define a nuclear or elementary family as consisting of a father, mother
    and their children; a compound family as composed of the elementary
    families of a polygynous patriarch; a joint family as lineally related kins-
    folk occupying a single settlement and jointly subject to the authority of a
    common living male ascendant; and an extended family as the dispersed
    form corresponding to a joint family (RAI, 1971: 70-2).
5   Inside the gate Akbar Jan wrote some lines in chalk in 1972 which survive:
    'Heard melodies are sweet those unheard are the sweetest.' Keats lives in
    one of the most remote parts of the world. The lines are inspired from the
    ode 'On a Grecian Urn', 'Heard melodies are sweet, but those unheard/Are
    sweeter; therefore ye soft pipes, play on' (Keats, 1975: 534-5).
6   Nearby the village to the north-west is the geographical area called Wacha
    Jawar (Map 2) mentioned in the 1935 campaign (Elliott, 1968). The
    Mohmand Rifles chose the site where the British camped for their tempor-
    ary headquarters in 1973-4.
7   His expenses on digging have amounted to over Rs. 50 a day for the last six
    months; two men paid Rs. 10 daily to work below the earth's surface, one
    man Rs. 5 for labour above ground, plus the full cost of their meals and the
    cost of dynamite at Rs. 10 a stick.
8   Mazullah and Ranra elders recounted how Shahzada built his new village on
    Malok land in the 1930s. Shahzada wished to buy one and a half acres from
    the Malok but they refused, so the political administration locked up Sar
    Gul in Shabkadar. The action worked and Shahzada got his village. It
    is only fair to recall that Mazullah has been a life-long enemy of Shahzada.

9   The small cannon which Shahzada's father used in the 1930s and which helped change the balance of agnatic power in Shati Khel stands in a separate room by the *hujra*. It is wheeled out to be displayed or used on rare occasions as one of the prized possessions of the region.

10 Said Mir, who died in 1940, and his son Pasham Gul, who died in 1973, feature in Chapter 7 in the lineage conflict of the 1930s in Shati Khel.

11 The Ranra Khel, in spite of their name, meaning 'light', prefer to remain in darkness and without electricity rather than submit to Shahzada by grovelling to him for it.

12 More recently there is a tendency to display printed posters brought from Peshawar and nailed on the mud wall declaring the *kalima*, 'There is no God but Allah and Muhammad is His Prophet' (Ranra and Bela mosques).

13 It may also be called smoke (*lugay*) signifying that separate food is cooked or a door (*tambagar*) that can be knocked on.

14

		TAM	SAM
A1	sub-section:	Musa, Ranra, Malok	Kado, Madar, Jano, Do, Sabah
A2	section:	Shati	Khalil
A3	sub-clan:	Wali Beg	Kasim
A4	clan:	Halimzai	Tarakzai
A5	tribe:	Mohmand	Mohmand
B	affiliated lineages:	Ganjian	
C	religious groups:	Sayyeds, Mians, Mullahs	
D	occupational groups:	carpenters, barbers, black-smiths.	

15 The simplicity of rituals in *nang* society contrast with those in *qalang* society where marriage functions pass through complex stages involving ritual and expenditure (Barth, 1972: 38–9). For instance, the engagement in *nang* is an informal commitment, often just the 'word' but in *qalang* an elaborate ceremony (ibid.: 38).

16 Pukhtun groups living across the Indus, as in Hazara, not only write *haq mehr* but honour it in cases of divorce and separation (Hussain, 1958: 13). Similarly, inter-tribal marriages are common even between Gujar non-Pukhtun males and Swati Pukhtun girls (ibid.: 13).

17 *Badal* meaning exchange as distinct from revenge.

9 Economic structure and lineage ideology

1   Polanyi (1968b:122) sums up the respective positions thus: the Substantivist economic approach (1) derives from fact (2) implies neither choice nor insufficiency of means (3) implies power of gravity and (4) laws of nature (Bohannan, P. 1959; Bohannan, P. and L., 1968; Bohannan and Dalton, 1962; Dalton, 1961, 1962, 1965, 1967, 1968, 1969; Meillasoux, 1964, 1972; Polanyi, 1944, 1966, 1968a and b; Polanyi *et al.*, 1957; Sahlins, 1968, 1969). The Formalist approach (1) derives from logic (2) has sets of rules referring to choices between alternative uses of insufficient means (3) has the power of syllogism and (4) derives from the laws of the mind (Burling, 1962; Cancian, 1966; Deane, 1953; Epstein, 1962; Firth, 1964, 1966, 1970; Hill, 1963, 1965; LeClair, 1962; Salisbury, 1962). The title of Cancian's paper 'Maximization as norm, strategy and theory' (1966) clearly states the Formalist position. Volumes containing both viewpoints are standard academic fare (Firth, 1970; LeClair and Schneider, 1968).

2   To quote a Frontier official 'Among Pathans generally the possession of a gun has always been a mark of prestige – a sort of tribal Rolls Royce' (Pettigrew, 1965: 82).

3   Professor Lambton discussing types of labour contracts in the Bela *hujra* explained that *dehqan* is a Persian word. The implication is that it is a non-Pukhto word and, in *nang* society, remains an external concept.

4   Fifty-four out of 692 people (260 Shati Khel and 432 Bela Mohmandan).

5   As a matter of interest, Hussain Khan (junior lineage) averaged 177 monthly and Hamesh Gul (senior lineage) 57, which further confirms my argument.

6   His annual income of Rs. 100,000 is divided by 25, the number of consumption units in his household, which comes to Rs. 4,000 annually and 333 monthly.

7   I am assuming that the rate of inflation over this period is negligible and does not distort comparative analysis. As the rites involved equally important members of the household they are equally weighted in terms of expenditure figures.

8   The question is a hypothetical one as mistresses or concubines do not exist among the Mohmand and *nang* society, unlike *qalang* groups within which they have been observed (Barth, 1972: 50).

10 Encapsulating systems and tribal strategy

1   Howell believes the word is supposed to have originated from *cacadores* (hunters), the name given to irregular units organized by Wellington during the Spanish campaigns against Napoleon and subsequently brought to India and incorporated into the Tribal Areas later in the century (Coen, 1971: 209). It is now a standard word in the Pukhto language.

2   The *khassadars* are an important form of patronage. They work for one month and are on official leave the next month. Their basic pay of Rs. 100 with allowances comes to about Rs. 210 monthly. They also receive one set of clothing and one pair of shoes annually. They provide their own guns and ammunition. Their charter is vague. They are to protect the roads and other government installations and they operate on the basis of territorial responsibility. For example, in 1974 when the Scouts' telephone-wires were cut the sum was deducted from the pay of the *khassadars* who were on duty (and were commonly believed to be the culprits). Needless to add, wires were never cut again in the Agency. *Khassadars* man the check-posts, where tribesmen deposit their guns before leaving for the District and reclaim them on return, and operate the 'political lock-up' at Ekka Ghund (constructed in 1974). *Khassadaries* are given to Maliks who usually recommend their sons. The importance of a Malik is judged by the number of *khassadars* he can obtain from the administration. Both Shahzada and Abdullah have had about twelve *khassadars* allotted to their sub-sections.

3   In spite of my attempts to locate a copy of the Frontier Crimes Regulation at Ekka Ghund in the Political Agent's office I constantly drew a blank. I was repeatedly assured that 'it must be in the Commissioner's office in Peshawar'.

4   Parliamentary politics are still largely external to TAM and SAM and therefore I shall restrict my comment on the Agency to a footnote. The first members of the Provincial Assembly were Yusuf Mohmand and Jabar, the father of Said Qahar, both Tarakzais in 1956. From 1962 to 1965 Akbar Khan, a non-Mohmand, and up to 1968 Jamshed were members.

In 1970 Akbar Khan became the first member of the National Assembly to represent the Mohmand Agency. The political officer who conducted the first elections in 1956 described the situation to me:

> Yusuf Mohmand and Jabar were the first members in Mohmand history. The entire tribe boycotted the elections as a gesture of rejecting attempts to 'absorb' them or change their 'free' status quo. The tribes fixed two lac [200,000] rupees as fine and also the burning of the houses of any one who participated. We were locked in the Shabkadar fort with some 20 Maliks while hundreds of Mohmands outside holding the Holy Koran threatened us. Many threw bricks into the compound. Until then no one had been beyond Yusuf Khel. We quickly terminated the proceedings by declaring two of the 20 Maliks present as elected.

Since then the membership has become prestigious and lucrative. In 1977 there were 6,098 Maliks on the electoral list and in the elections the successful member of the National Assembly, a Musa Khel Baezai businessman living in Peshawar, is said to have paid up to Rs. 2,000,000 to the Maliks for his victory. He paid Shahzada about Rs. 60,000 for 'safe conduct' in the Agency. Shahzada's sons were paid separately to 'escort' the candidate. Shahzada used the candidate's car, ostensibly to canvass for him, which he later reluctantly returned after extracting a further payment from him. To cap it all Shahzada voted for Khanzada, a Halimzai rival, rather than for a Baezai outside the clan.

5   Iftekhar was at school with me at Burn Hall, Abbottabad, where he passed his Senior Cambridge examination.

6   Under Islamic law two shares are given to males for every one given to a female issue.

7   Although this was the year when Sattar Mohmand of Takhtbahai, discussed in the previous section, took his Bachelor of Arts degree it is important to point out that Khanzada was still very much a tribal Mohmand maintaining regular contact with the place of his birth, Sangar, and its politics.

8   *Sabq the madrassay wai*
de para the paisey wai
pe janat ke ba ye zai nawi
pe dozahk ka ba ghota wahi.

(You are learning at the English school
you are learning for money
there will be no place in heaven for you
and for this you will be hanging in hell.)

9   The general ignorance of national figures in rural areas is a little recognized fact in developing countries and the despair of the urbanized literati and nationalists. For example, many Indian villagers 'did not know the names of Mahatma Gandhi and Jawaharlal Nehru' (Dube, 1965: 232).

10   It was significant that Belawals replied to the questions of Professor Lambton in Urdu. Obviously they identified Urdu as the universal and external language which foreigners 'ought' to understand.

11   The Deputy Commissioner was at school with me and a friend and kindly obliged.

12   Apart from numerous other Mohmand villages in the Daudzai Thana (mentioned earlier) I also visited Khalil Mohmand villages to the south-west of Peshawar, between the Frontier Constabulary forts of Bara and Mackeson, and situated in the District but juxtaposed to the Afridis of the Khyber

Agency. Khalil and Mohmand are cousins in the Ghoriah Khel lineage as may be recalled from earlier chapters. Khalil villages are poor and there are no walls encircling them or the houses. There are no towers or guns visible. They are vulnerable to Afridi encroachments from the hills. They are vulnerable as peasants can be in the face of aggressive tribesmen and have been completely out of contact with their cousins in the hills for generations. Their peasantization process noted in the last century (Holmes, 1887: 1,470; Merk, 1898: 1) is complete.

13 Mentioned earlier as a soldier in the Frontier Constabulary at Bara fort.
14 *Lote* is a corruption of note meaning money among the Mohmand.
15 For similar reasons such concepts have dropped out of *qalang* vocabulary and are generally not recognized in, for example, Swat.

11 Economic development and encapsulation

1 Appreciating their delicate role in the area and the sensitivities of the Halimzai, the Mohmand Rifles maintained a low profile. 'Recce' or *gasht* was never off the main road and even local supplies were purchased by Mohmand soldiers. As a result not a single incidence of a clash with a local group has been reported in spite of their presence in such large numbers at Yusuf Khel.
2 Land prices in Bela have also increased rapidly. In the 1950s when Hussain Khan began to buy his land, prices were Rs. 1,000 to 2,000 per acre. In 1977 the price of good land was about Rs. 20,000 per acre.
3 Emigration to the Arab States reached such a proportion that the *Khyber Mail* (12 October 1976) titled a leader 'Gulf Area Workers' and observed 'there are as many as 700 people going every week to the Persian Gulf area from the region of Hangu alone'.
4 'Visa' has been colloquially incorporated into Pukhto in the 1970s as *eza*.
5 I also discuss the Society as a case-study in a separate paper (Ahmed, forthcoming f).
6 The Project Director of the Daudzai IRDP Centre was the Director of the Pakistan Academy for Rural Development in Peshawar. The problems of the Daudzai area were generally identified as salinity, waterlogging, flood and soil erosion (Khan, A. H., 1975; Khan, S. S., 1975: 6). The total area of the Thana is about 80 square miles with a population of 96,000 based on the 1972 census and contains 89 villages. The average cultivated land per household is 2.3 acres (PARD, vol. 11, no. 2, 1974: 4, 5), slightly higher than the Bela average.
7 It is important to repeat a point here that I have already made regarding occupational groups. While *qasabgars* may not feature on the tribal charter within society, they identify with the dominant clan with which they are affiliated and are tacitly accepted by it as one of them for purposes of definition to the outside world. As a result the entire population of Bela is classified as 'Mohmand' in the PARD figures and indeed such blanket ethnic definitions are applied to the other villages.
8 It would appear that such cavalier attitudes to cooperative money are common among tribal groups on the subcontinent (Bailey, 1964).

Bibliography

The references cited are divided into (1) original sources: primary sources and published government records, (2) secondary sources: published books, articles and theses and (3) newspapers. The following abbreviations have been employed:

BEE: Board of Economic Enquiry, University of Peshawar
C & MG: *Civil and Military Gazette*, Lahore
JRAI: *Journal of the Royal Anthropological Institute*, London
PARD: Pakistan Academy for Rural Development, Peshawar
RAI: Royal Anthropological Institute, London.
RAIN: *Royal Anthropological Institute News*, London

(1) ORIGINAL SOURCES

(i) *Primary sources*

HAMID, F. (not dated), 'Socio-cultural traits' and 'Political organization of the Pathans', unpublished papers.

Home Department, Government of NWFP, Tribal Research Cell: 'Mohmand Affairs', 1901–15. Chief Commissioner's Office, File 181.

Home Department, Government of NWFP, Tribal Research Cell: 'Mohmand Situation', 1916–23, File 191.

Home Department, Government of NWFP, Tribal Research Cell: 'Mohmand Situation', 1927, File 258.

Home Department, Government of NWFP, Tribal Research Cell: 'Mohmand Situation', 1932–5, File 220.

Home Department, Government of NWFP, Tribal Research Cell: 'Frontier Constabulary Reports', 1930–40.

North-West Frontier (1903), 'Mohmand Affairs', Political and Secret Department, correspondence from Viceroy (Simla) to London, no. 1,552, pts 1 and 2, India Office Library, London.

North-West Frontier (1908), 'Demarcation of Mohmand boundary, Mohmand Expedition 1908, Mohmand Operations 1908, Mohmand Rising 1908', India Office Library, London.

(ii) *Published official records*

Administration report of the NWFP from 9 Nov 1901 to 31 March 1903 (1903), NWFP Government Press, Peshawar.

Border Publicity Organization, Government of Pakistan (1972–6), *Mohmand Agency*, Pukhto pamphlets, monthly and quarterly publications on the Tribal Areas, Peshawar.

Census Report of Tribal Agencies (1961), Government of Pakistan, Islamabad.

Census Report of Tribal Agencies (1971), Government of Pakistan, Islamabad.

Federally Administered Tribal Areas Census 1972, Bulletin 2, vol. 5, Interior Division, Government of Pakistan, Islamabad.

Frontier Crimes Regulation, 1901, validated 1954, Government of Pakistan, Peshawar.

Gazetteer 1883–4, *Kohat District*, Punjab Government, Calcutta.

General Staff (1926), *Military Report on the Mohmand Country*, Government of India, Calcutta.

Government of Pakistan (1975), *Socio-economic survey of Buner*, Narcotics Control Board, May, Islamabad.

HOLMES, A. L. E. (ed.) (1887), *Gazetteer of the North-West Frontier from Bajaur to the Indus Kohistan on the north to the Mari Hills on the south*, 4 vols, Government Central Branch Press, Simla.

HOWELL, E. (1931), *Mizh: a monograph on Government's relations with the Mahsud Tribe*, Government of India Press, Simla.

KING, L. W. (1900), *Monograph on the Orakzai country and clans*, Punjab Government Press, Lahore.

MACGREGOR, C. M. (1873), *Central Asia: North-West Frontier of British India: Topography, ethnography, statistics and history*, Part One, vol. 2, Superintendent of Government Printing, Calcutta.

MASON, A. H. (1884), *Record of the expeditions against the North-West Frontier tribes* (for Government), Whiting, London.

MERK, W. R. H. (1898), *Report on the Mohmands*, Punjab Government Press, Lahore.

North-West Frontier (1901), Parliamentary Papers (Great Britain), XLIX, NWF: *Curzon's Minute*.

North-West Frontier (1908), *East India: NWF: papers regarding Orakzai and Mohmand operations*, His Majesty's Stationery Office, London.

North-West Frontier Province (1908), *Imperial Gazetteer of India*, Provincial Series, NWFP, Calcutta.

North-West Frontier Province (1937–8), *Border Administration Reports, NWFP*.

Operations of the Mohmand Field Force (1897), Government of India.

Parliamentary Papers (1898), *Military Operations on the North-West Frontiers of India*, vol. 2. Papers regarding British relations with the neighbouring tribes of the North-West Frontier of India and the military operations undertaken against them during the year 1897–1898, Her Majesty's Stationery Office, London.

(2) SECONDARY SOURCES

(i) *Published books and articles*

ADDY, P. and AZAD, I. (1973), 'Politics and culture in Bengal', in *New Left Review*, no. 79, May–June, London; reprinted in R. Blackburn (ed.) (1975), *Explosion in a Subcontinent*, Penguin Books, Harmondsworth.

AHMAD, A. (1964), *Studies in Islamic culture in the Indian environment*, Oxford University Press.

AHMAD, I. (ed.) (1973), *Caste and social stratification among the Muslims*, Manohar Book Service, Delhi.

AHMAD, M. T. (1962), *Social organization of Yusufzai Swat: a study in social change*, Punjab University Press.

AHMAD, S. (1973), 'Peasant classes in Pakistan', in K. Gough and H. P. Sharma (eds), *Imperialism and revolution in South Asia*, Monthly Review Press.

AHMAD, S. (1977), *Class and power in a Punjabi village*, Monthly Review Press.

AHMED, A. S. (1973a), *A strategy for cooperation: a study of the North-West Frontier Province*, BEE, Peshawar.

AHMED, A. S. (1973b), *Mansehra: a journey*, Ferozsons, Pakistan.

AHMED, A. S. (1975), *Mataloona: Pukhto proverbs*, Oxford University Press, Karachi.

AHMED, A. S. (1976), *Millennium and charisma among Pathans: a critical essay in social anthropology*, Routledge & Kegan Paul, London.

AHMED, A. S. (1977a), *Social and economic change in the Tribal Areas*, Oxford University Press, Karachi.

AHMED, A. S. (1977b), *Pieces of green: the sociology of change in Pakistan*, Royal Book Co., Karachi.

AHMED, A. S. (1978a), Comment in *Current Anthropology*, vol. 19, no. 1 (March), p. 222.

AHMED, A. S. (1978b), 'The colonial encounter on the North-West Frontier Province: myth and mystification', in *Asian Affairs*, vol. ix, pt. III (October), London; revised version in *Journal of the Anthropological Society of Oxford*, Oxford, vol. IX, No. 3, Michaelmas 1978.

AHMED, A. S., *Tribal strategies and the organization of international trading networks: an analysis of the Bara market* (forthcoming a).

AHMED, A. S., *Red, white and black: the colour symbolism of Pukhtuns* (forthcoming b).

AHMED, A. S., *Mians and markets among the Mohmand* (forthcoming c).

AHMED, A. S., *The saints of Tirah: the economic base of religious leadership* (forthcoming d).

AHMED, A. S., *Taxonomy of Pukhtun groups* (forthcoming e).

AHMED, A. S., 'Lineage politics and development schemes: a case-study from the North-West Frontier Province', paper read at SSRC workshop on Development Anthropology at University of Sussex, 1–2 July 1978, reprinted in S. Pastner (ed.),

Cultural Anthropology in Pakistan, (forthcoming f).

AHMED, A. S. and AHMED, Z., 'Tor and mor: binary and opposing models of Pukhtun femalehood', in T. S. Epstein and S. P. F. Senaratne (eds), *Rural women: Asian case-studies*, Pergamon, Oxford (forthcoming).

ALAVI, H. (1965), 'Peasants and revolution', in R. Miliband and J. Saville (eds), 1968, *The Socialist Register*. Reprinted in K. Gough and H. Sharma (eds), 1973, *Imperialism and revolution in South Asia*, Monthly Review Press.

ALAVI, H. (1971), 'The politics of dependence: a village in West Punjab', in *South Asian Review*, vol. 4, no. 2 (January).

ALAVI, H. (1972), 'Kinship in West Punjab villages', in *Contributions to Indian Sociology*, New Series, no. VI.

ALAVI, H. (1973), 'Peasant classes and primordial loyalties', in *Journal of Peasant Studies*, vol. 1, no. 1 (October).

ALI, M. (1966), *and then the Pathan murders*, University Book Agency, Peshawar.

ALLEN, C. (ed.) (1977), *Plain tales from the Raj*, Futura Publications, London.

ASAD, T. (1970), *The Kababish Arabs*, Hurst, London.

ASAD, T. (1972), 'Market model, class structure and consent: a reconsideration of Swat political organization', in *MAN*, vol. 7, no. 1 (March).

ASAD, T. (ed.) (1973), *Anthropology and the colonial encounter*, Ithaca Press, London.

ASHRAF, K. (1962), *Tribal people of West Pakistan: a demographic study of a selected population*, BEE, Peshawar.

AYROUT, H. H. (1963), *The Egyptian peasant*, trans. J. A. Williams, Beacon Press, Boston.

BABAR, Z. M. (1922), *Babar Nama*, trans. A. S. Beveridge, Luzac, London; reprinted in 1975 by Sange Meel Publications, Chawk Urdu Bazaar, Lahore.

BAILEY, F. G. (1957), *Caste and the economic frontier*, Manchester University Press.

BAILEY, F. G. (1960), *Tribe, caste and nation*, Manchester University Press.

BAILEY, F. G. (1961), 'Tribe and caste in India', in *Contributions to Indian Sociology*, October.

BAILEY, F. G. (1964), 'Capital, saving and credit in Highland Orissa (India)', in R. Firth and B. S. Yamey (eds), *Capital, saving and credit in peasant societies*, Aldine, Chicago.

BAILEY, F. G. (1970), *Stratagems and spoils*, Basil Blackwell, Oxford.

BAILEY, F. G. (1973), 'The peasant view of the bad life', in T. Shanin (ed.), *Peasants and peasant societies*, Penguin Books, Harmondsworth.

BALANDIER, G. (1972), *Political anthropology*, Penguin Books, Harmondsworth.

BALANDIER, G. (1974), 'A dynamist approach to Social Anthropology', seminar at the School of Oriental and African Studies, 28 October, London.

BANGASH, A. (1972), 'Class struggle, not a tribal war', in *Pakistan Forum*, 2, nos 9 and 10, June–July, pp. 14–18.

BARTH, F. (1953), *Principles of social organization in Southern Kurdistan*, Universitets Etnografiske Museum Bulletin no. 7, Oslo.

BARTH, F. (1959), 'Segmentary opposition and the theory of games: a study of Pathan organization', in *JRAI*, 89, pt 1.

BARTH, F. (1961), *Nomads of South Persia*, George Allen and Unwin, London.

BARTH, F. (ed.) (1963), *The role of the entrepreneur in social change in Northern Norway*, Scandinavian University Books; first published in *Arbook for Universitet* in Bergen Humanistick Series, Bergen University Press.

BARTH, F. (1968), 'Capital, investment and the social structure of a pastoral nomad group in South Persia', in E. E. LeClair and H. K. Schneider (eds), *Economic anthropology*, Holt, Rinehart and Winston, New York.

BARTH, F. (1970), 'Pathan identity and its maintenance', in F. Barth (ed.), *Ethnic groups and boundaries: the social organization of culture difference*, George Allen and Unwin, London.

BARTH, F. (1971a), 'Models of social organization', Occasional Paper, *RAI*, no. 23.

BARTH, F. (1971b), 'The system of social stratification in Swat, North Pakistan', in E. R. Leach (ed.), *Aspects of caste in South India, Ceylon and North-West Pakistan*, Cambridge University Press.

BARTH, F. (1972), *Political leadership among Swat Pathans*, Athlone Press, London.

BELLEW, H. W. (1864), *A general report on the Yusufzai*, Government Press, Lahore.

BELLEW, H. W. (1867), *A grammar of the Pukkhto or Pushto language*, W. H. Allen, London.

BELLEW, H. W. (1880), *The races of Afghanistan*, W. Thacker, London.

BELSHAW, C. S. (1965), *Traditional exchange and modern markets*, Prentice-Hall, Englewood Cliffs, N.J.

BENDIX, R. (1960), *Max Weber: an intellectual portrait*, Heinemann, London.

BENEDICT, R. (1961), *Patterns of culture*, Routledge & Kegan Paul, London.

BENHAM, F. (1948), *Economics*, Pitman, London.

BÉTEILLE, A. (ed.) (1974), *Social inequality: selected readings*, Penguin Books, Harmondsworth.

BÉTEILLE, A. (1977), *Inequality among men*, Basil Blackwell, Oxford.

BIDDULPH, C. E. (1890), *Afghan poetry of the seventeenth century*, Kegan Paul, Trench Trubner, London.

BLACKBURN, R. (ed.) (1975), *Explosion in a Subcontinent*, Penguin Books, Harmondsworth.

BOHANNAN, L. (1952), 'A genealogical charter', *Africa*, vol. xxii, no. 4, pp. 301-15.

BOHANNAN, L. (1970), 'Political aspects of Tiv social organization', in J. Middleton and D. Tait (eds), *Tribes without rulers*, Routledge and Kegan Paul, London.

BOHANNAN, L. and BOHANNAN, P. (1953), *The Tiv of Central Nigeria*, Ethnographic Survey of Africa, International African Institute, London.

BOHANNAN, P. (1957), *Justice and judgement among the Tiv*, Oxford University Press, New York.

BOHANNAN, P. (1959), 'The impact of money on an African subsistence economy', in *The Journal of Economic History*, no. 19, pp. 491-503.

BOHANNAN, P. and BOHANNAN, L. (1968), *Tiv economy*, Northwestern University Press, Evanston, Ill.

BOHANNAN, P. and DALTON, G. (eds) (1962), *Markets in Africa*, Northwestern University Press, Evanston, Ill.

BOISSEVAIN, J. (1974), *Friends of friends: networks, manipulators and coalitions*, Basil Blackwell, Oxford.

BOTTOMORE, T. B. (1962), *Sociology: a guide to problems and literature*, Allen & Unwin, London.

BURLING, R. (1962), 'Maximization theories and the study of economic anthropology', in *American Anthropologist*, vol. 64, pp. 802-21.

BURNES, A. (1834), *Travels into Bokhara*, John Murray, London.

BURNES, A. (1961), *Cabool: a personal narrative of a journey to and residence in that city, in the years 1836-8*, Ferozsons, for Government of West Pakistan, Lahore; originally printed John Murray, 1843.

CANCIAN, F. (1966), 'Maximization as norm, strategy and theory: a comment on programmatic statements in economic anthropology', in *American Anthropologist*, vol. 68 (April), pp. 465-70.

CAPLAN, L. (1970), *Land and social change in East Nepal*, University of California Press, Berkeley and Los Angeles.

CAPLAN, P. (1972), *Priests and cobblers: a study of social change in a Hindu village in Western Nepal*, Intertext Books, Aylesbury, Bucks.

CAROE, O. (1965), *The Pathans*, Macmillan, London.

CAROE, O. (1977), review of Ahmed 1977a in *Asian Affairs*, vol. VIII (October), pp. 352-3.

CHAUDHURI, N. C. (1965), *The continent of Circe: being an essay on the peoples of India*, Chatto & Windus, London.

CHURCHILL, W. S. (1972), *Frontiers and wars*, Penguin Books, Harmondsworth.

COEN, T. C. (1971), *The Indian Political Service*, Chatto & Windus, London.

COHEN, A. (1969), *Custom and politics in urban Africa*, Routledge & Kegan Paul, London.

COHEN, A. (1972), 'Cultural strategies in the organization of trading diasporas', in C. Meillasoux (ed.), *The development of indigenous trade and markets in West Africa*, Oxford University Press.

COHEN, A. (1974), *Two-dimensional man: an essay on the anthropology of power and symbolism in complex societies*, Routledge & Kegan Paul, London.

COLSON, E. (1971), 'Contemporary tribes and the development of nationalism', in J. Helm (ed.), *Essays on the problem of tribe*, American Ethnological Society, University of Washington Press.

COON, C. S. (1952), *Caravan: the story of the Middle East*, Jonathan Cape, London.

CURZON, G. N. (1906), *Speeches as Viceroy and Governor-General of India*, John Murray, London.

DALTON, G. (1961), 'Economic theory and primitive society', in *American Anthropologist*, vol. 63, no. 1 (February).

DALTON, G. (1962), 'Traditional production in primitive African economies', in *The Quarterly Journal of Economics*, 76, pp. 360-78.

DALTON, G. (1965), 'Primitive money', in *American Anthropologist*, vol. 67, pp. 44-65.

DALTON, G. (ed.) (1967), *Tribal and peasant economies: readings in economic anthropology*, Natural History Press, New York.

DALTON, G. (ed.) (1968), *Primitive, archaic, and modern economies: essays of Karl Polanyi*, Anchor Books, New York.

DALTON, G. (1969), 'Theoretical issues in economic anthropology', in *Current Anthropology*, 10, pp. 63-101.

DALTON, G. (1971), *Economic development and social change: the modernization of village communities*, Natural History Press, New York.

DARLING, M. L. (1925), *The Punjab peasant in prosperity and debt*, Oxford University Press.

DARLING, M. L. (1930), *Rusticus loquitur or the old light and the new in the Punjab village*, London.

DARLING, M. L. (1934), *Wisdom and waste in the Punjab village*, Oxford University Press.

DATTA, K., CHAUDHURI, H. R. and MAJUMDAR, R. C. (1956), *An advanced history of India*, Macmillan, London.

DAVIES, C. C. (1975), *The problem of the North-West Frontier, 1890-1908*, Curzon Press, London.

DEANE, P. (1953), *Colonial social accounting*, Cambridge University Press.

DICHTER, D. (1967), *The North-West Frontier of West Pakistan*, Oxford University Press.

DOLE, G. E. (1971), 'Tribe as the autonomous unit', in J. Helm (ed.), *Essays on the problem of tribe*, American Ethnological Society, University of Washington Press.

DUBE, S. C. (1960), 'Approaches to the tribal problem in India', in *Journal of Social Research*, vol. 3, no. 2, Ranchi.

DUBE, S. C. (1965), *Indian village*, Routledge & Kegan Paul, London.

DUMONT, L. (1970), *Homo Hierarchicus: the caste system and its implications*, Paladin, London.

DUPREE, L. (1977), 'On two views of the Swat Pushtuns', review of Ahmed 1976 in *Current Anthropology*, 18 (September), pp. 514-16.

DUPREE, L. and ALBERT, L. (eds) (1974), *Afghanistan in the 1970s*, Praeger, New York.

DURKHEIM, E. (1951), *Suicide*, Free Press, Glencoe, Ill.

EDWARDES, H. B. (1851), *A year on the Punjab frontier, in 1848-49*, vols I and II, Richard Bentley, London; reprinted by Ferozsons, Lahore, for Government of West Pakistan, 1963.

EDWARDS, M. W. (1977), 'An eye for an eye: Pakistan's wild frontier', *National Geographic*, vol. 151, no. 1 (January), Washington D.C.

EGLAR, Z. (1960), *A Punjabi village in Pakistan*, Columbia University Press.

ELKIN, A. P. (1943), *The Australian aborigines*, Angus & Robertson, Sydney and London.

ELLIOTT, J. G. (1968), *The Frontier 1839-1947: the story of the North-West Frontier of India*, Cassell, London.

ELPHINSTONE, M. (1972), *An account of the kingdom of Caubul*, vols I and II, Oxford University Press, Karachi.

ENEVOLDSEN, J. (n.d.), *Sound the bells, O moon, rise and shine*, University Book Agency, Peshawar.

ENGELS, F. (1970), 'The origins of the family, private property and the state', in K. Marx and F. Engels, *Selected works*, vol. 3, Progress Publishers.

EPSTEIN, T. S. (1962), *Economic development and social change in South India*, Manchester University Press.

EPSTEIN, T. S. (1969), 'The data of economics in anthropological analysis', in A. L. Epstein (ed.), *The craft of social anthropology*, Tavistock, London.

EPSTEIN, T. S. (1973), *South India: yesterday, today and tomorrow*, Macmillan, London.

EVANS-PRITCHARD, E. E. (1937), *Witchcraft, oracles and magic among the Azande*, Oxford University Press.

EVANS-PRITCHARD, E. E. (1940), *The Nuer: the description of the modes of livelihood and political institutions of a Nilotic people*, Oxford University Press.

EVANS-PRITCHARD, E. E. (1962), 'Anthropology and history', in *Essays in social anthropology*, Faber & Faber, London.

EVANS-PRITCHARD, E. E. (1970), 'The Nuer of the Southern Sudan', in Fortes and Evans-Pritchard (eds), *African political systems*, Oxford University Press.

EVANS-PRITCHARD, E. E. (1973), *The Sanusi of Cyrenaica*, Oxford University Press.

FALLERS, L. A. (1971), 'Are African cultivators to be called "peasants"?' in G. Dalton (ed.), *Economic development and social change*, Natural History Press, New York.

FARIS, J. C. (1973), 'Pax Britannica and the Sudan: S. F. Nadel', in T. Asad (ed.), *Anthropology and the colonial encounter*, Ithaca Press, London.

FIRTH, R. (1936), *We, the Tikopia, a sociological study of kinship in primitive Polynesia*, Allen & Unwin, london.

FIRTH, R. (1959), *Social change in Tikopia*, Humanities Press, New York.

FIRTH, R. (1964), 'Capital, saving and credit in peasant societies: a view-point from economic anthropology', in R. Firth and B. Yamey (eds), *Capital, saving and credit in peasant societies*, Aldine, Chicago.

FIRTH, R. (1966), *Malay fishermen: the peasant economy*, Routledge & Kegan Paul, London.

FIRTH, R. (ed.) (1970), *Themes in economic anthropology*, ASA Monograph 6, Tavistock, London.

FORTES, M. (1945), *The dynamics of clanship amng the Tallensi*, Oxford University Press.

FORTES, M. (1958), 'Introduction', in J. R. Goody (ed.), *The developmental cycle in domestic groups*, Cambridge University Press.

FORTES, M. and EVANS-PRITCHARD, E. E. (eds) (1970), *African political systems*, Oxford University Press.

FOX, R. (1967), *Kinship and marriage, an anthropological perspective*, Penguin Books, Harmondsworth.

FRASER-TYTLER, W. K. (1969), *Afghanistan*, Oxford University Press.

FREEDMAN, M. (1958), *Lineage organization in southeastern China*, Athlone Press, London.

FREEDMAN, M. (1966), *Chinese lineage and society*, Athlone Press, London.

FRIED, M. H. (1971), 'On the concepts of "tribe" and "tribal society"', in J. Helm (ed.), *Essays on the problem of tribe*, American Ethnological Society, University of Washington Press.

FÜRER-HAIMENDORF, C. von (1939), *The naked Nagas*, Methuen, London.

FÜRER-HAIMENDORF, C. von (1962), *The Apa Tanis and their neighbours*, Free Press, New York.

FÜRER-HAIMENDORF, C. von (1976), 'Historical processes in the light of anthropological restudies', The Presidential Address, 3 November, *RAI*.

FÜRER-HAIMENDORF, C. von (1977), 'The changing position of tribal populations in India', in *RAIN*, no. 22 (October).

GEERTZ, C. and H. (1964), 'Teknonymy in Bali: parenthood, age-grading and genealogical amnesia', in *JRAI*, 94, pp. 94-108. See also P. Bohannan and J. Middleton (eds), *Marriage, family and residence*, Natural History Press, New York.

GELLNER, E. (1969a), *Saints of the Atlas*, Weidenfeld & Nicolson, London.

GELLNER, E. (1969b), 'A pendulum swing theory of Islam', in R. Robertson (ed.), *Sociology of religion*, Penguin Books, Harmondsworth.

GELLNER, E. (1969c), 'Introduction', in G. Ionescu and E. Gellner (eds), *Populism its meaning and national characteristics*, Weidenfeld & Nicolson, London.

GERTH, H. H. and MILLS, C. W. (trs and eds) (1961), *From Max Weber: essays in sociology*, Routledge & Kegan Paul, London.

GILSENAN, M. (1973), *Saint and Sufi in modern Egypt*, Oxford University Press.

GLUCKMAN, M. (1961), 'Ethnographic data in British social anthropology', in *Sociological Review*, 9, pp. 5-17.

GLUCKMAN, M. (1969), 'Introduction', in A. L. Epstein (ed.), *The craft of social anthropology*, Tavistock, London.

388   *Bibliography*

GLUCKMAN, M. (1970), 'The kingdom of the Zulu of South Africa', in Fortes and Evans-Pritchard (eds), *African political systems*, Oxford University Press.

GLUCKMAN, M. (1971), *Politics, law and ritual in tribal society*, Basil Blackwell, Oxford.

GODELIER, M. (1967), 'System, structure and contradiction in capital', in R. Miliband and J. Saville (eds), *The Socialist Register*, Merlin, London.

GODELIER, M. (1975), 'Modes of production, kinship and demographic structures', in M. Bloch (ed.), *Marxist analyses and social anthropology*, ASA Studies, Malaby Press, London.

GODELIER, M. (1977), *Perspectives in Marxist anthropology*, Cambridge University Press.

GOODWIN, B. (1969), *Life among the Pathans (Khattaks)*, Owl Printing Co., Tollesbury, Essex.

GOODWIN, B. (n.d.), *More stories of life among the Pathans (Khattaks)*, privately published, Peshawar Road, Rawalpindi, and 56 Addison Avenue, London.

GOODY, J. R. (1972), *Domestic groups*, Reading, Mass., Addison Wesley.

GOODY, J. R. and TAMBIAH, S. J. (1973), *Bridewealth and dowry*, Cambridge University Press.

GOUGH, K. and SHARMA, H. P. (eds) (1973), *Imperialism and revolution in South Asia*, Monthly Review Press, New York and London.

GREGORIAN, V. (1969), *The emergence of modern Afghanistan*, Stanford University Press.

GUHA, B. S. (1951), 'The Indian aborigines and their administration', in *Journal of the Asiatic Society*, Science 17.

HAMNETT, I. (1970), 'A social scientist among technicians', in *IDS Bulletin*, 3, 1 (October).

HART, D. M. (1976), *The Aith Waryaghar of the Moroccan Rif*, Wenner-Gren Foundation, no. 55, University of Arizona Press.

HAY, W. R. (1934), 'The Yusufzai state of Swat', in *The Geographical Journal*, vol. 84, no. 3.

HERSKOVITS, M. J. (1962), 'Preface', in Bohannan and Dalton (eds), *Markets in Africa*, Northwestern University Press, Evanston, Ill.

HILL, P. (1963), 'Markets in Africa', in *The Journal of Modern African Studies*, vol. 1, no. 4.

HILL, P. (1965), *A plea for indigenous economics: the West African example*, Economic Development Institute, University of Ibadan.

HITCHCOCK, J. T. (1958), 'The idea of the martial Rajput', in *Journal of American Folklore* (July–September).

HITCHCOCK, J. T. (1966), *The Magars of Banyan Hill*, Holt, Rinehart and Winston, New York.

HITTI, P. K. (1977), *History of the Arabs*, Macmillan, London.

HOEBEL, E. A. (1958), *Man in the primitive world*, McGraw-Hill, New York.

HOLLAND, H. (1958), *Frontier doctor: an autobiography*, Hodder & Stoughton, London.

HONIGMANN, J. J. (1964), 'Tribe', in *Dictionary of the social sciences*, published under auspices of UNESCO.

HOWELL, E and CAROE, O. (trs) (1963), *The poems of Khushal Khan Khattak*, Pashto Academy, University of Peshawar.

HUNTER, G. and BOTTRALL, A. (eds) (1974), *Serving the small farmer: policy choices in Indian agriculture*, Croom Helm, London.

HUNTER, G., BUNTING, A. H. and BOTTRALL, A. (eds) (1976), *Policy and practice in rural development*, Croom Helm, London.

HUSSAIN, M. (1958), *A socio-economic survey of village Baffa in the Hazara District*, BEE, Peshawar.

IBBETSON, D. C. J. (1883), *Outlines of Panjab ethnography, being extracts from the Panjab Census Report of 1881 treating of religion, language and caste*, Government Printing, Calcutta.

INAYATULLAH, K. and SHAFI, Q. M. (1964), *Dynamics of development in a Pakistani village*, PARD, Peshawar.

IONESCU, G. and GELLNER, E. (eds) (1969), *Populism its meaning and national characteristics*, Weidenfeld & Nicolson, London.

JAMES, W. (1973), 'The anthropologist as reluctant imperialist', in T. Asad (ed.), *Anthropology and the colonial encounter*, Ithaca Press, London.

JOSHI, V. C. (ed.) (1975), *Ram Mohun Roy and the process of modernization in India*, Vikas, Delhi.

KEATS, J. (1975), *Keats: the complete poems*, Longman, London.

KEPPEL, A. (1911), *Gun-running on the Indian North-West Frontier*, John Murray, London.

KHAN, A. H. (1975), *A second review of the Daudzai Pilot Project 1974–75*, PARD, August.

KHAN, F. and KHAN, M. A. (1964a), *Socio-economic survey of village Turangzai*, publication no. 18, BEE, Peshawar.

KHAN, F. (1964b), *Institutional rural credit in Mardan and Peshawar Districts*, publication no. 19, BEE, Peshawar.

KHAN, G. J. (1972), *Development of Tribal Areas*, publication no. 80, BEE, Peshawar.

KHAN, M. and SHAH, F. (1973), *Facts and figures: Daudzai Markaz IRDP*, PARD, Peshawar.

KHAN, S. S. (1975), *Daudzai project: a case study*, PARD, Peshawar.

KHATOON, Z. (1966), *Institutional agricultural credit in the former NWFP*, publication no. 29, BEE, Peshawar.

KUPER, A. (1974), 'Critical applied anthropology: urban unemployment and rural productivity in Jamaica', *Ethnos*, nos 1–4, Ethnographical Museum of Sweden, Stockholm.

LACKNER, H. (1973), 'Colonial administration and social anthropology: Eastern Nigeria 1920–1940', in T. Asad (ed.), *Anthropology and the colonial encounter*, Ithaca Press, London.

LAMB, D. (1977), 'Preserving a primitive society', in *The Sociological Review*, vol. 25, no. 4, New Series (November).

LAWRENCE, T. E. (1962), *Seven pillars of wisdom*, Penguin Books, Harmondsworth.

LEACH, E. R. (1940), *Social and economic organization of the Rowanduz Kurds*, London School of Economics.

LEACH, E. R. (1951), 'The structural implications of matrilateral cross-cousin marriage', in *JRAI*.

LEACH, E. R. (1971a), *Rethinking anthropology*, Athlone Press, London.

LEACH, E. R. (1971b), *Aspects of caste in South India, Ceylon and North-West Pakistan*, Cambridge University Press.

LEACH, E. R. (1977), *Political systems of highland Burma: a study of Kachin social structure*, Athlone Press, London.

LeCLAIR, E. E. (1962), 'Economic theory and economic anthropology', in *American Anthropologist*, 64, pp. 1,179–1,203.

LeCLAIR, E. E. and SCHNEIDER, H. K. (eds) (1968), *Economic anthropology: readings in theory and analysis*, Holt, Rinehart and Winston, New York.

LELE, U. (1975), *The design of rural development: lessons from Africa*, Johns Hopkins University Press, Baltimore.

LEWIS, I. M. (1961), *A pastoral democracy*, Oxford University Press.

LEWIS, I. M. (1962a), 'Historical aspects of genealogies in Northern Somali societal structure', in *Journal of African History*, 3, pp. 35–48.

LEWIS, I. M. (1962b), 'Lineage continuity and modern commerce in North Somaliland', in P. Bohannan and G. Dalton (eds), *Markets in Africa*, Northwestern University Press, Evanston, Ill.

LEWIS, I. M. (1969a), 'Conformity and contrast in Somali Islam', in *Islam in Tropical Africa*, Oxford University Press.

LEWIS, I. M. (1969b), 'Problems in the comparative study of unilineal descent', in M. Banton (ed.), *The relevance of models for social anthropology*, ASA monograph no. 1, Tavistock, London.

LEWIS, O. (1958), *Village life in Northern India: studies in a Delhi village*, University of Illinois Press, Urbana.

LORIMER, J. G. (1934), *Customary law of the main tribes in the Peshawar District*, revised by J. G. Acheson, vol. XVII, NWFP Government Press, Peshawar.

LYALL, A. (1882), *Asiatic studies: religious and social*, First Series, London.

MACKENZIE, D. N. (1960), 'Khushal Khan – the national poet of the Afghans', in *Journal of the Royal Central Asian Society*, London.

MACKENZIE, D. N. (1965), *Poems from the devan of Khushal Khan Khattak*, Allen & Unwin, London.

MAINE, H. (1861), *Ancient law*, John Murray, London.

MAINE, H. (1871), *Village communities in the East and the West*, London.

MAIR, L. (1972), *An Introduction to social anthropology*, Oxford University Press.

MAJUMDAR, D. N. (1958), *Races and cultures in India*, Asia Publishing House, Bombay.

MALINOWSKI, B. (1964), *Argonauts of the Western Pacific*, Routledge & Kegan Paul, London.

MANDELBAUM, D. G. (1956), 'Social groupings', in H. L. Shapiro (ed.), *Man, culture and society*, Oxford University Press.

MAO TSE-TUNG (1967), 'Report on an investigation of the peasant movement in Hunan', in *Selected works of Mao Tse-tung*, vol. I, Foreign Language Press, Peking.

MARRIOTT, Mck. (1955), 'Social structure and change in a U.P. village', in M. N. Srinivas (ed.), *India's villages*, Calcutta.

MARX, K. (1951), 'The Eighteenth Brumaire of Louis Bonaparte', in Marx-Engels, *Selected works*, vol. I, Foreign Languages Publishing House, Moscow.

MASON, P. (1976), *A matter of honour*, Penguin Books, Harmondsworth.

MASTERS, J. (1965), *Bugles and a tiger*, Four Square, London.

MAYER, A. C. (1966), 'The significance of quasi groups in the study of complex societies', in M. P. Banton (ed.), *The social anthropology of complex societies*, Tavistock, London.

MAYER, A. C. (1970), *Caste and kinship in Central India*, Routledge & Kegan Paul, London.

MAYER, P. (1961), *Townsmen or tribesmen*, Oxford University Press.

MEAD, M. (1974), *Male and female*, Penguin Books, Harmondsworth.

MEILLASOUX, C. (1964), *Anthropologie économique des Gouro de Côte d'Ivoire*, Mouton, Paris.

MEILLASOUX, C. (ed.) (1971), *The development of indigenous trade and markets in West Africa*, Oxford University Press.

MEILLASOUX, C. (1972), 'From reproduction to production: a Marxist approach to economic anthropology', in *Economic Sociology*, vol. I, pp. 93–105.

MERTON, R. K. (1968), *Social theory and social structure*, enlarged ed., Free Press, New York.

MIAN, N. I. (1956), *A preliminary economic survey of the Tribal Areas adjoining West Pakistan*, publication no. 6, BEE, Peshawar.

MIANGUL, A. W. (1962), *The story of Swat*, Ferozsons, Pakistan.

MIDDLETON, J. (1960), *Lugbara religion*, Oxford University Press.

MIDDLETON, J. and TAIT, D. (eds) (1970), *Tribes without rulers*, Routledge & Kegan Paul, London.

MILLER, C. (1977), *Khyber: the story of the North-West Frontier*, Macdonald and Jane's, London.

MISDAQ, N. (1976), review of Ahmed 1976 in *Sussex essays in anthropology*, vol. 2, no. 1 (Autumn), pp. 56-8, University of Sussex.

MOHMAND, D. M. K. (1968), *On a foreign approach to Khushal: a critique of Caroe and Howell*, Maktabah-i-Shaheen, Peshawar.

MONTAGNE, R. (1930), *Les Berbères et la Makhzen au Sud du Maroc*, Paris.

MONTAGNE, R. (1931), *La vie sociale et la vie politique des Berbères*, Paris.

MORAES, D. (1960), *Gone away: an Indian journal*, Heinemann, London.

MORAES, D. (1974), *Matter of people*, André Deutsch, London.

MORGAN, L. H. (1871), *Systems of consanguinity and affinity of the human family*, Washington.

MORGAN, L. H. (1878), *Ancient society*, Henry Holt, New York; new ed. (1964), L. A. White (ed.), Harvard University Press.

MORGENSTIERNE, G. (1927), 'An etymological vocabulary of Pashto', *Det Norske Videnskaps – Akademi i Oslo*, II. Hist-Filos, Klasse, no. 3.

MOYNAHAN, B. (1976), 'The free Frontier: warriors of the Khyber Pass', in *Sunday Times*, Magazine, 21 March, London.

MYRDAL, G. (1967), *Asian drama*, 3 vols, Pantheon.

MYRDAL, G. (1970), *The challenge of world poverty*, Penguin Books, Harmondsworth.

MYRDAL, G. (1971), 'The principle of circular and cumulative causation', in G. Dalton (ed.), *Economic development and social change*, Natural History Press, New York.

NADEL, S. F. (1942), *A black Byzantium: the kingdom of the Nupe of Nigeria*, Oxford University Press.

NADEL, S. F. (1947), *The Nuba,* Oxford University Press.

NAIPAUL, V. S. (1964), *An area of darkness*, André Deutsch, London.

NAIPAUL, V. S. (1977), *India: a wounded civilization*, André Deutsch, London.

NARAYAN, R. K. (1956), *Next Sunday*, Orient Paper Backs, New Delhi.

NARAYAN, R. K. (1969), *My dateless diary*, Orient Paper Backs, New Delhi.

NAROLL, R. (1964), 'On ethnic unit classification', in *Current Anthropology*, vol. 5, no. 4, pp. 283-312.

NEHRU, J. (1960), *The discovery of India*, Meridian Books, London.

NEIVA, A. H. (1964), Comments on Naroll, *Current Anthropology*, vol. 5, no. 4, pp. 302-3.

NICHOLAS, R. W. (1963), 'Village factions and political parties in rural West Bengal', in *Journal of Commonwealth Political Studies*, vol. II, no. 1 (November).

NICHOLAS, R. W. (1965), 'Factions: a comparative analysis', in M. Banton (ed.), *Political systems and the distribution of power*, Tavistock, London.

NORTH, R. E. (1946), *The literature of the North-West Frontier of India: a select bibliography*, Peshawar.

OXAAL, I., BARNETT, T. and BOOTH, D. (eds) (1975), *Beyond the sociology of development*, Routledge & Kegan Paul, London.

PARD (1974), *A Review of Daudzai pilot project 1972–74*, vol. 11, no. 2, Peshawar.

PARD (1975–6), *Daudzai Progress Report*, no. 13, Peshawar.

PARKIN, D. J. (1972), *Palms, wine and witnesses*, Intertext Books, Aylesbury, Bucks.

PARSONS, T. (ed.) (1947), 'Introduction', in Max Weber, *The theory of social and economic organization*, Free Press, New York.

PARSONS, T. (1949), *The structure of social action*, Free Press, New York.

PASTNER, S. and PASTNER, C. M. (1972), 'Agriculture, kinship and politics in Southern Baluchistan', in *MAN*, vol. 7, no. 1 (March).

PEHRSON, R. N. (1966), *The social organization of the Marri Baluch*, compiled and analysed from his notes by Fredrik Barth, Viking Fund Publications in Anthropology, no. 43, Chicago.

PENNELL, T. L. (1909), *Among the wild tribes of the Afghan Frontier*, Seeley, London.

PETERS, E. (1960), 'The proliferation of segments in the lineage of the Bedouin of Cyrenaica', in *JRAI*, vol. 90, pp. 29–53.

PETTIGREW, H. R. C. (1965), *Frontier Scouts*, privately published Clayton Road, Selsey, Sussex.

PITT, D. C. (ed.) (1976), *Development from below: anthropologists and development situations*, Mouton, The Hague.

POLANYI, K. (1944), *The great transformation*, Rinehart, New York.

POLANYI, K. (1966), *Dahomey and the slave trade*, University of Washington Press, Seattle.

POLANYI, K. (1968a), *Primitive, archaic, and modern economies: essays of Karl Polanyi*, ed. G. Dalton, Anchor Books, Doubleday, New York.

POLANYI, K. (1968b), 'The economy as instituted process', in E. E. LeClair and H. K. Schneider (eds), *Economic anthropology*, Holt, Rinehart and Winston, New York.

POLANYI, K., ARENSBERG, C. M. and PEARSON, H. W. (eds) (1957), *Trade and market in the early empires: economies in history and theory*, Free Press, Glencoe, Ill.

RADCLIFFE-BROWN, A. R. (1970), 'Preface' to Fortes and Evans-Pritchard (eds), *African political systems*, Oxford University Press.

RAHMAN, A. (1900), *The life of Abdur Rahman, Amir of Afghanistan*, edited by Mir Munshi S. M. Khan, vols I and II, John Murray, London.

RAI (1971), *Notes and queries on anthropology*, revised and rewritten by a committee of the RAI, Routledge & Kegan Paul, London.

RAVERTY, H. G. (1860), *A grammar of the Pukhto, Pushto or 'language of the Afghans'*, Williams and Norgate, London.

RAVERTY, H. G. (1862), *Selections from the poetry of the Afghans*, London.

RAVERTY, H. G. (1888), *Notes on Afghanistan and part of Baluchistan: geographical, ethnographical and historical*, Eyre & Spottiswoode, London.

REY, P. P. (1975), 'The lineage mode of production', in *Critique of Anthropology*, no. 3 (Spring), London.

RIDGEWAY, R. T. I. (1918), *Pathans*, Government Press, Calcutta.

ROBERTS, F. M. (1897), *Forty-one years in India*, London.

ROBERTSON, G. S. (1899), *Chitral – the story of a minor siege*, Methuen, London.

SAHIBZADA, M. I. (1968), *Socio-economic changes in the rural areas of the NWFP region*, publication no. 40, BEE, Peshawar.

SAHLINS, M. D. (1968), *Tribesmen*, Prentice-Hall, for University of Michigan.

SAHLINS, M. D. (1969), 'On the sociology of primitive exchange', in M. Banton (ed.), *The relevance of models for social anthropology*, ASA, monograph no. 1, Tavistock, London.

SAHLINS, M. D. (1974), *Stone age economics*, Tavistock, London.

SALE, Lady (1843), *A journal of the disasters in Afghanistan*, John Murray, London.

SALISBURY, R. F. (1962), *From stone to steel*, Melbourne University Press, for Australian National University.

SERVICE, E. R. (1966), *The hunters*, Prentice-Hall, Englewood Cliffs, N.J.

SHANIN, T. (ed.) (1973), *Peasants and peasant societies*, Penguin Books, Harmondsworth.

SMITH, M. G. (1956), 'On segmentary lineage systems', in *JRAI*, vol. 86.

SMITH, M. G. (1960), *Government in Zazzau*, Oxford University Press.

SMITH, V. A. (1958), *Oxford history of India*, Oxford University Press.

SOUTHALL, A. W. (1953), *Alur society*, W. Heffer, Cambridge.

SPAIN, J. W. (1962), *The way of the Pathans*, Robert Hale, London.

SPAIN, J. W. (1963), *The Pathan borderland*, Mouton, The Hague.

SPIRO, M. E. (1973), 'Religion: problems of definition and explanation', in M. Banton (ed.), *Anthropological approaches to the study of religion*, ASA, monograph no. 3, Tavistock, London.

SRINIVAS, M. N. (1952), *Religion and society among the Coorgs of South India*, Oxford University Press.

SRINIVAS, M. N. (1966), *Social change in modern India*, University of California Press.

SRINIVAS, M. N. (1974), review of T. S. Epstein 1973, in *South Asian Review*, vol. 7, no. 3 (April).

STACEY, M. (1970), *Methods of social research*, Pergamon Press, Oxford.

STARR, L. A. (1920), *Frontier folk of the Afghan border and beyond*, Church Missionary Society, London.

STARR, L. A. (1924), *Tales of Tirah and Lesser Tibet*, forewords by Lord Rawlinson and Sir John Maffey, edited by Basil Mathews, Hodder and Stoughton, London.

STEIN, A. (1929), *On Alexander's track to the Indus: personal narrative of explorations to the North-West Frontier of India*, Macmillan, London.

STEWARD, J. H. (1955), *Theory of culture change*, University of Illinois Press, Urbana.

STIRLING, P. (1965), *A Turkish village*, Weidenfeld & Nicolson, London.

SWINSON, A. (1967), *The North-west Fronter, 1839–1947*, London.

TAPPER, R. L. (1974a), 'Durrani', in *Family of Man*, pt 27, vol. 2, pp. 733–7, London.

TAPPER, R. L. (1974b), 'Nomadism in modern Afghanistan: asset or anachronism?', in L. Dupree and L. Albert (eds), *Afghanistan in the 1970s*, Praeger, New York.

TAVAKOLIAN, B. M. (1976), 'The role of cultural values and religion in the ecology of middle eastern pastoralism', in *Anthropology*, B, University of California, Los Angeles.

TERRAY, E. (1972), *Marxism and primitive societies: two studies*, Monthly Review Press, New York.

TERRAY, E. (1975a), 'Technology, tradition and the state', in *Critique of Anthropology*, no. 3 (Spring), London.

TERRAY, E. (1975b), 'Classes and class consciousness in the Abron kingdom of Gyaman', in M. Bloch (ed.), *Marxist analyses and social anthropology*, Malaby Press, London.

TRIMINGHAM, J. S. (1973), *The Sufi orders in Islam*, Oxford University Press.

VELSEN, J. V. (1964), *The politics of kinship*, Manchester University Press, for the Rhodes-Livingstone Institute.

VELSEN, J. V. (1969), 'The extended-case method and situational analysis', in A. L. Epstein (ed.), *The craft of social anthropology*, Tavistock, London.

VITEBSKY, P. (1978), 'Political relations among the Sora of India', seminars at School of Oriental and African Studies, London.

WARBURTON, R. (1900), *Eighteen years in the Khyber 1879–1898*, John Murray, London.

WARD, B. E. (1969), 'Varieties of the conscious model: the fishermen of South China', in M. Banton (ed.), *The relevance of models for social anthropology*, ASA, monograph no. 1, Tavistock, London.

WATT, W. M. (1961), *Islam and the integration of society*, Routledge & Kegan Paul, London.

WAX, R. H. (1971), *Doing fieldwork, warning and advice*, University of Chicago Press, Chicago and London.

WEBER, M. (1947), *The theory of social and economic organization*, edited by T. Parsons, Free Press, New York.

WEBER, M. (1960), *Max Weber: an intellectual portrait*, R. Bendix, Heinemann, London.

WEBER, M. (1961), *From Max Weber: essays in sociology*, translated and ed. H. H. Gerth and C. W. Mills, Routledge & Kegan Paul, London.

WEBER, M. (1962), *The Protestant ethic and the spirit of capitalism*, Allen & Unwin, London.

WEBER, M. (1966), *The sociology of religion*, Methuen, London.

WEBER, M. (1968), *Economy and society*, edited by G. Roth and C. Wittich, 3 vols.

WINTER, E. H. (1973), 'Territorial groupings and religion among the Iraqw', in M. Banton (ed.), *Anthropological approaches to the study of religion*, ASA Monograph no. 3, Tavistock, London.

WITTFOGEL, K. (1957), *Oriental despotism: a comparative study of total power*, Yale University Press.

WOLF, E. R. (1966), *Peasants*, Prentice-Hall, Englewood Cliffs, N.J.

WOLF, E. R. (1969a), 'On peasant rebellions', in *International Social Science Journal*, vol. XXI, no. 2, reprinted in T. Shanin (ed.) (1973), *Peasants and peasant societies*, Penguin Books, Harmondsworth.

WOLF, E. R. (1969b), *Peasant wars of the twentieth century*, Harper & Row, New York.

WOLF, E. R. (1971), 'The Spanish in Mexico and Central America', in G. Dalton (ed.), *Economic development and social change*, Natural History Press, New York.

WOODRUFF, P. (1965), *The men who ruled India*, vol. 1: *The founders*; vol. 2: *The guardians*, Jonathan Cape, London.

WOODRUFF, P. (1976), see Mason P., 1976.

WYLLY, H. C. (1912), *From the black mountain to Waziristan*, Macmillan, London.

YORKE, M. (1974), 'A tribal political system: a case-study among the Ho of Southern Singbhum in Eastern India', seminars at School of Oriental and African Studies, London.

YOUNG, G. (1977), 'The haunted pass' in *Observer*, Magazine, 16 October.

(ii) *Theses*

BAHA, L. (1968), *The administration of the NWFP 1901-1919*, history of Ph.D thesis, School of Oriental and African Studies, London.

KAKAR, M. H. (1968), *The consolidation of the central authority in Afghanistan under Amir Abdal-Rahman 1880-1896*, history M.Phil thesis, School of Oriental and African Studies, London.

MOHMAND, J. S. (1966), *Social organization of Musa Khel Mohmands*, M.A. thesis, University of Punjab, Pakistan.

PASTNER, C. (1971), *Sexual dichotomization in society and culture: women of Panjgur Baluchistan*, Ph.D thesis, Brandeis University, USA.

TAPPER, R. L. (1971), *The Shahsavan of Azarbaijan: a study of political and economic change in a Middle Eastern tribal society*, Ph.D thesis, School of Oriental and African Studies, London.

(3) NEWSPAPERS

Civil and Military Gazette, English daily, Lahore.

Dawn, English daily, Karachi.

Jihad, Urdu daily, Peshawar.

Khyber Mail, English daily, Peshawar.

Mashriq, Urdu daily, Peshawar and Rawalpindi.

Pakistan Times, English daily, Lahore and Rawlpindi.

Statesman, English daily, Delhi.

The Times, English daily, London.

Index